P9-EEP-932

DATE DUE

			PRINTED IN U.S.A.

SOMETHING
ABOUT THE
AUTHOR

ISSN 0276-816X

SOMETHING ABOUT THE AUTHOR

**Facts and Pictures about Authors
and Illustrators of Books for Young People**

EDITED BY
ANNE COMMIRE

VOLUME 57

 Gale Research Inc.

DETROIT • NEW YORK • FORT LAUDERDALE • LONDON

Riverside Community College
Library
4800 Magnolia Avenue
Riverside, California 92506

REF
PN
1009
A1C6
V. 57

Editor: Anne Commire

Associate Editors: Agnes Garrett, Helga P. McCue

Assistant Editors: Dianne H. Anderson, Elisa Ann Ferraro, Eunice L. Petrini, Linda Shedd

Sketchwriters: Catherine Coray, Marguerite Feitlowitz, Mimi H. Hutson, Deborah Klezmer, Dieter Miller

Researcher: Catherine Ruello

Editorial Assistants: Joanne J. Ferraro, Marja T. Hiltunen, June Lee, Susan Pfanner

Production Manager: Mary Beth Trimper

External Production Associate: Laura McKay

External Production Assistant: Anthony J. Scolaro

Internal Production Supervisor: Laura Bryant

Internal Production Associate: Louise Gagné

Internal Production Assistants: Shelly Andrews, Sharana Wier

Art Director: Arthur Chartow

Keyliner: C. J. Jonik

Special acknowledgment is due to the members of the *Something about the Author Autobiography Series* staff who assisted in the preparation of this volume.

Copyright © 1989 by Gale Research Inc. All rights reserved.

Library of Congress Catalog Card Number 72-27107

ISBN 0-8103-2267-6

ISSN 0276-816X

Printed in the United States

Contents

Introduction

As the only ongoing reference series that deals with the lives and works of authors and illustrators of children's books, *Something about the Author (SATA)* is a unique source of information. The *SATA* series includes not only well-known authors and illustrators whose books are most widely read, but also those less prominent people whose works are just coming to be recognized. *SATA* is often the only readily available information source for less well-known writers or artists. You'll find *SATA* informative and entertaining whether you are:

—a student in junior high school (or perhaps one to two grades higher or lower) who needs information for a book report or some other assignment for an English class;

—a children's librarian who is searching for the answer to yet another question from a young reader or collecting background material to use for a story hour;

—an English teacher who is drawing up an assignment for your students or gathering information for a book talk;

—a student in a college of education or library science who is studying children's literature and reference sources in the field;

—a parent who is looking for a new way to interest your child in reading something more than the school curriculum prescribes;

—an adult who enjoys children's literature for its own sake, knowing that a good children's book has no age limits.

Scope

In *SATA* you will find detailed information about authors and illustrators who span the full time range of children's literature, from early figures like John Newbery and L. Frank Baum to contemporary figures like Judy Blume and Richard Peck. Authors in the series represent primarily English-speaking countries, particularly the United States, Canada, and the United Kingdom. Also included, however, are authors from around the world whose works are available in English translation, for example: from France, Jean and Laurent De Brunhoff; from Italy, Emanuele Luzzati; from the Netherlands, Jaap ter Haar; from Germany, James Krüss; from Norway, Babbis Friis-Baastad; from Japan, Toshiko Kanzawa; from the Soviet Union, Kornei Chukovsky; from Switzerland, Alois Carigiet, to name only a few. Also appearing in *SATA* are Newbery medalists from Hendrik Van Loon (1922) to Paul Fleischman (1989). The writings represented in *SATA* include those created intentionally for children and young adults as well as those written for a general audience and known to interest younger readers. These writings cover the spectrum from picture books, humor, folk and fairy tales, animal stories, mystery and adventure, science fiction and fantasy, historical fiction, poetry and nonsense verse, to drama, biography, and nonfiction.

Information Features

In *SATA* you will find full-length entries that are being presented in the series for the first time. This volume, for example, marks the first full-length appearance of Carole Byard, J. Irving Crump, Maggie S. Davis, Lisa Eisenberg, Michael Grater, Cathy Guisewite, Carole and Bruce Hart, and William Kennedy.

Obituaries have been included in *SATA* since Volume 20. An Obituary is intended not only as a death notice but also as a concise view of a person's life and work. Obituaries may appear for persons who have entries in earlier *SATA* volumes, as well as for people who have not yet appeared in the series. In this volume Obituaries mark the recent deaths of William R. Cox, Nancy Hale, Ruth Manning-Sanders, Ursula Nordstrom, Edwin C. Reichert, and others.

Revised Entries

Since Volume 25, each *SATA* volume also includes newly revised and updated entries for a selection of *SATA* listees (usually four to six) who remain of interest to today's readers and who have been active enough to require extensive revision of their earlier biographies. For example, when Beverly Cleary first appeared in *SATA* Volume 2, she was the author of twenty-one books for children and young adults and the recipient of numerous awards. By the time her updated sketch appeared in Volume 43 (a span of fifteen years), this creator of the indefatigable Ramona Quimby and other memorable characters had produced a dozen new titles and garnered nearly fifty additional awards, including the 1984 Newbery Medal.

The entry for a given biographee may be revised as often as there is substantial new information to provide. In this volume, look for revised entries on Arnold Adoff, Ezra Jack Keats, Steven Kellogg, Norma Klein, and Kylie Tennant Rodd.

Illustrations

While the textual information in *SATA* is its primary reason for existing, photographs and illustrations not only enliven the text but are an integral part of the information that *SATA* provides. Illustrations and text are wedded in such a special way in children's literature that artists and their works naturally occupy a prominent place among *SATA*'s listees. The illustrators that you'll find in the series include such past masters of children's book illustration as Randolph Caldecott, Walter Crane, Arthur Rackham, and Ernest H. Shepard, as well as such noted contemporary artists as Maurice Sendak, Edward Gorey, Tomie de Paola, and Margot Zemach. There are Caldecott medalists from Dorothy Lathrop (the first recipient in 1938) to Stephen Gammell (the latest winner in 1989); cartoonists like Charles Schulz ("Peanuts"), Walt Kelly ("Pogo"), Hank Ketcham ("Dennis the Menace"), and Georges Rémi ("Tintin"); photographers like Jill Krementz, Tana Hoban, Bruce McMillan, and Bruce Curtis; and filmmakers like Walt Disney, Alfred Hitchcock, and Steven Spielberg.

In more than a dozen years of recording the metamorphosis of children's literature from the printed page to other media, *SATA* has become something of a repository of photographs that are unique in themselves and exist nowhere else as a group, particularly many of the classics of motion picture and stage history and photographs that have been specially loaned to us from private collections.

Indexes

Each *SATA* volume provides a cumulative index in two parts: first, the Illustrations Index, arranged by the name of the illustrator, gives the number of the volume and page where the illustrator's work appears in the current volume as well as all preceding volumes in the series; second, the Author Index gives the number of the volume in which a person's biographical sketch, Brief Entry, or Obituary appears in the current volume as well as all preceding volumes in the series. These indexes also include references to authors and illustrators who appear in *Yesterday's Authors of Books for Children* (described in detail below). Beginning with Volume 36, the *SATA* Author Index provides cross-references to authors who are included in *Children's Literature Review*.

Starting with Volume 42, you will also find cross-references to authors who are included in the *Something about the Author Autobiography Series* (described in detail below).

What a *SATA* Entry Provides

Whether you're already familiar with the *SATA* series or just getting acquainted, you will want to be aware of the kind of information that an entry provides. In every *SATA* entry the editors attempt to give as complete a picture of the person's life and work as possible. In some cases that full range of information may simply be unavailable, or a biographee may choose not to reveal complete personal details. The information that the editors attempt to provide in every entry is arranged in the following categories:

1. The "head" of the entry gives

   —the most complete form of the name,
   —any part of the name not commonly used, included in parentheses,
   —birth and death dates, if known; a (?) indicates a discrepancy in published sources,
   —pseudonyms or name variants under which the person has had books published or is publicly known, in parentheses in the second line.

2. "Personal" section gives

   —date and place of birth and death,
   —parents' names and occupations,
   —name of spouse, date of marriage, and names of children,
   —educational institutions attended, degrees received, and dates,
   —religious and political affiliations,
   —agent's name and address,
   —home and/or office address.

3. "Career" section gives

   —name of employer, position, and dates for each career post,
   —military service,
   —memberships,
   —awards and honors.

4. "Writings" section gives

   —title, first publisher and date of publication, and illustration information for each book written; revised editions and other significant editions for books with particularly long publishing histories; genre, when known.

5. "Adaptations" section gives

   —title, major performers, producer, and date of all known reworkings of an author's material in another medium, like movies, filmstrips, television, recordings, plays, etc.

6. "Sidelights" section gives

   —commentary on the life or work of the biographee either directly from the person (and often written specifically for the *SATA* entry), or gathered from biographies, diaries, letters, interviews, or other published sources.

7. "For More Information See" section gives

   —books, feature articles, films, plays, and reviews in which the biographee's life or work has been treated.

How a *SATA* Entry Is Compiled

A *SATA* entry progresses through a series of steps. If the biographee is living, the *SATA* editors try to secure information directly from him or her through a questionnaire. From the information that the biographee supplies, the editors prepare an entry, filling in any essential missing details with research. The author or illustrator is then sent a copy of the entry to check for accuracy and completeness.

If the biographee is deceased or cannot be reached by questionnaire, the *SATA* editors examine a wide variety of published sources to gather information for an entry. Biographical sources are searched with the aid of Gale's *Biography and Genealogy Master Index*. Bibliographic sources like the *National Union Catalog*, the *Cumulative Book Index*, *American Book Publishing Record*, and the *British Museum Catalogue* are consulted, as are book reviews, feature articles, published interviews, and material sometimes obtained from the biographee's family, publishers, agent, or other associates.

For each entry presented in *SATA*, the editors also attempt to locate a photograph of the biographee as well as representative illustrations from his or her books. After surveying the available books which the biographee has written and/or illustrated, and then making a selection of appropriate photographs and illustrations, the editors request permission of the current copyright holders to reprint the material. In the case of older books for which the copyright may have passed through several hands, even locating the current copyright holder is often a long and involved process.

We invite you to examine the entire *SATA* series, starting with this volume. Described below are some of the people in Volume 57 that you may find particularly interesting.

Highlights of This Volume

ARNOLD ADOFF......lived in a house filled with newspapers and magazines where "everyone read a great deal, and held to opinions with great passion." Small wonder that, as he grew older, Adoff became politically active. He was arrested for fighting "to protect civil liberties on campus" in the fifties. The desire to focus on his writing led him to a Greenwich Village apartment (three of its four walls were painted chocolate brown), where he supported himself "with substitute teaching and spent the rest of my time writing and going to jazz clubs." He also spent time with another young writer from Ohio, Virginia Hamilton, whom he married in 1960. The two joined in the civil rights causes of the early sixties. Recognizing that "our national bibliography was not sufficiently representative of black writers and that the balance had to be addressed," Adoff compiled his first anthology of black poetry, *I Am the Darker Brother: An Anthology of Modern Poems by Negro Americans*. With each new anthology that Adoff produced, his "passion for the task intensified." Besides collecting poetry, he also writes his own; his book of poems, *Black Is Brown Is Tan* was one of the first children's books to deal directly with growing up in an interracial family. It was written with his own children in mind. In addition to writing, Adoff and his wife team-teach using their own books as classroom tools.

E. M. FORSTER......was a young English writer on vacation in Florence when he overheard a conversation between two English ladies about another English woman who had married a much younger Italian, socially far beneath her. "This sorry bit of twaddle stuck in my mind. I worked at it until it became alive and grew into a novel of contrasts." It was called *A Room with a View*. Although it was well received when it was published in 1908, in the author's opinion, it wasn't his best novel; *Howards End* was "my best novel and approaching a good novel." A trip to India and a meeting with the Rajah of Dewas provided source material for another book. While working as private secretary to the Rajah, Forster worked on his book about the country he loved. When *A Passage to India* was finished, the author claimed, "I shall never write another novel....But I shall go on writing."

CATHY GUISEWITE......was fortunate to have parents who encouraged her to be creative. "Most mothers tape their children's work to the refrigerator door. Mine would send them off to the Museum of Modern Art," she said. Fortunately, her mother's support didn't end with childhood but was the impetus Guisewite needed to send her comic-strip doodlings to the syndicates. When Universal Press Syndicate accepted what became the "Cathy" strip, Guisewite "ran out and bought several books on how to draw cartoon characters." The drawing got easier; "Cathy" became so popular with her readers that it was adapted into many specialty items: T-shirts, aprons, mugs, etc., all created by "artist" Guisewite. "I think this is the opportunity that writers dream about," says Guisewite. "To write from life. That's the richest material."

EZRA JACK KEATS......started painting "when I was about four years old. I really dedicated myself to what I did, avidly and lovingly. I drew on and colored in everything that came across my path, with the indulgent approval of my mother." Despite three scholarships to art schools, Keats could not continue his formal art training, but found work as a mural painter on W.P.A. projects during the Depression. His first illustration assignments were for magazines, then book covers, and, finally, children's books. Two things bothered the young artist during those years that he illustrated other people's books: "In many of the manuscripts...there was a peculiar quality of contrivance and rigid structure; the other was that I never got a story about Black people." So, in 1961 he wrote and illustrated a story about a small black boy, Peter. "I really found myself when I produced *The Snowy Day* which won the Caldecott Award for the best children's book of the year," said Keats. Peter was the subject of other books, which used collage illustrations to enhance the stories. Author and illustrator of more than twenty-two children's books, Keats hoped that they would be "inspiring books for all children; about all children—the tall and short, fat and thin, dark and light, beautiful and homely."

STEVEN KELLOGG......told stories and illustrated them for his younger sisters. "I think I drew my way through elementary school." Growing up, he had great hopes of becoming a naturalist-illustrator because he wanted to combine his love of drawing with his love of animals. His enthusiasm never faltered during his school years. "When it was time for college I was...accepted by Rhode Island School of Design" with a full scholarship which "made my attendance possible." After graduation, Kellogg taught etching at American University in Washington, D.C., and began writing and illustrating. "The picture book is an art form that is designed specifically for children, but I feel it can be appreciated and enjoyed by all ages....The special thing about the picture book is that it's a combination of both words and pictures, and the two of them work together to tell the story. I write with the illustration and with the words as well, and try to make the two of them dance together to tell the story."

GARY LARSON......had a brother who was distantly related to Count Dracula. "I was his lab for exploring various forms of torture. Since we were latchkey kids, every day from three to five-thirty became Survival Time." Oddly enough, for a boy who lived in terror, he was fascinated by anything that crawled—snakes, lizards, salamanders, etc. He recreated swamps in the backyard, hauled sand to the basement to duplicate the Mojave Desert, and had his mother read "over and over again 'Mr. Bear Squash You All Flat.'" His interest in science continued through school, although he majored in communications in college "because I didn't want to teach." While working as an animal cruelty inspector for the Seattle Humane Society, Larson drew a cartoon for the *Seattle Times* entitled "Nature's Way," the forerunner of "The Far Side," a cartoon strip that first appeared in the *San Francisco Chronicle* in 1980. It has become a regular feature in more than seven hundred newspapers, with six million books sold, and has inspired greeting cards, posters, coffee mugs, calendars, and T-shirts. "I've been swept along by the merchandising monster," says its creator. Larson believes adamantly in following his own instincts. "In this 'yuppified' day and age, there is no substitute for doing something you enjoy."

These are only a few of the authors and illustrators that you'll find in this volume. We hope you find all the entries in *SATA* both interesting and useful.

Yesterday's Authors of Books for Children

In a two-volume companion set to *SATA, Yesterday's Authors of Books for Children (YABC)* focuses on early authors and illustrators, from the beginnings of children's literature through 1960, whose books are still being read by children today. Here you will find "old favorites" like Hans Christian Andersen, J. M. Barrie, Kenneth Grahame, Betty MacDonald, A. A. Milne, Beatrix Potter, Samuel Clemens, Kate Greenaway, Rudyard Kipling, Robert Louis Stevenson, and many more.

Similar in format to *SATA, YABC* features bio-bibliographical entries that are divided into information categories such as Personal, Career, Writings, and Sidelights. The entries are further enhanced by book illustrations, author photos, movie stills, and many rare old photographs.

In Volume 2 you will find cumulative indexes to the authors and to the illustrations that appear in *YABC*. These listings can also be located in the *SATA* cumulative indexes.

By exploring both volumes of *YABC*, you will discover a special group of more than seventy authors and illustrators who represent some of the best in children's literature—individuals whose timeless works continue to delight children and adults of all ages. Other authors and illustrators from early children's literature are listed in *SATA*, starting with Volume 15.

Something about the Author Autobiography Series

You can complement the information in *SATA* with the *Something about the Author Autobiography Series (SAAS)*, which provides autobiographical essays written by important current authors and illustrators of books for children and young adults. In every volume of *SAAS* you will find about twenty specially commissioned autobiographies, each accompanied by a selection of personal photographs supplied by the authors. The wide range of contemporary writers and artists who describe their lives and interests in the *Autobiography Series* includes Joan Aiken, Betsy Byars, Leonard Everett Fisher, Milton Meltzer, Maia Wojciechowska, and Jane Yolen, among others. Though the information presented in the autobiographies is as varied and unique as the authors, you can learn about the people and events that influenced these writers' early lives, how they began their careers, what problems they faced in becoming established in their professions, what prompted them to write or illustrate particular books, what they now find most challenging or rewarding in their lives, and what advice they may have for young people interested in following in their footsteps, among many other subjects.

Autobiographies included in the *SATA Autobiography Series* can be located through both the *SATA* cumulative index and the *SAAS* cumulative index, which lists not only the authors' names but also the subjects mentioned in their essays, such as titles of works and geographical and personal names.

The *SATA Autobiography Series* gives you the opportunity to view "close up" some of the fascinating people who are included in the *SATA* parent series. The combined *SATA* series makes available to you an unequaled range of comprehensive and in-depth information about the authors and illustrators of young people's literature.

Please write and tell us if we can make *SATA* even more helpful to you.

Acknowledgments

Grateful acknowledgment is made to the following publishers, authors, and artists for their kind permission to reproduce copyrighted material.

AVON BOOKS. Cover illustration from *It's Not What You Expect* by Norma Klein. Copyright © 1973 by Norma Klein./Cover illustration by Gehm from *Taking Sides* by Norma Klein. Copyright © by Norma Klein. Both reprinted by permission of Avon Books.

CHRONICLE FEATURES. Cartoon by Gary Larson from *Bride of the Far Side* by Gary Larson. Copyright © 1980, 1981, 1982, 1983, 1984 by the Chronicle Publishing Company./ Cartoon by Gary Larson from *The Far Side Gallery* by Gary Larson. Copyright © 1980, 1981, 1982, 1983, 1984 by the Chronicle Publishing Company./ Cartoon by Gary Larson from *Beyond the Far Side* by Gary Larson. Copyright © 1983 by the Chronicle Publishing Company. All reprinted by permission of the Chronicle Publishing Company.

CONTINUUM PUBLISHING CO. Sidelight excerpts from *Black Women Writers at Work*, edited by Claudia Tate. Copyright © 1983 by Claudia Tate. Reprinted by permission of The Continuum Publishing Company.

COWARD-MCCANN, INC. Illustration by Bruce Degen from *Commander Toad and the Space Pirates* by Jane Yolen. Text © 1987 by Jane Yolen. Illustration © 1987 by Bruce Degen. Reprinted by permission of Coward-McCann, Inc.

THOMAS Y. CROWELL. Jacket art by Denise Saldutti from *My Brother Ange* by Mary McCaffrey. Text © 1982 by Mary McCaffery. Jacket art and illustration © 1982 by Denise Saldutti. Reprinted by permission of Thomas Y. Crowell, a subsidiary of Harper & Row, Publishers, Inc.

CROWN PUBLISHERS, INC. Photograph by Flip and Debra Schulke from *Your Future in Space* by Flip and Debra Schulke and Penelope and Raymond McPhee. Text © 1986 by Penelope McPhee. Photo © 1986 by Flip and Debra Schulke. Reprinted by permission of Crown Publishers, Inc.

ANDRE DEUTSCH LTD. Illustration by Francis Mosley from *The Rich Kid* by Bill Gillham. Text © 1984 by Bill Gillham. Illustrations © 1984 by Francis Mosley. Reprinted by permission of Andre Deutsch Ltd.

DIAL BOOKS FOR YOUNG READERS. Illustration by Simms Taback from *Fishy Riddles* by Katy Hall and Lisa Eisenberg. Text © 1983 by Katy Hall and Lisa Eisenberg. Illustrations © 1983 by Simms Taback./ Illustration by Steven Kellogg from *Pinkerton, Behave* by Steven Kellogg. Copyright © 1979 by Steven Kellogg./ Illustration by Steven Kellogg from *Matilda Who Told Lies and Was Burned to Death* by Hilaire Belloc. Text © by Alfred A. Knopf Co. Illustrations © 1970 by Steven Kellogg./ Illustration by Steven Kellogg from *The Mystery of the Stolen Blue Paint* by Steven Kellogg. Copyright © 1981 by Steven Kellogg./ Illustration by Steven Kellogg from *The Orchard Cat* by Steven Kellogg. Copyright © 1972 by Steven Kellogg./ Illustration by Steven Kellogg from *Much Bigger Than Martin* by Steven Kellogg. Copyright © 1976 by Steven Kellogg./ Illustration by Steven Kellogg from *The Mysterious Tadpole* by Steven Kellogg. Copyright © 1977 by Steven Kellogg. All reprinted by permission of Dial Books for Young Adults.

DINOSAUR PUBLICATIONS. Illustration by Helen Herbert from *Dizzy Duncan* by Suzy Siddons. Text © 1979 by Suzy Siddons. Illustrations © 1979 by Helen Herbert. Reprinted by permission of Dinosaur Publications/William Collins, Sons & Company Ltd.

DODD, MEAD & CO. Sidelight excerpts from "Carole Byard," in *Black Artists of the New Generation* by Elton C. Fax./Illustration by Joyce Audy dos Santos from *Mrs. Peloki's Snake* by Joanne Oppenheim. Text © 1980 by Joanne Oppenheim. Illustrations © 1980 by Joyce Audy dos Santos. Both reprinted by permission of The Putnam Publishing Group.

DOUBLEDAY & CO., INC. Illustration by Carole Byard from *Willy* by Helen H. King. Copyright © 1971 by Helen H. King./Jacket illustration by Margo Herr from *To Die in Italbar* by Roger Zelazny. Copyright © 1973 by Roger Zelazny. Both used by permission of Doubleday, a division of Bantam, Doubleday, Dell Publishing Group Inc.

DOVER PUBLICATIONS, INC. Illustration by Henry Anelay from *The Mother's Picture Alphabet*, with introduction by Peter Stockham. Copyright © 1974 by Dover Publications, Inc. Reprinted by permission of Dover Publications, Inc.

EDICIONES DEL NORTE. Cover illustration by Mark Spencer from *La Insurreccion* by Antonio Skarmeta. Copyright © by Antonio Skarmeta. Reprinted by permission of Ediciones del Norte.

FAWCETT BOOKS. Cover illustration from *Snapshots* by Norma Klein. Copyright © 1984 by Norma Klein. Reprinted by permission of Random House.

FOUR WINDS PRESS. Illustration by David Wiesner from *Kite Flier* by Dennis Haseley. Text © 1986 by Dennis Haseley. Illustrations © 1986 by David Wiesner. Reprinted by permission of Four Winds Press, an imprint of Macmillan Publishing Company.

GREENWILLOW BOOKS. Illustration by Ezra Jack Keats from *Louie* by Ezra Jack Keats. Copyright © 1975 by Ezra Jack Keats. / Illustration by Lynn Sweat from *Amelia Bedelia and the Baby* by Peggy Parish. Text © 1981 by Margaret Parish. Illustrations © 1981 by Lynn Sweat. Both reprinted by permission of Greenwillow Books, an imprint of William Morrow and Company.

HARCOURT BRACE JOVANOVICH, INC. Sidelight excerpts from *Two Cheers for Democracy* by E. M. Forster. Copyright 1951 by E. M. Forster; renewed 1979 by Donald Parry. / Sidelight excerpts from *The Hill of Devi* by E. M. Forster. Copyright 1953 by E. M. Forster. / Sidelight excerpts and photographs from *E. M. Forster: A Life* by P. N. Furbank. Copyright © 1977, 1978 by P. N. Furbank. All reprinted by permission of Harcourt Brace Jovanovich, The Society of Authors, and Edward Arnold Ltd. / Jacket design by Richard Mantel from *Fielder's Choice: An Anthology of Baseball Fiction* edited by Jerome Holtzman. Copyright © 1979 by Jerome Holtzman. / Illustrations by Janet Stevens from *The Cabbages Are Chasing the Rabbits* by Arnold Adoff. Text © 1985 by Arnold Adoff. Illustrations © 1985 by Janet Stevens. All reprinted by permission of Harcourt Brace Jovanovich.

HARPER & ROW, PUBLISHERS, INC. Jacket painting detail by Benny Andrews from "Trash" which appears in *The Poetry of Black America*, edited by Arnold Adoff. Copyright © 1973 by Arnold Adoff. / Illustration by Emily Arnold McCully from *Black Is Brown Is Tan* by Arnold Adoff. Text © 1973 by Arnold Adoff. Illustrations © 1973 by Emily Arnold McCully. / Illustration by Ezra Jack Keats from *Peter's Chair* by Ezra Jack Keats. Copyright © 1967 by Ezra Jack Keats. / Illustration by Ezra Jack Keats from *A Letter to Amy* by Ezra Jack Keats. Copyright © 1968 by Ezra Jack Keats. All reprinted by permission of Harper & Row, Publishers, Inc.

HOLIDAY HOUSE. Illustration by Stephen Gammell from *The Best Way to Ripton* by Maggie S. Davis. Text © 1982 by Barbara Steincrohn Davis. Illustrations © 1982 by Stephen Gammell. / Illustration by Barbara McClintock from *Potbellied Possums* by Elizabeth Winthrop. Text © 1988 by Elizabeth Winthrop Mahoney. Illustrations © 1977 by Barbara McClintock. Both reprinted by permission of Holiday House.

HOUGHTON MIFFLIN. Sidelight excerpts from an article "The Site of Memory," by Toni Morrison from *Inventing the Truth*, edited by William Zinsser. Reprinted by permission of Houghton Mifflin.

UNIVERSITY OF ILLINOIS PRESS. Sidelight excerpts from *Alive and Writing*, edited by Larry McCaffery and Sinda Gregory. Reprinted by permission of University of Illinois Press.

INDIANA UNIVERSITY PRESS. Sidelight excerpts from *Folklorists Progress* by Stith Thompson. / Illustration by Franz Altschuler from *One Hundred Favorite Folktales*, chosen by Stith Thompson. Copyright © 1968 by Indiana University Press. Reprinted by permission of Indiana University Press.

J. B. LIPPINCOTT. Cover and inside illustration by Troy Howell from *Friend Dog* by Arnold Adoff. Text © 1980 by Arnold Adoff. Illustrations © 1980 by Troy Howell. / Illustration by Steve Kuzma from *Sports Pages* by Arnold Adoff. Text © 1986 by Arnold Adoff. Illustrations © 1986 by Steven Kuzma. All reprinted by permission of J. B. Lippincott, a subsidiary of Harper & Row, Publishers, Inc.

LOTHROP, LEE & SHEPARD BOOKS. Illustration by John Steptoe from *All the Colors of the Race* by Arnold Adoff. Text © 1982 by Arnold Adoff. Illustrations © 1982 by John Steptoe. Reprinted by permission of Lothrop, Lee & Shepard Books, a subsidiary of William Morrow and Company.

LUTTERWORTH PRESS. Jacket illustration from *Alf Gorilla* by Michael Grater. Copyright © 1986 by Michael Grater. Reprinted by permission of Lutterworth Press, Cambridge, England.

MACMILLAN PUBLISHING CO. Frontispiece by Benny Andrews from *I Am the Darker Brother: An Anthology of Modern Poems by Black Americans* by Arnold Adoff. Copyright © 1968 by Macmillan Publishing Company./Illustration by Stephen Gammell from *The Old Banjo* by Dennis Haseley. Text © 1983 by Dennis Haseley. Illustrations © 1983 by Stephen Gammell./Illustration by Bruce Degen from *Better Not Get Wet, Jesse Bear* by Nancy White Carlstrom. Text © 1988 by Nancy White Carlstrom. Illustrations © 1988 by Bruce Degen. All reprinted by permission of Macmillan Publishing Company.

METHUEN. Sidelight excerpts from *How Writers Write* by Pamela Lloyd, amended by Steven Kellogg. Reprinted by permission of Methuen.

WILLIAM MORROW & CO. Jacket illustration by Maria Horvath from *Chileno!* by Antonio Skarmeta. Copyright © 1979 by Hermann Luchterhand Verlag GmbH & Co. Translation © 1979 by William Morrow and Company. Reprinted by permission of William Morrow and Company.

PANTHEON. Cover illustration from *Mom, the Wolfman and Me* by Norma Klein. Copyright © 1972 by Norma Klein. Reprinted by permission of Random House.

POCKET BOOKS. Cover illustration from *What It's All About* by Norma Klein. Copyright © 1975 by Norma Klein./Cover illustration from *Tomboy* by Norma Klein. Copyright © 1978 by Norma Klein./Cover illustration from *A Honey of a Chimp* by Norma Klein. Copyright © 1980 by Norma Klein./Cover illustration from *Robbie and the Leap Year Blues* by Norma Klein. Copyright © 1981 by Norma Klein. All reprinted by permission of Simon & Schuster.

CHARLES SCRIBNER'S SONS. Illustration by Carole M. Byard from *Under Christopher's Hat* by Dorothy M. Callahan. Text © 1972 by Dorothy M. Callahan. Illustrations © 1972 by Carole M. Byard. Reprinted by permission of Charles Scribner's Sons, an imprint of Macmillan Publishing Company.

SIMON & SCHUSTER. Jacket painting by Sonja Lamut and Nenad Jakesvic from *Eye of Cat* by Roger Zelazny. Copyright © 1982 by The Amber Corporation./Jacket illustration from *Unicorn Variations* by Roger Zelazny. Copyright © 1983 by The Amber Corporation. Both reprinted by permission of Simon & Schuster.

STEMMER HOUSE. Illustration by Caren Caraway from *The Cucumber Princess* by Jan Wahl. Text © 1981 by Jan Wahl. Illustrations © 1981 by Caren Caraway. Reprinted by permission of Stemmer House Publishers, Inc.

UNIVERSAL PRESS SYNDICATE. Sidelight excerpts from "Frontispiece," by Gary Larson from *The Far Side Gallery*./Cartoons by Gary Larson from *The Far Side Gallery 2* by Gary Larson. Copyright © 1980, 1981, 1982, 1983, 1984 by the Chronicle Publishing Company; 1984, 1985, 1986 by Universal Press Syndicate./Cartoon by Gary Larson from *Valley of the Far Side* by Gary Larson. Copyright © 1985 by Universal Press Syndicate./Cartoon by Cathy Guisewite from *The Salesclerk Made Me Buy It* by Cathy Guisewite. Copyright © 1983 by Universal Press Syndicate./Cartoon by Cathy Guisewite from *My Cologne Backfired* by Cathy Guisewite. Copyright © 1984 by Universal Press Syndicate./Cartoon by Cathy Guisewite from *Two Pies. One Fork.* by Cathy Guisewite. Copyright © 1985 by Universal Press Syndicate./Cartoon by Cathy Guisewite from *I'll Pay $5000 for a Swimsuit That Fits Me!!!* by Cathy Guisewite. Copyright © 1985 by Universal Press Syndicate./Cartoon by Cathy Guisewite from *It Must Be Something in the Ink* by Cathy Guisewite. Copyright © 1986 by Universal Press Syndicate./Cartoon by Cathy Guisewite from *A Hand to Hold, An Opinion to Reject* by Cathy Guisewite. Copyright © 1987 by Universal Press Syndicate. All reprinted by permission of Universal Press Syndicate.

VICTOR BOOKS. Cover illustration by Myron Sahlberg from *Mad Dog of Lobo Mountain* by Lee Roddy. Copyright © 1986 by Lee Roddy./Cover illustration by Myron Sahlberg from *The Mystery of the Black Hole Mine* by Lee Roddy. Both reprinted by permission of Victor Books/Scripture Press Publications, Inc.

THE VIKING PRESS. Illustration by Ezra Jack Keats from *The Snowy Day* by Ezra Jack Keats. Copyright © 1962 by Ezra Jack Keats./Illustration by P. K. Roche from *Jump All the Morning: A Child's Day in Verse*, selected by P. K. Roche. Copyright © 1984 by P. K. Roche./Illustration by P. K. Roche from *At Christmas Be Merry*, selected by P. K. Roche. Copyright © 1986 by P. K. Roche./Jacket illustration from *Quinn's Book* by William Kennedy. Copyright © 1988 by Viking Penguin, Inc. All rights reserved. All reprinted by permission of Viking Penguin, Inc., a division of Penguin Books USA, Inc.

WASHINGTON SQUARE PRESS. Cover illustration from *The Bluest Eye* by Toni Morrison. Copyright © 1970 by Toni Morrison. Reprinted by permission of Simon & Schuster.

WESTMINSTER/JOHN KNOX PRESS. Jacket illustration by Richard Horwitz from *Tiger Terwilliger* by James L. Summers. Copyright © MCMLXIII by James L. Summers. Reprinted by permission of Westminster/John Knox Press.

ALBERT WHITMAN & CO. Illustration by Blanche Sims from *Sometimes I Wish I Were Mindy* by Abby Levine and Sarah Levine. Text © 1986 by Abby Levine and Sarah Levine. Illustrations © 1986 by Blanche Sims. Reprinted by permission of Albert Whitman & Company.

WORKMAN PUBLISHING. Illustration by Sandra Boynton from *Christmastime* by Sandra Boynton. Copyright © 1987 by Sandra Boynton. Reprinted by permission of the author.

Sidelight excerpts from "The Gentle World of Ezra Jack Keats," by Erma Perry, September, 1971, in *American Artist*. Reprinted by permission of *American Artist*./ Sidelight excerpts from "An Interview with William Kennedy," by Kay Bonnetti, American Audio Prose Library, 1984. Copyright © American Audio Prose Library. Reprinted by permission of American Audio Prose Library./Sidelight excerpts from an article "More Realism for Children," by Norma Klein, April, 1975, in *Top of the News*. Copyright © 1975 by the American Library Association. Reprinted by permission of the American Library Association./ Sidelight excerpts from an article "Being Banned," by Norma Klein, Spring, 1985, in *Top of the News*. Copyright © 1985 by the American Library Association. Reprinted by permission of the American Library Association./Album cover photograph by Ken Duncan from *Free to Be...You and Me*. Copyright © 1983 by Marlo Thomas./ Album cover illustration by Laurie Glick from *Free to Be...You and Me*. Copyright © 1983 by Arista Records, Inc. Reprinted by permission of Arista Records, Inc./ Sidelight excerpts and photographs from *The Autobiography of Kylie Tennant: The Missing Heir* by Kylie Tennant. Copyright © 1986 by Kylie Tennant./ Jacket design by Arthur Brocksopp from *Summer's Tales 2*, edited by Kylie Tennant. Both reprinted by permission of Curtis Brown Pty, Ltd./Illustration by Diane Dollar from *The Adventures of Space Baby* by Diane Dollar. Copyright © 1987 by Diane Dollar. Reprinted by permission of the author./Illustration by Joyce Audy dos Santos from *Piskies, Spriggans, and Other Magical Beings*, retold by Shirley Climo. Illustration copyright © 1981 by Joyce Audy dos Santos. Reprinted by permission of Joyce Audy dos Santos.

Sidelight excerpts from "Steven Kellogg - Teachers' Co-Conspirator," January, 1986, in *Early Years*./Illustration by Ezra Jack Keats from *John Henry, an American Legend* by Ezra Jack Keats. Copyright © 1965 by Ezra Jack Keats. Reprinted by permission of the Ezra Jack Keats Foundation, Inc./Sidelight excerpts from "Narrative Motif-Analysis as a Folklore Method," by Stith Thompson, Vol. LXIV, No. 161, in *F. F. Communications*./Sidelight excerpts from "The Beauty of Being a Late Bloomer," by Bel Kaufman, June, 1986, in *50 Plus*. Copyright © 1986 by Bel Kaufman. Reprinted by permission of Bel Kaufman./Illustration by William Heaslip from *The Cloud Patrol* by Irving Crump./Sidelight excerpts from "Caldecott Award Acceptance," by Ezra Jack Keats, August, 1963 in *The Horn Book Magazine*. Reprinted by permission of The Horn Book, Inc./Sidelight excerpts from "Collage," by Ezra Jack Keats, June, 1964, in *The Horn Book Magazine*. Reprinted by permission of The Horn Book, Inc./ Sidelight excerpts from "Critical Decisions: Reflections on the Changing Role of a Children's Book Reviewer," by Elaine Moss, April, 1984, in *The Horn Book Magazine*. Reprinted by permission of The Horn Book, Inc./Sidelight excerpts from "How Winning the Pulitzer Has Changed One Writer's Life," by William Kennedy, January 1, 1985, in *Life Magazine*. Reprinted by permission of *Life Magazine*./Jacket illustration by Glen Baxter from *Charlie Malarkey and the Belly-Button Machine* by William Kennedy and Brendan Kennedy. Text © 1986 by Brendan and William Kennedy. Illustrations copyright © 1986 by Glen Baxter. Little, Brown and Company./Sidelight excerpts from "Roger Zelazny" in *Speaking of Science Fiction: The Paul Walker Interviews*. Reprinted by permission of Luna Publications.

Sidelight excerpts from an article "Honesty Is Author's Policy for Children's Books," by Margo Huston, March 28, 1974, in *The Milwaukee Journal*. Reprinted by permission of *The Milwaukee Journal*./Cover illustration from *Sula* by Toni Morrison. Copyright © 1973 by Toni Morrison./Cover illustration from *Tar Baby* by Toni Morrison. Copyright © 1981 by Toni Morrison./Cover illustration from *Song of Solomon* by Toni Morrison. Copyright © by Toni Morrison. New American Library./Sidelight excerpts from an article "And Now, the Real

Cathy," by Millie Ball, June 8, 1986, in *The New Orleans Times-Picayune*. Reprinted by permission of *The New Orleans Times-Picayune*./Detail art by David Shannon from September 13, 1987 in *The New York Times Book Review*. Copyright © 1987 by The New York Times Company. Reprinted by permission of The New York Times Company./Sidelight excerpts from "The Far Side of Science," by Sheridan Warrick, October/December, 1985, in *Pacific Discovery*. Reprinted by permission of *Pacific Discovery*./Sidelight excerpts from "The Mischievous Mind of Gary Larson," by Tim Appelo, September, 1987, in *Pacific Northwest*. Reprinted by permission of *Pacific Northwest*./Sidelight excerpts from an article "A Cartoonist on the Wild Side," by Dan Geringer, September 18, 1984, in *Philadelphia Daily News*. Reprinted by permission of *Philadelphia Daily News*.

Photograph by Don Bierman from *Inside Hockey* by Stan Mikita with George Vass. Copyright © 1971 by Stan Mikita. Henry Regnery Company./Sidelight excerpts from an article "Cathy and 'Cathy': A Lot in Common," by Judy J. Newmark, September 5, 1982, in *St. Louis Post Dispatch*. Copyright © 1982 by *St. Louis Post Dispatch*. Reprinted by permission of *St. Louis Post Dispatch*./Sidelight excerpts from "How Cartoonist Cathy Guisewite Makes Us Laugh at Life's Little Frustrations," by Cork Miller, May, 1983, in *Seventeen*. Reprinted by permission of *Seventeen*./Sidelight excerpts from "Creatures from the Black Cartoon," by Peter Richmond, September 24, 1987, in *Rolling Stone*. Copyright © 1987 by Straight Arrow Publishers, Inc. Reprinted by permission of Straight Arrow Publishers, Inc./Sidelight excerpts from "First Day of School," by Bel Kaufman, September/October, 1981, in *Today's Education*. Reprinted by permission of *Today's Education*./Illustration by Ezra Jack Keats from *Whistle for Willie* by Ezra Jack Keats. Copyright © 1964 by Ezra Jack Keats./Cover photo by Margaret Bourke-White from *Ironweed* by William Kennedy./Illustration from *O Albany!* by William Kennedy. Copyright © 1983 by William Kennedy. Viking Penguin./Sidelight excerpts from an article "William Kennedy," by Curt Suplee, December 28, 1983, in *The Washington Post*. Copyright © 1983 by *The Washington Post*. Reprinted by permission of *The Washington Post*.

PHOTOGRAPH CREDITS

Maggie S. Davis: Nessie Summers; Michael Grater: Cory Bevington; Bruce Hart: Alan Singer; Helen Herbert: John Aldous Photography; Ezra Jack Keats: copyright © 1983 by Lois Dreyer; Brendan Kennedy (with William Kennedy): Jerry Bauer; William Kennedy: copyright © 1988 by Thomas Victor; Norma Klein: copyright © by Jerry Bauer; Barbara Ann Porte: Teresa Miller; Kylie Tennant Rodd: Vic Johnson, Associated Newspapers; Paul Russell: Daniel Hill; Antonio Skarmeta: copyright © by Isolde Ohlbaum; Peter Stockham: Mark Gerson; Barbara M. Walker: Edward Walker.

SOMETHING ABOUT THE AUTHOR

ADOFF, Arnold 1935-

PERSONAL: Born July 16, 1935, in New York, N.Y.; son of Aaron Jacob (a pharmacist) and Rebecca (Stein) Adoff; married Virginia Hamilton (a writer), March 19, 1960; children: Leigh Hamilton, Jaime Levi. *Education:* City College of New York (now City College of the City University of New York), B.A., 1956; Columbia University, further study, 1956-58; New School for Social Research, poetry workshops, 1965-67. *Politics:* "Committed to change for full freedom for all Americans." *Religion:* "Freethinking Pragmatist." *Home:* 750 Union St., Yellow Springs, Ohio 45387. *Office:* Arnold Adoff Agency, P.O. Box 293, Yellow Springs, Ohio 45387.

CAREER: Poet, anthologist and writer; Board of Education, New York, N.Y., teacher in Harlem and upper west side of Manhattan, 1957-69; Arnold Adoff Agency, Yellow Springs, Ohio, literary agent, 1977—. Instructor in federal projects at New York University, Connecticut College, and other institutions; lecturer at colleges throughout the country; visiting professor, Queen's College, Flushing, N.Y., 1986-87; consultant in children's literature, poetry, and creative writing. Member of Planning Commission, Yellow Springs; "general agitator" for full equality in education, jobs, and housing. *Military service:* New York National Guard.

AWARDS, HONORS: I Am the Darker Brother was selected one of Child Study Association of America's Children's Books of the Year, 1968, *City in All Directions*, 1969, and *Sports Pages*, 1986; *It Is the Poem Singing into Your Eyes* was selected one of *School Library Journal*'s Best Children's Books, 1971, and *Black Is Brown Is Tan*, 1973; Notable Children's Trade Book in the Field of Social Studies from the Children's Book Council and the National Council for Social Studies, 1974, and one of International Reading Association and Children's Book Council's Children's Choices, 1985, both for *My Black Me*; Brooklyn Art Books for Children Citation from the

Brooklyn Museum and the Brooklyn Public Library, 1975, for *MA nDA LA; It Is the Poem Singing into Your Eyes* was chosen one of New York Public Library's Books for the Teen Age, 1980, 1981, and 1982; Jane Addams Children's Book Award Special Recognition from the Jane Addams Peace Association, 1983, for *All the Colors of the Race*.

WRITINGS:

JUVENILE POETRY, EXCEPT AS NOTED

Malcom X (juvenile biography; ALA Notable Book; illustrated by John Wilson), Crowell, 1970.
MA nDA LA (picture book; ALA Notable Book; illustrated by Emily Arnold McCully), Harper, 1971.
Black Is Brown Is Tan (illustrated by E. A. McCully), Harper, 1973.
Make a Circle Keep Us In: Poems for a Good Day (illustrated by Ronald Himler), Delacorte, 1975.
Big Sister Tells Me That I'm Black (illustrated by Lorenzo Lynch), Holt, 1976.
Tornado! Poems (illustrated by R. Himler), Delacorte, 1977.
Under the Early Morning Trees: Poems (illustrated by R. Himler), Dutton, 1978.
Where Wild Willie (illustrated by E. A. McCully), Harper, 1978.
Eats: Poems (illustrated by Susan Russo), Lothrop, 1979.
I Am the Running Girl (illustrated by R. Himler), Harper, 1979.
Friend Dog (illustrated by Troy Howell), Lippincott, 1980.
OUTside/INside Poems (illustrated by John Steptoe), Lothrop, 1981.
Today We Are Brother and Sister (illustrated by Glo Coalson), Lothrop, 1981.
Birds: Poems (illustrated by T. Howell), Lippincott, 1982.
All the Colors of the Race: Poems (ALA Notable Book; illustrated by J. Steptoe), Lothrop, 1982.

ARNOLD ADOFF

The Cabbages Are Chasing the Rabbits (illustrated by Janet Stevens), Harcourt, 1985.
Sports Pages (illustrated by Steve Kuzma), Lippincott, 1986.
Greens, Morrow, 1988.
Chocolate Dreams, Lothrop, 1988.
Flamboyant, Harcourt, 1988.

*EDITOR; ANTHOLOGIES FOR YOUNG ADULTS AND ADULTS, EX-
CEPT AS NOTED*

*I Am the Darker Brother: An Anthology of Modern Poems by
Negro Americans* (ALA Notable Book; illustrated by Benny
Andrews), Macmillan, 1968.
Black on Black: Commentaries by Negro Americans, Mac-
millan, 1968.
City in All Directions: An Anthology of Modern Poems (illus-
trated by Donald Carrick), Macmillan, 1969.
*Black Out Loud: An Anthology of Modern Poems by Black
Americans* (juvenile; ALA Notable Book; illustrated by
Alvin Hollingsworth), Macmillan, 1970.
Brothers and Sisters: Modern Stories by Black Americans,
Macmillan, 1970.
*It Is the Poem Singing into Your Eyes: An Anthology of New
Young Poets,* Harper, 1971.
*The Poetry of Black America: An Anthology of the Twentieth
Century* (ALA Notable Book), Harper, 1973.
My Black Me: A Beginning Book of Black Poetry (juvenile;
ALA Notable Book), Dutton, 1974.
Celebrations: A New Anthology of Black American Poetry (ALA
Notable Book), Follett, 1977.

Contributor of articles and reviews to periodicals.

WORK IN PROGRESS: Poetry, picture books, anthology of
women's poetry, anthology of American Indian poetry. A series of autobiographical novels. "Most of the material has to
do with my parents and grandparents coming to this country
from Russia and their life in the South Bronx. Much of my
old neighborhood—Kelly Street, Fox Street—was utterly de-
stroyed in the 1970s. All of the tales are told from the viewpoint of a thirteen-year-old male. The stories owe a lot to folk
literature where truth and exaggeration blend into one; where
fact and fancy tend to blur. This is the first time I've attempted

to write extended prose fiction. For years the novel form terrified me, because I have worked in the relatively short forms
of poetry."

SIDELIGHTS: Born July 16, 1935 in New York City, son of
an immigrant father who left his native border town of Russia
and Poland to settle in the South Bronx. A rich immigrant
heritage was imprinted on the young Adoff. "My father told
marvellous stories of *shtetl* life and his early years in lower
Manhattan. But in our home, as in so many others, the emphasis was on being American with a keen sense of Jewish,
even though there was very little religious orientation. There
was a tradition of liberal, free-thinking females in the family.
My mother was involved in Zionist and civil rights causes. I
recall when a black Baptist congregation reclaimed a derelict
church in our neighborhood, my mother playing her violin,
welcoming the new congregation.

"From an early age, women have played an extraordinarily
important part in my life. I was raised by women who were
extremely vital not only in the home but outside as well. My
mother was passionately active on behalf of the Israeli Pioneer
Women, a group aligned with the Labor Party whose main
function it was to raise funds for hospitals, ambulances and
various good works in Israel. My maternal grandmother would
never allow me to join the Boy Scouts, because they wore
uniforms and carried knives—for her, a sure sign of creeping
fascism. These were women who brought a great deal of the
outside world into our home, often in subtle ways. Their cooking was one example. Recipes in our house originated from
Russia, Poland, Germany, Hungary, Roumania. As I grew
older, I came to recognize which dishes came from where. A
small thing, perhaps, but nonetheless a way of maintaining
traditions, keeping the heritage alive, and of being conscious
of a huge world beyond our windows.

"My family was vocal. Everyone talked at once, all the time.
Everyone read a great deal, and held to their opinions with
great passion. Discussions were volatile, emotional as well as
intellectual—all those energies rolled into one. In order to hold
status within the family, you had to speak loudly and articu-
lately on such burning topics as economics, socialism, the Soviet Union, and how to be assimilated into the larger society
without losing one's Jewishness. There was always a sense of
temporariness in being a Jew in America (in being a Jew anywhere, for that matter). I suppose that on some level we were
waiting for the next pogrom to turn the corner of 172nd Street
and Boston Road. The house was always full of newspapers
and magazines—*PM* (a socialist paper), the *Forward* (in which
Isaac Singer originally published so much of his work), the
Star, the *New Yorker.* My grandmother, however, drew the
line at the funnies, which were strictly verboten. Too low-
brow. So adamant was she about that that she refused to buy
the Sunday editions of the newspapers.

"My father's pharmacy, a focal point in our neighborhood
life, was a block away from where we lived. He was there
from early in the morning until quite late in the evening. As
a young child I liked to play behind the counter, dipping crepe
paper in water to create colored waters which I would then
mix, pretending they were pharmacist's chemicals. I also counted
pills, compounded salves and delivered prescriptions, becoming very familiar with the musty odor in the apartments of old
people who had been sick and shut in for a long time. In lots
of ways, the pharmacy was a bellwether. One window display
I'll never forget went up during World War II: ostensibly for
a particular roach spray, it portrayed Hitler, Stalin, and Mussolini as roaches. The pharmacy was also a locus for collections for the war—cardboard (which the store had in great

arnold adoff

friend dog

illustrated by

troy howell

(Cover illustration by Troy Howell from *Friend Dog* by Arnold Adoff.)

And I can brush your coat and hug so hard. ■ (From *Friend Dog* by Arnold Adoff. Illustrated by Troy Howell.)

Arnold Adoff and Virginia with their children.

quantities) was particularly valuable. I was the undisputed 'cardboard king' of the neighborhood war effort.

"Ours was a mixed working class neighborhood—Polish, Irish, Italian, Jewish, and German—of garment people, shop people, and union people. We children played together in the streets and on the stoops during kite-flying season, stick-ball season, marble season. I suspect the fellows who sold toys to the local candy store made up the seasons, depending on what they could get from the wholesalers. My brother and I were never allowed to own bonafide sports equipment. Our family was not atypical in this. Parents expected their sons to grow up to become doctors, lawyers, accountants. There were strict quotas in medical and law schools in those days, so Jews had to do exceedingly well just to have a shot at admission. The dirtiest words in my family were 'truck driver,' even before the teamsters. If you didn't go to college and do well, then you would go to hell, not to be eternally consumed by flames, but to lead the unending life as a truck driver.

"From the age of ten or so, I started attending a neighborhood Zionist school, where we studied the Old Testament and, of course, Zionism as well as other aspects of Jewish history and culture. I went there after school, and when I was older, in the evenings. I also took courses at the Jewish Teacher's Seminary and People's University, another Zionist educational institution. These schools were important to me not only because I was intensely interested in things Jewish, but because, unlike my high school, there were girls. I realized early on that girls generally were much more mature than boys their age. I gravitated toward girls with literary and artistic interests and they became my closest friends.

"I went to Stuyvesant High School on Fourteenth Street in Manhattan with the intention of becoming a doctor. I soon discovered that I was a wash-out at organic chemistry and

similar subjects, and had to rethink my career plans, such as they were. I felt like a fish out of water at that school because I was not a scientist in the depths of my soul. Perhaps the best thing about Stuyvesant was that it was relatively far from home. I took the Third Avenue El down from the Bronx and then the subway. This was during the late forties and early fifties when the city was safe and no thought was given to danger. My happiest memories are of Stuyvesant Center on Fridays, 'St. Paramount's Day,' when we cut school to spend the afternoon at the movies.

"Our house was filled with music. My mother played the violin, my aunt sang, the radio played opera, gospel, and jazz. I began to see our culture as segregated. What was called 'American culture' most often did not include black or Latino culture. I started sneaking into jazz clubs when I was sixteen, beginning at Birdland, where Sarah Vaughan, Dizzie Gillespie and Tito Puente often played, to the Village Vanguard, Jimmy Ryan's and Eddie Condon's. I remember seeing Mingus, Max Roach, Bud Powell, Lester Young and Charlie Parker sharing the same tiny stage playing at each other's throats. Enough genius electricity to burn Birdland down. There were places that featured Dixieland where the midnight ritual was everyone dancing to 'When the Saints Come Marching In.' Later I would go to the Apollo and the Cotton Club, both in Harlem. By the time I graduated high school, jazz was the only music I listened to. It pushed out the boundaries of my world.

"I was still at odds about what I wanted to do and what I should do: become a poet or a pharmacist like my father. I continued to write poetry, and enrolled in the Columbia University School of Pharmacy. I became so unhappy with my choice, however, that I ran away from home in the most literary sense imaginable, leaving no note, but my copy of Thomas Wolfe's *You Can't Go Home Again* opened to a salient passage. Instead of going to school that day, I packed a bag, went

i am white　the milk is white　i am not the color
of the milk　i am white　the snow is white　i am not
the color of the snow

(From *Black Is Brown Is Tan* by Arnold Adoff. Illustrated by Emily Arnold McCully.)

to the bus station and bought a ticket for Chicago, the only
other city that existed for New Yorkers. I had in mind to get
a job, become an adult, write poetry. I got a room in a sleazy
hotel, went to a bar for a Singapore Sling and bought a pair
of chinos. Then I called my parents (nice Jewish boy that I
was, I didn't want to worry them). 'Study anything you want,
but COME HOME!' I went home on the next train, and enrolled at City College.

"They didn't have creative writing programs in those days,
and I was still intensely interested in politics, so I majored in
history. I minored in literature, but was loathe to major in it
lest I end up a flunky poet/English teacher. My plan was to
become a history professor and write poetry. City College was
truly an amazing place during the 1950s. One of my teachers
was Richard Myers, who argued Brown vs. Topeka Board of
Education [the landmark school desegregation case]. I learned
tremendous amounts of Constitutional law. I was passionate
about my studies in history. I also wrote for the college newspaper and literary magazine. Writers important to me at that
time were e.e. cummings, Gertrude Stein, and Langston Hughes
whose work led me to other black poets and writers. Of course
Joyce loomed large, as did Dylan Thomas. We loved Bernard
Shaw for his politics and vegetarianism. We would sit for
hours in the college cafeteria arguing about poets and poetry.

"A seminal event for me in college was the opportunity to
meet Charles Mingus, who had been invited to lecture by the
jazz club, of which I was president. Without a doubt, he was
the most impressive person I had ever met. From then on, I
went to see him wherever he played, and we got to know each
other. In time, he would become my spiritual father.

"As always, I was politically active. It is a myth that the fifties
was a decade during which nothing much happened. It was
far from a quiet time. A number of us were arrested for fighting to protect civil liberties on campus. The Students for Democratic Action picketed in Baltimore to protest the fact that
blacks were not allowed to eat at the same lunch counters as
whites. There were FBI agents on campus.

"I applied to Columbia's Political Science Department for
graduate work. I was totally committed at the time, but the
counselor who interviewed me said, 'This isn't your field. You
won't graduate from here and go on to be a professor. You'll
become a writer.' 'No,' I insisted. 'I want to go here. Really,
really.' My grades were excellent, my parents could afford the
tuition, he relented. But he turned out to be right, and I've
often wondered at his prescience. I did all the required course-
work for a Ph.D. in American history, but left unfinished my
dissertation on the Federal Emergency Relief Administration
and the New Deal, 1932-33. Again, the teachers I had were
phenomenal—Richard Hoffstedter, my academic advisor, won
a Pulitzer Prize while I was there; Henry Steele Commager
was my thesis advisor.

"In grad school I had a job teaching seventh-grade social studies at a *yeshiva* in the Brownsville section of Brooklyn. One

(From *I Am the Darker Brother: An Anthology of
Modern Poems by Black Americans* by Arnold Adoff.
Illustrated by Benny Andrews.)

The Poetry of Black America

Anthology of the 20th Century

The Poetry of Black America

Adoff

Harper & Row

Introduction by Gwendolyn Brooks

Edited by Arnold Adoff

(Jacket painting detail from ''Trash'' by Benny Andrews from *the Poetry of Black America,* edited by Arnold Adoff.)

hundred thirty-five dollars every two weeks, and we had to cash the checks in Brooklyn. If I took my check up to the Bronx to cash it at my father's drugstore, by the time it went through the banks, it would bounce. This was a very poor *yeshiva*. However, it was quite an interesting place as many of the students were from as far away as South America. The job also gave me confidence knowing I could stay alive outside grad school. This was important, because after two years I wanted to leave. The desire to live independently and focus on my writing had become overpowering.

''I moved to the Village, rented an apartment across from New York University, painted three of its four walls chocolate brown and began to live. I supported myself with substitute teaching and spent the rest of my time writing and going to jazz clubs. I also became Mingus' manager. He taught me much about living. I have a trunk full of notes from this period—things Mingus said and did, and running chronicles of the Village club scene. I haven't opened it since the fifties, but plan to use much of the material in the second book in my new series of autobiographical novels.

''I met Virginia Hamilton through Mingus in 1958. She, too, was living in the East Village working on a novel. I had heard about this brilliant young writer from Ohio, but nothing I had been told quite prepared me for the rarity of the woman. She was a ninety-eight-pound, fresh-faced Ohio farm girl, wore an extremely unusual boyish black-and-white plaid coat and boots and had marvellous curly hair, which she cut herself. She embodied all my ideals of an independent woman: she could think, she was a writer, she was an artist. Mingus had a crush on Virginia as well, but while he was involved playing his long sets, I spent time talking with her. One night we left a club with Mingus and as we pulled up to her door, I asked for her phone number. She whispered it in my ear. I didn't say another word to anyone until I got home, so intent was I on

keeping it in my memory. As soon as I got in, I called her (this must have been four in the morning), and what does a poet do when he's trying to impress the woman of his dreams? Well, he reads her his poetry, which I did, not realizing that Virginia had no heat in her apartment and was freezing to death while I declaimed. The next day I went over to her place, and we weren't separated again until 1963 when she went to the hospital to have our first child. We were married in 1960.

''I was staying up all night in the clubs, sleeping mornings and teaching public school in the afternoons, which wasn't leaving me enough time for writing. So I cut back on the music scene and focused on my poetry. The Village was a vibrant community of painters, writers, musicians who would meet in the coffeehouses and talk art. As a poet I have been more influenced by musicians and painters than by other writers. People who see my very early work, in which I used no capital letters, say, 'Oh, yes, you were reading cummings.' But I didn't read cummings until later. My reasons then for not using capital letters had to do with certain surrealist paintings I saw at the Museum of Modern Art. Man Ray was an important influence, as was Picasso, the Russian Constructivists and other painters and sculptors influenced by technology and things industrial. I was very excited by collaborations between visual artists and writers, particularly by their *livres d'art* published in Europe.

''Shortly after Virginia and I were married, we went to Paris for one month and then to Spain for six. We rented a little house near Torremolinos, and settled in with our two green Olivettis, she working on an adult novel, I on my poetry. In 1965, we again went to Argeles-sur-Mer, a tiny village on the Mediterranean coast of France, near Spain for six months of uninterrupted writing. This time we took our two-year-old daughter, Leigh, eleven suitcases, a trunk, and a teddy bear tied to a stroller. The French had never seen a child carried in a gerry-pack and because I carried Leigh around on my back most of the time, or pushed her in the stroller, they assumed she was congenitally unable to walk. We took a short break and went to Paris, during which time our daughter took her first steps. We later learned that when we returned to Argeles-sur-Mer, people thought a miracle had been worked for Leigh at Lourdes.

''One day I brought home a magazine with the famous photograph of the black man throwing a firebomb in Watts. That forced us to think seriously about whether we wished to remain in Europe. Virginia is black, our children brown—we felt somehow that it would be wrong to stay. Besides, it all seemed very exciting and we didn't want to be removed from the action. So we returned to New York, where we threw ourselves into our work and as much political work as we could handle.

''I resumed collecting black literature, which I had begun in the late 1950s and early 1960s teaching in Harlem and on Manhattan's Upper West Side. I would dig up old magazines like *Dial* and look for specifically black periodicals like *Opportunity, Urban League, Negro Digest, Black Digest, Black World,* most of which no longer exist. I'd haunt bookshops all over town. One of my favorites was University Books on Fourteenth Street on the ninth floor of an old building. You'd get out of the old freight elevator and there you would be in the center of this wonderful world of things African.''[1]

''As a teacher I had students who wanted life in those dusty classrooms. They wanted pictures of themselves inside themselves. I began to bring some in. I was the dealer. The pusher of poems and stories. Plays and paintings. Jazz and blues. And my students began to push on me. To deal their sounds

My knee is only sprained. ■ (From *Sports Pages* by Arnold Adoff. Illustrated by Steve Kuzma.)

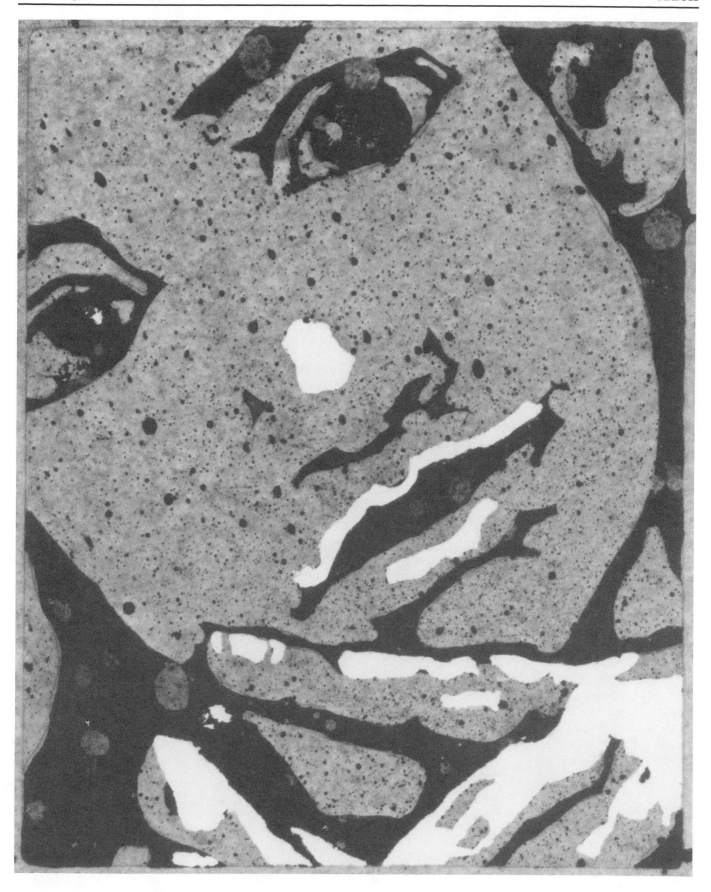

Remember: long ago before people moved and migrated, and mixed and matched. ■ (From
All the Colors of the Race by Arnold Adoff. Illustrated by John Steptoe.)

and write their poems. And I was made to become serious about myself. To get my head together and attempt to go beyond the classrooms and students and schools. To go beyond the racist textbooks and anthologies that were on the shelves and in the bookstores.''[2]

"One day I asked a friend, who was an editor at Macmillan, to make some copies for one of my classes. While standing at the machine, she read the poems and was overwhelmed by their quality and importance. She 'smelled' a book, in other words, and arranged for me to meet with the editor-in-chief of the house. The time was right. People in publishing were beginning to recognize that our national bibliography was not sufficiently representative of black writers and that the balance had to be addressed. There was a good deal of money around then for such projects as anthologies of black poetry. My first book, which was published in 1968, was *I Am the Darker Brother: An Anthology of Modern Poems by Negro Americans.*

"My history training served me well with the anthologies. My research skills were well honed, and I had a natural historical perspective, which is very helpful when you're working with a lot of material from different periods. Doing an anthology is a bit like solving a mystery: instead of being 'hot on the trail' of criminals, one is in 'hot pursuit' of clues to literary movements and submovements. I went to extraordinary efforts to track down poets whose work had appeared in little magazines thirty or more years ago. Sometimes, poets were pleased to be 'rediscovered,' but sometimes they preferred to be left alone, allowed to go out of print, saying that their poetry

'belonged to a different time, a different life.' It's an interesting phenomenon, poets who disappear—an unsettling phenomenon.

"I saw *I Am the Darker Brother* as the end of my anthologizing, but it was just the beginning. With every anthology, I uncovered more and more material. Each pointed to the need for yet another. And my own passion for the task intensified. *The Poetry of Black America* is the largest anthology of black verse ever published in the United States. It contains six hundred poems, although my manuscript consisted of three thousand poems that richly deserved to be included. The final choices were among the most agonizing selections I have ever had to make.''[1]

"I want my anthologies of Black American writing to make Black kids strong in their knowledge of themselves and their great literary heritage—give them facts and people and power. I also want these Black books of mine to give knowledge to White kids around the country, so that mutual respect and understanding will come from mutual learning. We *can* go beyond the murders and muddles of the present.

"Children have to understand that the oversimplifications they get in classrooms, along with the token non-White artists represented, are not the true American literature. Melvin Tolson stands with Robert Frost as does Robert Hayden with Robert Lowell. The great force and numbers of the current, most exciting generation of Black writers in the history of this country is overwhelming to the White educator, textbook writer,

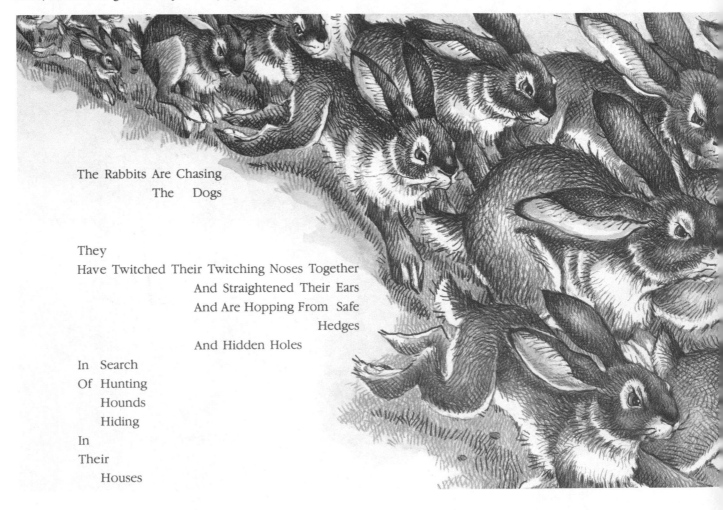

The Rabbits Are Chasing
    The   Dogs

They
Have Twitched Their Twitching Noses Together
            And Straightened Their Ears
            And Are Hopping From Safe
                     Hedges
            And Hidden Holes

In Search
Of Hunting
    Hounds
    Hiding
In
Their
    Houses

and guardian-of-the-culture who wish to preserve the mainstream culture in its basic White dress. But for those who want the truth, for themselves and for their students, using an anthology is the first step to discovery. The anthology then leads to individual works of the writers."[3]

Adoff does not consider himself a spokesperson for the black community. "Blacks and other so-called minorities have too many outside spokespersons. They're quite capable of speaking on their own behalf. I never want to be caught in that trap, and have stayed away from reviewing books by black authors or writing critical essays on literary works by blacks. I have no intention of encroaching on the terrain of black intellectuals and black writers.

"The negative aspect of doing so many anthologies was that people came to think of me primarily as an anthologizer, which made it difficult to get my first books of poetry published and reviewed. The publishing media, it seems, has trouble with people who wear more than one hat. I, however, have always thought of myself as a poet first.

"Shortly after we returned from France in 1965 I enrolled in the New School to study poetry with Jose Garcia Villa, an absolutely brilliant Philippine-American poet. Jose became my second spiritual father, and I studied with him for several crucial years. He talked about creating a poetry that was as pure as music. In one of his books, a comma separates every word—his so-called 'experiments.' His extremism based on an exhaustive knowledge of the art and craft of poetry set him apart.

"A poem must have form and physical shape which should serve to promote its message. I use the image of invisible rubber bands pulling the reader's eye from the last letter of the last word in the first line down to the first letter of the first word in the last line. The eye should be able to travel freely, and not get hung up on any clanking chains holding the work together. The music of language greatly affects meaning—most obvious where a given line is broken. I hate to see poetry reprinted in newspapers or magazines that adhere to a strict prose format and indicate line breaks with slashes. A poem printed like prose automatically loses its intrinsic meaning. Ideally, each poem should be read three times: for meaning; for rhythm; for technical tricks. My poems demand active participation.

"My first book, *MA nDA LA,* is a poem about the music of the 'ah' vowel sound. Logically, the poem makes no sense and is not supposed to. I sent it to my editor at Macmillan, who sent it back because she didn't understand it. I then sent it to editor Ursula Nordstrom, who also didn't understand it but thought that 'it sings, and we love it, and we're going to try to find an illustrator.' They found the ideal artist in Emily McCully. She gave the poem a racial, geographic and social context, none of which is in the poem."[1]

Adoff's second book of original poetry, *Black Is Brown Is Tan,* was one of the first children's books published in this country to deal directly with growing up in an interracial family. "Of course I was thinking of my children. The book is for them, and, really, for all the beautiful interracial kids in

Cottontails Of Courage

                 Shout

Rabbits Of The Field
            Come
               Out
And
Together We Can Bite
             Back
That
Pack Of Dogs So Mean
The
Way We Bite   A Cabbage
           Or A Bean

(From *The Cabbages Are Chasing the Rabbits* by Arnold Adoff. Illustrated by Janet Stevens.)

the world. Gentle though it may be, it was the target of a citizens vigilante group in a suburb of New Haven, Connecticut. Too embarrassed to admit racist undertones, they argued against the book because I used no capitalization. Happily, this group did not prevail. Other books of mine have been similarly attacked, but have always been ultimately saved from censorship."[1]

His original collections consist of books of poems on a particular subject, like *Eats, Tornado! OUTside/INside Poems* or *Birds,* and books of poems from the viewpoint of a particular character, like *I Am the Running Girl* or *Sports Pages.* "*Sports Pages* I consider a breakthrough. Not only did I manage to work in a longer form of a combination of poetic prose and poetry, but I was able to deal with some autobiographical material using individual voice in the midst of organized activity.

"Individual poems start out as a teasing rhythm or an elusive hint of melody in my ear. From these initial fragments is born the language of my poems. It can be a slow, laborious, and mysterious process. It is not unusual for them to go through seventy-five drafts. I tell my students that I have a 'learner's permit' in poetry (I've been writing poetry for over forty years). I still question, still feel unsure. This is, afterall, part of being a poet. With each attempt he sees the world for the first time. Too, the creative process plays on dualities: normal/abnormal, sane/insane, happy/sad, vulnerable/guarded. The tension between these polar opposites can tear you apart.

"A duality I consciously play within my work is the 'mundane' and the 'fantastical.' A lot of my poems have to do with normal, everyday things, like eating a Hostess Twinkie every day of your life. What counts is not eating the Twinkie, but the perspective of the act. I happen to believe that eating a Hostess Twinkie can be a fantastical experience. Anything can be a fantastical and even mystical experience. It all depends on the way you look at it. Children understand this concept very well.

"I began writing for kids because I wanted to effect a change in American society. I continue in that spirit. By the time we reach adulthood, we are closed and set in our attitudes. The chances of a poet reaching us are very slim. But I can open a child's imagination, develop his appetite for poetry, and most importantly, show him that poetry is a natural part of everyday life. We all need someone to point out that the emperor is wearing no clothes. That is the poet's job.

"I know, too, that I write for children because the child in me is still very much alive. A book that will forever remain dear to my heart is *It Is the Poem Singing into Your Eyes,* an anthology of poems by young people. I was able to convince a publisher to accept mail from young poets from all over the country, which normally they are most hesitant to do. I sent flyers to schools, put notices in the *New York Times Book Review* and similar publications, and, lo and behold, we got over six thousand submissions. The tragedy—and I do consider it a tragedy—is that I was allowed to publish only one hundred poems. There were many, many, many poems that were absolutely superb. Most of the poems in the book were by sixteen- and seventeen-year-olds, and some by ten-year-olds. One of the poets, August Wilson, is now a Pulitzer Prize-winning playwright. The title of the volume was suggested by one of my young correspondents. I loved her statement—a poem truly does sing into your eyes and then on into your mind and soul."[1]

Adoff lives with Virginia Hamilton and their children in Yellow Springs, Ohio. "Virginia teases me that I 'kidnapped' her twice to Europe; the third time she 'kidnapped me' to her home

town where most of her family still lives. We bought some land behind her parents' farm, built a house and settled in. Sometimes I marvel to find myself living here after so many years as an inveterate New Yorker. I liked the idea that our kids could walk across the fields to their grandmother's house for homemade cookies. Antioch College in Yellow Springs creates a lot of literary and artistic activity here. For that matter, a wife who is a brilliant novelist and two kids who are talented musicians, create a lot of scintillating activity within my own walls.

"During the academic year, we keep an apartment in New York City. For the last couple of years, Virginia and I have been distinguished visiting professors at Queens College. We team-teach, using only our own books. Most of our students are professional teachers who are living in the world of children, which makes the process stimulating and immediate for all of us. They can apply something we taught in class the day before. The department has a special relationship with the Louis Armstrong School in Queens, a magnet for the arts. Each year Queens College sponsors a conference on children's literature, attracting the best and brightest authors in the field."[1]

A legendary teacher, Adoff has written extensively on his experiences and methods. "If you really want to write," he advises, "you must read, read, read. Steep yourself in the field of children's literature, if that is what you want, or if you want to be a novelist, read many novels. Set aside some daily time for writing. Assign yourself long- and short-term writing and reading projects. Discipline yourself. I recognize the worth of writing workshops, although writing is a solitary activity. For one thing, it's nice to be in the company of other writers, to deal with deadlines, and to subject your work to criticism. However, avoid, like the plague, any writing teacher who emphasizes the importance of 'self-expression.' Self-expression is not positive. A diary is for self-expression and similar forms of spilling guts. A poem is a work of art. And any poet, be it a ten-year-old kid or a poet with forty years of practice, should have in mind to make a work of art."[1]

FOOTNOTE SOURCES

[1]Based on an interview by Marguerite Feitlowitz for *Something about the Author.*
[2]Arnold Adoff, "Preface," *The Poetry of Black America,* Harper, 1973.
[3]Lee Bennet Hopkins, editor, "Arnold Adoff," *More Books by More People,* Citation, 1974.

FOR MORE INFORMATION SEE:

Kirkus Review, April 15, 1970.
Horn Book, April, 1970, June, 1970, February, 1972, December, 1972, August, 1982 (p. 420).
Publishers Weekly, July 13, 1970 (p. 86ff), August 26, 1988 (p. 88).
Bulletin of the Center for Children's Books, September, 1970.
New York Times Book Review, September 6, 1970, January 23, 1972.
Martha E. Ward and Dorothy A. Marquardt, *Authors of Books for Young People,* second edition, Scarecrow, 1971.
Top of the News, January, 1972 (p. 152ff), winter, 1981 (p. 192ff).
Judith Wagner, "More Vivid Than Daylight," *Cincinnati Enquirer,* January 5, 1975.
Antioch Review, fall, 1975.
Authors in the News, Volume 1, Gale, 1976.
Doris de Montreville and Elizabeth D. Crawford, editors, *Fourth Book of Junior Authors and Illustrators,* H. W. Wilson, 1978.
Washington Post Book World, November 11, 1979.
Children's Literature in Education, Volume 11, number 3, 1980.

Arnold Adoff, *All the Colors of the Race*, Lothrop, 1982.
School Library Journal, March, 1982, May, 1986 (p. 86), June/July, 1988 (p. 107).
Interracial Books for Children Bulletin, number 1, 1983, number 6, 1984.
Language Arts, April, 1983, March, 1985 (p.235ff).
D. L. Kirkpatrick, editor, *Twentieth-Century Children's Writers*, St. Martin's, 1983.
Children's Literature Review, Volume VII, Gale, 1984.
Lion and the Unicorn, Volume 10, 1986 (p. 9ff).

TOM BAHTI

BAHTI, Tom 1926-1972

PERSONAL: Born June 23, 1926, in South Range, Mich.; died in 1972; son of Eino and Alice (Howe) Bahti; married Margaret Pack, August 16, 1949; children: Mark, Kurt, Tani. *Education:* University of New Mexico, B.A., 1949. *Residence:* Tucson, Arizona.

CAREER: Author, illustrator, lecturer, artist, shopkeeper, and columnist. *Awards, honors:* Caldecott Honor Book from the American Library Association, 1973, for *When Clay Sings;* Awards from the University of Arizona Tucson Indian Center.

WRITINGS:

An Introduction to Southwestern Indian Arts and Crafts (photos by K. Camille den Dooven), KC Publications, 1964, revised edition, 1983.
Southwestern Indian Tribes, KC Publications, 1968.
Southwestern Indian Ceremonials, KC Publications, 1970.

ILLUSTRATOR

Byrd Baylor, *Before You Came This Way*, Dutton, 1969.
B. Baylor, *When Clay Sings*, Scribner, 1972, reissued, 1987.

SIDELIGHTS: When Clay Sings, written by Byrd Baylor, earned a posthumous Caldecott Honor for illustrator Tom Bahti. Known as an anthropologist and well-known judge of Indian arts and crafts, he had lectured and written articles on the subject.

BALES, Carol Ann 1940-

PERSONAL: Born November 19, 1940, in St. Louis, Mo.; daughter of Ella T. (Schierbaum) Kothe. *Education:* University of Missouri, A.B., 1963, B.J., 1963. *Politics:* Independent. *Home:* Box 5, Route 1, Wentzville, Mo. 63385.

CAREER: Free-lance photographer and writer for local and national publications, 1965—.

WRITINGS:

Kevin Cloud: Chippewa Boy in the City, Reilly & Lee, 1972.
A Chinatown Sunday: The Story of Lillian Der, Reilly & Lee, 1973.
Tales of the Elders: A Memory Book of Men and Women Who Came to America as Immigrants, 1900-1930 (young adult), Follett, 1977.

Contributor of articles and photographs to periodicals, including *Saturday Review, Life International, TransAction*, and *Chicago Tribune*.

WORK IN PROGRESS: A book on American Indians living in the city.

BOYNTON, Sandra (Keith) 1953-

PERSONAL: Born April 3, 1953, in Orange, N.J.; daughter of Robert Whitney and Jeanne Carolyn (Ragsdale) Boynton; married James Patrick McEwan (a writer), October 28, 1978. *Education:* Yale University, B.A., 1974; graduate study at the University of California-Berkeley Drama School, 1974-75, and Yale University School of Drama, 1976-77. *Religion:* Quaker. *Agent:* Edite Kroll, 31 East 31st St., Apt. 2E, New York, N. Y. 10016.

CAREER: Author, illustrator, cartoonist. Recycled Paper Products, Inc., Chicago, Ill., designer of greeting cards, 1974—, vice-president, 1980—. *Member:* Cartoonists Guild. *Awards, honors:* Irma Simonton Black Award from the Bank Street College of Education, 1986, for *Chloe and Maude;* Children's

(From *Moo, Baa, La La La* by Sandra Boynton. Illustrated by the author.)

Choice Award from the Children's Book Council and the International Reading Association, for *Hester in the Wild*.

WRITINGS:

*ALL SELF-ILLUSTRATED JUVENILE PICTURE BOOKS, EXCEPT AS
INDICATED*

Hester in the Wild, Harper, 1979.
Hippos Go Berserk, Little, Brown, 1979.
If at First. . . (Junior Literary Guild selection), Little, Brown,
1980.
But Not the Hippopotamus, Simon & Schuster, 1982.
The Going to Bed Book, Simon & Schuster, 1982.
Opposites, Simon & Schuster, 1982.
Moo, Baa, La La La, Simon & Schuster, 1982.
A Is for Angry: An Animal and Adjective Alphabet, Workman,
1983.
A to Z, Simon & Schuster, 1984.
Blue Hat, Green Hat, Simon & Schuster, 1984.
Doggies, Simon & Schuster, 1984.
Horns to Toes (and in Between), Simon & Schuster, 1984.
Chloe and Maude, Little, Brown, 1985.
Good Night, Good Night, Random House, 1985.
Hey! What's That?, Random House, 1985.

OTHER; SELF-ILLUSTRATED

Gopher Baroque and Other Beastly Conceits (cartoons), Dutton, 1979.
The Compleat Turkey, Little, Brown, 1980.
Chocolate: The Consuming Passion, Workman, 1982.
Don't Let the Turkeys Get You Down, Workman, 1986.
Christmastime, Workman, 1987.

ILLUSTRATOR

Jamie McEwan, *The Story of Grump and Pout*, Crown, 1988.

SIDELIGHTS: Well known for her greeting cards that feature anthropomorphic creatures, Boynton has also written clever adult books filled with her cartoons and books for young children. Born in Orange, New Jersey, the illustrator-cartoonist grew up in Philadelphia, where she attended Germantown Friends School (where her father taught English) and then earned her B.A. degree from Yale University.

While at Yale, she took a course in illustrating children's books from Maurice Sendak. "I don't think he remembers me,"[1] commented Boynton. She remembers, however, that Sendak

Six hippos show up with a quest. ■ (From *Hippos Go Berserk* by Sandra Boynton. Illustrated
by the author.)

told her that she could do much better. "He said, 'This looks like greeting card art.'"[1]

Sendak was right. Her illustrations were appropriate for the first greeting cards that she created in the summer of 1974 to earn money for graduate school. With the assistance of an uncle who had a printing business and had agreed to print up sets of her gift and greeting cards, Boynton sold 10,000 of them to East Coast craft shops. At the end of the summer, she went to a trade show in New York City and talked to greeting card companies. She found a fledgling young company, Recycled Paper Products, which was run by two Amherst College graduates who were combining ecology and business, to produce her cards. Combining whimsical animals and wry humor, Boynton's cards appealed to a wide variety of people. "One thing I do know is that, against all the rules, forty per cent of my sales are attributable to men. The industry never thought of them as card buyers, but I'm apparently hitting that market.

"One of my Valentine's Day cards, one of my particular favorites, is a card that says, 'I know that no mass-produced card could ever express the unique, enduring, profound feeling I have for you.' And then on the inside it says, 'But I also know that you would have throttled me unmercifully if I didn't get you one.' The interesting thing about that card is that I doubt there was one female who sent it to a male. No matter how much you get away from stereotypes, I guess there is still that kind of relationship where the woman expects a card and the man doesn't see the point. This particular card really hit on that.

"Another difference about my cards is that right now my friendship cards are selling almost as much as birthday, which by any wisdom of the industry just doesn't happen. But I think there's a need for them. People only have so many birthdays, but when you want to communicate with someone and you don't have time to write a long letter, and a short note would be sort of offensive, the perfect thing is a card that has no occasion. There are so many sentiments that other card companies weren't hitting—anything from 'I'm depressed' to 'long-distance relationships. . .aren't easy.' I love doing these cards because you can never run out of permutations of people's interactions with each other.

"I must admit that sometimes I've been tempted to do a card that meant absolutely nothing to me, just to see what would happen with it. Maybe I shouldn't say this, but some of my cards have been printed with the wrong message or with something left off and they still sold well. I've thought about doing that intentionally just to see what would happen, but to find out that it would sell anyway might be too depressing.

"There have also been some other cards that I thought would have absolutely no market and ended up doing very well, for no apparent reason. I did one recently that had a pig running across saying, 'Quack, quack, quack, quack.' And then a turkey runs across saying, 'Oink, oink, oink, oink.' Then a rabbit runs across saying, 'Moo, moo.' And then in the last frame a turkey says, 'Arf?' That's it. When you open it up it says, 'If you understand this card please write and explain.' The point of the card then is that there really is no point, except maybe to get someone to write to you."[2]

Besides greeting cards, her animals appear on calendars, posters, towels, stuffed animals, T-shirts, mugs and stationery. She is also an author of numerous books for children and adults. Boynton "works in binges." "It's gotten so much easier. I've become a better artist, for one thing. It's pleasing to be so fluent at something—it's a feeling of power."[3]

DECEMBER
PERSONALITY OF THE MONTH

SANTA "ST. NICK" CLAUS

AGE: 1,706

RESIDES: North Pole

PROFESSION: Part-time Philanthropist

MOST INFLUENTIAL BOOK: Spiegel Catalog

QUOTE: "I think it's not so important what others say about you, as long as you truly believe in yourself."

DRINK: About 60 million glasses of milk every December 24.

(From *Christmastime* by Sandra Boynton. Illustrated by the author.)

She works a forty-hour week from her studio next to her Lakeview, Connecticut farmhouse which she shares with husband Jamie McEwan, a writer and a former Olympic bronze medalist in whitewater canoeing, and three children. "I always knew I would never work for anybody—it would be impossible for me."[3]

Boynton works at a fairly fast pace, but ". . .I won't compromise my work just to do something to sell."[1]

One popular Boynton cartoon shows a pig in a tutu doing ballet exercises on a rail fence. The caption reads, "Ambition knows no bounds."

"My animals are not people. But they are not really animals, either.

"They are philosophers."[1]

Their creator describes herself as a ". . .humorist. I guess any good humorist is a philosopher. But that seems too pretentious to say about myself."[1]

Boynton has written numerous books for younger children, including *Hippos Go Berserk* in which she reveals her ear for nonsense rhyme. Not only a counting book but a visual tool as well, *Hippos Go Berserk* was described by *Wilson Library Journal* as ". . .a small, unpretentious book, but a special one in terms of overall unity, not to mention its warmth and whimsicality. . . .The total effect is light, airy, and tender." The old adage of "try, try again" is spotlighted in *If at First. . . .*

The desperate attempts of an orange mouse to push a purple elephant up a hill sets the stage for a book that can be enjoyed as much by adults as by children.

Other children's books written and illustrated by Boynton include *Hester in the Wild, Moo, Baa, La La La, Opposites, The Going to Bed Book, But Not the Hippopotamus,* and *A Is for Angry: An Adjective and Animal Alphabet.* Most recently, Boynton illustrated her husband's book, *The Story of Grump and Pout.*

FOOTNOTE SOURCES

[1]Victoria Irwin, "Sandra Boynton Takes the Cake with 'Hippo Birdy, Two Ewes. . . ,'" *Christian Science Monitor,* December 30, 1980.
[2]Ann Marie Lipinski, "When It Comes to Turkey Jokes, Sandra Boynton's a Real Card," *Chicago Tribune,* November 27, 1980.
[3]Laurie A. O'Neill, "Illustrator Finds Seventy-six Ways to Say 'I Love You,'" *New York Times,* February 13, 1983.

FOR MORE INFORMATION SEE:

Deborah Mesce, "Boynton's Salutations Are Real Cards," *Houston Post,* March 19, 1981.
Sarah Fritschner, "What a Card," *Washington Post,* April 3, 1983.
Linda Matchan, "Greetings! The Woman behind Those Animal Cards," *Boston Globe,* April 8, 1986 (p. 11).
Paula Span, "When You Care to Send the Very Whimsical," *San Francisco Chronicle,* April 22, 1986.
P. Span, "Boynton: From Dilettante to Star, Riding a Hippo," *Detroit News,* May 4, 1986 (p. 1B).
Marilyn A. Harris and Marc Frons, "She Cares Enough to Battle the Very Biggest," *Business Week,* July 21, 1986 (p. 96).
Barbara Mayer, "Cartoonist Goes from Cards to Sheets and Clothes," *Detroit News,* September 11, 1986.
David Hinckley, "Jingle Bears and Hippo Gnu Boynton Book," *Daily News* (New York), November 29, 1987.

BYARD, Carole (Marie)   1941-

PERSONAL: Born July 22, 1941, in Atlantic City, N.J.; daughter of William (a construction worker) and Viola Eugenia (Longdon) Byard. *Education:* Attended Fleisher Art Memorial, 1961-63; Phoenix School of Design, diploma, 1968; studied lithography with H. Morimoto. *Address:* 463 West St., New York, N.Y. 10014.

CAREER: Artist and illustrator. Phoenix School of Design, New York City, instructor in life drawing and basic drawing, 1968-71; Studio Museum in Harlem, New York City, instructor of figure drawing and illustration, 1972-73; Metropolitan Museum of Art, New York City, instructor in drawing and painting, 1974; New York Foundation for the Arts, New York City, instructor of drawing and painting, 1978; Baltimore School for the Arts, Md., instructor of drawing and painting and department head of visual arts, 1980-84; Maryland Institute College of Art, Baltimore, instructor of foundation drawing, 1983; Parsons School of Design, New York City, faculty member, 1988—. Lecturer, demonstrator, and workshop leader, 1977-88. Commissioned works include a religious mural for House of Light, Ibadan, Nigeria, 1972, and a panel for Kwanza celebration, Studio Museum in Harlem, New York City, 1973-74; artist-in-residence, Studio Museum in Harlem, New York City, 1972-73, New York Foundation for the Arts, 1978, and Blue Mountain Center, N.Y. 1985; president, Darshan (pub-

lisher of original fine art prints), 1974—; mural artist, New Jersey State Council on the Arts, 1976; U.S. artist participant, Festival of African Culture, Lagos, Nigeria, 1977.

EXHIBITIONS: Black Artist Guild, New York City, 1971; "From Life," University of Rhode Island, 1971; "Where We At, Black Women Artists," Weusi Nyumba Ya Sanna Gallery, New York City, 1972; Gallery 1199, New York City, 1972, 1975, 1978; Westbeth Gallery, New York City, 1972; Bedford-Stuyvesant Restoration Center, New York City, 1972; The East, New York City, 1972; University of Ibaden, Nigeria, 1972; "Mother and Child," RTP Inc., New York City, 1973; Studio Museum in Harlem, New York City, 1973, 1974, 1979, 1985; "Blacks: U.S.A. Now," New York Cultural Center, New York City, 1973; "Black Artists Graphic Exhibition," Union Carbide, New York City, 1973; "Tenth World Festival of Youth and Students against War and Facism," Berlin, Germany, 1973; "In Her Own Image," Fleisher Art Memorial, Philadelphia, Pa., 1974; Janet Carter Gallery, New York City, 1974, 1976, 1977; "On Site," New York State Building, 1974; "Children of Africa," American Museum of Natural History, New York City, 1974-75.

"A Black Perspective on Art," Black Enterprise Magazine, 1975; "Black Women Artists," 1975; "Contributing Black Artists," Black Enterprise Magazine, 1976; Howard University Gallery of Art, Washington, D.C., 1976, 1980; "Intergrafik," Berlin, Germany, 1976, 1980; "We the People," El Museo del Barrio, New York City, 1976; "Migrations: African-American Printmakers," travelling exhibition through South America, 1976-77; "Fourteen Afro-American Artists," Pratt Institute Gallery, New York City, 1976; "Carole Byard: Spells and Spirits," University of Massachusetts, Amherst, 1977; "Festival of African Culture Exhibition," Nigeria, West Africa, 1977; Amherst College, Amherst, Mass., 1977; "Two African American Artists," Atlantic City Art Gallery, N.J., 1978; "Black Enterprise Magazine Print Exhibit," New York City, 1978; "Bayou Classic," New Orleans, La., 1978; "Festival of African Culture Reunion Exhibition," Black Arts Consortium, New York City, 1979; "The Child," Gallery 62, New York City, 1979-80; "Prints and Drawings, Carole Byard," Institute of International Education, United Nations Plaza, New York City, 1979-80; Smithsonian Institution Traveling Exhibition, 1979-84.

"Voices Beyond the Veil," University of Maryland, Baltimore, 1980; "The Nineteen Seventies," Museum of Afro-American Artists, Boston, Mass., 1980; "Contributing Artists," Black Enterprise Magazine, New York City, and Craftery Gallery, Hartford, Conn., 1980; Alcazar Gallery, Baltimore School for the Arts, Md., 1981-84; "Carole Byard/James Denmark—Roots in Art," Scarsdale, N.Y., 1981; "Visual Conversations—East Coast/West Coast," Sparc Gallery, Venice, Calif., 1983; "Art against Apartheid," Westbeth Gallery/ Abyssinian Baptist Church, New York City, 1984.

Pickard Smith Gallery, University of California, Santa Cruz, 1985; Columbia Museum, S.C., 1985; "Carole Byard" (one-woman show), Reese Palley Gallery, Atlantic City, N.J., 1985; "Visions of the World," Women's Center, New York City, 1986; "Liberty," Westbeth Gallery, New York City, 1986; "Expressions African-Art against Apartheid," Fashion Moda, Bronx, N.Y., 1987; "Concrete Crisis," Exit Art, New York City, 1987; "Home," Goddard Riverside Center, New York City, 1987; "Artists' Book Exhibitions," Houston Museum, Tex., 1988; "Pleides and Friends," Pleides Gallery, New York City, 1988; "Praisesong for Charles," Outdoor Sculptural Installation, Art Awareness, Lexington, N.Y., 1988; "Coast to Coast," Franklin Furnace, N.Y., 1988; "The Family in Contemporary Art," Nexus Gallery, Philadelphia, Pa., 1989.

CAROLE BYARD

MEMBER: Black Artists Guild, Westbeth Graphic Artists. *Awards, honors:* Ford Foundation Travel Grant, 1972, for study at the Institute of International Education; Unique New Yorker Art Award, 1978; Coretta Scott King Award for Illustration from the American Library Association, 1978, for *Africa Dream,* and 1980, for *Cornrows;* National Black Child Development Institute Award, 1981; Visual Art Fellowship from the National Endowment for the Arts, 1985; Art Awareness Artist-in-Residence Grant, 1988; Collaborative Grant, with Madeleine Yayodele Nelson, from New American Radio, 1990.

ILLUSTRATOR:

JUVENILE

Helen H. King, *Willy,* Doubleday, 1971.
Phumla, *Nomi and the Magic Fish: A Story from Africa,* Doubleday, 1972.
Dorothy M. Callahan, *Under Christopher's Hat,* Scribner, 1972.
Lee Po, reteller, *The Sycamore Tree and Other African Tales,* Doubleday, 1974.
Tobi Tobias, *Arthur Mitchell* (biography), Crowell, 1975.
Eloise Greenfield, *Africa Dream,* John Day, 1977.
Lessie J. Little and E. Greenfield, *I Can Do It by Myself,* Crowell, 1978.
Camille Yarbrough, *Cornrows,* Coward, 1979.
Adjai Robinson, *Three African Tales,* Putnam, 1979.
E. Greenfield, *Grandmama's Joy,* Collins, 1980.
Phillip Mendez, *The Black Snowman,* Scholastic, 1989.
Mildred Pitts Walker, *Have a Happy By,* Lothrop, 1989.

SIDELIGHTS: "I was born and raised in Atlantic City, New Jersey."

"Our house was always full of relatives—cousins, aunts, uncles—and lots of love. My brother and I grew up very close. Our mother died when we were very young. Our father raised us with the help of our grandmother and other relatives. William Byard, my father, was the type of person everyone loved. He was warm, kind, soft spoken as well as a hard worker."[1]

As a child, Byard was interested in reading and spelling. She discovered drawing in the fourth grade—her first creative effort was a copy of Myron's "Discus Thrower." "Though I was pleased with the result, I kept the drawing as a very personal secret. And I used every chance I could get to do something more in art than what was assigned in school. This, too, became a private and secret kind of mystery for me."[1]

During her high school years, Byard became aware of racial and social prejudice. "My father had been laid off when his job, under government control, was transferred back to civilian hands. He'd been driving heavy equipment in the construction industry and was replaced by a white union worker."[1]

Her exceptional artistic talent was noticed by an art teacher who encouraged her to pursue a career in art. "Through my guidance counsellor, Mrs. Gerard was able to direct me to an art scholarship to the Columbus College of Art in Columbus, Ohio. I didn't even have the bus fare to Columbus. As badly as I wanted to be a painter I had to be realistic. My father had

(From *Under Christopher's Hat* by Dorothy M. Callahan. Illustrated by Carole M. Byard.)

been laid off his job. So I wrote the school in Columbus asking if they would hold the scholarship for me until I could get enough money to get there and use it. They agreed and I got a job and began putting some money away.''[1] Byard worked as a resort hotel chambermaid and later as a factory worker. She was slowly accumulating enough money for art school.

Nineteen-year-old Byard helped to support her family with a civil service job and attended art school in Philadelphia part-time. ''After high school, my earliest formal art education was at the Fleisher Art Memorial in Philadelphia, Pennsylvania. The two years I spent at Fleisher were wonderful and gave me the courage to pursue my childhood dream of becoming a fine artist.''

''I used to get to Fleisher Memorial before the school opened, as much as one-and-a-half hours early. And I'd stand outside and wait. As it began to grow cold, a black woman, who was the housekeeper, let me sit inside completely alone in that grottolike interior until the basement where I took my sculpture class was opened.''[1]

Four years later, Byard sold her car and quit her job so that she could move to New York City and attend art school there. ''I arrived in New York City in 1964 to study at the New York Phoenix School of Design (which later became Pratt Manhattan Center). As a full-time student for four consecutive years, I was awarded a full tuition merit scholarship.''

''. . .I was twenty-three years old. Phoenix was strict and heavy on academics. You learned basic drawing and you practiced no tricks—no beards, dungarees, or long hair at that time.''

''I got other jobs in the school—in the office—the library—everything to make it possible for me to pay for my education.

I even had a job pasting cloth swatches in sample books—a job that provided my carfare.''[1]

Upon graduation from Phoenix, Byard accepted a position at the school, first as an assistant instructor in basic drawing and later as a full instructor teaching life drawing, pen and ink, and painting. ''Since graduating in 1968, I have enjoyed a career as a painter and graphic artist. Gaining experience as an educator in colleges and special arts training schools, I have developed skills as an arts instructor and administrator. Teaching, lecturing, exhibiting and traveling has heightened my political awareness and broadened my social vision.

''Since the early 1970s, my work has been exhibited in a number of major and alternative gallery spaces. My career and work is regularly featured in books, periodicals and film documentaries, the most recent being *IKON* magazine which featured a portfolio of my drawings.

'''Blacks: USA Now,'' a 1973 New York Cultural Center exhibition, is a memorable early exhibition. Of equal importance to my career was the 1979 exhibition, 'Impressions/Expressions: Black American Graphics,' which opened at the Studio Museum in Harlem. This show later travelled around the country for five years under the sponsorship of the Smithsonian Institution.''

Byard became a founding member of the Black Artists Guild in 1971, and in 1972 visited Africa. ''I applied for a Ford Motors grant. . .and was amazed to get it. The grant was set up to cover black artists and five of us were chosen. Charles Russell, Quincy Troupe, Jackie Early, and Terry Morgan were the four others. Our grants were for travel anywhere in the world and I chose Africa. I traveled alone. And I went to Senegal, Ghana, Ethiopia, and Egypt—carrying with me my

(From *Cornrows* by Camille Yarbrough. Illustrated by Carole Byard.)

travel easel and paints. That trip to Africa was the most moving event in my life.

"Nobody knew specifically where I was going—when I'd be arriving—and there was no one to meet me at any place along the way. I was just overwhelmed at being able to do this by myself. . . .And everyone was most friendly toward me. I met and stayed with a Nigerian family in a village near Ibadan, and I found it hard to leave them on account of the communication and friendship we established with each other. They were my 'family' as long as I was with them.''[1]

In 1980, Byard received the Coretta Scott King Award for her illustrations for *Cornrows*. Her own work has been exhibited in galleries in Massachusetts, New York and Philadelphia. About her work, she once remarked: "I'd like for my work to grow so that many people could gain something from it. I would like to just continue painting. And I'd like to confront those things that I would have looked at earlier as obstacles and see them as learning posts or stop posts from which I can keep on going.

". . .I am interested in making art available to more people. . .like publishing some of my lithographs and telling other artists how to raise money through exploiting their own works. And as I become involved with illustrating books I realize that art has a lot of power.''[1]

"'Visual Conversations—East Coast/West Coast,' at Sparc Gallery of Venice, California in 1983 also marked an important point in my career as the first opportunity to exhibit my early 'Rent Drawings.' "These images are inspired by the memory of my loving father who worked as hard as two men all his life, yet never acquired a moments respite in knowing a sense of security in one essential fact of life: a place to be. Upon his death fifteen years ago, I inherited his neat collection of a lifetime of rent receipts, a material testament to his being here. From this locus, I see the homeless everywhere and I cannot dismiss the hills and valleys they have travelled. I know that their struggle is mine.

"These drawings are stylized images of perseverance. Rent or torn cloth symbolizes internal and external forces we strive to overcome. These pieces celebrate survival and a continuous universal struggle to triumph over obstacles. I search for the power and sense of one simple gesture, one motion and emotion to bear witness to a portion of social madness and inner strength in modern times. These drawings are charcoal or monochromatic pastel figures. They celebrate the strength of the

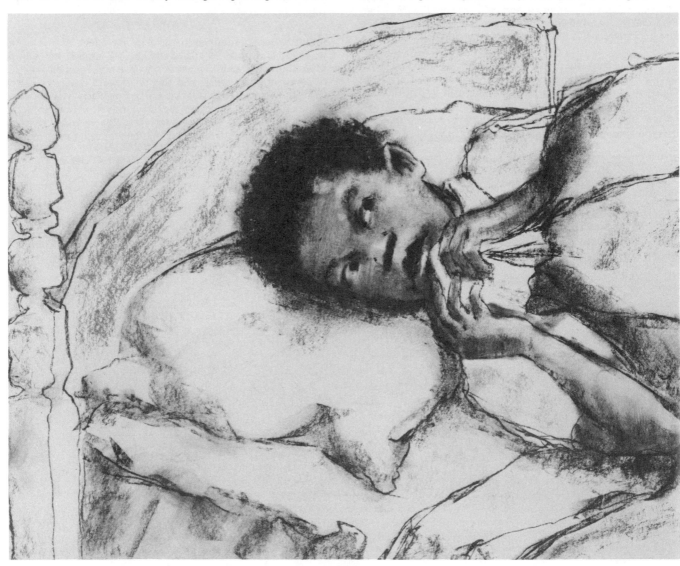

(From *Willy* by Helen H. King. Illustrated by Carole Byard.)

spirit within. Some of these drawings are executed on large stretched raw linen canvases.

"The 'Home Exhibition' at Goddard Riverside in 1987 was the beginning of an opportunity to exhibit my sculptural installations. This was a tremendous challenge which strengthened and encouraged me in my new direction.

"I created 'Praisesong for Charles,' an outdoor sculptural installation in Lexington, New York. It was my first opportunity to create a site specific outdoor piece. What a joy it was to work on such a large scale.

"'Praisesong for Charles' is a chorus of earth mask figures dedicated to the memory of the spiritual, creative and living nature of the artist, Charles Abramson. Set in a quiet glade surrounded by three walls of trees and a very old building, the tip of the triangular surface shape faces the path entrance to the area. I excavated a slope that descends three feet down at the forward tip. All of the soil removed was then used to extend the slope in the rear, creating a soft hill above ground.

"'Praisesong' was created in the Catskill Mountains of indigenous materials, with the exception of the Calabashes, which are from California. The materials used were all gathered from the local area: natural clay from the hills and fields, soil, sand and stones from the stream, and weathered wood from the river banks wed this sculptural installation to its environment.

"From 1980 to 1984, I was chair of the visual arts department of the Baltimore School for the Arts, a highly acclaimed senior high school in the Baltimore City public school system. This pioneering work involved creating, planning, developing, staffing and administering the school's model four-year fine arts curriculum from its inception through the graduation of three classes by June of 1984. I loved this job. It was wonderful working with so many talented young people. After four and one-half years I resigned to return to New York City to devote more time to my studio art and in particular to the work I had begun in Baltimore.

"In February of 1988, I returned to teaching as a faculty member at Parsons School of Design. The art history/philosophy course I have developed examines the work of artists Kathe Kollwitz, Charles White, and Valerie Maynard within the social/political climate of their lives.

"Through the years, I have collaborated periodically with Madeleine Yayodele Nelson, founder and director of 'Women of the Calabash,' an African Percussion Ensemble. Presently, she is assisting me in the development of a vocal sound piece inspired by my sculptures. In March of 1989, 'Women of the Calabash' will perform one of our vocal collaborations with my sculptural installation at Henry Street Gallery. We have received funding from New American Radio to explore and further develop for radio presentation the 'Sounds of the Sculpture' collaborations.

"In the fall of 1985, I was awarded a Visual Arts Fellowship from the National Endowment for the Arts. This grant came during an intensive period of growth and development in my work, enabling me to work extensively on my 'Rent Drawings.' This period has spawned the new direction of my present efforts, which includes painting and sculptural installations. My recent residence at 'Art Awareness' in Lexington, New York has reinforced my commitment to working in three dimensions."

FOOTNOTE SOURCES

¹Elton C. Fax, "Carole Byard," *Black Artists of the New Generation*, Dodd, 1977. Amended by Carol Byard.

FOR MORE INFORMATION SEE:

Barbara Cohen, "Careers" (filmstrip), Harcourt, 1974.
"Two Women Who Paint," *Daily World*, March, 1974.
"Brush and Chisel" (documentary), NBC-TV, November, 1975.
"An Artist's Lifestyle," *Black Enterprise*, December, 1975.
"Blacks and the Arts," *New York Post*, February 7, 1976.
Wilson Library Bulletin, October, 1976.
"Byard in Baltimore," *In the Arts*, winter, 1983.
Denise Bartelo, "Carole Byard," *CLA: The Bulletin*, fall, 1985.
IKON, winter/summer, 1986, Volume 8, 1988.

CARAWAY, Caren 1939-

PERSONAL: Born August 8, 1939, in Madison, Wis., daughter of Jesse Claude (an architect) and Frances (in accounting; maiden name, Fritz) Caraway; married Frank Dameron Leach, Jr., (an architect and designer), August 5, 1961 (divorced, 1979); married James Gilbert Quast (a planner), January 1, 1980; children: (first marriage) Larc, Tanya. *Education:* Art Institute of Chicago, B.F.A., 1961; attended University of Wisconsin, 1984-85. *Home:* Rt. 1, Avoca, Wis. 53506. *Office:* University of Wisconsin—Extension, Madison, Wis. 53703.

CAREER: Free-lance designer, photographer, and painter, 1961—; Greenbriar Papers, Spring Green, Wis., owner and designer, 1969-76; Himalayan Institute, Glenview, Ill., art director, 1974-75; The Valley Studio, Spring Green, teacher, 1976-77, director of apprentice industries, 1977-79; free-lance writer and illustrator, 1979—; University of Wisconsin—Extension, Madison, advisor, 1984-85, project designer and computer artist, 1986—. *Member:* Clyde Community Club. *Awards, honors:* Has received various art fair awards for drawings; Author/Artist of the Year from the Children's Reading Roundtable of Chicago, 1981, for a juvenile book.

WRITINGS:

SELF-ILLUSTRATED

The Beginner's Guide to Quilting: Easy-to-Make Coverlets, Pillows and Hangings, McKay, 1980.

CAREN CARAWAY

The tiny girl quickly shook the rag picker awake. ■ (From *The Cucumber Princess* by Jan Wahl. Illustrated by Caren Caraway.)

(Reteller) *Beauty and the Beast,* Stemmer House, 1980.

(Reteller) Jacob Grimm and Wilhelm Grimm, *Snow White and the Seven Dwarfs,* Stemmer House, 1980.

Zodiac Designs to Color, Stemmer House, 1980.

(Reteller) J. Grimm and W. Grimm, *Cinderella,* Stemmer House, 1981.

(Reteller) J. Grimm and W. Grimm, *Sleeping Beauty,* Stemmer House, 1981.

Applique Quilts to Color, Stemmer House, 1981.

Pieced Quilt Designs to Color, Stemmer House, 1981.

Mayan Designs to Color, Stemmer House, 1981.

Tarot Designs to Color, Stemmer House, 1981.

The Mola Design Coloring Book, Stemmer House, 1981.

(Reteller) *Dick Whittington's Cat,* Stemmer House, 1982.

(Reteller) J. Grimm and W. Grimm, *Hansel and Gretel,* Stemmer House, 1982.

Northwest Coast Indian Designs to Color, Stemmer House, 1982.

Designs of the South Pacific, Stemmer House, 1983.

Peruvian Textile Designs, Stemmer House, 1983.

Southeast Asian Textile Designs, Stemmer House, 1983.

Southwest Indian Designs, Stemmer House, 1983.

Aztec and Other Mexican Indian Designs, Stemmer House, 1984.

Plains Indian Designs, Stemmer House, 1984.

Northeast Woodland Indian Designs, Stemmer House, 1984.

African Art of Nigeria and the Cameroons, Stemmer House, 1984.

African Designs of the Guinea Coast, Stemmer House, 1985.

Designs of Hawaii and Easter Island, Stemmer House, 1985.

African Designs of the Congo, Stemmer House, 1986.

African Designs from the Congo, Nigeria, the Cameroons and the Guinea Coast, Stemmer House, 1987.

ILLUSTRATOR

Rudolph Ballantine, Allen Weinstock and Swami Rama, *Yoga and Psychotherapy,* Himalayan International Institute, 1974.

The Yoga Way, Volumes I and II, Himalayan International Institute, 1974.

Jan Wahl, *The Cucumber Princess,* Stemmer House, 1981.

Laura Greene and Eve Dicker, *The First Book of Sign,* F. Watts, 1981.

Lani Van Ryzin, *Patch of Earth,* Messner, 1981.

Arleen Lorrance, *Born of Love,* LP Publications, 1981.

Joseph Martinez, *Combat Mime,* Nelson-Hall, 1982.

Diane Kennedy Pike, *The Process of Awakening, an Overview,* LP Publications, 1985.

A. Lorrance, *Images,* LP Publications, 1985.

L. Greene and E. Dicker, *Sign Language Talk,* F. Watts, 1988.

ADAPTATIONS:

''The Cucumber Princess'' (filmstrip with cassette), Society for Visual Education, 1982.

WORK IN PROGRESS: Computer animation of children's stories.

SIDELIGHTS: "I am particularly interested in traveling to other countries and exploring remote regions where the culture is less influenced by that of the United States and Europe, and the environment shows the least evidence of disturbance by man.

"Many of my books were done to give a global perspective on what is traditionally considered to be art. Others are concerned with the spiritual aspects of human life. Most of my drawings illustrate natural subjects, but many of my paintings are large abstracts with metalflake and metallic powders. Others reflect my life-long interest in Arabian horses. My photographs are of nature or other cultures, taken on such occasions as the Holy Week festivities of Guatemalan villages, a backpack trek through the Andes on the Inca Trail to Macchu Picchu, Peru, or a mountain flight to Mt. Everest.

"I was born into a family closely associated with Frank Lloyd Wright for four generations. An artist's environment is reflected in his work, so I live in a beautiful area where I can draw nourishment from the meadows and woods and our animals. My husband and I raise Arabian horses, have dogs and cats, wild birds at window feeders, and deer in the fields.

"To sum up, I can say most of my work, in any media, is concerned with human kinship with the earth, the brother/sisterhood of all living beings, and the relationship of the human to the divine."

HOBBIES AND OTHER INTERESTS: Plants, classical music, crystals, metaphysics.

FOR MORE INFORMATION SEE:

Arabian Express, March, 1985.
Arabian Visions, January, 1986.

CARTER, Peter   1929-

PERSONAL: Born August 13, 1929, in England; son of Percy (a seaman) and Evelyn (a spinner; maiden name, Giles) Carter; married Gudrun Willege (a photographer), February 17, 1974. *Education:* Wadham College, Oxford, M.A., 1962. *Religion:* Anglican. *Home:* Ilmington, Warwickshire, England.

CAREER: Writer. Worked a wide variety of jobs ranging from construction work to road making, office work to school teaching. Churchwarden at St. Barnabas Church, Birmingham, 1973-76. *Awards, honors:* Guardian Award runner-up, 1974, for *The Gates of Paradise; The Black Lamp* was selected one of Child Study Association of America's Children's Books of the Year, 1975; Carnegie Medal Commendation from the British Library Association, 1978, for *Under Goliath;* Guardian Award, 1981, and chosen one of New York Public Library's Books for the Teen Age, 1982, both for *The Sentinels;* Young Observer/Rank Teenage Fiction Award from *Young Observer,* 1983, for *Children of the Book.*

WRITINGS:

The Black Lamp (novel), Oxford University Press, 1973, T. Nelson, 1975.
Madatan (novel), Oxford University Press, 1974.
The Gates of Paradise (novel), Oxford University Press, 1974.
Mao (biography), Oxford University Press, 1976, Viking, 1979.
Under Goliath (illustrated by Ian Ribbons), Oxford University Press, 1977.
The Sentinels, Oxford University Press, 1980.

Children of the Book (illustrated by Richard Jervis; maps by Barry Rowe), Merrimack, 1982.
Bury the Dead, Oxford University Press, 1986, Farrar, Straus, 1987.

TRANSLATOR

Mira Lobe, *The Snowman Who Went for a Walk* (illustrated by Winfried Opgenoorth), Oxford University Press, 1981.
Grimms' Fairy Tales (illustrated by Peter Richardson), Oxford University Press, 1982.
M. Lobe, *Valerie and the Good-Night Swing* (illustrated by W. Opgenoorth), Oxford University Press, 1983.
Wolf Harranth, *My Old Grandad* (illustrated by Christina Opperman-Dimov), Merrimack, 1984.

SIDELIGHTS: An extensive traveler, Carter has visited the United States, Canada, India, the Middle East and Europe. "I write because I enjoy it."

HOBBIES AND OTHER INTERESTS: Rock climbing, cricket, bird watching.

CHAMBERS, John W.   1933-

PERSONAL: Born September 29, 1933, in New York, N.Y.; son of Robert A. (a lawyer) and Jean (a writer; maiden name, Wheeler) Chambers; married Margaret Powell, 1960 (divorced, 1969); married Carole Griffith (an actress), 1969; children: (first marriage) Margaret Watson, John Powell. *Education:* Yale University, B.A., 1957; Columbia University, M.A., 1961. *Politics:* Independent. *Religion:* Protestant. *Home and office:* 109 Division Ave., Blue Point, N.Y. 11715. *Agent:* Joan Daves, 59 East 54th St., New York, N.Y. 10022.

CAREER: Wykeham Rise School, Washington, Conn., teacher, 1962-69; worked at odd jobs, 1969-71; free-lance writer, 1969—; Morrell & Co. (retail wine outlet), Nye, N.Y., began as salesman, became manager, 1971-85; Winebow, Inc. (wholesale wine distributors), New York, N.Y., sales representative, 1985—. *Military service:* U.S. Army, 1973-75.

WRITINGS:

JUVENILE NOVELS

Fritzi's Winter (illustrated by Carole K. Odell), Atheneum, 1979.
Finder, Atheneum, 1981.
Showdown at Apple Hill, Atheneum, 1982.
Footlight Summer, Atheneum, 1983.
Fire Island Forfeit, Atheneum, 1984.
The Colonel and Me, Atheneum, 1985.

Wine columnist for *Medical Tribune,* 1978-84. Contributor of articles and stories to magazines.

WORK IN PROGRESS: Tuxedo Tom, a story about a cat, set on Fire Island; an adult mystery novel; *Clambo's Revenge,* a juvenile mystery set on Fire Island; *How We Got Daddy Back,* a juvenile domestic novel.

SIDELIGHTS: "My writing career developed as an outgrowth of storytelling to my children. *Fritzi's Winter* was written to be read aloud to them, then revised for publication. Three of my books are set on Fire Island, a barrier beach off southern Long Island where I have a summer house. Early horseback riding experiences led to *The Colonel and Me,* and two years of summer theater resulted in *Footlight Summer.*

"I consider my primary object as a juvenile writer is to entertain. I believe stories should be imaginative and well narrated, with good characterization, and they should be upbeat. My characters act morally without being goody-goody, but I face them with moral crises that require decisions. I consider myself a realist, not a naturalist. I am not inclined to write about abortion, rape, and similar subject matter. There is all too much of this on television, in the movies, and in the newspapers. I think juvenile literature should offer an alternative, and I endeavor to do so."

COX, William R(obert)   1901-1988
(Willard d'Arcy, Mike Frederic, John Parkhill, Joel Reeve, Wayne Robbins, Roger G. Spellman, Jonas Ward)

OBITUARY NOTICE: See sketch in *SATA* Volume 46: Born April 14, 1901, in Peapack, N.J.; died of congestive heart failure, August 7, 1988, at his home in Los Angeles, Calif. Editor and author. Cox was eighty-seven years old at the time of his death. His wife, Casey, said that he died at his typewriter while working on his eighty-first novel, "Cemetery Jones and the Tombstone Wars." During a writing career that spanned six decades, Cox produced novels for adults and young adults and contributed more than one thousand stories to such magazines as *Saturday Evening Post, Collier's,* and *Cosmopolitan.* He began his writing career as a sports reporter in the early twenties and specialized in sports stories, mysteries, and westerns, often writing under one of a number of pen names. During the era of the pulp magazines, he was said to have averaged 600,000 published words a year for fourteen years.

His books for young readers include *Five Were Chosen: A Basketball Story;* (under pseudonym Joel Reeve) *Goal Ahead; The Backyard Five; The Unbeatable Five; The Running Back; Game, Set, and Match; Battery Mates; Home Court Is Where You Find It;* and *The Fourth of July Kid.* His other books include *Luke Short and His Era, The Sixth Horseman, Gunsharp,* and *Johnny Bear.* In addition, Cox wrote screenplays and scripts for more than one hundred television programs, among them "Fireside Theater," "Bonanza," "Zane Grey Theater," and "Route 66." He also edited *Rivers to Cross,* a collection of stories by members of the Western Writers of America, an organization of which he was a one-time president. His manuscripts are collected at the University of Oregon and the University of Wyoming.

FOR MORE INFORMATION SEE:

Martha E. Ward and Dorothy A. Marquardt, editors, *Authors of Books for Young People,* second edition, Scarecrow Press, 1971.
The Writers Directory: 1988-1990, St. James Press, 1988.

OBITUARIES

Chicago Tribune, August 12, 1988.
Los Angeles Times, August 12, 1988.
New York Times, August 12, 1988.

CRUMP, J(ames) Irving   1887-1979

PERSONAL: Born December 7, 1887, in Saugerties, N.Y.; died July 3, 1979, in Hackensack, N.J.; son of William Russell and Emma F. (Peters) Crump; married Marguerite Duryea Whitney, April 4, 1910 (died, 1969); children: Marguerite Whitney, James Irving. *Education:* Attended Columbia Uni-

versity. *Politics:* Republican. *Religion:* Baptist. *Residence:* Oradell, N.J.

CAREER: Author. Associate editor, *Edison Monthly,* 1912-14; editor, *Boys' Life,* 1915-23, 1935-52; managing editor, *Pictorial Review,* 1923-24; author and writer for radio. Past member of Board of Education and Library Board of Trustees, both in Oradell, N.J. *Member:* Ulster Company Society of New York, Omega Gamma Delta.

WRITINGS:

Jack Straw in Mexico: How the Engineers Defended the Great Hydro-Electric Plant (illustrated by Leslie Crump), McBride, Nast, 1914.
Jack Straw, Lighthouse Builder (illustrated by L. Crump), R. M. McBride, 1915.
The Boys' Book of Firemen, Dodd, 1916.
The Boys' Book of Policemen, Dodd, 1917.
The Boy Scout Fire Fighters (illustrated by Charles L. Wrenn), Barse & Hopkins, 1917.
The Boys' Book of Mounted Police, Dodd, 1917.
Conscript 2989: Experiences of a Drafted Man (illustrated by H. B. Martin), Dodd, 1918.
Og: Son of Fire (illustrated by Charles Livingston Bull), Dodd, 1922.
The Boys' Book of Forest Rangers, Dodd, 1924.
Og: Boy of Battle (illustrated by C. L. Bull), Dodd, 1925.
The Boys' Book of Arctic Exploration, Dodd, 1925.
The Boys' Book of the U.S. Mails, Dodd, 1926.
The Boys' Book of Airmen (with an introduction by Richard E. Byrd), Dodd, 1927.
The Boys' Book of Coast Guards, Dodd, 1928.
The Pilot of the Cloud Patrol (illustrated by William Heaslip), Grosset, 1929.
The Cloud Patrol (illustrated by W. Heaslip), Grosset, 1929.
Mog, the Mound Builder (illustrated by Remington Schuyler), Dodd, 1931.
Craig of the Cloud Patrol (illustrated by W. Heaslip), Grosset, 1931.
The Boys' Book of Fisheries, Dodd, 1933.

As Lindy sprang at him, he tripped over a chock and went down on his back. ■ (From *The Pilot of the Cloud Patrol* by Irving Crump. Illustrated by William Heaslip.)

The Boys' Book of Newsreel Hunters, Dodd, 1933.
"Making" the School Newspaper, Dodd, 1933.
The Boys' Book of Cowboys, Dodd, 1934.
(With John W. Newton) *Our Police,* Dodd, 1935.
Og of the Cave People (illustrated by Jack Murray), Dodd, 1935.
(With J. W. Newton) *Our Airmen,* Dodd, 1936.
(With J. W. Newton) *Our G-Men,* Dodd, 1937.
Our Firemen, Dodd, 1938.
Scouts to the Rescue, Rand McNally, 1939.
(With Norman Maul) *Our Airliners,* Dodd, 1940.
Our Movie Makers, Dodd, 1940.
Out of the Woods (short stories; illustrated by Enos B. Comstock), Dodd, 1941.
Our United States Secret Service, Dodd, 1942.
Our Marines, Dodd, 1944.
Teen-Age Boy Scout Stories (illustrated by Ronald Gaschke), Lantern Press, 1948, reissued, Grosset, 1961.
Our Oil Hunters, Dodd, 1948.
(Editor) *Dog Stories,* T. Nelson, 1949.
(Editor) *Adventure Stories,* T. Nelson, 1950.
Our Tanker Fleet, Dodd, 1952.
(Editor) *Book of Scout Stories,* Doubleday, 1952.
Our Army Engineers, Dodd, 1954.
Our State Police, Dodd, 1955.
The Birdsong Boys (illustrated by Cyrus Le Roy Baldridge), Friendship Press, 1955.
Our Merchant Marine Academy, Kings Point, Dodd, 1958, reissued, Greenwood Press, 1975.
Our United States Coast Guard Academy, Dodd, 1961, reissued, Greenwood Press, 1975.
(With son, James Irving Crump) *Dragon Bones in the Yellow Earth,* Dodd, 1963.
Og: Son of Og, Dodd, 1965.
Biography of a Borough—Oradell [Oradell, N.J.], 1969.

Also author of *The Boys' Book of Railroads,* 1917, "The Great War" series (five volumes), "Adventures in Birdland" (five volumes), and with Dan Beard, *The Black Wolf Pack.* Author of radio shows, including "Jack Armstrong, All American Boy," "Og, Son of Fire," and a serial dramatization of *Treasure Island.* Contributor of stories and articles to periodicals, including *Adventure, Collier's, Cowboy Stories, Leslie's, Publishers Weekly, Munsey, Metropolitan, Boys' Life, American Boy, Western Stories, Redbook, Ranch Romances,* and *Ace High.*

ADAPTATIONS:

"Scouts to the Rescue" (movie series), starring Jackie Cooper, Universal, 1938-39.

SIDELIGHTS: Best known for his boys' books and as editor of the official publication of the Boy Scouts, *Boy's Life* magazine, Crump was born on December 7, 1887, in Saugerties, N.Y. "I was born and brought up for a considerable period on the outskirts of that little town in the shadow of the Catskill Mountains, and there I learned to love the field and woods and streams and books that dealt with adventure out of doors."[1]

He also learned to love writing stories "full of adventure."[1] He was an avid reader, "though never a particularly good student."[1] Although his father tried to interest him in a career in stocks and bonds, young Crump was determined to be a writer. His first short story was sold to *Collier's* magazine in 1912, which launched his career as a writer of books for young people. By 1915 he had combined writing with editing by accepting the position of managing editor of *Boys' Life,* a post he held for a total of twenty-five years.

During his long and distinguished career, Crump became a popular author of boys' stories and one of America's foremost

As he slung his leg over the side there was a sound of feet on the gravel. ■ (From *The Cloud Patrol* by Irving Crump. Illustrated by William Heaslip.)

literary figures. He wrote more than thirty books, 500 radio programs, dozens of plays and numerous magazine articles. "My work in the boys' field has always had a strong appeal to me. Though I have contributed to many adult magazines and at one time was managing editor of *Pictorial Review,* my interest was always in writing for boys."[1]

During most of his adult life, Crump lived in Oradell, New Jersey, where he was a Boy Scout adult volunteer. He died at the age of ninety-two in Hackensack, N. J., after a short illness.

FOOTNOTE SOURCES

[1]"Irving Crump," *Junior Book of Authors,* second edition, edited by Stanley J. Kunitz and Howard Haycraft, H. W. Wilson, 1951.

FOR MORE INFORMATION SEE:

Books, January 2, 1938.
New York Times, August 10, 1941.
New York Herald Tribune, March 2, 1952.
Kirkus, July 15, 1955.
W. O. G. Lofts and D. J. Adley, *The Men behind Boys' Fiction,* Howard Baker, 1970.
Martha E. Ward and Dorothy A. Marquardt, *Authors of Books for Young People,* 2nd edition, Scarecrow, 1971.

OBITUARIES

New York Times, July 4, 1979.
AB Bookman's Weekly, July 30, 1979.

DAVIS, Maggie S.   1943-
(M. E. Cooper, Barbara Steincrohn Davis, Emma Davis)

PERSONAL: Born May 30, 1943, in Hartford, Conn.; daughter of Peter Joseph (a physician and author) and Patti (a radio songstress and pianist; maiden name, Chapin) Steincrohn; married Alan J. Davis, September 1, 1963 (divorced, 1976); married Arnold Greenberg (a poet and bakery owner), June 27, 1982; children: (first marriage) Joel, Jenny; stepchildren:

MAGGIE S. DAVIS

David, Julie, Dan and Joe (twins). *Education:* Attended Connecticut College for Women (now Connecticut College), 1960-61; University of Miami (Florida), A.B., 1963, University of Florida, M.A., 1965; graduate study at University of Miami, and Florida International University. *Home:* P.O. Box 981, Blue Hill, Me. 04614. *Agent:* Sue Cohen, Writers House, 21 West 26th St., New York, N.Y. 10010.

CAREER: Reese Air Force Base, Lubbock, Tex., director of nursery, 1967; University of Miami Reading Clinic, Miami, Fla., teacher of learning-disabled children, 1967-68; McGlannan Language Arts Center, Miami, teacher of learning-disabled children, 1967-73; Association for Children with Learning Disabilities, Miami, director of training workshops, 1969-73; author, 1971—; Citizens Dispute Settlement Center, Miami, counselor, public relations representative, 1977-79; freelance editor and rewrite specialist, New York, 1981-86; The Left Bank Bakery and Cafe, Blue Hill, Me., co-owner. Poets-in-the-Schools Program, Miami, 1973; host of radio talk show, "Tribute: A Program for and about Women," Long Island, N.Y., 1983.

WRITINGS:

JUVENILE

(Under pseudonym Barbara Steincrohn Davis) *Scrubadubba Dragon* (illustrated by Carroll Dolezal), Steck Vaughn, 1971.
(Under pseudonym Barbara Steincrohn Davis) *Forest Hotel: A Counting Story* (illustrated by Benvenuti), Golden Press, 1972.
Grandma's Secret Letter (illustrated by John Wallner), Holiday House, 1982.
The Best Way to Ripton (illustrated by Stephen Gammell; Junior Literary Guild selection), Holiday House, 1982.
Rickety Witch (illustrated by Kay Chorao), Holiday House, 1984.
(Under house pseudonym M. E. Cooper) *Something New,* Scholastic, 1987.
(Under pseudonym Emma Davis) *A Dog for Jessie,* Scholastic, 1988.
The Rinky-Dink Cafe, Simon & Schuster, 1988.

ADULT

Blooming! Choices of a Growing Woman, Acropolis, 1981.

Also contributor to periodicals, including *New Jersey Outdoors* and *Delaware Valley News.*

WORK IN PROGRESS: A ten-chapter novel for beginning readers; books for children, ages six to nine, inspired by the folklore, environment, history, and people of Maine.

SIDELIGHTS: "As an only child, I read hungrily every day to propel myself out of loneliness and into fantasy worlds. I wrote stories, too, to fill the alone times. I filled diaries. Always, I eavesdropped on my mother and father's conversations. Words were my best company. (That should have been clue enough that I would be a writer.) But it wasn't until I had children of my own that what had been a flickering interest exploded into a full-blown passion, fed—as I look back now—by my many career paths (secretary, teacher, trainer, mediator, counselor, waitress, talk-show host, editor. . .).

"Because of the hopscotch nature of my life till recently, I never had my own office to write in. My knees, I'm sure, have been permanently affected from my sitting cross-legged on my bed, typing—scores of pages and files teetering all around me. And, of course, there were the times I assumed

"The best way is the simple way," said the pig. ■ (From *The Best Way to Ripton* by Maggie S. Davis. Illustrated by Stephen Gammell.)

the same position in front of shelves in libraries' children's rooms, or on the top bunk of my motor home (houseboat, too), or by the pond on the working farm we lived on, or on a rock at low tide in a cove in Maine (my heart's home and the state I have promised myself I will stay put in forever). In fact, I'm still searching for the perfect permanent writing spot. In the meantime, bless my lap-top computer and tiny printer.

"For me, writing (especially children's books) is essential to my soul's survival. (If only I could draw the scenes I see in my mind!) Most of the time, I'd rather write than eat (except when tempted, during a bout of writer's block, by our bakery-cafe's appealing goodies).

"Although I've written and published poems and magazine articles and a book for women, I have—during the past few years—singlemindedly given my heart and time to writing for children. My friends tease me. They say that even at parties for adults, I'm more than likely to be found off in a corner with children and the family dog. I have found much wisdom in those corners, I believe, and *certainly* much fun.

"Talking with and writing for children nourishes the child in *me*. I never want to lose her.

"I plan to be working on books rooted in Native American history, tradition and spirituality, for it is the Indians' attitude toward our earth which, in these difficult times, can best help to preserve it.

"I am gently and carefully clearing land I bought. In the spring I will be building a simple cabin so that AT LAST! I will have a FIXED spot to write in!"

HOBBIES AND OTHER INTERESTS: Reading, gardening, hiking, singing, knitting, dancing. "Also, I guess I would call myself an environmental activist."

FOR MORE INFORMATION SEE:

Miami News (Fla.), November 17, 1971.
New York Times, September 5, 1982, December 23, 1984.
Delaware Valley News, October 11, 1984.

DEGEN, Bruce 1945-

PERSONAL: Born June 14, 1945, in Brooklyn, N.Y.; married Christine Bostard (a teacher and illustrator); children: Benja-

Poking, soaking, hey hey
Getting wet is okay
For you, cup.

(From *Better Not Get Wet, Jesse Bear* by Nancy White Carlstrom. Illustrated by Bruce Degen.)

min, Alexander. *Education:* Cooper Union, B.F.A., 1966; Pratt Institute, M.F.A., 1975. *Home:* 101 Clark St., Brooklyn, N.Y. 11201.

CAREER: Author and illustrator. Has worked as an art teacher in New York City High Schools, and as a director of an artists' lithography studio in Ein Hod, Israel. Teacher of life-drawing, printmaking, and calligraphy to advanced high school students and adults. *Awards, honors: Little Chick's Big Day* was selected a Children's Choice by the International Reading Association and the Children's Book Council, 1982, and *My Mother Didn't Kiss Me Good-Night,* 1985; Garden State Children's Book Award, Easy-to-Read Category, from the New Jersey Library Association, 1983, for *Commander Toad in Space; Jamberry* was selected one of *Booklist*'s Children's Reviewers' Choices, 1983; *Jamberry* was selected one of Child Study Association of America's Children's Books of the Year, 1985, and *The Josefina Story Quilt,* 1987.

WRITINGS:

SELF-ILLUSTRATED CHILDREN'S BOOKS

Aunt Possum and the Pumpkin Man (Junior Literary Guild selection), Harper, 1977.
The Little Witch and the Riddle, Harper, 1980, large print edition, 1980.
Jamberry, Harper, 1983.

ILLUSTRATOR

Malcolm Hall, *Forecast* (Junior Literary Guild selection), Coward, 1977.
Stephen Krensky, *A Big Day for Sceptres,* Atheneum, 1977.
M. Hall, *Caricatures,* Coward, 1978.
Carol Chapman, *Ig Lives in a Cave,* Dutton, 1979.
Judy Delton, *Brimhall Turns to Magic* (Junior Literary Guild selection), Lothrop, 1979.
Marjorie Weinman Sharmat, *Mr. Jameson and Mr. Phillips,* Harper, 1979.
Claudia Louise Lewis, *Up and Down the River: Boat Poems,* Harper, 1979.
Jane Yolen, *Commander Toad in Space* (Junior Literary Guild selection), Coward, 1980.
Charlotte Herman, *My Mother Didn't Kiss Me Good-Night,* Dutton, 1980.
Donald J. Sobol, *Encyclopedia Brown's Second Record Book of Weird and Wonderful Facts,* Delacorte, 1981.
Mary Kwitz, *Little Chick's Big Day,* Harper, 1981.
Clyde Robert Bulla, *Dandelion Hill,* Dutton, 1982.
J. Yolen, *Commander Toad and the Planet of the Grapes,* Coward, 1982.
Joel L. Schwartz, *Upchuck Summer,* Delacorte, 1982.
M. Hall, *Deadlines,* Coward, 1982.
M. Kwitz, *Little Chick's Breakfast,* Harper, 1983.
J. Yolen, *Commander Toad and the Big Black Hole,* Coward, 1983.
Lyn Littlefield Hoopes, *Daddy's Coming Home!,* Harper, 1984.

They have watched lots and lots and lots of movies. ■ (From *Commander Toad and the Space Pirates* by Jane Yolen. Illustrated by Bruce Degen.)

J. Yolen, _Commander Toad and the Dis-Asteroid_ (Junior Literary Guild selection), Coward, 1985.

Joseph Slate, _Lonely Lula Cat,_ Harper, 1985.

Bonnie Pryor, _Grandpa Bear,_ Morrow, 1985.

J. L. Schwartz, _Best Friends Don't Come in Threes,_ Dell, 1985.

Eleanor Coerr, _The Josefina Story Quilt,_ Harper, 1986.

J. Yolen, _Commander Toad and the Intergalactic Spy_ (Junior Literary Guild selection), Coward, 1986.

Diane Stanley, _The Good-Luck Pencil,_ Four Winds, 1986.

B. Pryor, _Grandpa Bear's Christmas,_ Morrow, 1986.

Nancy White Carlstrom, _Jesse Bear, What Will You Wear?_ (Junior Literary Guild selection), Macmillan, 1986.

Joanna Cole, _The Magic School Bus: At the Waterworks,_ Scholastic, 1986.

(With wife, Chris Degen) Aileen Lucia Fisher, _When It Comes to Bugs: Poems,_ Harper, 1986.

Larry Weinberg, _The Forgetful Bears Meet Mr. Memory,_ Scholastic, 1987.

J. Cole, _The Magic School Bus: Inside the Earth,_ Scholastic, 1987.

J. Yolen, _Commander Toad and the Space Pirates,_ Putnam, 1987.

N. W. Carlstrom, _Better Not Get Wet, Jesse Bear,_ Macmillan, 1988.

L. Weinberg, _The Forgetful Bears Help Santa,_ Scholastic, 1988.

Joan L. Nixon, _If You Were a Writer,_ Four Winds, 1988.

Mike Thaler, _In the Middle of the Puddle,_ Harper, 1988.

Jan Wahl, _Tim Kitten and the Red Cupboard,_ Simon & Schuster, 1988.

J. Cole, _The Magic School Bus: Inside the Body,_ Scholastic, in press.

ADAPTATIONS:

"Jamberry" (cassette), Live Oak Media, 1986.

SIDELIGHTS: "I have always loved books. As a child I would love to go to the library. If it was a nice day I wouldn't wait until I got home to read my books. I had to stop in the little park and begin my books under a tree. I had always been a city kid. My early contact with nature was raising flowers from two-cent packets of seeds.

"But some summers we spent in the country and those were the most intense memories of my childhood. Stoopball is pale beside catching fish, frogs, snakes, salamanders, and poison ivy. My love of nature comes from these happy summers. One of the most educational aspects of Cooper Union was their country campus in New Jersey, where I hiked, looked and learned.

"I try to convey some of this awareness in my books. When I draw I try to remember what I reacted to most as a child. People often ask me why I use animals. I think it is because they allow an easy fantasy identification, and the change of scale is cozy and attractive to children."

DOLLAR, Diane (Hills)   1933-

PERSONAL: Born April 25, 1933, in Kansas City, Mo.; daughter of Henry Allen (a sales representative) and Daisy (a teacher and counselor; maiden name, Sweeney) Hills; married John Paul Dollar (an assistant dean of engineering), September 3, 1955; children: Allison Ann, Matthew Allen. _Education:_ Kansas State College, B.S., 1955; Kansas State University,

M.A., 1967; Kansas University, M.F.A., 1986. _Politics:_ "Yellow Dog Democrat." _Religion:_ Episcopalian. _Home:_ 1719 Fairchild, Manhattan, Kan. 66502. _Office:_ Art Department, Kansas State University, Manhattan, Kan. 66502.

CAREER: Kansas State University, Manhattan, Kan., instructor, 1967-87, assistant professor, 1987—. Lecturer and demonstrator of illustration and painting in elementary schools. Designer and execution of signage and publicity, Grand County Theatre Association, Grand Lake, Colo., 1975—; consultant, Fine Arts Society at Kansas State Penitentiary, Lansing, 1985—; executive board member, Kansas Council on Crime and Delinquency, 1987. _Exhibitions:_ Kansas Artist's Exhibition, 1967; Kansas Federation of Art (traveling exhibition), 1968; Kansas State University Faculty Traveling Exhibition, 1973-74; Kansas Artist-Craftsman Show, Lawrence, 1975; Kansas State University Faculty Exhibition, Union Gallery, Manhattan, 1975-78, 1982—; Kansas Landscape Photography, Wichita Art Association, Wichita, Kan., 1983; Kansas State University, 1983; (one-person show) Carnegie Art Gallery, Dodge City, Kan., 1984; Great Bend Art Center, Great Bend, Kan., 1984; Lawrence Public Library, Lawrence, Kan., 1986; Strecker Gallery, Manhattan, Kan., 1986; The Exceptional Dream Gallery, Tokepa, Kan., 1987; Manhattan Town Center Grand Opening, Kan., 1987; Faculty Exhibition, Hutchinson Art Center, Hutchinson, Kan., 1988. _Awards, honors:_ Honorable mention from the Photographer's Forum for Best of College Photography, 1980; many awards from art exhibitions; grants to run programs for developmentally disabled adults, 1975, 1977, 1978.

WRITINGS:

SELF-ILLUSTRATED

The Adventures of Space Baby, Professor Publishing, 1987.

ILLUSTRATOR

Lida Helson and Anna Fiske, _Building Language Skills,_ Educators Publishing, 1971.

L. Helson and A. Fiske, _Readiness for Reading,_ Educators Publishing, 1971.

Joan McNeil, _People: Patterns and Puzzles,_ Kendall-Hunt, 1975.

S. M. Hoffman, _What's under That Rock?,_ Atheneum, 1985.

Helen Harwell, _Candy, the Zoo Truck,_ Colonial Press, 1989.

Also author of "The Grand Saga," a musical theater production based on the history of Grand County, Colorado. Contributor of illustrations to _Kansas Quarterly,_ 1975—; contributor to _Pet Parade_ (magazine), 1982. Cartoonist for _Kansas State Collegian,_ 1967-68.

WORK IN PROGRESS: Illustrations for a pre-school book, _Basic Strokes,_ by W. Bradley Twitty, for _Teaching the Language Arts,_ by Frederick L. Westover, and for _The Story of Merle,_ all for Colonial Press.

SIDELIGHTS: "Today, as a university teacher, I am very much aware of what a blessing it was to grow up in a home where art was considered a worthy activity. In fact, I expect I'll be a genuine fanatic on the subject before I retire from the classroom. It's hard to imagine what direction I would have taken if it hadn't been for the wonderful Sunday afternoons we spent, my brother David and I, surrounded by paper and drawing tools, entertaining ourselves while the adults were doing boring things like 'having a little nap.'

"We lived a few doors from the city park and didn't grow up recluses, but when the Kansas winters turned very cold there

DIANE DOLLAR

was nothing more pleasant than to sit down by the fireplace and draw or make folded paper houses filled with carefully colored furniture that was made of folded paper. I was never bored when I spent afternoons designing clothes for my paper dolls using patterned paper from discarded wallpaper sample books. We were even permitted to paint in the living room if we were very careful with the material.

"If my brother, whom we all called Skip, was on hand to participate we often spent the afternoon making up our own newspapers. I did the illustrations for articles, Skip would write. He was two years older and had that much more experience in writing. He knew about things like the war that was going on and about spies who were lurking about waiting to steal important military secrets from nearby Fort Riley. I wasn't good at drawing tanks and guns but I could do a decent spy or landscape where the war was taking place.

"My career in the world of art was set early. My first grade teacher took my drawing of a cow to a teacher's conference because she knew they wouldn't believe a first grader had done it. I must have clung to that success because even then I knew I was not going to do well with other subjects like arithmetic. I loved to read, write and draw. I was not at all bothered by appearing before an audience to recite or to play a role. But I did not enjoy memorizing things that had only one answer. The arts were definitely my best hope for recognition in the first grade.

"Skip had other alternatives. He was very good in every subject in school. He was an honor student and eventually re-

ceived his doctorate in psychology. I knew that he could become anything he wanted. For the most part I didn't worry about becoming anything in particular. I coasted through school accepting accolades for my May baskets and valentines.

"When Skip and I were both given chemistry sets, I soon concluded that chemistry would be fun only if a person could add the chemicals by color and wait for a reaction instead of having to depend upon a formula. Skip made things like powders that would flair up in beautiful colors, perfumes that almost smelled good, and a few things that were functional but smelled very bad. He understood the logic of it all. Fortunately for everyone in the house I ran through my less exotic collection of chemicals before I discovered a truly explosive mixture. They did not offer to replace my set when I ran out of possible combinations.

"At school I volunteered a lot to do the posters and pictures when there was a request. I thought that the only reason no one else wanted those jobs was because they could do the 'hard stuff.' I was truly amazed, when I went to college, to learn that there were people who could not draw at all.

"My first degree from college was in commercial art. My interest in fine arts was tempered by the thought that to be very successful as a painter or a sculptor one had to start with a concept or an idea that was to be explored thoroughly. My interest was in making handsome art. But to do a series of works dealing with the same point of view lost something for me. Getting through graduate school with a focus in painting

Space Baby sleeps anywhere when it is nap time. ■
(From *The Adventures of Space Baby* by Diane Dollar. Illustrated by the author.)

was a real challenge. I liked to paint—and draw—and work in three dimensions. I planned happenings, painted theatre sets and illustrated university publications. Creating a body of work in one area was difficult.

"As it turns out. . .the illustration business allows for the variety in which I am most interested and leaves time to run off to Colorado in the summer to work for a theatre company which I helped to organize. (Colorado in the summer is a lot more pleasant than Kansas.)

"Teaching supports my art habit. It also forces me to stay organized. Keeping a class schedule makes keeping a studio schedule easier. Teaching others makes staying aware of current art a necessity. And it is something I enjoy doing. Besides, if I were alone in my studio for extended periods of time, I'd probably deflate like a slowly leaking balloon. There'd be too little coming in to replace what was going out.

"Of the illustrations I have done I am most fond of the pictures in the children's publications. Most recently I did a coloring book that is sold with a doll I designed. The doll was created out of an idea by a friend, Beverly Williams.

"In some circles coloring books are considered an unacceptable way to do art when you're little. But along with the cutting and folding, writing and drawing, Skip and I also had a few very special coloring books. I seldom got them out when I had friends in to play. They did not color in a manner which I found acceptable for my favorite books. We were expected to share our toys graciously and since that meant watching someone color badly in my Walt Disney coloring book I solved

the problem by not getting it out except when I was the only one interested in coloring.

"Perhaps the *Space Baby* coloring book is part of a need to once in a while color inside the lines. The doll and book were an interesting project to do. The pictures had to be single line drawings. No shade, no shadows are included. That's for the person who owns the book to add.

"The book called *What's under That Rock* was also fun to do. When I was asked to do this book about bugs and snakes I wasn't sure I could do it well because those type critters have never been my favorite. They are either too slippery or they look like they'd bite. But when I got started and found I could include the children and the dog instead of just the bugs and snakes, I began to enjoy it.

"One of my favorite books was *Winnie the Pooh*. I borrowed the idea of the map from the inside cover of the Pooh books and included something similar in the bug book. Then, for the most part, the children and dog seen in the background are roaming about places that can be found on the map in the front of the book. The dog in the pictures is our dog Nip whom we had when we were growing up. It became a very nostalgic experience.

"All the time I was growing up there was a lady who lived next door who thought that we did everything better than anyone else she could think of. I knew that she was prone to exaggeration where Skip and I were concerned. But it didn't hurt to be told by someone other than your parents, who are supposed to like you anyway, that you were special. Her name was Edna Beckman, and Edna told me many times that one should think of the thing you liked to do for fun and then major in that in college. Then going to work would never be a problem.

"Well, obviously Edna had some credibility. She was certainly right about making your hobby your job. And if she was right about that. . .as I know she was. . .than maybe Skip and I were almost as amazing as she said. Or maybe we were just lucky to have grown up without television and to have been told once in a while that we were all right. After that everything else seemed like a hobby.

"Because there are so many good exhibitions of art in Chicago, Kansas City, Dallas, and Denver, I periodically organize trips to visit galleries. The students and area folks make up the passenger list. I get to see the shows too. For four years I have gone with students and others to England—London, Bath and Stratford. We visit galleries, theaters and 'do' London for two weeks between fall and spring semesters."

HOBBIES AND OTHER INTERESTS: Theater, music.

DOREN, Marion (Walker) 1928-

PERSONAL: Born July 10, 1928, in Glen Ridge, N.J.; daughter of Robert M. S. (in advertising) and Marion (an artist; maiden name, Lockwood) Walker; married George V. Doren (a musician and teacher), April 15, 1950; children: Anne Doren Krupsky, Martin V., Keith D., Laurie Doren Camillucci. *Education:* Connecticut College for Women (now Connecticut College), B.A., 1949; attended Central Connecticut State College, 1949, Southern Connecticut State College, 1949-50, Framingham State College, 1963-80, and College of Charleston, 1983. *Politics:* Liberal. *Religion:* Unitarian. *Home:* 750 Wakendaw Blvd., Mount Pleasant, S.C. 29464. *Agent:* Liza Pu-

MARION DOREN

litzer, Kirchoff/Wohlberg, Inc., 866 United Nations Plaza, New York, N.Y. 10017.

CAREER: Hand Elementary School, Madison, Conn., teacher, 1949-50; Missouri Historical Society, St. Louis, lecturer, 1950; Bigelow Elementary School, Marlborough, Mass., teacher, 1962-64; Mary E. Finn Elementary School, and Margaret A. Neary Elementary School, Southborough, Mass., teacher, 1965-81; writer, 1981—. *Member:* National League of American Penwomen (historian, 1986-89), Society of Children's Book Writers, Charleston Women's Network, Newcomers East of the Cooper, Southborough Teachers' Association. *Awards, honors: Post and Courier* Prize, 1983, for story "The Christmas I Remember Best;" Fiction Award from the South Carolina Arts Commission, 1986, for short story "Green Wishes"; Christopher Award, 1987, and Mark Twain Award List, and Juvenile Fiction Contest Award from the National League of American Penwomen, both 1988, all for *Borrowed Summer.*

WRITINGS:

Borrowed Summer (juvenile), Harper, 1986.

Contributor of articles and stories to periodicals, including *Berkshire Sampler, Discovery, Today's Christian Parent, True Love, Modern Romances,* and *Horsemen's Yankee Pedlar.*

WORK IN PROGRESS: Rich Little Poor Girl; Nell of Blue Harbor, to be published by Harcourt; *A Pony in the Field.*

SIDELIGHTS: "When I hit New York, diploma in hand, I was ready to write copy for anyone. Instead I was advised to go to Katie Gibbs, work for fifteen years in the secretarial pool, and then I might be chosen to write. I took a course in education, married, had four children, and wrote in secret. For most of my adult life I was involved with my own children and the children in my classes, so it was natural to begin by writing for them.

"I write mostly about the importance of the family, and try to give my young characters some control in keeping the family together. Young people are bombarded by negative and unpleasant facts, and I feel they need more positive role models.

"After so many years of being controlled by school bells, it is a new experience to set my own schedule. I have been influenced mainly by women writers who have faced the same dilemmas I have, balancing child-raising, working, and writing. *Borrowed Summer,* the result of having to put my mother in a nursing home, spent three years traveling from editor to editor. I write for children, not markets or editors, and this will probably make me the Grandma Moses of the writing world."

HOBBIES AND OTHER INTERESTS: "Over the years I raised horses along with children, gardened, played violin in amateur orchestras, and made clothes. Now I am redoing a house, painting the interior. I walk every day checking on the water turkeys, great blue herons, and egrets. I play bridge, do word games, and enter contests, ride my bike and swim. We have supported a foster child since the sixties. Our latest, Eliazar, lives in El Salvador."

EISENBERG, Lisa　1949-

PERSONAL: Born April 19, 1949, in Flushing, N.Y.; daughter of Charles (a social worker) and Agnita (an educational administrator; maiden name, Greisen) Wright; married Theodore Eisenberg (a professor of law), November 27, 1971; children: Katherine, Ann, Thomas. *Education:* Swarthmore College, B.A., 1971. *Home:* 203 The Parkway, Ithaca, N.Y. 14850. *Agent:* Sheldon Fogelman, 10 East 40th St., New York, N.Y. 10016.

CAREER: Kindergarten teacher in Washington, D.C., 1973-74; Scholastic Magazines, New York City, editor, 1974-76; Harcourt Brace Jovanovich, Inc., New York City, editor, 1976-77; Bowmar/Noble Publishers, Inc., Los Angeles, Calif., editor, 1977-79; free-lance writer, 1979—. *Member:* Authors Guild. *Awards, honors: Fishy Riddles* was selected one of Library of Congress' Books of the Year, and one of Child Study Association of American's Children's Books of the Year, both 1983.

WRITINGS:

JUVENILE

Mystery at Snowshoe Mountain Lodge, Dial, 1987.
Mystery at Bluff Point Dunes, Dial, 1988.
Leave It to Lexie, Viking, 1989.

JUVENILE; ALL WITH KATY HALL

Chicken Jokes and Puzzles, Scholastic Book Services, 1976.
A Gallery of Monsters (illustrated by Joe Mathieu), Random House, 1980.
Fishy Riddles (illustrated by Simms Taback), Dial, 1983.
Pig Jokes and Puzzles, Scholastic Book Services, 1983.
Buggy Riddles (illustrated by S. Taback), Dial, 1986.
One Hundred and One Bug Jokes (illustrated by Don Orehek), Scholastic, 1987.
One Hundred and One School Jokes, Scholastic, 1987.
One Hundred and One Ghost Jokes, Scholastic, 1988.

"LAURA BREWSTER" MYSTERY SERIES; YOUNG ADULT

House of Laughs, Pitman, 1978.
Falling Star, Pitman, 1978.
Killer Music, Pitman, 1978.
Tiger Rose, Pitman, 1978.
Golden Idol, Pitman, 1978.
Fast Food King, Pitman, 1978.

Why are fish so smart?

They are always in schools.

(From *Fishy Riddles* by Katy Hall and Lisa Eisenberg.
Illustrated by Simms Taback.)

"SOUTH CITY COPS" SERIES; YOUNG ADULT

Hit Man, Fearon, 1984.
Kidnap, Fearon, 1984.
The Payoff Game, Fearon, 1984.

ADAPTATIONS:

"Fishy Riddles" (read-along cassette), Live Oak Media, 1984.

SIDELIGHTS: "In my writing I combine an interest in children, education, and, most importantly, humor."

HOBBIES AND OTHER INTERESTS: Skiing, reading mysteries.

FORSTER, E(dward) M(organ)   1879-1970

PERSONAL: Born January 1, 1879, in London, England; died of a stroke, June 7, 1970, in Coventry, England; son of Edward Morgan Llewellyn (an architect) and Alice Clara (Whichelo) Forster. *Education:* King's College, Cambridge, B.A. (second-class honors in classics), 1900, B.A. (second-class honors in history), 1901, M.A., 1910. *Residence:* King's College, Cambridge University, Cambridge, England.

CAREER: Working Men's College, London, England, lecturer, for a period beginning in 1907; Red Cross volunteer in Alexandria, Egypt, 1915-19; literary editor for the *Daily Herald*, London, England; served as private secretary to the Ma-

harajah of Dewas State Senior, India, 1921; writer and lecturer, 1921-70. Annual Clark Lecturer at Cambridge University, beginning, 1927, Rede Lecturer, Cambridge, 1941, W. P. Ker Lecturer, University of Glasgow, 1944; lecture tour of United States, 1947. Member of general advisory council, British Broadcasting Corp., and writer of numerous broadcasts; past vice-president of the London Library. *Member:* American Academy of Arts and Letters (honorary corresponding member), Bavarian Academy of Fine Arts (honorary corresponding member), Cambridge Humanists (president), Reform Club.

AWARDS, HONORS: Tukojirao Gold Medal, Dewas State Senior, India, 1921; James Tait Black Memorial Prize, and Prix Femina/Vie Heureuse, both 1925, both for *A Passage to India;* Fellow, King's College, Cambridge, England, 1927-1930; LL.D., University of Aberdeen, 1931; Benson Medal, Royal Society of Literature, 1937; honorary fellow, King's College, Cambridge, 1946-70; Litt.D., University of Liverpool, 1947, Hamilton College, 1949, Cambridge University, 1950, University of Nottingham, 1951, University of Manchester, and Leyden University, both 1954, University of Leicester, 1958; Tukojimo III Gold Medal; Order of Companion of Honour to the Queen, 1953; Companion of Royal Society of Literature, 1961; Order of Merit, 1969.

WRITINGS:

Where Angels Fear to Tread (novel), Blackwood, 1905, Knopf, 1920.
The Longest Journey (novel), Blackwood, 1907, Knopf, 1922, Holmes & Meier, 1984.
A Room with a View (novel), Edward Arnold, 1908, Putnam, 1911, new edition, Vintage Books, 1986.
Howards End (novel), Putnam, 1910, later edition, Buccaneer Books, 1984.
The Celestial Omnibus and Other Stories, Sidgwick & Jackson, 1911, Knopf, 1923.
The Story of the Siren (short story), Hogarth Press, 1920.

E. M. FORSTER

The Government of Egypt (history), Labour Research Department, 1921.

Alexandria: A History and a Guide, W. Morris, 1922, 3rd edition, Doubleday-Anchor, 1961.

Pharos and Pharillon (history), Knopf, 1923, 3rd edition, Hogarth Press, 1961.

A Passage to India (novel), Harcourt, 1924, new edition, Meier, 1978.

Anonymity: An Enquiry, Hogarth Press, 1925, Norwood, 1978.

Original Letters from India, edited by Eliza Fay, Hogarth Press, 1925, new edition, 1986.

Aspects of the Novel (Clark Lecture, 1927), Harcourt, 1927.

The Eternal Moment and Other Stories, Harcourt, 1928.

A Letter to Madan Blanchard (belles lettres), Hogarth Press, 1931, Harcourt, 1932.

Goldsworthy Lowes Dickinson (biography), Harcourt, 1934, new edition, Edward Arnold, 1945.

Abinger Harvest (essays), Harcourt, 1936.

What I Believe (political), Hogarth Press, 1939, Folcroft, 1970.

Reading as Usual (criticism), 1939, Folcroft, 1970.

Nordic Twilight (political), Macmillan (London), 1940, Norwood, 1978.

England's Pleasant Land (pageant play; first produced in Surrey, England, July 9, 1938), Hogarth Press, 1940.

Virginia Woolf (criticism; Rede Lecture, 1941) Harcourt, 1942.

The Development of English Prose between 1918 and 1939 (criticism; W. P. Ker Lecture, 1944), Jackson (Glasgow), 1945.

The Collected Tales of E. M. Forster (previously published as *The Celestial Omnibus* and *The Eternal Moment*), Knopf, 1947, new edition, Modern Library, 1968 (published in England as *Collected Short Stories of E. M. Forster,* Sidgwick & Jackson, 1948, new enlarged edition published as *The New Collected Short Stories* (large print), G. K. Hall, 1986.

(Author of libretto with Eric Crozier) *Billy Budd: An Opera in Four Acts* (based on the novel by Herman Melville; music by Benjamin Britten), Boosey & Hawkes, 1951, revised edition, 1961.

Two Cheers for Democracy (essays), Harcourt, 1951.

Desmond MacCarthy, Mill House Press, 1952.

The Hill of Devi, Harcourt, 1953, new edition, 1985 (published in England as *The Hill of Devi: Being Letters from Dewas State Senior,* Edward Arnold, 1953).

Battersea Rise (first chapter of *Marianne Thornton*), Harcourt, 1955.

Marianne Thornton: A Domestic Biography, 1797-1887, Harcourt, 1956.

E. M. Forster: Selected Writings, edited by G. B. Parker, Heinemann Educational, 1968.

Albergo Empedocle and Other Writings (previously unpublished material, written 1900-15), edited by George H. Thomson, Liveright, 1971.

Maurice (novel), Norton, 1971.

The Life to Come and Other Stories, Norton, 1972, republished as *The Life to Come and Other Short Stories,* 1972.

The Arbinger Edition of E. M. Forster, 13 volumes, edited by O. Stallybrass and E. Heine, E. Arnold, 1972-83, Holmes & Meier, 1973-84.

A View without a Room (essay), Albondocani Press, 1973.

The Lucy Novels: Early Sketches for "A Room with a View," edited by O. Stallybrass, Holmes & Meier, 1973.

The Manuscripts of "Howards End," edited by O. Stallybrass, Holmes & Meier, 1973.

Goldsworthy Lowes Dickinson and Related Writings, edited by O. Stallybrass, Holmes & Meier, 1973.

Aspects of the Novel and Related Writings, edited by O. Stallybrass, Holmes & Meier, 1974.

E. M. Forster's Letters to Donald Windham, privately printed, 1975.

A Commonplace Book, Scolar, 1978, new edition, edited by Philip Gardner, Stanford University Press, 1985.

The Machine Stops and Other Stories (illustrated by Alan Gilham), abridged by S. H. Burton, Longman, 197(?).

The Manuscripts of "A Passage to India," edited by O. Stallybrass, E. Arnold, 1978, Holmes & Meier, 1979.

Only Connect: Letters to Indian Friends, edited by Syed Hamid Husain, Arnold-Heinemann, 1979.

Arctic Summer and Other Fiction, E. Arnold, 1980, Holmes & Meier, 1981.

Selected Letters of E. M. Forster: Volume 1, 1879-1920, edited by Mary Lago and P. N. Furbank, Harvard University Press, 1983.

The Hill of Devi and Other Indian Writings, edited by E. Heine, Holmes & Meier, 1983.

Foster-Masood Letters, edited by Jalil Ahmad Kidwai, Ross Masood Education and Culture Society of Pakistan, 1984.

Selected Letters of E. M. Forster: Volume II, 1921-1970, edited by M. Lago and P. N. Furbank, Harvard University Press, 1984.

Calendar of the Letters of E. M. Forster, compiled by M. Lago, Mansell, 1985.

Also author of plays, "The Heart of Bosnia," 1911, and "The Abinger Pageant," 1934, and script for film, "Diary for Timothy."

CONTRIBUTOR

Arnold W. Lawrence, editor, *T. E. Lawrence by His Friends,* J. Cape, 1937.

Hermon Ould, editor, *Writers in Freedom,* Hutchinson, 1942.

George Orwell, editor, *Talking to India,* Allen & Unwin, 1943.

Peter Grimes: Essays, John Lane, 1945.

H. Ould, editor, *Freedom of Expression: A Symposium,* Hutchinson, 1945.

"Harnham," Forster's home 1904-1925.

Forster at Crag House, 1949.

S. Radhakrishnan, *Mahatma Gandhi: Essays and Reflections on His Life and Work,* 2nd edition, Allen & Unwin, 1949.

Hermon Ould: A Tribute, [London], 1952.

The Fearful Choice: A Debate on Nuclear Policy, conducted by Philip Toynbee, Wayne State University Press, 1959.

Also contributor to *Aspects of England,* 1935, and *Britain and the Beast,* 1937.

AUTHOR OF INTRODUCTION

(And notes) Virgil, *The Aeneid,* 2 volumes, translated by E. Fairfax Taylor, Dent, 1906.

(And notes) Eliza Fay, *Original Letters from India, 1799-1815,* Harcourt, 1925.

Constance Sitwell, *Flowers and Elephants,* J. Cape, 1927.

George Crabbe, Jr., *The Life of George Crabbe,* Oxford University Press, 1932.

Maurice O'Sullivan, *Twenty Years A-Growing,* Chatto & Windus, 1933.

Mulk Raj Anand, *Untouchable,* Wishart, 1935.

Alec Craig, *The Banned Books of England,* Allen & Unwin, 1937.

K. R. Srinivasa Iyengar, *Literature and Authorship in India,* Allen & Unwin, 1943.

Goldsworthy Lowes Dickinson, *Letters from John Chinaman and Other Essays,* Allen & Unwin, 1946.

Huthi Singh, *Maura,* Longmans, Green, 1951.

Zeenuth Futehally, *Zohra,* Hind Kitabs (Bombay), 1951.

Peter Townsend, editor, *Cambridge Anthology,* Hogarth Press, 1952.

Forrest Reid, *Tom Barber,* Pantheon, 1955.

(And notes) William Golding, *Lord of the Flies,* Coward, 1955.

G. L. Dickinson, *The Greek View of Life,* University of Michigan Press, 1958.

D. Windham, *The Warm Country,* Hart-Davis, 1960.

Guiseppe Tomasi di Lampedusa, *Two Stories and a Memory,* translated by A. Colquhoun, Pantheon, 1962.

Frank Sargeson, *Collected Stories,* MacGibbon & Kee, 1965.

Work is represented in collections, including *The Challenge of Our Time,* Percival Marshall, 1948, and *Fairy Tales for Computers,* Eakins Press, 1969. Contributor to journals and periodicals, including *Listener, Independent Review, Observer, New Statesman, Nation, Albany Review, Open Window, Athenaeum, Egyptian Mail,* and *Horizon.* Forster's works have been translated into twenty-one languages.

ADAPTATIONS:

A Room with a View (play; adapted by Stephen Tait and Kenneth Allott), produced in Cambridge, England, February, 1950, Edward Arnold, 1951; (television dramatization) BBC-TV, April 15, 1973; (motion picture) Merchant Ivory, 1986.

''A Passage to India'' (play; adapted by Santha Rama Rau), produced in London, England, 1960, Ambassador Theatre (New York), January, 1962; (television; adapted by John Maynard), produced by BBC-TV, broadcast by NET, 1968, (cassette), Newmann Communications, 1984; (movie) Columbia, 1984.

King's College in the 1890's.

Where Angels Fear to Tread (play; adapted by Elizabeth Hart), S. French, 1963.

"Howards End" (play; adapted by Lance Sieveking and Richard Cottrell), produced in London, 1967; (television; adapted by Pauline Macaulay; starring Glenda Jackson), BBC-TV, April, 1970; (three-part radio drama), Radio-4 (London), September 1985.

"A Passage to E. M. Forster" (play; based on his works; compiled by William Roerick and Thomas Coley), produced in New York, N.Y. at Theatre de Lys, October 26, 1970.

"The Longest Journey" (play), Lampa Theatre (London), August, 23, 1974.

"The Obelisk" (television), BBC-TV, October 13, 1977.

"The Celestial Omnibus" (recording), American Forces Radio and Television Service, 1978.

"Maurice" (motion picture), Merchant Ivory, 1987.

SIDELIGHTS: **January 1, 1879.** Forster was born in London, England, the only child of Alice Clara (Lily) Whichelo and Edward Morgan Llewellyn Forster, an architect. His name had been registered as Henri, but at his christening "the old verger asked my father what the baby was to be called, and he, distrait, gave his own name, Edward Morgan. This the verger wrote down on a piece of paper. My maternal grandmother held me at the font. When the clergyman asked her what I was to be called she became afraid of the sound of her voice in a sacred edifice, and indicated the piece of paper. My mother, in a distant pew, heard the announcement with horror. I had been registered one way and christened another. What on earth was to happen. It turned out after agitated research that the christening had it, so Edward I am."[1]

After his father died of tuberculosis, young Forster was brought up almost exclusively by the women in the family and various maids. His great Aunt Marianne was particularly intent on managing his and his mother's lives. "I realised without being told, that I was in the power of a failing old woman who wanted to be kind but she was old and each visit she was older. How old was she? Born in the reign of George the Fourth, my mother thought. 'More likely Edward the Fourth' cried I."[1]

"Those early years made a deep impression which no amount of suburbianism or travel has dispelled. When I think of England it is of the countryside, and I still think of her thus though so little of our countryside remains. And my patriotism, which is very steady, is loyalty to the place where I happen to belong. It doesn't go any further...."[2]

The family, considering him of delicate constitution, was overprotective, coddling him and dressing him in frilly outfits with his hair in long curls. His mother recalled: "We have rather a life of it if we do anything baby doesn't like....He calls us 'monstrous crows and rats,' and when his grandmother asked him 'not to do it' he said 'I shall, Mrs piece of suet.

"[He has]...such a stupid habit of throwing things for no reason in the world—he had just flung my prayer book and hymn book across the room and when we were with Laura he

(Dust jacket illustration from the British edition of *Howards End* by E. M. Forster.)

all but knocked down some valuable vases by throwing a sofa cushion at them. . . .''[1]

Great Aunt Marianne died at the age of ninety-one and left Forster 8,000 pounds (approximately $2,000). The interest on this amount was to be used for his education and at the age of twenty-five he was to receive the capital. ''I am grateful to Marianne Thornton; for she and no one else made my career as a writer possible, and her love in a most tangible sense followed me beyond the grave.''[3]

1890. Sent to preparatory school, Kent House, in Eastbourne, he was bullied by the other boys, who called him ''Mousie.'' Painfully homesick and ''I feel so very nervous somehow. I don't know why it is but perhaps it is excitement, but lately I have always been taking the dark side of things. I have never been like it before, but it is not at all nice. It is very much like despondency; I am afraid I shall miss the train in the morning. . .afraid I shall lose my tickets; those are instances of the kind of state of mind I am in; it is not so bad in the day-time as at night, then I cry a lot. I also have. . .a kind of forboding that something dreadful will happen before the holidays. . . .The worst of school is that you have nothing and nobody to love, if I only had somebody; I shall be much happier.''[4]

1892. Sent for the summer term to the ''The Granger,'' a local school. ''Two of the boys in my dormitory last night kept on taking my pillow, and wetting my clothes; so I bore it for a long time and then when they began hitting me and hurting my face, I thought 'no more of this' and I slapped their faces. So they say they will take it out on me this evening. Let them do it!, but I shan't go at them with my fists closed till they do the same to me. And I believe the reason for this is that I did not bring back any grub on Sunday. I don't feel at all worried about it, but I am threatened with all the school setting on to me to morrow. I rather hope they do, and I don't intend

to stand still and be bullied; and perhaps I shall get on better afterwards. . . .''[1] His mother withdrew him and brought him home.

Moved to Tonbridge where he enrolled in Tonbridge School as a dayboy. Because those who attended as dayboys were branded as socially inferior by the boarders and staff, Forster was bullied more extensively than in previous school experiences. As a schoolmate recounted years later: ''Forster? The writer? Yes, I remember him. A little cissy. We took it out on him, I can tell you. . . .''[1]

1897. Entered King's College, Cambridge. ''Body and spirit, reason and emotion, work and play, architecture and scenery, laughter and seriousness, life and art—these pairs which are elsewhere contrasted were there fused into one. People and books reinforced one another, intelligence joined hands with affection, speculation became a passion, and discussion was made profound by love.''[5]

''The education I received in those far-off and fantastic days made me soft and I am very glad it did, for I have seen plenty of hardness since, and I know it does not even pay. . . .But though the education was humane it was imperfect, inasmuch as. . .none of us realised our economic position. In came the nice fat dividends, up rose the lofty thoughts, and we did not realise that all the time we were exploiting the poor of our country and the backward races abroad, and getting bigger profits from our investments than we should. We refused to face this unpalatable truth. I remember being told as a small boy, 'Dear, don't talk about money, it's ugly'—a good example of Victorian defence mechanism.''[6]

''It was Cambridge that first set me off writing. . . .At one time my tutor. . .suggested to me that I might write. He did it in a very informal way. He said in a sort of drawling voice 'I don't see why you should not write,' and I being very diffident was delighted at this remark and thought, after all why shouldn't I write? And I did. It is really owing to Wedd and to that start at Cambridge that I have written. I might have started for some other reason.

''[Cambridge] is not a place in which a writer ought to remain. I am quite sure he ought to go out into the world and meet more types, I was going to say meet people of more classes, but of course in Cambridge you can now meet people of all classes, but mostly selected intellectuals. It is most necessary for the writer, and for everyone else, to go all over the place. That is my general feeling.''[7]

October, 1901. Forster and his mother embarked on a one-year voyage to Italy, Sicily, and Austria. ''I missed nothing—neither the campaniles, nor the crooked bridges over dry torrent beds, nor the uniformity of blue sky, nor the purple shadows of the mountains over the lake. But I knew that I must wait for many days before they meant any thing to me or gave me any pleasure. We—that is I—are never too tired or unhappy to record, and while we are young a little time purges away our frailties and leaves us with the pure gold. But I would rather have the pure gold at once.''[1]

Their days were filled with museums, galleries and churches. His mother's concern was for Forster's health, impracticality, absent-mindedness and occasional clumsiness: first he sprained his ankle, then he broke his arm walking up the steps of St. Peter's.

In Florence, Forster began to work on a new novel. His early version called ''Lucy'' evolved into *A Room with a View*. ''In a hotel lounge one day—at Siena or that sort of place—I ov-

"Rooksnest," the model for *Howards End*.

erheard an English lady talking to another English lady about a third English lady who had married an Italian far beneath her socially and also much younger, and how most unfortunate it was. This sorry bit of twaddle stuck in my mind. I worked at it until it became alive and grew into a novel of contrasts.''[2]

Back in London, mother and son took up residence at the Kingsley Hotel in Bloomsbury and Forster began giving weekly classes in Latin at the Working Men's College. He was to teach there for more than twenty years, developing friendships with students, participating in the college's social activities and writing for the college journal.

1904. Moved into a house in Weybridge which he shared with his mother and grandmother. "I worry. . .about myself. I write so slowly, and I think not so well. It is impossible to work at Cambridge: here I'm dull and fairly bright.

"Is it impossible to live with old people without deteriorating?

"My life is now straightening into something rather sad & dull to be sure, & I want to set it & me down, as I see us now. Nothing more great will come out of me. I've made my two discoveries—the religious about 4 years ago, the other in the winter of 1902—and the reconstruction is practically over. If I'm wrecked now it will be on little things—idleness, irritability, & still more, shyness. Self-consciousness will do for me if I'm not careful—drive me into books, or the piano. The truth is I'm living a very difficult life: I never come into contact with any one's work, & that makes things difficult. I may

sit year after year in my pretty sitting room, watching things grow more unreal, because I'm afraid of being remarked. . . .It begins to look that I'm not good enough to do without regular work. . . .A few people like my work, but most of them like me. As to lecturing. . .I'm not good at it. . . .I still want, in all moods, the greatest happiness but perhaps it is well it should be denied me. . . .Unimportant as my youth has been, it's been less unimportant than I expected & than other people think. And ardently as I desire beauty & strength & a truer outlook, I don't despise myself, or think life not worth while.''[1]

1905. Went to Germany as a tutor. "I wanted to learn some German and do some writing, and a Cambridge friend put me in touch with his aunt. She was English (born in Australia actually) and she had married an aristocratic Pomeranian landowner. She was, furthermore, a well-known and gifted authoress, who wrote under the name of Elizabeth. Her *Elizabeth and Her German Garden* was widely read, and her three eldest girls had become household words in many a British household. . . .I was one of a series of tutors. . .and I was to pick up in exchange what German I could. At first I feared I should not get the job, for I met none of her requirements: refused to come permanently, could not give all my time, could not teach mathematics or anything except English. But the more difficulties I raised the warmer grew Elizabeth's letters. She begged me to come when I liked and as I liked. She trusted I should not find Nassenheide dull, and she asked me to be so good as to bring her from London a packet of orris root.

"My arrival occurred on April 4, 1905. . . . came to the long low building I was presently to know under sunlight. The bell

Forster, in Mahratta turban.

pealed, a hound bayed, and a half-dressed underservant un-locked the hall door and asked me what I wanted. I replied, 'I want to live here'. . . .And presently I stood in the presence of the Countess herself. . . .

"The discomforts of my arrival seemed to have lowered me in her opinion: indeed I lost all the ground I had gained through refusing to come. Glancing up at my tired and peaked face, she said in her rather grating voice, 'How d'ye do, Mr. Forster. We confused you with the new housemaid. . . .Can you teach the children, do you think? They are very difficult. . .oh yes Mr. Forster, very difficult, they'll laugh at you, you know. You'll have to be stern or it'll end as it did with Mr. Stokoe.' I gave her the packet of orris root, which she accepted as only her due, and the interview ended.

"Subsequently our relations became easy and she told me that she had nearly sent me straight back to England there and then, since I was wearing a particularly ugly tie. I do not believe her. I was not. She had no respect for what may be called the lower forms of truth. Then we spoke of some friends of hers whom I had met in Dresden. 'They don't like me,' she said. I replied: 'So I saw.' This gave her a jump.

"So my arrival was on the tough side. Still all went well, and all around us stretched the German countryside. . . .When I began to look about me I was filled with delight.

"It was the country, the flat agricultural surround, that so ravished me. . . .

"I had a little room which got the morning sun, so that I could sit in my bath and be shone upon. . . .

"My teaching duties were only an hour a day. I had abundant leisure for my German and my writing and was most considerately treated if I asked for leave. . .our pupils, delightful and original and easy. . .their mother, delightful and original and occasionally difficult.

"It is curious that Germany, a country which I do not know well or instinctively embrace, should twice have seduced me through her countryside. I have described the first occasion. The second was half a century later when I stayed in a remote hamlet in Franconia. . . .The two districts resembled each other in their vastness and openness and in their freedom from industrialism. They were free from smoke and wires, and masts and placards, and they were full of living air: they remind me of what our own countryside used to be before it was ruined.

"The tragedy of England is that she is too small to become a modern state and yet to retain her freshness. The freshness has to go. Even when there is a National Park it has to be mucked up. Germany is anyhow larger, and thanks to her superior size she may preserve the rural heritage that smaller national units have had to scrap—the heritage which I used to see from my own doorstep in Hertfordshire when I was a child, and which has failed to outlast me."[8]

1907. *The Longest Journey* published. "All I write is, to me, sentimental. A book which doesn't leave people either happier or better than it found them, which doesn't add some permanent treasure to the world, isn't worth doing. (A book *about* good and happy people may be still better but hasn't attracted me yet so much.) This is my 'theory,' and I maintain it's sentimental. . . ."[2]

"Though critics do not think highly of it. It is sometimes dismissed as a failure. Yet I like it most because it is so close to me. . .to what I am."[9]

October 14, 1908. *A Room with a View* released to warm reviews. "It *is* gratifying when those who know the world and men at work can find a book by me not sloppy nor unconnected with life. . . .I can't write down 'I care about love, beauty, liberty, affection, and truth,' though I should like to.

"I don't at all know about [*A Room with a View*]. It is slight, unambitious, and uninteresting, but—in rather an external way—the characters seem more alive to me than any others that I have put together. The publisher is much pleased—which is all to the bad, I admit—and I have got good terms. Have tried to get it taken in America, but that was no go. 'Not sufficiently compelling for a transatlantic audience.' Which, I admit, is all to the good. . . .The thing comes out in October, and will probably gratify the home circle, but not those whose opinions I value most."[1] The book was not a commercial success.

October 18, 1910. *Howards End* was ". . .my best novel and approaching a good novel. Very elaborate and all pervading plot that is seldom tiresome or forced, range of characters, social sense, wit, wisdom, colour. Have only just discovered why I don't care for it: not a single character in it for whom I care. . . .Perhaps the house in *H.E.*, for which I did once care, took the place of people and now that I no longer care for it, their barrenness has become evident. I feel pride in the achievement, but cannot love it, and occasionally the swish of the skirts and the non-sexual embraces irritate. . . ."[1]

Began a deep friendship with Florence Barger with whom he could also discuss his homosexuality. She was to become one of his close female friends. "She loves me and I her, and reverence her without feeling ashamed of my useless-

The Lomas Rishi Cave served as the model for the Marabar Caves in "A Passage to India."

ness. . . .Very great happiness, and must try not to impose on her and tout for sympathy."[1]

October, 1912. Departed for India, leaving his mother in Italy for a vacation. The Rajah of Dewas was to have a great impact on Forster's life, and they met many times. "The Rajah has just been talking to me, cross-legged and barefoot on a little cane chair. We had a long talk about religion. . . .Indians are so easy and communicative on this subject, whereas English people are mostly offended when it is introduced, or else shocked if there is a difference of opinion. His attitude was very difficult for a Westerner. He believes that we—men, birds, everything—are part of God, and that men have developed more than birds because they have come nearer to realising this. . . .

"He is really a remarkable man, for all this goes with much practical ability and a sense of humour. In the middle of a chat he will suddenly pray, tapping his forehead and bobbing on his knees, and then continuing the sentence where he left it off; 'On days when one feels gratitude, it is well to show it,' he said.

"He was certainly a genius and possibly a saint, and he had to be a king."[10]

November, 1915. Left for Alexandria, Egypt. "I am liking my work out here. I am what is called a 'Red Cross Searcher':— that is to say I go round the Hospitals and question the wounded soldiers for news of their missing comrades. It is depressing in a way, for if one does get news about the missing it is generally bad news. But I am able to be of use to the wounded soldiers themselves in various unofficial ways. . . .

"I live in a comfortable hotel here, and start out about 10.0., returning for lunch and finishing about 7.0. In the evening I write my reports which go—ultimately—to the relatives in England and to the War Office. The Red X is a semi-military organisation, so, though technically a civilian, I wear officer's uniform, and get various privileges and conveniences. . . .I have one or two friends here, and the regular and definite work has stopped me thinking about the war, which is a mercy, for in England I very nearly went mad.

"I do not like Egypt much—or rather, I do not see it, for Alexandria is cosmopolitan. But what I have seen seems vastly inferior to India, for which I am always longing in the most persistent way, and where I still hope to die. It is only at sunset that Egypt surpasses India—at all other hours it is flat, unromantic, unmysterious, and godless—the soil is mud, the inhabitants are of mud moving, and exasperating in the extreme: I feel as instinctively not at home among them as I feel instinctively at home among Indians. . . .

"It is useless to make plans when at any moment one may be submarined or conscripted. . . .All that I cared for in civilisation has gone forever, and I am trying to live without either hopes or fears—not an easy job, but one keeps going some how."[4]

January, 1919. Returned to England. "Isn't it awful how all the outward nonsense of England has been absolutely untouched by the war—still this unbroken front of dress-shirts and golf. I'm damned if I know what bucks one up. . . ."[4]

In need of money, Forster began working in literary journalism. Wrote approximately a hundred articles and reviews for *Nation, Daily News, Herald* and *Athenaeum*. "I am happiest when busy. How fatuous! I see my middle age as clearly as middle age can be seen. Always working, never creating. Pleasant to all, trusting no one. A mixture of cowardice and sympathy. Blaming civilization for my failure. At the end of these activities begins a great pain, after which death, but I

(From the movie "A Passage to India," starring Judy Davis and Victor Banerjee. Released by Columbia Pictures in 1984, it won two Academy Awards.)

cannot realize such things. . . .I long for something of which youth was only a part. I don't see what it is clearly yet, but know what keeps me from it. I am not vain, but I am sensitive to praise and blame: this is bad. Is it just the aimiable [*sic*] journalist—who can't even write as soon as he looks into his own mind.''[11]

1921. Returned to India to work as private secretary to the Rajah. ''The day after my arrival we had a bewildering interview and [the Maharajah] assigned me my duties: gardens, tennis courts, motors, Guest House, Electric House. None of these had much to do with reading or writing, my supposed specialities. I had an office (hours 7-11 and 4-5). All the post was to pass through my hands. These were not the duties which I had expected or for which I was qualified, but this did not disturb us, and he spent most of the interview in writing me out lists of the dignitaries of state. They fell into four categories: the Ruling Family, the great Maratha nobles, the secondary nobles, and the lesser nobles, who bore the title of Mankari: 'in this last lot you will be the first.' Reverting to the ruling Family, he emphasized the names and titles of his brother, his son, his brother's wife, his aunt, and his own absent wife. These were the highest in the land: I was to salaam with two hands and the whole hand, and to extend similar courtesies to the Dewan, the A.G.G. and the P.A. These last two were British officials. I was to regard myself when meeting them as an Indian. But I began by this time to get a little mixed—far from clear for instance as to the composition of the all-powerful council of State. 'Wait a minute!' he cried. On he swept, descending to individual Mankaris and

clerks and mysterious persons called 'Eighteen Offices' or 'Horse Doctor.'

'' 'I shall never get all this right,' I said.

'' 'Oh yes, you will. Besides it does not matter in the least, except in the case of Brother and those others whom I have specially mentioned.'. . .

''The suite he assigned me was on the first floor at the end of the drawing-room wing: bedroom, sitting room, anteroom, bathroom, all decently furnished in the European style. It was reached either by a verandah along the inner side of the courtyard, or by a staircase that descended straight into the garden and was sometimes, though not often, locked at the bottom, or by an outside verandah which communicated with the bedroom. It was not very private, but what was? We all of us lived in a passage, the Ruler included. I usually slept on the roof, facing Devi. . . .''[10]

Forster returned to Weybridge ''. . .to come back to an ugly house a mile from the station, an old, fussy, exacting mother, to come back having lost your Rajah, without a novel, and with no power to write one—this is dismal, I expect, at the age of 43.''[11]

He continued working on one of his unfinished novels. ''I began this novel before my 1921 visit [to India], and took out the opening chapters with me, with the intention of continuing them. But as soon as they were confronted with the country they purported to describe, they seemed to wilt and go dead

Forster in his rooms at King's College, 1950.

and I could do nothing with them. I used to look at them of an evening in my room at Dewas, and felt only distaste and despair. The gap between India remembered and India experienced was too wide. When I got back to England the gap narrowed, and I was able to resume. But I still thought the book bad, and probably should not have completed it without the encouragement of Leonard Woolf."[10]

"[*A Passage to India*] is done at last and I feel—or shall feel when the typing's over—great relief. I am so weary, not of working but of not working; of thinking the book bad and so not working, and of not working and so thinking it bad: that vicious circle. Now it is done and I think it good. Publishers fall into ecstasies! But I know much about publishers. . .and sent them those chapters that are likely to make them ecstatic, concealing the residue in the W. C. until the contracts are signed. They unite, though, in restraining their joy until the autumn. I'm afraid it won't come out till then."[12]

"I shall never write another novel. . .—my patience with ordinary people has given out. But I shall go on writing. I don't feel any decline in my 'powers.'"[13]

"I have wondered—not whether I was getting down or up, which is too difficult, but whether I had moved at all since King's [College]. King's stands for personal relationships, and these still seem to me the most real things on the surface of the earth, but I have acquired a feeling that people must go away from each other (spiritually) every now and then, and improve themselves if the relationship is to develop or even endure. *A Passage to India* describes such a going away—preparatory to the next advance, which I am not capable of describing. It seems to me that individuals progress alternately by loneliness and intimacy. . . ."[12]

There were some accusations from political and social circles that the book was not fair in dealing with its subject. "Isn't 'fair-mindedness' dreary! A rare achievement, and a valuable one, you will tell me, but how sterile in one's own soul. I fall in love with Orientals, with Anglo-Indians—no: that is roughly my internal condition, and all the time I had to repress the consequences, or fail to hold the scales. Where is truth? It makes me so sad that I could not give the beloved a better show. One's deepest emotions count for so little as soon as one tries to describe external life honestly, or even readably. . . .

"As to what qualifies a man to write a novel dealing with India, to what extent blue-book accuracy is desirable, to what extent intensity of impression and sensitiveness, is a controversial question, and one on which gibes are apt to be exchanged. I have only been to the country twice (year & a half in all), and only been acquainted with Indians for eighteen years, yet I believe that I have seen certain important truths. . . ."[11]

1925-1926. Moved into West Hackhurst with his mother, though she resisted. He described himself as: "Famous, wealthy, miserable, physically ugly—red nose enormous, round patch in middle of scalp which I forget less than I did and which is brown when I don't wash my head and pink when I do. Face in the distance. . .is toad-like and pallid, with a tiny rim of hair along the top of the triangle. My stoop must be appalling yet I don't think much of it, indeed I still don't think often. *Now* I do, and am surprised I don't repel more generally: I can still get to know any one I want and have that illusion that I am charming and beautiful. Take no bother over nails or teeth but would powder my nose if I wasn't found out. Stomach increases, but not yet visible under waistcoat. . . .Eyes & probably hearing weaker."[11]

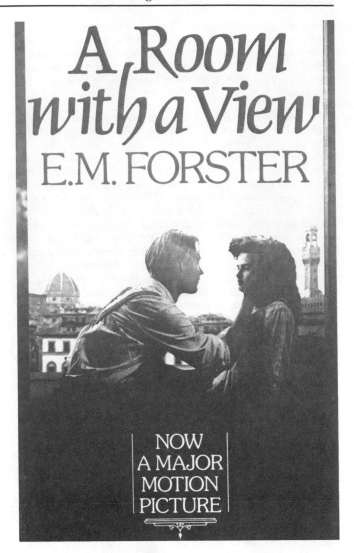

(Cover from the paperback edition of *A Room with a View* by E. M. Forster.)

Forster experienced emotional difficulty with his mother and was plagued with waves of melancholy. "The fact that I don't create, or get idler, is depressing me, even to the point of making me self-conscious and disinclining me to see certain people. . . .I don't know what to do with my existence, my memory's worse, my vitality probably less, and yet I am feeling perfectly well—unless the sense that I couldn't face anything except what I actually do face is a sign of morbidity. There is no doubt that work would put every thing right, but what work?

"I never felt work was a duty—indeed, the less one adds to civilisation the longer perhaps it will take to topple over. But not to feel intact, not to [be] able to expose oneself to certain contacts because of self-consciousness—that really is an aweful [sic] nuisance, and I spend a good deal of time now with people who are (vaguely speaking) my inferiors, and to whom I can very easily be kind."[12]

1930. "I am now fifty-one, and perhaps the fact that I'm awfully young in some ways make difficulties that wouldn't come to people who bow themselves down all of a piece."[12]

Struck up a close friendship with police officer Bob Buckingham. "I'm quite sure that his feeling for me is something he has never had before. It's a spiritual feeling which has extended to my physique."[11]

Regularly reviewed books on BBC Radio. "It is nice getting all this money, as I have been losing investments like everyone else in the last few months. Now I shall be rich again, as I have not been for a long time, and I am not again making the mistake of investing, or even of letting it lie in the Bank. I shall bury it to be disinterred as wanted...."[12]

"The ugly habit has crept on me. I bring myself to the front by saying jokingly that I am rich, poor, have made good terms in America, paid a lot at a restaurant; and a man who has had real worries over money rebukes me. 'A thing to use if one's got it'—I have always preached that, yet I am letting it use me, and take hold of me where I feel safest, through my sense of humour."[11]

"One of the evils of money is that it tempts us to look at it rather than at the things that it buys. They are dimmed because of the metal and the paper through which we receive them. That is the fundamental deceitfulness of riches, which kept worrying Christ. That is the treachery of the purse, the wallet and the bank-balance, even from the capitalist point of view. They were invented as a convenience to the flesh, they have become a chain for the spirit. Surely they can be cut out, like some sorts of pain. Though deprived of them the human mind might surely still keep its delicacy unimpaired, and the human body eat, drink and make love."[6]

"Life is certainly odd," Forster wrote to a friend during World War II. "And what I resent is that it must be making *me* so odd, and people elsewhere...still odder. It does not seem natural that I should have interrupted this letter to call out to my mother (aged 88) to keep away from glass, that she should have transmitted the warning in calm tones while packing me up some margarine, and that I should have gone on with this letter equally calmly. One adapts oneself to conditions, and it is depressing that one should, for it means that one is failing to notice them."[11]

"I am tearing up papers and fill the wastepaper basket nightly, mostly with old letters. I don't know what to do with my unpublished stories, of which there are an untidy bunch. They are mostly frivolous, many would be repelled by them, and I don't really know whether they are any good."[12]

1945. "Mother is dead. Peacefully, while I was spooning her some lunch on Sunday, and the famous death-rattle wasn't too bad. I said 'Can you hear me?' and she nodded. I think there was something deeper between us than I knew, for the shock is worse than I expected. I can't explain—or could explain all too well, being a writer—but it has to do with the greatness of love and one's own smallness...."[12] "I partly died when [she] did, and must smell sometimes of the grave.—I have noticed and disliked that smell in others occasionally."[11]

Returned to India. "I feel like a sponge which has been dropped back into an ocean whose existence it had forgotten."[11]

1946. Upon his return home, King's College offered to make him an honorary fellow, giving him residence at the college. His first weeks were uncomfortable. "There is no privacy, and people are always pestering one to be interesting."[11]

He soon acclimatized, however, reconnecting with the Apostles Society and mingling with undergraduates. "I have no mystic faith in the people. I have in the individual. He seems to me a divine achievement and I mistrust any view which belittles him. If anyone calls you a wretched little individual—

and I've been called that—don't you take it lying down. You are important because everyone else is an individual too—including the person who criticises you. In asserting your personality you are playing for your side."[6]

1947. Invited by Harvard University to give a lecture at their "Symposium on Music Criticism." "An extraordinary invitation, really. I'm to speak on 'The Raison d'Etre of Criticism in the Arts,' revealing whether or not criticism is any use....Actually, it was jolly smart of the Harvard people to find out that I'm fond of music. England hasn't got onto it yet. The Harvard people wrote that they liked something I said about Beethoven's Fifth in my novel *Howards End,* which came out in 1910. I was so grateful for their perspicacity that I accepted their invitation at once. Of course, I've always fancied that I am rather better than the average music listener in comprehension. . . .

"America has been awfully kind to my books. But admiration can be a little frightening you know. I understand there are some very deep readers of mine at Harvard and I'm a bit uneasy about facing them. It's unsettling to have people going over your work with a magnifying glass and turning up hidden meanings.

"All I seem to write any more is little essays. But I must say I keep right on looking at things from a novelist's point of view.

"Perhaps an idea will come along."[14]

"I have refused $25,000 from Fox Films for the movie rights of *A Room with a View.* Stimulated by my refusal, they offer more....Nothing would have survived of the original except my name, and if I had tried to control the production I should have broken my heart at Hollywood...."[12]

"America is rather like life. You can usually find in it what you look for. If you look for skyscrapers or cowboys or cocktail parties or gangsters or business connections or political problems or women's clubs, they will certainly be there. You can be very hot there or very cold. You can explore the America of your choice by plane or train, by hitch-hike or on foot. It will probably be interesting, and it is sure to be large.

"I went there for the first time at the age of sixty-eight. By sixty-eight one is so to speak a pilgrim grandfather who knows very clearly what to look for when he disembarks. I had no doubt as to what I wanted to discover in America. It was to provide me with scenery and individuals. The scenery was to be of two sorts—gigantic and homely. The individuals were not to be representative—I never could get on with representative individuals—but people who existed on their own account and with whom it might therefore be possible to be friends. That is the America I looked for and was to find. My visit was a complete success from my own point of view."[6]

1953. Received the Order of Companions of Honour to the Queen. "All went well between myself and the queen yesterday. I was alone with her for about ten minutes—she was quite an ickle thing, very straight and charming, stood with her back to a huge fire, gave me a very handsome decoration in a case...and we talked about this and that very pleasantly. She shook hands to start and to finish, and I threw in some bows, and occasionally threw in Your Majesty or Ma'am. She was much better at the chat than I was. I liked her very much indeed. Finally she rang a buzzer in the mantel piece and I retired. It was a state dining room I think, which was gold, and very long. She looked tiny at the end of it, dressed in

(From the movie ''A Room with a View,'' starring Helena Bonham Carter and Maggie Smith. Winner of three Academy Awards, it was produced by Merchant Ivory in 1986.)

blue. I drove up to the Palace in a taxi and departed from it on foot.''[12]

1960-1963. Stage adaptation of *A Passage to India* by Santha Rama Rau premiered in London. ''Though you might not think so, this is not the first time I have trodden the stage. On the previous occasion it was that of Covent Garden: then I only had to bow. Tonight's undertaking is more difficult. . . .How good the actors were. And how pleased I was that there were so many of them. I am so used to seeing the sort of play which deals with one man and two women. They do not leave me with the feeling I have made a full theatrical meal. They are excellent in many ways, but they do not give me the impression of the multiplicity of life. . . .As a member of the audience I have on occasion been thanked by the actors for being so good. It did not arouse in me any great emotion. All the same, it is a pretty thought, so I will give you my bow.''[12]

June 7, 1970. Died of a stroke. He had left instructions that he was to be ''disposed of'' wherever he was at the time of his death, without any religious observances. Forster was cremated and his ashes scattered on Buckingham's rose bed.

''I suppose such views and beliefs that I have, have come out incidentally in my books. . . .Anyone who has cared to read

my books will see what high value I attach to personal relationships and to tolerance and, I may add, to pleasure. Pleasure one is not supposed to talk about in public however such one enjoys it in private. But if I have had any influence I should be very glad that it had induced people to enjoy this wonderful world into which we are born, and of course to help others to enjoy it too.''[7]

FOOTNOTE SOURCES

[1]P. N. Furbank, *E. M. Forster: A Life, Volume I,* Harcourt, 1977.

[2]E. M. Forster, *The Hill of Devi,* E. Arnold, 1983.

[3]E. M. Forster, *Marianne Thornton: A Domestic Biography, 1797-1887,* Harcourt, 1956.

[4]Mary Lago and P. N. Furbank, editors, *Selected Letters of E. M. Forster, Volume I, 1879-1920,* Belknop Press, 1983.

[5]Francis King, *E. M. Forster and His World,* Thames & Hudson, 1978.

[6]E. M. Forster, *Two Cheers for Democracy,* Harcourt, 1951.

[7]David Jones, ''E. M. Forster on His Life and His Books,'' *Listener,* January 1, 1959.

[8]E. M. Forster, ''Recollections of Nassenheide,'' *Listener,* January 1, 1959.

(From the movie ''Maurice,'' starring Rupert Graves. Produced by Merchant Ivory, 1987.)

⁹V. A. Shahane, "A Visit to Mr. E. M. Forster," *Quest* (Bombay), spring, 1967.

¹⁰E. M. Forster, *The Hill of Devi*, Harcourt, 1953.

¹¹P. N. Furbank, *E. M. Forster: A Life, Volume II*, Harcourt, 1978.

¹²M. Lago and P. N. Furbank, editors, *Selected Letters of E. M. Forster, Volume II, 1921-1970*, Belknop Press, 1977.

¹³E. M. Forster, *The Life to Come and Other Stories*, Norton, 1972.

¹⁴"Tourist," *New Yorker*, May 3, 1947.

FOR MORE INFORMATION SEE:

BOOKS

Frank Swinnerton, *The Georgian Literary Scene*, Dent, 1938, revised edition, 1951.

Rose Macaulay, *The Writings of E. M. Forster*, Harcourt, 1938, new edition, Barnes & Noble, 1970.

Lionel Trilling, *E. M. Forster*, New Directions, 1943, 2nd revised edition, 1965.

Austin Warren, *Rage for Order*, University of Chicago Press, 1948.

John K. Johnstone, *The Bloomsbury Group: A Study of E. M. Forster, Lytton Strachey, Virginia Woolf, and Their Circle*, Noonday, 1954.

Stanley J. Kunitz, editor, *Twentieth Century Authors*, 1st supplement, H. W. Wilson, 1955.

Morton Dauwen Zabel, *Craft and Character*, Viking, 1957.

James McConkey, *The Novels of E. M. Forster*, Cornell University Press, 1957.

Malcolm Cowley, editor, *Writers at Work: The Paris Review Interviews*, first series, Viking, 1958.

H. J. Oliver, *The Art of E. M. Forster*, Cambridge University Press, 1960.

Mark Schorer, editor, *Modern British Fiction*, Oxford University Press, 1961.

Karl Watts Gransden, *E. M. Forster*, Grove, 1962, revised edition, Oliver & Boyd, 1970.

F. C. Crews, *E. M. Forster: The Perils of Humanism*, Princeton University Press, 1962.

John Beer, *The Achievement of E. M. Forster*, Chatto, 1962, Barnes & Noble, 1963.

James Hall, *The Tragic Comedians: Seven Modern British Novelists*, Indiana University Press, 1963.

John Edward Hardy, *Man in the Modern Novel*, University of Washington Press, 1964.

Alan Wilde, *Art and Order: A Study of E. M. Forster*, New York University Press, 1964.

K. Natwar-Singh, editor, *E. M. Forster: A Tribute*, Harcourt, 1964.

Current Biography Yearbook, 1964, H. W. Wilson, 1964.

David Shusterman, *The Quest for Certitude in E. M. Forster's Fiction*, Indiana University Press, 1965.

B. J. Kirkpatrick, *A Bibliography of E. M. Forster*, Hart-Davis, 1965, revised edition, 1968.

Wilfred Stone, *The Cave and the Mountain: A Study of E. M. Forster*, Stanford University Press, 1966.

Malcolm Bradbury, editor, *Forster: A Collection of Critical Essays*, Prentice-Hall, 1966.

George H. Thomson, *The Fiction of E. M. Forster*, Wayne State University Press, 1967.

Norman Kelvin, *E. M. Forster*, Southern Illinois University Press, 1967.

Vasant Anant Shahane, editor, *Perspectives on E. M. Forster's "A Passage to India,"* Barnes & Noble, 1968.

Laurence Brander, *E. M. Forster: A Critical Study*, Hart-Davis, 1968.

Denis Godfrey, *E. M. Forster's Other Kingdom*, Barnes & Noble, 1968.

Frederick P. W. McDowell, *E. M. Forster*, Twayne, 1969, revised edition, 1982.

H. H. Anniah Gowda, *A Garland for E. M. Forster*, Literary Half-Yearly (Mysore, India), 1969.

Oliver Stallybrass, editor, *Aspects of E. M. Forster: Essays and Recollections Written for His Ninetieth Birthday, January 1, 1969*, Harcourt, 1969.

Andrew Rutherford, *Twentieth Century Interpretations of "A Passage to India,"* Prentice-Hall, 1970.

June P. Levine, *Creation and Criticism: "A Passage to India,"* University of Nebraska Press, 1971.

Alfred Borrello, *An E. M. Forster Dictionary*, Scarecrow, 1971.

James McConkey, *The Novels of E. M. Forster*, Archon Books, 1971.

Martial Rose, *E. M. Forster*, Arco, 1971.

A. Borrello, *An E. M. Forster Glossary*, Scarecrow, 1972.

Carolyn Riley, editor, *Contemporary Literary Criticism*, Gale, Volume I, 1973, Volume II, 1974, Volume III, 1975, Volume IV, 1975.

P. Gardner, editor, *E. M. Forster: The Critical Heritage*, Routledge & Kegan Paul, 1974.

John Colmer, *E. M. Forster: The Personal Voice*, Routledge & Kegan Paul, 1975.

John Sayre Martin, *E. M. Forster: The Endless Journey*, Cambridge University Press, 1976.

F. P. W. McDowell, editor, *E. M. Forster: An Annotated Bibliography of Writings about Him*, Northern Illinois University Press, 1977.

Jane Lagoudis Pinchin, *Alexandria Still: Forster, Durrell and Cavafy*, Princeton University Press, 1977.

G. K. Das, *Forster's India*, Macmillan (London), 1977, Rowman & Littlefield, 1978.

Philip Gardner, *E. M. Forster*, Longman, 1978.

Francis E. King, *E. M. Forster and His World*, Scribner, 1978.

G. K. Das and J. Beer, editors, *E. M. Forster, a Human Exploration: Centenary Essays*, New York University Press, 1979.

Robin Jared Lewis, *E. M. Forster's Passages to India*, Columbia University Press, 1979.

V. A. Shahane, *Approaches to E. M. Forster: A Centenary Volume*, Arnold-Heinemann (New Delhi), 1981.

J. S. Herz and Robert K. Martin, editors, *E. M. Forster: Centenary Revaluations*, Macmillan (London), 1982.

Barbara Rosecrance, *Forster's Narrative Vision*, Cornell University Press, 1982.

Elmer Borklund, *Comtemporary Literary Critics*, 2nd edition, Gale, 1982.

British Writers, Volume 6, Scribner, 1983.

Christopher C. Brown and William B. Thesing, *English Prose and Criticism, 1900-1950*, Gale, 1983.

Dictionary of Literary Biography, Volume 34, Gale, 1985.

H. F. Oxbury, *Great Britons: Twentieth-Century Lives*, Oxford University Press, 1985.

David Dowling, *Bloomsbury Aesthetics and the Novels of Forster*, Macmillan (London), 1985.

J. Beer, *"A Passage to India": Essays in Interpretation*, Macmillan (England), 1986.

Graham Chainey, *A Literary History of Cambridge*, University of Michigan Press, 1986.

Judith Scherer Herz, *The Short Narratives of E. M. Forster*, Macmillan (England), 1987.

PERIODICALS

Forum, December, 1927.

Atlantic Monthly, November, 1927 (p. 642), January, 1949 (p. 60).

E. M. Forster, "Breaking Up," *Spectator*, July 28, 1933.

Criterion, October, 1934.

Scrutiny, September, 1938.

Theology, April, 1940.
New York Times Book Review, June 29, 1947, June 19, 1949, December 29, 1968 (p. 1), October 10, 1970 (p. 2), January 8, 1984 (p. 3), May 5, 1985 (p. 12), February 23, 1986 (p. 11).
P. N. Furbank and F. J. H. Haskell, "The Art of Fiction I: E. M. Forster," *New Republic,* October 5, 1949 (p. 17), January 11, 1964 (p. 15), June 20, 1970 (p. 28).
Paris Review, spring, 1953.
Newsweek, October 26, 1953 (p. 119), January 13, 1969 (p. 52).
New York Herald Tribune Book Review, May 20, 1956 (p. 2).
Encounter, November, 1957, February, 1980 (p. 51), September/October, 1985 (p. 43).
New Yorker, September 19, 1959 (p. 61), April 2, 1984 (p. 130).
Modern Fiction Studies, autumn, 1961 (p. 258), summer, 1967 (p. 195), winter, 1983 (p. 623).
Times Literary Supplement, June 22, 1962, November 14, 1975 (p. 1356), November, 1980 (p. 1294), November 18, 1983 (p. 1267).
Theoria, June 15, 1963 (p. 17).
Commonweal, February 21, 1964 (p. 635), September 21, 1973 (p. 506).
Mademoiselle, June, 1964.
Criticism, winter, 1964 (p. 70).
Vogue, January 1, 1965 (p. 12).
New York Public Library Bulletin, May, 1967 (p. 283).
Observer, June 14, 1970.
Christian Science Monitor, June 18, 1970.
Nation, June 29, 1970, November 11, 1978 (p. 500).
Listener, July 9, 1970.
Christian Century, July 22, 1970.
New York Review of Books, July 23, 1970, October 12, 1978 (p. 6).
Books and Bookmen, August, 1970.
Journal of Aesthetics and Art Criticism, fall, 1971 (p. 101).
Extrapolation, May, 1976 (p. 172).
Time, November 6, 1978 (p. 113), December 31, 1984 (p. 57).
New Leader, November 20, 1978 (p. 14).
New Statesman, November 14, 1980 (p. 21).
International Fiction Review, winter, 1980 (p. 46).
Modern Language Quarterly, June, 1981 (p. 166).
London, July, 1981 (p. 94).
Modern Philology, August, 1981 (p. 45), August, 1982 (p. 61).
Prose Studies, December, 1982 (p. 326).
Journal of Modern Literature, March, 1983 (p. 109).
Twentieth Century Literature, summer/fall, 1985 (p. 170).
Commentary, September, 1985 (p. 48).
Modern Language Review, October, 1985 (p. 817).
Variety, August 26, 1987 (p. 15).

OBITUARIES

New York Times, June 8, 1970 (p. 1).
Times (London), June 8, 1970 (p. 8).
Washington Post, June 8, 1970.
New Statesman, June 12, 1970.
L'Express, June 15-21, 1970.
Antiquarian Bookman, June 22, 1970.
Time, June 22, 1970 (p. 72).
Newsweek, June 22, 1970 (p. 84).
Publishers Weekly, June 22, 1970 (p. 42).

COLLECTIONS

E. M. Forster Archive at King's College Library, King's College, Cambridge, England.
Humanities Research Center, University of Texas.

GRATER, Michael 1923-

PERSONAL: Born September 8, 1923, in London, England; son of Bertie (a transport clerk) and Lucy (Humphreys) Grater; married Ruth Silvestre (an actress and a singer); children: Adam, Matthew. *Education:* Attended the University of London, 1947-51. *Home:* 117 Rodenhurst Rd., London SW4 8AF, England. *Agent:* Deborah Rogers Ltd., 20 Powis Mews, London W11 1JN, England.

CAREER: Inner London Education Authority, London, England, art teacher, 1952-64; writer, 1961—; University of London, London, lecturer in art and design education, 1964-84. Consultant and writer for BBC (British Broadcasting Corporation) Schools Television, 1970-80; visiting professor at the University of Long Island, 1976-80. *Military Service:* Royal Armoured Corps, 1941-46.

WRITINGS:

Make It in Paper: A Simple Introduction to Paper Sculpture for Children, Teachers, and Students, Mills & Boon, 1961, published in the U.S. as *Make It in Paper: Three-Dimensional Paper Projects,* Dover, 1983.
One Piece of Paper, Taplinger, 1963.
Paper Faces, Mills & Boon, 1967, Taplinger, 1968, published as *Complete Book of Paper Mask Making,* Dover, 1984.
Paper People, Mills & Boon, 1969.
Paper Play, Taplinger, 1972.
Cut and Colour Toys and Decorations, Dover, 1974.
Cut and Colour Paper Masks, Dover, 1975.
Cut and Make Monster Masks in Full Color, Dover, 1978.
Cut and Fold Paper Spaceships, Dover, 1978.
Creative Paper Toys and Crafts, Dover, 1981.
Cut and Fold Extraterrestrial Invaders, Dover, 1983.
Green-Eyed Ghost Cat (self-illustrated), Piccadilly Press, 1984.
Alf Gorilla, Lutterworth Press, 1986.
(With Marc Sewell) *Cut and Fold an Old English Village,* Dover, 1987.
Fun Faces, Macdonald, 1987.
Fun Figures, Macdonald, 1987.
Fun Movers, Macdonald, 1987.
Fun Models, Macdonald, 1987.
Papercraft Projects with One Piece of Paper, Dover, 1987.
Alf Gorilla Adrift, Lutterworth Press, 1988.
On Sunday the Giant, Ginn, 1988.
On Monday the Giant, Ginn, 1988.
On Tuesday the Giant, Ginn, 1988.
On Wednesday the Giant, Ginn, 1988.
On Thursday the Giant, Ginn, 1988.
On Friday the Giant, Ginn, 1988.

ILLUSTRATOR

Harry Gilbert, *A Vampire in the Computer,* Piccadilly Press, 1986.

WORK IN PROGRESS: Alf Gorilla and the Battersea Gang.

SIDELIGHTS: "I write and illustrate books for children because I like books, I like children, I like writing and I like drawing.

"I began writing when I was a young art teacher, not long returned from war service in Europe. As a student I met a Polish refugee who had studied in Warsaw. He introduced me to the traditional Polish craft of paper cutting and to paper sculpture which, although taught in the Warsaw Academy, was hardly known as a subject in Western Europe.

MICHAEL GRATER

"The post-war interest in child art and the understanding of the value of individual expression as an educational activity made working as an art teacher exciting, but having been partly trained as a wood-carver and in three-dimensional crafts, I saw that there was a need to open the two-dimensional activity in child art into wider areas—into sculpture as well as painting. Since paper and cards were available in all schools these seemed to be an obvious starting point, and I wrote my first book, *Make It in Paper,* in 1961. I have been adding new titles ever since.

"As I progressed from schools into work with students and adults I knew that learning should be fun and should also be as three-dimensional as possible, and that in education we should go on to work in as many materials as were available.

"It has taken me a long time with much experiment, many lectures and working sessions with students and teachers in Europe, the Far East and in the USA, many television programmes and a few books to realize that many of the materials which are thrown away every day are exactly right for children to work with. They cost nothing and with the right sort of guidance can be used by children of all ages in fun and learning projects. I am trying to demonstrate this in detail in my latest series, the *Michael Grater Fun to Make* series, published by Macdonald.

"I write and illustrate fiction for children because, having bought an old farmhouse in Aquitaine, in southwest France, I spend long periods away from my well-equipped London studio. Having spent several years rebuilding the house I can now sit in the sun when I am there, looking down a vine-covered

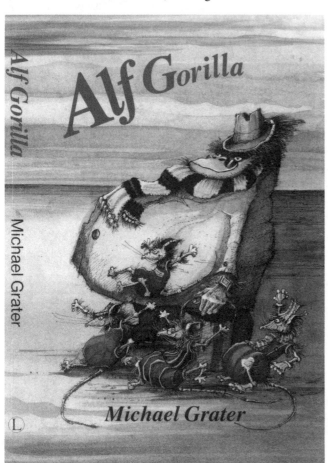

(Jacket illustration from *Alf Gorilla* by Michael Grater.)

valley and without risk of interruption—and I can write and illustrate stories. That is the practical reason. You do not need masses of equipment to accommodate an active imagination, but you do need a bit of peace.

"I am sure that to write for children you have to like children. You must clearly also like books, especially children's books. It was my pleasure always to read to my own children as they were growing, and sometimes to make up stories for them— or better still with them.

"I am not sure if it is talent or if it is experience and industry which make it possible for me to write and illustrate books for children. But I am sure that when I am doing it I am happy. The business of living—credit cards, automobiles, property and people is complex enough. If you can escape from it into the *MAGIC* of being a child again you are a privileged and fortunate person.

"I was brought up in London in a large, impecunious and happy family in a relatively stable and simple world. We had no TV, no electronic gadgetry, no pop, no commercial pressures; we had limited travel opportunity and probably a deeper personal focus on simple things. Times change certainly and we grow up. But the *MAGIC* of childhood through my involvement with children's books—where I am happy with my ghosts, my giants, my gorillas and the lines I make into words for them or into pictures—keeps me still a little bit young."

GUISEWITE, Cathy 1950-

PERSONAL: Surname rhymes with "rice-white"; born September 5, 1950, in Dayton, Ohio; daughter of William Lee (in advertising) and Anne (Duly) Guisewite. *Education:* University of Michigan, A.B., 1972. *Home:* Los Angeles, Calif. *Office:* c/o Universal Press Syndicate, 4900 Main St., Kansas City, Mo. 64112.

CAREER: Campbell-Ewald Advertising Agency, Detroit, Mich., writer, 1972-73; Norman Prady Ltd. (advertising agency), Detroit, writer, 1973-74; W. B. Doner & Co. (advertising agency), Southfield, Mich., writer, 1974-75, group supervisor, 1975-76, vice-president, 1976-77; Universal Press Syndicate, Mission, Kan., creator, author, and artist of "Cathy" comic strip, 1976—. Creator of "Cathy" novelty items. *Awards, honors:* L.H.D. from Rhode Island College, 1979, Eastern Michigan University, 1981, and Russell Sage College, 1986; Emmy Award from the Academy of Television Arts and Sciences, for best animated program, 1987, for "Cathy."

WRITINGS:

COLLECTIONS

The Cathy Chronicles, Andrews & McMeel, 1978.
What Do You Mean, I Still Don't Have Equal Rights?, Andrews & McMeel, 1980.
What's a Nice Single Girl Doing with a Double Bed?, Bantam, 1981.
I Think I'm Having a Relationship with a Blueberry Pie, Bantam, 1981.
It Must Be Love, My Face Is Breaking Out, Andrews & McMeel, 1982.
Another Saturday Night of Wild and Reckless Abandon, Andrews & McMeel, 1982.
A Mouthful of Breath Mints and No One to Kiss, Andrews & McMeel, 1983.
Climb Every Mountain, Bounce Every Check, Andrews & McMeel, 1983.

CATHY GUISEWITE

The Salesclerk Made Me Buy It, Fawcett, 1983.
Men Should Come with Instruction Booklets, Andrews & McMeel, 1984.
My Cologne Backfired, Fawcett, 1984.
I'll Pay $5,000 for a Swimsuit That Fits Me!!!, Fawcett, 1985.
Wake Me Up When I'm a Size Five, Andrews & McMeel, 1985.
Sorry I'm Late, My Hair Won't Start, Fawcett, 1986.
Stressed for Success, Fawcett, 1986.
Thin Thighs in Thirty Years, Andrews & McMeel, 1986.
It's More Than a Pregnancy. It's a Religion, Fawcett, 1986.
Two Pies. One Fork, Fawcett, 1987.
It Must Be Something in the Ink, Fawcett, 1987.
A Hand to Hold, an Opinion to Reject, Andrews & McMeel, 1987.
Why Do the Right Words Always Come Out of the Wrong Mouth?, Andrews & McMeel, 1988.

OTHER

Cathy's Valentine Day Survival Kit: How to Live through Another February 14th, Andrews & McMeel, 1983.
How to Get Rich, Fall in Love, Lose Weight, and Solve All Your Problems by Saying "No," Andrews & McMeel, 1983.
Eat Your Way to a Better Relationship, Andrews & McMeel, 1983.

ADAPTATIONS:

ANIMATED TELEVISION SPECIALS

"Cathy," CBS-TV, May 15, 1987.
"Cathy's Last Resort," CBS-TV, fall, 1988.

WORK IN PROGRESS: An animated television special for Valentine's Day, to be aired on CBS-TV, 1989.

SIDELIGHTS: Guisewite was born in Dayton, Ohio on **September 5, 1950.** "All my life my parents have been wildly enthusiastic about anything creative my sisters or I did. Every time we made a greeting card—and we almost always made our own—Mom would say, 'Oh, this is good enough to be published.' Most mothers tape their children's work to the refrigerator door. Mine would send them off to the Museum of Modern Art.

"When I was growing up, I resented my mom for not being the kind of mother who sat home baking all day. She didn't bake and she didn't knit, and I felt mothers should do those things. Mom tended to be more cosmopolitan than the other mothers I knew. She took us to art museums and foreign films, and I hated everything she dragged us to. I wanted a fat little mother baking cookies.

"But I have never doubted for a second that her children come first. She would stop anything and travel any distance if one of us needed her—and she has."[1]

1972. Received a B.A. in English from the University of Michigan.

(From *Two Pies. One Fork* by Cathy Guisewite. Illustrated by the author.)

1974. Began working as a writer at W. B. Doner and Co. (advertising agency), where by 1976 she had become vice-president. ''My career was going great, but I was miserable about my love life. Balancing those two have always been a major conflict for me. . . . So there I was, sitting around my apartment, snacking, waiting for this guy to call, and writing a depressing letter to my mother. I drew a picture of how I looked and another of how I'd look if the phone would ring. It made me see the humorous side of my situation.''[2]

''My mother had always taught me that the real strength of a person was her ability to move through a crisis—that every big crisis has a purpose and every little disappointment has a bright and wonderful side.''[3]

''But actually, my dad is the central sense of humor in the family. Both my parents have sickeningly cheerful attitudes. They always forced us to look for the bright side in any disaster. And that's how I do the strip.

''You just recreate your worst moments and think of a twist to make them feel better. That's my favorite part of my job.''[4]

''I spent a lot of evenings drawing out my frustrations and then I'd send the sketches home. They were simply a release. I didn't know I was creating a comic strip.''[3]

''My mother went to the library and researched comic-strip syndicates. She put them in order and typed up a list. I didn't want the syndicates to get a cover letter from my mom, so

when I thought she was getting serious, I sent a letter to the first one on the list.''[5]

Universal Press Syndicate accepted what was to become the ''Cathy'' strip. ''I've come to realize how amazing that day really was. I have talked to other cartoonists who've literally spent half their lives trying to get a syndicate to respond to their ideas and accept their comic strip for publication. . . .''[3] It was totally stunning in every way. I was shocked! I'm just as incoherent about it today as I was then.

''I stayed [with W. B. Doner and Co.] for about nine months after I started the strip, so it was hardly a sudden transition. I really only quit the agency when I was just exhausted—you know, it was a lot of work to try to do both. But I think I stayed at the agency partly because of the security of the routine I was in there and partly because I was sure that somebody would call me up and tell me they were just kidding about the comic strip!

''It was about six months between the time that I first heard from them and when the strip really started appearing. In the first few months they had me prepare six weeks' worth of strips so that their sales people could take them out and sell 'Cathy' to the newspapers. So I had a few months to work on the drawing, and they gave me a lot of guidance in that.''[6]

''I ran out and bought several books on how to draw cartoon characters. I took them home and studied and practiced. I felt that I already had a natural knack for showing emotion and

(From *A Hand To Hold, an Opinion To Reject* by Cathy Guisewite. Illustrated by the author.)

character in my drawings. If a comic figure felt sheepish or wishy-washy, the lines I drew would be wiggly, if the person was mad, the lines would be straight and hard. If a character was happy, the lines became soft and pleasant. If you try to 'feel' what you're drawing, it will work its way out to your hand.''[3]

''It used to take me an entire afternoon to get Cathy to walk across the room in one frame. Drawing anything was a totally new experience for me. It's gotten way, way easier.

''Mostly my art has been a result of personal trial and error. But I do look at other cartoonists' work and always have. For instance, if I have a scene with a lot of motion and a lot of commotion in it, I know that 'Beetle Bailey' often has strips like that where there's a big flurry of activity; I'll look back at those strips and see what the artist does that makes it look like that's happening. As far as people's expressions go, I think that I probably was most inspired by Charles Schulz and still am. He's wonderful at capturing great expressions with very few lines.''[6]

With ''Cathy'' in syndication, readers came to know and sympathize with the young woman executive who works for a company called ''Product Testing, Inc.'' ''Cathy is a woman who does not have it under total control and tends to run back to horrible relationships. There's a vulnerability in her that some feminists may not like. I feel you can be a feminist and still keep your insurance policy stuffed in your sock drawer.''[5]

''Cathy'' vascillates between serious dieting, and serious food binging. Furthermore, she's usually in conflict trying to meet pressure from her boss and her chauvinistic boyfriend, Irving, of whom Guisewite admits: ''I wouldn't pin him on any one man—he is every negative trait rolled into one. I tried to reform him a couple of times, but it didn't work. Guys like that don't change.''[4]

As for ''Cathy's'' best friend, an ardent feminist named Andrea: ''She's pretty much my conscience, saying, 'You know better.' In one of the best strips, Cathy says, 'I'll be fat for the rest of my life.' Andrea says, 'No, you don't have to be. You're the one in control.' 'I know,' Cathy says, 'That's why I'll always be fat.'

''It would be nice to see Andrea grappling with some problems of her own. But she'll always be the voice of authority.''[4]

Of ''Cathy's'' sweet and slightly crazy cousin, Cellophane, Guisewite said: ''My younger sister, Mickey, came to spend a couple of months with me a while ago, I was exposed to a whole new breed of music and clothes. Cellophane came from that. I did like her—I'm thinking of bringing her back.''[4]

Readers frequently ask how much of Guisewite is in ''Cathy.'' ''I'm pretty much a combination of Andrea and Cathy in the strip, but I'm most like Cathy in that I see both sides of everything.''[3]

''Cathy is my more emotional side. I think I'm a little more together than her. I think I'm a combination of great self-confidence and total insecurity sort of at once.''[7]

''Periodically I'm better at everything than Cathy is, but when I'm not, I can be like she is or worse. I can be frantically organized, like I'll spend days working on an address book while the whole world around me is crumbling.''[8]

''When the comic strip first began, I was horrified with the idea of calling it 'Cathy.' ''[3] ''The syndicate wanted me to stay

(From *It Must Be Something In the Ink* by Cathy Guisewite. Illustrated by the author.)

with Cathy because they liked the idea that it was true to life. I thought it would be a good idea to call her something else. I went through all the name-your-baby books and tried everything.''[5]

''Not only did the character resemble me a little physically, but what I was writing about was quite personal. I didn't want friends calling me up the next day, saying 'Idiot, why did you say that about yourself?'

''In the early days, she spent a lot of time getting dumped on. Cathy was a kind of doormat, because that's the way it was at that point in *my* life. Of course, Cathy will never have it all together. She has many weaknesses. Her character is built on them.

''I have an obsession with food—something anyone who's eaten a hot-fudge sundae while hiding in a closet will understand. I let my obsession rub off on Cathy.''[3] ''A lot of my material is based on my neuroses. If all that vanished, it would be 'bye-bye career.' ''[9]

''I have a way to use every disaster in my life now. That's one of the nicest things and probably one of the problems, too: I can't just wallow in my misery all the time; I have a responsibility to turn it into material. But it's a real blessing.

The more chaotic and trauma-filled my life is, the better my work is!''[6]

Some think ''Cathy'' is Guisewite's way of commenting on a woman's role in today's society. ''But what I am really writing about is gum wrappers and why I dropped the hair dryer in the toilet on the day it was important for me to look nice at the office meeting. I don't write about the big picture and the emerging new woman. What Cathy is doing is floundering in the middle of her ideals or concepts: traditionalism and feminism. She likes what she sees in both areas so she is walking down the middle. Because many of us are walking the same line, it makes us laugh.

''For instance, Cathy is looking at an ad for 'Creamy-Dreamy Lipstick' and tells her feminist friend, Andrea, that she wants to get some. Andrea screams, 'That's chauvinistic capitalism at its worst. All they are selling is sex, hope and dreams!' Cathy grins and says, 'I'll take it.'''[3]

''It's a confusing time. . . .We're getting a lot of different signals. I was just getting used to the 'Me Decade,' starting to revel in putting other people's needs second, when suddenly they pulled the rug out from under me by proclaiming the '80s the 'We Decade,' with the family unit making a comeback.''[9]

''The problem with the concept of the 'New Woman' is that she is too perfect. . . .The women I read about in magazines and see on television are self-confident, self-assured, dynamic business people and they are also cheery homemakers and understanding nonsexist mothers.

''It's a wonderful idea, but most of us feel we are not living up to it. We feel frustrated with our little failures, and then we want to give up and say forget it. In a nice way, Cathy evokes a lot of empathy. She makes us feel we're not the only ones with problems.''[3]

Guisewite believes much of her inspiration comes from her mother, and from their close, sometimes volatile relationship. ''I'm more like her than my sisters are. Like her, I'm essentially quiet and private. I'm also strong in some ways because I've modeled myself after her.

''The only problem I've had with my mother is that I see myself in her so much that I tend to be crabbiest around her. I am truly even-tempered. I never yell or snap at anybody— except her. Since I see myself in her—and *I* want to be perfect—I want *her* to be perfect, and I can't stand it when she isn't. When I snap, it's almost like being impatient with myself.

''Fortunately, my mother is very down-to-earth and has a wonderful sense of humor. If she didn't, I couldn't do what I do with Cathy's mother! She's got an especially good sense of humor about the contradictions she lays out for me—cheering my career, yet waiting for the day when I get married, settle down and start my real life.''[4]

She finds that women like her mother are some of her most avid readers. ''I'd say the second biggest group of mail I get is from women the age of the mothers of women my age. Some are writing to say that the mother-daughter relationship

Guisewite with a life-size ''Cathy'' doll and her dog, Trolley. ■ (Los Angeles Times Photo.)

in 'Cathy' has really meant a lot to them and their daughters and that the strip has really become like a sounding board for them with each other. And many mothers or women who are a little bit older than Cathy write to say that they are identifying not with the mother but with Cathy because she's a lot like them or a lot like they were. I also hear increasingly from men. Not that many men come right out and say that they are identifying with Irving, but a lot say they have a girlfriend just like Cathy; that Cathy has really helped them understand what's going on with women. Some write to say that they feel a lot like Cathy themselves; that her anxieties and frustrations are not all that different from men's.

"Specifically, people comment on the mother-daughter relationship a lot. Many letters come in on the food strips. It just depends on the person who's writing. If somebody happens to be in a relationship crisis around the time that Cathy is, then they're writing about that.

"I think people can interpret what's going on however they'd like. Once I had Cathy fly to St. Louis to spend the weekend with somebody she had met and I remember, after that, hearing from a mother and daughter. They both wrote to me at the same time. They had had a discussion about what had happened that weekend: The mother was sure that the boy had put Cathy up in a nice hotel somewhere and the daughter

(From *I'll Pay $5,000 for a Swimsuit That Fits Me!!!* by Cathy Guisewite. Illustrated by the author.)

read. . .that she was going there to spend the weekend at his place. They both were equally convinced that the way they saw it was the way it happened, and that is fine with me."[6]

Besides the strip, Guisewite is also the creator of several specialty items, such as T-shirts, aprons, mugs, and iron-on transfers, all based on the "Cathy" characters. "They take a lot of time, considering that it used to take me every waking minute of the day to get the strip done and now we're doing products for about thirty different companies. You know, it's the old business of it takes as long as you have to do it, I guess. I really like doing designs for the merchandise. I think that some of the things are very appropriate to the characters, and that has been an exciting area for me to get into. I know that some people just turn over the rights and don't get that involved. I've become obsessed with getting totally involved with every project, so I put a lot more time into it than is probably necessary. But I love it.

"I am always at the office by 8:30 or 9:00 and begin panicking immediately about what's most overdue on that particular day. Sometimes it's the comic strip. I usually send the strip. . .in groups of two weeks, so, as that deadline gets close, that's all I do. Some days that deadline is not so pressing but the deadlines for merchandise that we're doing are pressing, and I'll work on those, I work by myself in the mornings; in the afternoons a secretary and her baby come in, and also a graphic designer. He does mechanical work for the merchandise: He'll get type set or do coloring or stat things. He has taken a lot of the detail work off my hands for the licensed products we're doing."[6]

Even with help, deadlines can be a problem. "I haven't sent a piece of mail in the last five years that wasn't Federal Express."[9] "Panic is just part of a cartoonist's life, though an idea always comes. Sometimes, I just have to force it a bit."[3]

1978. Guisewite published *The Cathy Chronicles,* the first of several collections of her comic strip. Other titles include: *It Must Be Love, My Face Is Breaking Out,* and *A Mouthful of Breath Mints and No One to Kiss.* "I don't actually keep them in the theme of the title. We've gotten into a pattern now of doing a book a year, so I go through the strips, and pull out ones that I do not ever want to see in print again; but otherwise, in the books, I try to keep them in chronological order and from a certain period."[6]

1980. Moved from the Midwest to Santa Barbara, California, and lived by herself in a Victorian house where her mother would visit and make herself at home. "She visits me in Santa Barbara and I don't think she ever leaves my house. She just works on projects—anything she thinks I need done: reorganizing my cupboards, cleaning my closets, taking care of paperwork. She makes the meals and packages any leftovers in individual servings to freeze for when she's gone. She also encloses any opened packages in my cupboard in plastic bags. After she's been here awhile, everything in the house is wrapped up.

"I'm touched by how much she wants to help."[1]

But Santa Barbara proved too small to provide anonymity: "I need to be able to go to a bank and scream at the teller and not have them go, 'Oh, you're the one who does the comic strip.'"[8] So she relocated to Los Angeles. "I wanted to expand my horizons. I'm still not going outside much, but at least sitting in my house, I get a feeling there's a lot going on out there.

"I still have my health club that I don't go to. I'm told that a supermarket on Ventura Boulevard is a great place on Thursday nights, but since you know that, who wants to go?"

"I don't own a bathing suit. They make size 5 suits for babies. . . .Everybody in California is size 5. But you have to be a perfectly toned, perfectly tanned size 5. No normal person, would wear a bathing suit in California."[8]

The distance hasn't diminished her relationship with "Mom." "I still call Mom long distance and ask her what I should wear on a date. Then I get annoyed because she lives 2,500 miles away and isn't familiar with my clothes, . . .or I tell her about a guy I see only a few times and get angry because she asks me about him for the next five years."[2]

"It's a constant contradiction of loving and worshipping her, and being horrified as I see myself turning into her. Every week I say I'm nothing like her and that I'm going to lead my own life, and fifteen minutes later I'm calling to ask what to wear. . . .It's awful. I think a lot of people really relate to it, to that contradiction of dependence and independence. She still says I moved to California to put distance between us."[8]

"She's the greatest support system in the world. The sense of being loved, that no matter what I do, someone thinks I'm wonderful has made it possible for me to strive and succeed."[2]

Though being a famous cartoonist has its advantages, "this is probably the best of both worlds, because I get the recognition of people knowing my name, but nobody knows what I look like, so I can look like a pig when I go to the grocery store."[7]

Guisewite finds her old neuroses haven't disappeared—they've only become inspiration for her strip. "I used to be heavier. And I still turn to food in times of crisis. But now I'll eat steamed vegetables for a week instead of a box of frozen doughnuts I haven't bothered to defrost!

". . .The food themes are near and dear to my heart. You can be pretty sure, if you see Cathy eating in a strip it's because I couldn't think of anything to write and consoled myself with food."[4]

"I got in the habit, when I was overweight, of always buying clothes at least one size smaller than I am, 'cause I thought then, 'I'm gonna lose weight; why waste the money on the correct size? I'll buy it one size smaller; it will motivate me.'. . .Now I'm my normal size, and I still buy clothes that are slightly too small for me."[7]

"I have every type of look in my closet. Every now and then I'll try the exotic, but then I'll stand there too humiliated to let anyone else see."[8]

(From *The Salesclerk Made Me Buy It* by Cathy Guisewite. Illustrated by the author.)

(From *My Cologne Backfired* by Cathy Guisewite. Illustrated by the author.)

(From the animated TV special, ''Cathy's Last Resort.'' Presented on CBS-TV, 1987.)

"Definitely any insecurities that I have, have been wonderful for my career. . . .So it puts me in the unfortunate position of never being able to just sit and wallow in misery, because some little part of me always has to be sort of entertained by it."[7]

"I've never gotten married. I think if I did, that would have to happen to Cathy, because I write the strip so much from my own point of view. The cartoon syndicate, in fact, is horrified by that possibility—it would destroy everything we've all worked for! So they manage to keep me busy enough to make sure it's not real likely."[4]

"As my friends have gotten married—and some of these were diehard singles—I've sensed my own feelings of desertion. I don't want Cathy to do that."[8] As a matter of fact, she likes being single. "It's given me a huge amount of freedom to really go for it in my career. I think that I have avoided relationships that threaten that."[7]

Even dating has its own set of pressures. "My mother. . .will talk to me about the virtues of independence and not having to depend on a man, and then she'll drag one of my sisters aside and say, 'Who is she going out with now? What does she think of him? Does he have possibilities?'"[10]

"This ticking biological clock business has taken the fun out of dating. Guys think, 'Oh, my God, she's thirty-six. If I take her out to dinner, she'll probably want me to marry her.' I'm so paranoid about seeming to act that way that I'm barely friendly to guys I really like."[2]

1987. "Cathy" appeared in an animated television special, and met with fine reviews. "I find it so liberating to get to carry on a conversation longer than four boxes.

"I think that Cathy will continue to grow and change and be affected by things as I am. This year, for instance, I did a series that lasted about two weeks on the fact that half the women in her office suddenly were pregnant. That's not a subject I would have done a couple of years ago, but this year I found that every time I turned around another woman I knew (who swore she would never get married or pregnant) had transformed herself. When I was doing some promotions, I talked to some other women about it and found that, in fact, that was something a lot of single women were experiencing: Their single friends were dropping like flies and becoming married mothers. So I thought it was a very appropriate subject to address.

"I can't think of too many other jobs where total strangers write you or meet you and say, 'I love what you do for a living!' That's a great kind of support to get. It really is very reassuring for me, and it's just nice. If I weren't fairly insecure myself I would never write the things I do, and getting that sort of feedback from people is great for me."[6]

"I think this is the opportunity that writers dream about—to write from life. That's the richest material. One of my greatest pleasures is having someone write to me and say, 'Cathy, you said it just right!'"[3]

FOOTNOTE SOURCES

[1]Mary James, "Cathy and Her Mom," _Woman's Day_, July 13, 1982.
[2]Lynn Emmerman, "Comic Relief from 'Cathy' and Her 'Mom,'" _Chicago Tribune_, May 10, 1987.
[3]Cork Miller, "How Cartoonist Cathy Guisewite Makes Us Laugh at Life's Little Frustrations," _Seventeen_, May, 1983.

[4]Judy J. Newmark, "Cathy and 'Cathy': A Lot in Common," _St. Louis Post-Dispatch_, September 5, 1982.
[5]Ann Japenga, "The Real-Life 'Cathy': A Cartoonist's Dream," _Los Angeles Times_, April 28, 1981.
[6]_Contemporary Authors_, Volume 113, Gale, 1985.
[7]Dan Sperling, "Cathy Guisewite: She Cashes in on Her Insecurities—Comically," _USA Today_, October 30, 1986.
[8]Millie Ball, "And Now, the Real Cathy," _New Orleans Times-Picayune_, June 8, 1986.
[9]Sally Koris, "Cartoons Are No Laughing Matter for Cathy Guisewite," _People_, July 5, 1982.
[10]Sylvia Rubin, "The Woman Behind 'Cathy,'" _San Francisco Chronicle_, November 29, 1982.

FOR MORE INFORMATION SEE:

Glamour, July, 1978, August, 1982.
Laurence J. Peter, "Peter's People," _Human Behavior_, January, 1979 (p. 68).
Rosemarie Robotham, "Funny Females in the Funny Pages," _Life_, September, 1982 (p. 90).
Jonathan Friendly, "Women's New Roles in Comics," _New York Times_, February 28, 1983.
Detroit Free Press, February 27, 1984.
Jonathan Alter, Linda Tibbetts, Michael Reese, and Holly Morris, "Comics in Yuppiedom," _Newsweek_, October 1, 1984 (p. 76).
Variety, May 27, 1987 (p. 82).
Lynn Emmerman, "Mom Makes Cathy Run in Comics and in Life," _St. Louis Post-Dispatch_, June 7, 1987.

HALE, Nancy   1908-1988

OBITUARY NOTICE—See sketch in _SATA_ Volume 31: Born May 6, 1908, in Boston, Mass.; died after suffering a stroke, September 24, 1988, in Charlottesville, Va. Painter, journalist, and author. Hale, whose parents were both working artists, was born and raised in Boston. Among her ancestors were Nathan Hale, the American Revolutionary hero, Edward Everett Hale, author of _The Man without a Country_, and Harriet Beecher Stowe, author of _Uncle Tom's Cabin_. When Hale was not quite eight years old, she asked to be given a printing press for her birthday. As soon as she received her wish she began to put out a family newspaper called the _Society Cat_. By eleven she had submitted a story to the _Boston Herald_, with a letter stating that "my purpose is remuneration."

During the five decades of her writing career Hale produced nineteen volumes of fiction, biography, and memoirs and numerous short stories documenting changing American upper-class manners. Educated in Boston art schools, Hale worked briefly as a painter before moving to New York City, where she worked as an assistant editor, first at _Vogue_, and later at _Vanity Fair_. In 1935 she held the distinction of being the _New York Times_'s first woman reporter. Her publications include the novels _The Young Die Good_, _The Prodigal Women_, and _Heaven and Hardpan Farm_; autobiographical essays _A New England Girlhood_ and _The Life in the Studio_, recollections of her painter mother; short story collections _The Earliest Dreams_, _Between the Dark and the Daylight_ and _The Empress's Ring_; a children's book, _The Night of the Hurricane_; a biography of the American painter Mary Cassett; two plays; and _The Realities of Fiction: A Book about Writing_. She found writing her children's book, _The Night of the Hurricane_, "surprisingly difficult. Children don't give a hair for effect," she said. "They only demand that a story be absolutely true emotionally."

Hale also edited _Discovery_, an anthology of three hundred years of New England writing, and contributed short stories to more than thirty anthologies and to magazines such as *American Mercury, Harper's Bazaar, McCall's,* and *New Yorker.* She received the O. Henry short story prize in 1933, the Benjamin Franklin Special Citation for Short Story Writers in 1958, and the Henry H. Bellaman Award for Literature in 1969. She once said that, "If you really are a writer, you will somehow *make* the time to write."

FOR MORE INFORMATION SEE:

Contemporary Novelists, 4th edition, St. Martin's, 1986.

OBITUARIES

New York Times, September 26, 1988.
Washington Post, September 27, 1988.

HARGROVE, James   1947-
(Jim Hargrove)

PERSONAL: Born May 7, 1947, in New York, N.Y.; son of Kenneth (a business machine executive) and Donna (a legal secretary and actuary; maiden name, Grace) Hargrove; married Cynthia Lyngas (a metallurgist), September 27, 1969; children: Andrea. *Education:* University of Illinois at Chicago Circle, B.A., 1969, Teaching Certificate, 1970; additional study at College of Lake County, 1981-82. *Office:* Book Productions Ltd., 519 Greenwood Dr., Round Lake Park, Ill. 60073.

CAREER: Imperial International Learning Corp., Kankakee, Ill., director of product development, 1971-77; Greatlakes Living Press Ltd., Waukegan, Ill., managing editor, 1977-78; Quality Books, Inc., Northbrook, Ill., editorial director, 1978-79; Book Productions Ltd., Round Lake Park, Ill., owner, 1979—. Producer of filmstrip series "Math Mystery Theater," 1975-76; creator and producer of media program "Arithme-toons," 1977; guest on radio and television programs. *Awards, honors:* Best of 1975-76 Award from *Learning,* for "Math Mystery Theater"; Honor Book from Children's Reading Round Table of Chicago, 1985, 1986, and 1987.

JAMES HARGROVE

WRITINGS:

JUVENILE, EXCEPT AS NOTED; UNDER NAME JIM HARGROVE

(With S. A. Johnson) *Mountain Climbing* (illustrated with photographs by John Yaworsky), Lerner, 1982.
Microcomputers at Work, Childrens Press, 1984.
Mark Twain: The Story of Samuel Clemens, Childrens Press, 1984.
Richard M. Nixon: The Thirty-Seventh President, Childrens Press, 1985.
Computer Wars (young adult), Childrens Press, 1985.
Daniel Boone: Pioneer Trailblazer, Childrens Press, 1985.
The Story of the Black Hawk War (illustrated by Ralph Canaday), Childrens Press, 1986.
Thomas Jefferson, Childrens Press, 1986.
Gateway to Freedom: The Story of the Statue of Liberty and Ellis Island, Childrens Press, 1986.
Enchantment of Belgium, Childrens Press, 1986.
Martin Van Buren, Childrens Press, 1987.
Dwight D. Eisenhower, Childrens Press, 1987.
Lyndon B. Johnson, Childrens Press, 1987.
Harry S. Truman, Childrens Press, 1987.
Steven Spielberg: Amazing Filmmaker, Childrens Press, 1988.
Abraham Lincoln, Childrens Press, 1988.
Nebraska, Childrens Press, 1988.
The Story of Presidential Elections, Childrens Press, 1988.
The Story of Watergate, Childrens Press, 1988.
The Story of the F.B.I., Childrens Press, 1988.
Nelson Mandela: South Africa's Silent Voice of Protest, Childrens Press, 1989.

OTHER; UNDER NAME JIM HARGROVE

(Editor) *The Official Guide to Disco Dance Steps,* Chartwell, 1978.
(With Patrick K. Snook) *Five Hundred Things to Do in Chicago for Free,* Follett, 1980.
(Contributor) Mike Michaelson, editor, *The Best of the Best in the United States,* National Bestseller, 1985.
(With Richard Whittingham) *The History of Western Springs,* Western Springs Historical Society, 1986.
(With R. Whittingham) *Skokie 1888-1988: A Centennial Celebration,* Village of Skokie, 1988.
(Contributor) M. Michaelson, editor, *New York Weekend Getaway Guide,* Dutton, 1989.

WORK IN PROGRESS: A book about the German Democratic Republic (East Germany), for Childrens Press "Enchantment of the World" series.

SIDELIGHTS: "My career as a writer is a continuing source of surprise. It began with an overwhelming desire to leave the editing business, a decision I've never regretted. Although I first co-authored an adult book about places to visit in and near Chicago (and packaged similar books for Houston, Atlanta, and Los Angeles), I soon found that my steadiest work involved writing books for youngsters, most published by Childrens Press. Subsequent work in the adult field has been limited to the roles of co-author, contributor, and for a number of sports books, ghostwriter."

HOBBIES AND OTHER INTERESTS: Computers, photography, canoeing, outdoor sports.

HART, Bruce   1938-

PERSONAL: Born January 15, 1938, in New York, N.Y.; son of Lou S. (a film exhibitor) and Dorothy (an amateur painter;

BRUCE and CAROLE HART

maiden name, Feins) Hart; married Carole Strickler (a writer and producer), July 6, 1963. *Education:* Syracuse University, A.B., 1959; Yale University, LL.D., 1962. *Residence:* New York, N.Y. *Agent:* The Agency, Dick Berman, 10351 Santa Monica Blvd., Los Angeles, Calif. 90025. *Manager:* Scott Shukat, 340 West 55th St., New York, N.Y. 10019. *Office:* The Laughing Willow Co., 200 West 86th St., New York, N.Y. 10024.

CAREER: Television writer and producer, lyricist, and author of books for young people. Writer for "Candid Camera" television series, Columbia Broadcasting System (CBS-TV), 1966; member of original writing staff of "Sesame Street" show, National Educational Television, 1969; co-producer, *Psychology Today* educational film series, 1970-71; writer, "The Masks We Wear," television news special, American Broadcasting Co. (ABC-TV), 1971; co-producer of music for record album "Free to Be...You and Me," 1972; co-developer, writer, lyricist, and producer (with Marlo Thomas and wife, Carole Hart) of "Free to Be...You and Me" television special, ABC-TV, 1974; co-headwriter (with C. Hart), "Dick Cavett Summer Show, CBS-TV, 1975; co-writer, director, lyricist and producer (with C. Hart) of movie "Sooner or Later," National Broadcasting Co. (NBC-TV), 1979; co-creator, lyricist, writer, and executive producer (with C. Hart) of "Hot Hero Sandwich" series, NBC-TV, 1979; co-writer (with C. Hart and Sherry Coben) of television special, "Oh, Boy! Babies!," NBC-TV, 1982; writer of movie, "Leap of Faith," CBS-TV, 1988. *Military service:* U.S. Naval Reserve, 1962-65, served with judge advocate general; became lieutenant.

MEMBER: American Guild of Authors and Composers; American Society of Composers, Authors, and Publishers; Directors Guild of America; Writers Guild of America; Authors Guild. *Awards, honors:* Recipient of three Cine (Council on International Nontheatrical Events) Gold Eagle Awards, 1970, for *Psychology Today* film series; Emmy Award from the National Academy of Television Arts and Sciences, 1970, for "Sesame

Street" pilot, "Sally Sees Sesame Street," and 1974, for "Free to Be...You and Me"; First Prize in the American Film Festival, 1972, for "Learning" for *Psychology Today;* Christopher Award, Peabody Award from the University of Georgia, and Merit Award from the National Conference of Christians and Jews, all 1974, all for "Free to Be...You and Me"; Gold Record from the Record Industry Association of America, 1974, for "Free to Be...You and Me," and 1980, for "Sooner or Later," and "You Take My Breath Away"; two Emmy Awards, 1979-80, for writing and production, both for series "Hot Hero Sandwich"; Christopher Award, Merit Award from the National Conference of Christians and Jews, and First Prize from the American, San Francisco and Atlanta Film Festivals, all 1981, all for "Oh, Boy! Babies!"

WRITINGS:

FOR YOUNG PEOPLE

(With Joe Raposo and Jeffery Moss) *The Sesame Street Songbook,* Simon & Schuster, 1971.
Sooner or Later Song Book, Big Three Music, 1979.

FOR YOUNG PEOPLE; WITH WIFE, CAROLE HART

(Editor with others) *Free to Be...You and Me,* McGraw, 1974.
Sooner or Later, Avon, 1978.
Age Ingrat, Avon, 1980.
Waiting Games (sequel to *Sooner or Later*), Avon, 1981.
Breaking Up Is Hard to Do, Avon, 1987.
Cross Your Heart, Avon, 1988.

Also lyricist for "Bang the Drum Slowly," "Can You Tell Me How to Get to Sesame Street," "For Those in Love," "Free to Be...You and Me," "One Way Ticket," "Sooner or Later," "Who Are You Now," and "You Take My Breath Away."

WORK IN PROGRESS: Writing and directing "Who Are You?," an interactive videodisc exhibit for the California Institute of Science and Technology in Los Angeles.

SIDELIGHTS: Television writer and author Bruce Hart originally studied law at Yale University. While there, he wrote songs and jokes for television comics. He also met his future wife, Carole.

Married in 1963, they settled in New York where they pursued their professional careers. In 1966 Hart was writing for the television program "Candid Camera" until Carole persuaded him to collaborate on some scripts for a new children's program called "Sesame Street." He co-wrote the words to the now famous "Sesame Street" theme song.

Besides "Sesame Street," the Harts produced educational film series and television specials, and wrote television movies and shows. They have also written several young adult books.

In 1974, Hart co-wrote and co-produced "Free to Be...You and Me," a multi-media television special using songs, stories, poems, animation, hand puppets, and live actors. The show, which was unanimously well-received, is a series of vignettes encouraging children to discover what they want to be outside of what boys do as boys and girls do as girls: boys can cry; girls can be construction workers or play football. Both sexes share the duties of life. The television special was based on the theme of the record released in 1972. It was produced by actress Marlo Thomas with the help of show biz friends such as Harry Belafonte, Dick Cavett, Carol Channing,

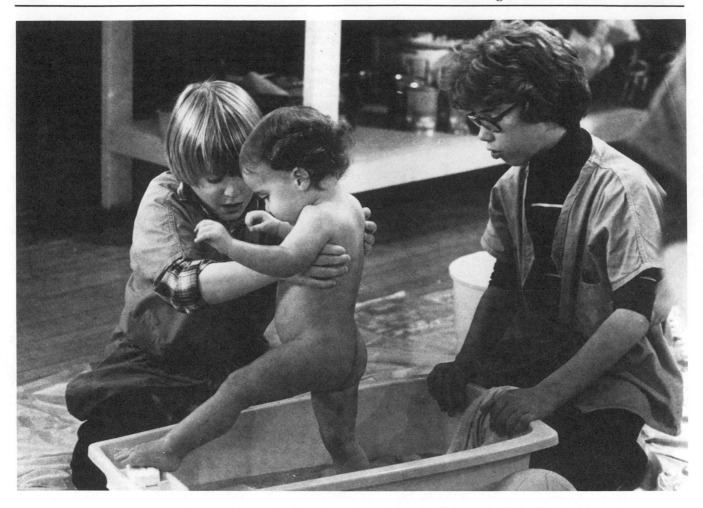

(From the television special "Oh, Boy! Babies!" Presented on NBC-TV, 1982. Photograph copyright © by Ken Howard.)

Mel Brooks, and Alan Alda who said: "The theme is a terrific idea. I've been a feminist for a long time, but this goes beyond that to a broader and truer meaning, which is freedom for everyone to follow his or her natural inclinations and talents."[1]

FOOTNOTE SOURCES

[1]Annette Grand, "Free to Be. . .You and Me," *Seventeen,* June, 1974.

FOR MORE INFORMATION SEE:

Victoria Everett, "Bruce and Carole Hart Give Teenagers Food for Thought in 'Hot Hero Sandwich,'" *People Weekly,* November 12, 1979.

HART, Carole   1943-

PERSONAL: Born April 30, 1943, in Paterson, N.J.; daughter of Abraham (a certified public accountant) and Florence (a homemaker; maiden name, Schatzberg) Strickler; married Bruce Hart (a producer, lyricist, writer, and director), July 6, 1963. *Education:* Barnard College, A.B. (with honors), 1965. *Residence:* New York, N.Y. *Agent:* Lynn Nesbit, International Creative Management, 40 West 57th St., New York, N.Y. 10019. *Office:* Hart, Thomas & Berlin Productions, Inc., 1211 Avenue of the Americas, New York, N.Y. 10036.

CAREER: Television writer and producer, and author of books for young people. Secretary to film director Frank Perry, 1964-65; Management Facilities, Inc. (a multi-media seminar firm), director, 1966-69; member of original writing staff of the "Sesame Street" show, National Educational Television, 1969; co-creator, writer, director, and co-producer, *Psychology Today* educational film series, 1970-71; associate producer and co-writer of television news special "The Masks We Wear," American Broadcasting Co. (ABC-TV), 1971; co-producer of record album "Free to Be. . .You and Me," 1972; head writer for "Woman of the Year" special, ABC-TV, 1974; co-creative consultant, "Captain Kangaroo," 1974; co-developer and producer (with Marlo Thomas and husband, Bruce Hart) of television special "Free to Be. . .You and Me," ABC-TV, 1974; co-headwriter (with B. Hart) and producer of "Dick Cavett Summer Show," Columbia Broadcasting System (CBS-TV), 1975; co-producer (with M. Thomas) of movie "It Happened One Christmas," ABC-TV, 1977; co-writer and producer (with B. Hart) of movie "Sooner or Later," National Broadcasting Co. (NBC-TV), 1979; co-creator and executive producer (with B. Hart) of "Hot Hero Sandwich" series, NBC-TV, 1979; producer and co-writer (with B. Hart and S. Coben) of television special "Oh, Boy! Babies!," NBC-TV, 1982; Hart, Thomas & Berlin Productions, Inc., New York, N.Y., founder, 1985—; executive producer with M. Thomas and Kathie Berlin of comedy pilot "Baby on Board," CBS-TV, and of television movie "Leap of Faith," CBS-TV, both 1988.

MEMBER: National Academy of Television Arts and Sciences, Writers Guild of America East, New York Women in

Film (board of directors). *Awards, honors:* Recipient of three Cine (Council on International Nontheatrical Events) Gold Eagle Awards, 1970, for *Psychology Today* film series; Emmy Award from the National Academy of Television Arts and Sciences, 1970, for "Sesame Street" pilot, "Sally Sees Sesame Street," and 1974, for "Free to Be. . .You and Me"; National Media Award from the American Psychological Association, and First Prize from American Film Festival, both 1972, both for "Learning" for *Psychology Today;* Gold Medal from Atlanta Film Festival, and certificate from the Columbus Film Festival, both 1972, both for "Information Processing," for *Psychology Today;* Christopher Award, Peabody Award from the University of Georgia, and Merit Award from National Conference of Christians and Jews, all 1974, all for "Free to Be. . .You and Me"; two Emmy Awards, 1979-80, for writing and production, both for series "Hot Hero Sandwich"; Christopher Award, Merit Award from the National Conference of Christians and Jews, First Prize from the American, San Francisco and Atlanta Film Festivals, all 1981, all for "Oh, Boy! Babies!"

WRITINGS:

FOR YOUNG PEOPLE

Delilah (short stories; illustrated by Edward Frascino), Harper, 1973.

FOR YOUNG PEOPLE; WITH HUSBAND, BRUCE HART

(Editor with others) *Free to Be. . .You and Me,* McGraw, 1974.
Sooner or Later, Avon, 1978.
Age Ingrat, Avon, 1980.
Waiting Games (sequel to *Sooner or Later*), Avon, 1981.
Breaking Up Is Hard to Do, Avon, 1987.
Cross Your Heart, Avon, 1988.

TELEVISION MOVIES; CO-CREATOR AND WRITER

"Christine and Me," NBC-TV, 1975.
"Assault with a Deadly Weapon," NBC-TV, 1976.
"Senior Prom," CBS-TV, 1977.
"Sooner or Later," NBC-TV, 1979.

TELEVISION SPECIALS; CO-CREATOR AND WRITER

"Free to Be. . .You and Me," ABC-TV, 1974.
"Taking Off," ABC-TV, 1974.
"The First Annual Show of the Year," ABC-TV, 1976.
"Oh, Boy! Babies!," NBC-TV, 1982.

Also author of *Source Book of American Corporate Insurance and Employee Benefit Management,* for the American Management Association.

SIDELIGHTS: "Although I don't write or produce exclusively for young people, I do find that my work aimed at this audience brings me the greatest satisfaction. Young readers and viewers (especially adolescents) are tough and discerning. They are also extremely responsive to honesty and quality. If you reach them, they let you know. If you touch them, chances are you'll be able to affect them in positive and lasting ways."

Carole Hart co-produced "Free to Be. . .You and Me," a record of original songs, poems, and narrative designed to debunk the stereotypical roles assigned to boys and girls as they grow up. The original idea came from actress Marlo Thomas who, after reading a bedtime story to her four-year-old niece, said: "The book made me furious—it was all about how boys are pilots and girls are stewardesses, boys are doctors and girls are nurses and—worst of all—boys invent things and girls use the things that boys invent. So I started to look for stories that

(From the Emmy award-winning series "Hot Hero Sandwich," which premiered on NBC-TV, November, 1979.)

(Detail from the album cover "Free to Be. . .You and Me." Photograph by Ken Duncan. Copyright © 1983 by Arista Records, Inc.)

(Detail from the album cover "Free to Be. . .You and Me." Illustrated by Laurie Glick. Copyright © 1983 by Arista Records, Inc.)

enlarged children's horizons, instead of limiting them. And I found only a few."[1]

The record was a tremendous success, selling more that 150,000 copies in two years. It was nominated for a Grammy Award, and the public requested more of "Free to Be. . .You and Me." In 1974, Hart, her husband, Bruce, and Marlo Thomas co-developed a television special modeled after the record; that same year it was published in book form. Both were nationally acclaimed and as Gloria Steinem, editor of *Ms.*, said: "This is a really helpful concept for children, for these are good stories with new kinds of rules that well help banish stereotyped images."[1]

FOOTNOTE SOURCES

[1]Annette Grand, "Free to Be. . .You and Me," *Seventeen*, June, 1974.

FOR MORE INFORMATION SEE:

Victoria Everett, "Bruce and Carole Hart Give Teenagers Food for Thought in 'Hot Hero Sandwich,'" *People Weekly*, November 12, 1979.

HASELEY, Dennis   1950-

PERSONAL: Surname rhymes with "paisley"; born June 28, 1950, in Cleveland, Ohio; son of Robert Carl (a sales executive) and Margaret (an account supervisor; maiden name, Boigner) Haseley; married Claudia Eleanore Lament (a child psychoanalyst), October 12, 1986. *Education:* Oberlin College, A.B., 1972; New York University, M.S.W., 1982. *Home:* 136 Prospect Park West, Apt. 6A, Brooklyn, N.Y. 11215. *Agent:* Marilyn Marlow, Curtis Brown Ltd., 10 Astor Place, New York, N.Y. 10003.

CAREER: Jewish Board of Family and Children's Services, New York, N.Y., therapist, 1982-86; author of books for children, 1982—; private practice in psychotherapy, 1984—; Personal Performance Consultants, New York, N.Y., therapist, 1987-88; Hunter College Employee Assistance Program, New

DENNIS HASELEY

York, N.Y., clinical supervisor, 1988—. Has also worked as a professional fund raiser, a community organizer, and a teacher. *Member:* Society of Children's Book Writers. *Awards, honors: The Old Banjo* was named one of New York Public Library's Children's Books, and one of Child Study Association of America's Children's Books of the Year, both 1983; Parents Choice Remarkable Book for Literature from the Parents' Choice Foundation, 1983, for *The Scared One; The Old Banjo* was one of American Bookseller's Pick of the Lists, 1983, and *The Kite Flier,* 1986; *The Kite Flier* was chosen a Notable Book in the Field of Social Studies by the National Council for Social Studies, 1986, and one of Child Study Association of America's Children's Books of the Year, 1987.

WRITINGS:

The Scared One (illustrated by Deborah Howland), Warne, 1983.
The Old Banjo (Junior Literary Guild selection; illustrated by Stephen Gammell), Macmillan, 1983.
The Pirate Who Tried to Capture the Moon (illustrated by Sue Truesdell), Harper, 1983.
The Soap Bandit (illustrated by Jane Chambless-Rigie), Warne, 1984.
The Kite Flier (illustrated by David Wiesner), Four Winds, 1986.
The Cave of Snores (illustrated by Eric Beddows), Harper, 1987.
The Counterfeiter (young adult novel), Macmillan, 1987.
My Father Doesn't Know about the Woods and Me (illustrated by Michael Hays), Atheneum, 1988.
Ghost Catcher (illustrated by Lloyd Bloom), Harper, 1989.

The Pirate Who Tried to Capture the Moon has been translated into French and Spanish. *The Old Banjo* has been translated into French.

ADAPTATIONS:

"The Old Banjo" (cassette; filmstrip with cassette), Random House, 1986.

WORK IN PROGRESS: A novel for children; several stories; several screenplays.

SIDELIGHTS: "I was brought up in Brecksville, Ohio. I wrote my first poem when I was six or seven. In high school, I rediscovered my interest in writing—mainly poetry—both then and later when I went to Oberlin College where I was an English major.

"While at Oberlin, I qualified to participate in a program that allowed me to spend a semester in New York City, studying with a professional writer. I had the good fortune to work with William Goldman (probably best known for *Butch Cassidy and the Sundance Kid*). I learned a lot more about writing stories.

"Following graduation from Oberlin, I had some poetry published in a number of small magazines. Even though I was staying with poetry, I noticed that all my poems seemed to tell stories. About the same time, I stumbled across a number of intriguing children's books—by Arnold Lobel, Maurice Sendak, and William Steig, among others. I felt there were possibilities in the picture book form that were quite exciting.

"The first picture book text I had accepted for publication was *The Scared One*. This story arose partly out of experiences I had working on a Native American Reservation in Northern Ontario. It's a story about a young Native American boy, who's trying to find his place in the world. Quite by accident, he finds a miraculous bird, which helps him to find his true

And now all the forgotten instruments are singing together. ■ (From *The Old Banjo* by Dennis Haseley. Illustrated by Stephen Gammell.)

strength and to recontact his strong history. There are some Sioux words in the text, which took a great deal of effort to find—and involved many trips to libraries and interviews with Native Americans in several U.S. cities where I lived at the time.

"I think a number of my books have a similarity to *The Scared One,* in that they represent journeys of discovery, often a character's journey within himself or across the gap that separates him from others.

"*The Pirate Who Tried to Capture the Moon* is about a rather nasty fellow—whom, by the way, I like a great deal—who wants to take over the world as he recognizes it. Being a pirate, that world is made up of various kinds of fantastic ships, and, of course, the biggest, most fantastic ship of all floating in the sky—the moon. Well, of course he can't capture the moon, but what the moon does is capture him, in a way: it shows him a much greater power than he is, and it's a power that's

on a much different level, not concerned with capturing and taking over things. This book was also published in French and Spanish. In French it's called *Le terrible chasseur de lune*—which translates as 'the terrible hunter of the moon,' also quite a nice title, I think.

"As I'm writing this, I'm thinking I should say something about where the idea for a story like *The Pirate. . .* or *The Scared One* comes from. I suppose that these characters represent aspects of myself: there's a part of me—or was a part of me—that felt like a young boy trying to find his place in the world. And there's another part of me that's like a pirate, I suppose. When I'm writing, I'm not thinking of this, of course. What happens is that some interesting character appears on the little movie screen in my mind, and the story goes on from there, with very many false starts and wrong turns and terrible ideas needing to get cleared out of the way. But during the writing process itself, when a character appears that I'm going to build my story around, it's almost like meeting some distant relation: they're vaguely familiar, they do have odd habits, you hope they'll present themselves in the best possible light, and, if not, you'll have to assist them.

"Needless to say, helping this character get on with doing what he needs to do, in the clearest possible way, involves a lot of rewriting. One of my picture book texts, finished, may be anywhere from four to eight typewritten pages. But I may have anywhere from twenty-five to fifty pages of typewritten drafts, or more. (These finished four to eight pages are then broken down by the editor, designer, and artist—sometimes with my suggestions—to form a picture book of usually thirty-two to forty pages.)

"*The Old Banjo*—which is about a farm full of musical instruments that no one plays anymore—was based on a couple of experiences. I lived for a time in rural Vermont. Behind my house was a barn, and in the barn was a piano, covered over with bales of hay. I also thought about all the people I knew who used to play instruments—including myself—who, as they grew older and busy with other things, hardly played the instruments anymore. In the book, the instruments get tired of waiting around for people like me to play them: they start playing themselves, and, in so doing, open up another side of life to the boy and his hard-working father who live on the farm. Why I chose a banjo as the major instrument—as the ring-leader, or the band-leader—I really can't say.

"*Kite Flier* is about a father who can best express his love for his son by making wonderful kites for the boy. This story is about the ways in which people express love for each other, and it's also about the gifts that fathers pass on to their sons.

"*The Cave of Snores* is also about fathers and sons. In this book a young man and his father are isolated from their fellow shepherds because of the father's loud snoring. However, it turns out that the snoring is a blessing in disguise, and when the father is prevented from snoring, disaster strikes their camp. It's only when the young man visits the mysterious Cave of Snores—and learns to snore himself—that things can be set right again. This story comes from my own experience—not that I'm a shepherd—but that my father snores, and I do, too, and a lot of people don't like it much. So I wrote a story about snoring being a hidden strength, being a kind of male thunder.

"In my picture book writing, I've been very fortunate in the artists that were chosen to do the illustrations for the books. However, I do have different images of the character in my mind when I write the stories. When I finally see the illustrations, it always comes as a shock. But then, after a little while, I feel much more friendly towards the illustrations. Now, when I think about the books I've written, I can only picture the characters and scenes the way they've been illustrated. And it's interesting to see another artist's interpretation of my written words. In *The Pirate Who Tried to Capture the Moon,* for instance, the illustrator, Sue Truesdell, developed a whole character study around the pirate's parrot, who wasn't even mentioned in my text, as I recall. But he's a charming parrot. And now I can't imagine the pirate without him.

"*The Counterfeiter,* a young adult novel, was based partly on stories I wrote a long time ago when I had my writing semester in New York City during my college days. This novel is about the difficulties of being an artist in a society that pays a lot more attention to money than to art. In the story, an adolescent boy, who's a gifted artist, decides to draw from scratch a five-hundred dollar bill in the hopes of cashing it in and becoming a success. Success in his view means taking out a beautiful girl on a wonderful, once-in-a-lifetime date. It was rather frightening to take on a novel: I'd been used to writing in

It looked like a human face with eyes faraway like stars. ■ (From *Kite Flier* by Dennis Haseley. Illustrated by David Wiesner.)

formats, as I've said, of four to eight typewritten pages, and here was a work that came out to be 275 pages typewritten. It was a lot of work...but very enjoyable, and gave me a chance to be both humorous and serious, which is a wonderful combination. So, in addition to picture books, I hope to be writing more novels.''

HOBBIES AND OTHER INTERESTS: Tennis, skiing, running.

FOR MORE INFORMATION SEE:

COLLECTIONS

De Grummond Collection at the University of Southern Mississippi.

HAUPTLY, Denis J(ames) 1945-

PERSONAL: Surname is pronounced *How*-plee; born November 6, 1945, in Jersey City, N.J.; son of John James and Genevieve (Dunt) Hauptly; married Elizabeth Howard (a civil engineer), December 21, 1968; children: Matthew Howard. *Education:* St. Michael's College, B.A., 1968; University of Notre Dame, J.D., 1972. *Home:* 42 Hewitt Ave., North Andover, Mass. 01845. *Office:* U.S. Sentencing Commission, 1331 Pennsylvania Ave., Washington, D.C. 20004.

CAREER: Junior high school teacher in Washington, D.C., 1968-69; attorney, 1972—; affiliated with U.S. Court of Appeals, Portland, Ore., 1972-73, U.S. Department of Justice,

DENIS J. HAUPTLY

Washington, D.C., 1973-81, U.S. Court of Appeals, Boston, Mass., 1981-85, and U.S. Sentencing Commission, Washington, D.C., 1985—; author. *Member:* American Bar Association, Oregon Bar Association. *Awards, honors:* Special Commendations from the U.S. Department of Justice, 1979 and 1981.

WRITINGS:

JUVENILE

The Journey from the Past: A History of the Western World, Atheneum, 1983.
In Vietnam, Atheneum, 1985.
A Convention of Delegates: The Creation of the Constitution, Atheneum, 1987.

SIDELIGHTS: ''I write history for children with an emphasis on the analysis of events. We spend a great deal of money and time preparing our bright children to build tools (from computers to bombs), and very little effort goes into teaching them how to choose what the tools should be used for. I hope that my writing helps bridge that gap.''

HERBERT, Helen (Jean) 1947-
(Jean Howat)

PERSONAL: Born September 30, 1947, in Market Drayton, Shropshire, England; daughter of William Lawson (an agricultural seedsman) and Isabel Marion (a homemaker; maiden name, Howe) Howat; married Adrian Robert Herbert, March 17, 1975 (divorced July, 1978); married Malcolm Gordon Graham-Cameron (a publisher and author of children's books), February 11, 1984. *Education:* Cambridge College of Arts and Technology, General Certificate of Education and Licentiate of the Society of Industrial Artists, 1974. *Politics:* Democratic Socialist. *Religion:* Humanist. *Home and office:* 10 Church St., Willingham, Cambridge CB4 5HT, England.

CAREER: Ordnance Survey, Southampton, England, cartographic draughtsman, 1967-69, Cambridge County Council, Cambridge, England, cartographic draughtsman, 1969-70; freelance painter/etcher, 1974—; free-lance illustrator of children's books, 1977—; Graham-Cameron Publishing, Cambridge, director, 1984—. *Exhibitions:* Cambridge Drawing Society, 1975-88; Sheringham Theatre Gallery, 1976, 1977; Saffron Walden Arts Centre (one-man), 1977; Royal Society of Painter Etchers, London, 1977; Old Fire Engine House, Ely, Cambridge, 1977, 1979, 1981, 1983, 1985; Royal Academy, London, 1977; Philip Francis Gallery, Sheffield, 1981-84. *Member:* Association of Illustrators, Society of Industrial Artists and Designers, Guild of Independent Publishers, Association of Independent Museums, Cambridge Professional Book Association, Cambridge Drawing Society, Children's Book Circle, Artist Subscriber to Royal Academy.

AWARDS, HONORS: Award from the United Kingdom Reading Association, 1978, for *Life on a Country Estate* and *Cats,* and 1981, for *My Babysitter;* Award from the National Book League, 1979, for *Home Sweet Home,* and 1981, for *Printing for Presents;* Award from the Design Centre, 1980, for *Buildings with Character* and *A Painting Book of Scotland,* 1981, for *Printing for Presents* and *The Old-Fashioned Nursery Painting Book,* and 1983, for *Animals in Famous Pictures;* Joint First Prize for Drawing from the Cambridge Drawing Society, 1981.

HELEN HERBERT

WRITINGS:

JUVENILE; SELF-ILLUSTRATED

A Painting Book of Scotland (coloring book), Dinosaur, 1980.
Buildings with Character (coloring book), Dinosaur, 1980.
Printing for Presents, Dinosaur, 1981.
The Old-Fashioned Nursery Painting Book, Dinosaur, 1981.
Gardens in Trust (coloring book), Dinosaur, 1982.
Animals in Famous Pictures (coloring book), Dinosaur, 1983.
Costumes Cut and Colour, Dinosaur, 1983.
At the Fair, Cambridge/Dinosaur, 1984.
The Clothes They Wore: Nineteenth and Twentieth Centuries,
    Cambridge University Press, 1986.

ILLUSTRATOR; JUVENILE

Althea (variant of Althea Braithwaite), *The Great Family Bar-*
    nado's, Dinosaur, 1977.
Teessa Morris-Suzuki, *Odo the Snail,* Dinosaur, 1978.
Mike Graham-Cameron, *Life on a Country Estate,* Dinosaur/
    National Trust, 1978, new edition published as *Life in an*
    Edwardian Country Household, 1983.
M. Graham-Cameron, *Cats,* Dinosaur, 1978.
Suzy Siddons, *Dizzy Duncan,* Dinosaur, 1979.
M. Graham-Cameron, *Home Sweet Home,* Dinosaur/National
    Trust, 1979, Merrimack, 1980, new edition published as
    Households through the Ages, Cambridge University Press/
    Dinosaur, 1983.
Judith Chaudhri, *My Friend Rab,* Dinosaur, 1980.
Althea, *Wearing Many Hats,* Dinosaur, 1980.
Maryan Macdonald, *No More Nappies,* Dinosaur, 1980.

Althea, *Riding on a Roundabout,* Dinosaur, 1981.
Althea, *My Babysitter,* Dinosaur, 1981.
Eileen Dunlop and Antony Kamm, *Edinburgh,* Cambridge/
    Dinosaur, 1982, new edition, Cambridge University Press,
    1985.
Althea, *Foxes,* Longman, 1982.
Althea, *Snails,* Longman, 1982.
(Under name Jean Howat) Althea, *I Have Asthma,* Dinosaur,
    1982.
Althea, *Fish,* Paul Wrigley, 1983.
Cherry Gilchrist, *Markets,* Cambridge/Dinosaur, 1983.
Jocelyn Dimbleby, *The Jocelyn Dimbleby Collection,* Sains-
    bury, 1984.
M. Graham-Cameron, *Rural Life in Roman Suffolk,* Graham-
    Cameron Publishing, 1984.
Mary Berry, *Cooking from Your Freezer,* Martin Books, 1985.
M. Graham-Cameron, *Shopping at the Co-op,* Graham-Cam-
    eron Publishing, 1985.
Adrienne Boston, *C'est a Vous,* Longman, 1986.
Valerie Chazan, *Kings Pantry Vegetarian Cook Book,* Silent
    Books, 1986.
Nellie Roberts, *The Clothes They Wore: Seventeenth and Eigh-*
    teenth Centuries, Cambridge University Press, 1986.
Heather Govier, *Buildings,* Macdonald, 1988.
Mike Rathbone, *Improve Your Teaching,* Scholastic, 1988.

WORK IN PROGRESS: Two children's books.

SIDELIGHTS: "At the age of ten, questioned by a gushing
enquirer about what I 'would be' when I grew up, I am re-

So he pulled down his sock and walked on. ■ (From *Dizzy Duncan* by Suzy Siddons. Illustrated by Helen Herbert.)

ported as quickly replying, 'I will be a famous artist.' The indulgent chuckles merely stiffened my resolve to show them!

"I was brought up in Scotland, and in spite of the accident of being born in England, I am Scottish. The tiny east coast town of St. Cyrus, where my parents had a rambling house a few yards from the prima donna North Sea, was the background to a very happy period in my childhood. I watched people, animals, houses, everything, but especially the sea in all its moods. The light in Scotland is pure, clear, unlike the light in the south, and its quality intensifies colour in such a way that I cannot forget it. All my pictures are bright. Whether the brush strokes are light or heavy, whether the pencil dents the paper or skates over it, the colour jumps out of the picture. That's how I see things, and it's because I grew up in northern light.

"As an adolescent, being out of the ordinary seemed normal to me. Other people thought in logical progressions—I thought in feelings which became pictures in my mind. I was hopeless at every subject at school except English and art. The other subjects were so dull; I only passed geography because my graphs and rift valley diagrams were pretty.

"As adulthood approached, small-town Scotland began to tighten around me, and I knew I had to escape south. At age eighteen, with some resistance from my parents, I took the train into a different world full of people with 'English' accents. I arrived in Southampton, its harbour still full of great liners, and went to work at the world's biggest and oldest map-making factory—The Ordnance Survey. I liked it and the people who worked there. In those days before computers had stolen a lot of the skill from human beings, we used to draw the maps with a dip-pen, some of us cleverly working our initials into the meticulously-drawn lines of elevation on our projects. I met the man who was to be my first husband there, and when he was sent to work in Cambridge, I went with him.

"I went to art school in Cambridge and, in spite of some dissatisfactions which I expressed by leading a deputation of students to the Head, I owe a lot to the Cambridge College of Art. It gave me the impetus to keep going in the face of difficult financial circumstances, struggling with student penury and living on spaghetti and sandwiches.

"When I graduated in 1974, I hopefully did the rounds of publishers. They mostly liked my work, but a few wanted to see my published material. When I said I hadn't any, they said they couldn't use me unless I was experienced—Catch 22! I returned from my third foray in Bloomsbury pretty disheartened and resolved to concentrate on fine art instead.

"During the next three years I worked steadily, painting, drawing, and etching. Mostly I painted and drew street scenes, lots of buildings, many in London, and with the pavements peopled with characters who were sometimes actually there, but more often, placed there from one of the hundreds of sketches done into discreet little books in cars and pubs and cattle markets and auction rooms. I think people are funny as well as nice, and a critic who said my work displayed 'gentle satire' probably got it right. I was all set to be a painter for the rest of my life when, in 1977, something happened to alter things.

"Some years earlier, at my finals exhibition of illustration work at art school, Althea Braithwaite, a talented children's writer and publisher, had seen and liked my work. Now she contacted me again to ask me to illustrate a book for Dinosaur Publications. It was a simple picture book on the history of a famous charity orphanage, Barnado's, and I took the job. This first step in illustrating children's books led to many more along the same path, and I started to get work from other editors, including Mike Graham-Cameron, co-founder of Dinosaur with Althea.

"In 1978 my first husband and I divorced, and six years later Mike and I were married. Many of the books we worked on together were historical, and the ones I liked doing best were the few titles he found time to write himself. This showed in the results, for it was these titles which, in the main, won acclaim.

"When Dinosaur went up for sale in 1984, Mike left them and, although it was a wrench for him, we set up our own publishing company, Graham-Cameron Publishing. Working out of a cunningly devised penthouse studio on top of our tiny Georgian cottage at the edge of the flat fenlands near Cambridge, we have started over again to build another kind of living.

"I'm sometimes torn between my work as an illustrator and my painting, and I am lucky, and glad, to have both. The strict framework imposed on illustration, often done to fit the author's ideas as expressed in his text, spilled over into my paintings for years and made it more defined and predictable than I wanted. I think 1985 was a breakthrough for me. I can now, at last, be structured in my illustrating work while still using imagination; and I can work with far fewer restraints in painting pictures but retain enough discipline to make them work."

HOBBIES AND OTHER INTERESTS: Collecting old (and new!) clothes, collecting bric-a-brac, cycling, running, dancing, reading, theatre, walking, galleries, looking around houses, dinner with friends, meeting new people.

FOR MORE INFORMATION SEE:

Creative Handbook, British Media Publications, 1987/88.
Writers' and Artists' Yearbook, Black, 1987.
Publishers Handbook, Grosvenor Press International, 1988.

HISCOCK, Bruce 1940-

PERSONAL: Born December 4, 1940, in San Diego, Calif.; son of Roy Burnett (a doctor) and Clara L. (a homemaker; maiden name, Hauser) Hiscock; married Mary Rebecca Habel

BRUCE HISCOCK

(divorced, 1972); married Nancy A. Duffy (divorced, 1988); children: (first marriage) Julia Anne, Frederick William. *Education:* University of Michigan, B.S., 1962; Cornell University, Ph.D., 1966. *Home:* 198 Ballou Rd., Porter Corners, N.Y. 12859.

CAREER: Dow Chemical Co., Midland, Mich., research chemist, 1966-68; Utica College of Syracuse University, Utica, N.Y., assistant professor of chemistry, 1968-71; Cornell University, Ithaca, N.Y., laboratory director and equine drug tester at Saratoga Harness Track, 1972-80; Saratoga Springs City Schools, Saratoga Spring, N.Y., substitute teacher, 1980—. *Member:* Saratoga County Arts Council, Lake George Arts Project, Albany League of Arts, Adirondack Mountain Club. *Awards, honors: Tundra* was chosen an Outstanding Science Trade Book for Children by the National Science Teachers Association and the Children's Book Council, and one of Child Study Association of America's Children's Books of the Year, both 1986.

WRITINGS:

JUVENILE; SELF-ILLUSTRATED

Tundra: The Arctic Land (Junior Literary Guild selection), Atheneum, 1986.
The Big Rock, Atheneum, 1988.

ILLUSTRATOR

Lorus J. Milne and Margery Milne, *Nature's Great Carbon Cycle,* Atheneum, 1983.
Pat Hughey, *Scavengers and Decomposers: Nature's Clean-Up Crew,* Atheneum, 1984.

James Jesperson and Jane Fitz-Randolph, *RAMs, ROMs, and Robots: The Inside Story of Computers,* Atheneum, 1984.

J. Jesperson and J. Fitz-Randolph, *From Quarks to Quasars: A Tour of the Universe,* Atheneum, 1987.

L. J. Milne and M. Milne, *Radioactivity,* Atheneum, 1989.

Contributor to magazines, including *American Artist* and *American Kennel Gazette.*

WORK IN PROGRESS: A natural history for young children, working title *The Big Tree;* a picture book "about Chloe, a little girl with lots of ideas."

SIDELIGHTS: "The inspiration for *Tundra* really began when I was eleven years old and moved from southern Michigan with my mother and stepfather to Shemya, Alaska, a small tundra-covered island in the outer Aleutians. It was a refueling stop for Northwest Airlines flights to Tokyo. For two years I roamed the windswept landscape, watching the Arctic fox, finding tiny flowers, and digging up Aleut artifacts on the beach. I spent much of this time alone, because there were no other children of school age on the island. I had no thoughts of writing a book at the time, and my reading concentrated mainly on practical things, like how to build crystal radios and kites.

"Later, I would follow those practical inclinations to a career in chemistry, although it occurred to me, when I was a junior at the University of Michigan, that writing and illustrating children's books would be a wonderful way to make a living. No one I talked to knew much about the field, so I let the idea slide and went on to earn a Ph.D. in chemistry at Cornell.

"I was newly married, immersed in my studies, and soon the delighted father of a girl and boy. I continued to do an occasional drawing, but when I began writing scientific papers, I found I liked working with words. I went on to jobs as a research chemist, a professor at Utica College of Syracuse University, and drug tester for race horses as the years went by, keeping the idea of children's books in the back of my mind.

"I put off any serious attempts at writing until I was in my thirties. Then I fell off the roof of a house I was building, and, confronted with my own mortality and several months in a cast, I began writing stories and working hard on my drawing. Years would pass before anything was published, but I found the work itself provided a freedom to wander about in my mind. It was completely fascinating.

"Now I live in a little cabin on the edge of the Adirondacks. I built it using stones and trees from the land, and it has turned out to be a composite of my life. It is a scientific design with passive solar heat and high-tech insulation, but it looks like something from *Little Red Riding Hood.* It is very cute, awfully tiny, and a great place to live and work on children's books. In many ways I lead a fairly simple life, but one that is rich in experience. I do a lot of programs with children, making kites and puppets, and I spend time every day in the woods with the birds and animals. At night, I watch the stars with a telescope or listen to the world on shortwave radio and knit sweaters. I travel often and far.

"The idea for *Tundra: The Arctic Land* came to me while visiting Rocky Mountain National Park. Looking at the alpine tundra plants, I began to wonder what the Arctic tundra, the land of the caribou, was like. I spent the next several months reading and taking notes on the tundra, but the most important part of my research was a long canoe trip in the barren lands of Canada. The writing did not become real to me until I had come face to face with the caribou, wolves, and musk-oxen. For several weeks I paddled through the unspoiled land, sketching flowers and animals, and slapping mosquitoes in the twenty-four-hour daylight. After I returned home I spent a year rewriting and illustrating the book.

"*The Big Rock,* on the other hand, is about this huge boulder that is just down the hill from my house. I was sitting there one day watching the woods and contemplating a story that had just been rejected. Suddenly it came to me, through the seat of my pants I suppose, that I should do a book about the rock itself. I began at once, making sketches and studying geology. I came to know the rock well and gradually pieced together its story over the past billion years."

FOR MORE INFORMATION SEE:

Booklist, July 1, 1986, November 1, 1988.
Bulletin of the Center for Children's Books, August, 1986, October, 1988.
School Library Journal, September, 1986.
Washington Post Book World, November 9, 1986.

HOLTZMAN, Jerome   1926-

PERSONAL: Born July 12, 1926, in Chicago, Ill.; son of Samuel and Dorothy (Sloan) Holtzman; married Marilyn Ryan, 1949; children: Arlene, Alice, Catherine, Janet, Merrill. *Education:* Attended University of Chicago, 1954-55. *Residence:* Evanston, Ill.

CAREER: Chicago Times, copy boy, 1943-44, reporter, 1946-57; *Chicago Sun-Times,* Chicago, Ill., baseball writer and columnist, 1957-81; *Chicago Tribune,* Chicago, Ill., baseball columnist, 1981-83. President and founder of Holtzman Press, Inc. *Military service:* U. S. Marines, 1944-46. *Awards, honors:* Stick o'Type Award from the Chicago Newspaper Guild, 1961, 1969, 1976; *Three and Two!* was chosen one of New York Public Library's Books for the Teenage, 1980, and *Fielder's Choice,* 1981.

JEROME HOLTZMAN

WRITINGS:

No Cheering in the Press Box, Holt, 1974.
(With Tom Gorman) *Three and Two!* (biography of Tom Gorman), Scribner, 1979.
(Editor) *Fielder's Choice: An Anthology of Baseball Fiction,* Harcourt, 1979.

Sports editor and adviser for *Encyclopaedia Britannica;* correspondent and columnist for *Sporting News,* 1958-78.

SIDELIGHTS: "I went to work as a copy boy for the old *Chicago Times* on June 25, 1943. I was supposed to graduate from high school that week, but I didn't because I flunked physics. You know why I flunked? Because I was sports editor of my high school paper, the *Crane Tech Chronicle,* and I was off covering games instead of going to physics class.

"I went into the Marines from 1944 to 1946, and when I came back the paper put me on the prep beat. I covered more than 200 high school football and basketball games a year for the next eleven years. I can still recite teams' lineups by heart and tell you what kids' jump shots looked like.

"They put me on baseball in '57. I'd go a half-season with the Cubs and a half-season with the White Sox. I did that at the *Sun-Times* until 1981 and at the *Trib* through [1983].

"For my first eighteen to twenty years on the beat it was a seven-days-a-week job, seven and one-half months a year. There were no vacations except for maybe a day or two at the All-Star Game break. People ask me how I could stand watching all those games, especially with the Cubs and Sox, who usually were lousy. I never minded it. I love baseball, and every game is different. When I found myself getting bored, it usually was because I wasn't watching the action. I could cure the boredom by watching harder.

"I didn't care if the team I was covering won or lost. What was important to me was writing a good story every day. I'd have bad days sometimes, like a ballplayer who goes 0-for-4, but the nice thing about being a beat man was that you could make it up with a good piece the next day.

"Sportswriters always were my heroes, which is one reason I did *No Cheering.* I wanted to talk to those older guys while I still could. Talking to them, I realized that I was doing about the same job they'd done forty years before.

"The game is about the same, except for the designated hitter and Astroturf. The DH is bad, but Astroturf is worse. I hate to see those balls bouncing over fielders' heads. They ought to rip it all out.

"Some players are jerks, and get sore if you write anything critical about them, but ninety-five per cent are content with fairness. Most ballplayers I've known have been pretty bright, you know—brighter than some sportswriters.

"I think sportswriting is better today than it used to be. Most papers have bigger staffs now, and editors aren't as paralyzed by television as they were when it first came out. For a while, they just wanted us to write about why things happened, because they assumed people watched the games on TV, but that was bad. It got to where we were telling people why without telling 'em what. Now, there's more description.

"Some fellows in the business are in love with their own words, but that's always been the case. I try to stay away from the big words. It's been my observation that the guys who use them most wind up saying the least.

(From *Fielder's Choice: An Anthology of Baseball Fiction,* edited by Jerome Holtzman. Jacket illustration by Richard Mantel.)

"Sports are so interesting—there's always so much going on—that it's a shame not to let your readers in on it. I always admired John Carmichael, of the old *Chicago Daily News.* I remember once, at spring training, he told me that he'd talked to Chuck Dressen, and that Dressen had given him a hell of a column. Most writers would have said they'd written a hell of a column about Dressen, but not John. He had things straight."[1]

FOOTNOTE SOURCES

[1] Frederick C. Klein, "The Quintessential Baseball Writer," *Wall Street Journal,* June 15, 1984.

JEZARD, Alison   1919-

PERSONAL: Born September 7, 1919, in Mayfield, Sussex, England; daughter of Stormont (an army colonel) and Alice (Angel) Bisset; divorced; children: Vanessa, Hilary, Gillian. *Education:* Attended St. Denis School, Edinburgh, Scotland, 1924-38. *Politics:* Conservative. *Religion:* Atheist. *Home and office:* Garden Flat, 57 Earl's Ave., Folkestone, England.

CAREER: Has taught at Schools in Folkestone, England, and at School of English Studies (for foreign students); writer of children's books.

WRITINGS:

Albert, Gollancz, 1968.
Stories of Willy Mouse, BBC Publications, 1969.

Albert in Scotland, Gollancz, 1969.
Albert and Henry, Gollancz, 1970.
Albert's Christmas (illustrated by Margaret Gordon), Gollancz, 1970.
Albert up the River, Gollancz, 1971.
Albert and Digger, Gollancz, 1972.
Albert and Tum Tum, Gollancz, 1973.
Albert Goes to Sea, Gollancz, 1973.
Albert, Police Bear, Gollancz, 1975.
Albert Goes Trekking, Gollancz, 1976.
Albert's Circus (illustrated by M. Gordon), Gollancz, 1977.
Albert Goes Treasure Hunting (illustrated by M. Gordon), Gollancz, 1978.
Albert on the Farm (illustrated by M. Gordon), Gollancz, 1979.

Contributor of humorous articles to magazines.

WORK IN PROGRESS: Wilberforce and the Witches.

HOBBIES AND OTHER INTERESTS: Embroidery, carving alabaster, travel.

FOR MORE INFORMATION SEE:

Listener, November 14, 1968.
Times Literary Supplement, October 16, 1969.
Books and Bookmen, December, 1969.
Mary Hobbs, "In Which Albert Has a Birthday," *Junior Bookshelf,* April, 1976.
Children's Literature Abstracts, September, 1976.

KAUFMAN, Bel

PERSONAL: Born in Berlin, Germany; came to the United States at age of twelve; daughter of Michael J. (a physician) and Lola (a writer; maiden name Rabinowitz) Kaufman; divorced; children: Jonathan Goldstine, Thea Goldstine. *Edu-*

BEL KAUFMAN

cation: Hunter College (now Hunter College of the City University of New York), B.A. (magna cum laude); Columbia University, M.A. (with highest honors). *Religion:* Jewish. *Home:* 1020 Park Ave., New York, N.Y. 10028. *Agent:* Attorney Maurice Greenbaum, 575 Madison Ave., New York, N.Y. 10022.

CAREER: Taught in New York City high schools for over thirty years; New School for Social Research, New York City, instructor in English, 1964; Borough of Manhattan Community College (now Borough of Manhattan Community College of the City University of New York), New York City, assistant professor of English, adjunct professor of English, 1964—. Taught creative writing workshops and seminars at the University of Rochester and the University of Florida. Lecturer; member, Advisory Commission of Performing Arts, Advisory Council Town Hall Foundation. *Member:* Authors League, Writer's Guild, P.E.N., Dramatists Guild, Commission on Performing Arts, Sholom Aleichem Foundation (board member), Phi Beta Kappa, English Graduate Union (Columbia), Phi Delta Kappan (editorial board).

AWARDS, HONORS: Plaques from the Anti-Defamation League and from the United Jewish Appeal; Doctor of Letters, Nasson College, 1965; Paperback of the Year Award for Fiction from the National Bestsellers Institute, 1966, for *Up the Down Staircase;* named to the Hall of Fame, Hunter College of the City University of New York, 1973; National Human Resource Award from the American Bicentennial Research Institute, 1974, for "professional and civic attainments"; Award for Best Articles on Education from the Educational Association of America, 1976, and 1979; named "Woman of the Year" by the Organization for Rehabilitation through Training, 1980, and Brandeis University, 1980, 1981; National Education Association/P.E.N. Short Story Contest Winner, 1983, for "Sunday in the Park"; selected one of the prominent Americans to meet with Gorbachev at the Soviet Embassy, 1987.

WRITINGS:

NOVELS

Up the Down Staircase, Prentice-Hall, 1964, new edition, 1988.
Love, Etc., Prentice-Hall, 1979.

Author of lyrics for musical "Peabody and the Mermaid," and of an episode of the television series, "Room 222." Translator of Russian poetry. Contributor to periodicals, including *Esquire, Saturday Review, Today's Education, Ladies' Home Journal, English Journal, McCall's,* and *New York Times.*

ADAPTATIONS:

"Up the Down Staircase," starring Sandy Dennis, Warner Bros., 1967.

WORK IN PROGRESS: Lyrics for a musical; a theatre piece about her grandfather, the Yiddish humorist Sholom Aleichem.

SIDELIGHTS: "I was born in Berlin, where my father was studying medicine. Russia, however, is the country of my childhood and Russian is my native language. . . ."[1]

One of Kaufman's childhood memories is of walking with her cousin Tamara and "our grandfather someplace in Switzerland, at a summer resort, each holding on to his hand. 'You see that forest?' He points to the distant woods. 'I've just given it to Tamarochka! You see that lake? I just gave it to Bellochka!' We skip with pleasure at his largess, as delighted as

Bel Kaufman at eighteen months, on grandfather Sholom Aleichem's lap.

we are with the funny rhymes he thinks up for us, and the secret languages he invents for us, and the little stories he makes up just for us, his grandchildren, that the rest of the world, which knows him as Sholom Aleichem, the famous writer, does not receive from him.

"I did not realize until later, after he had died, how much I had been given."[2]

"I was only three when he died, but there is one particular scene that has remained in my mind. We were at a zoo in Copenhagen. 'Papa Sholom Aleichem,' as we called him, rolled up a piece of paper into the shape of a cup, filled it with water from a nearby fountain and offered a drink to a monkey. The monkey refused. Papa Sholom Aleichem bent down and said to me in Russian: *'Ona isporchenaya'* ('she is spoiled'), then he refilled the cup and drank thirstily from it. I learned only much later that he was already suffering from one of his illnesses: diabetes insipidus. One of its symptoms is inordinate thirst. But he made a joke even of that. He wrote to my parents: 'Now I know I will never die of hunger. I'll die of thirst.'

"After a childhood spent in Russia, I arrived in New York at the age of twelve, knowing not a word of English.

"The late Sam Levenson used to say that all through life he felt as if he had begun school one day late and had never caught up. I had begun six years late.

"I was taken to the neighborhood public school by my mother, who knew no more English than I did and who acted as my interpreter in my brief interview with the principal. To determine if I could read, he handed my mother a primer that she

in turn gave me. I had been brought up on Russian classics, had just finished *War and Peace* (though I had skipped all the war chapters and read only the love story), but I could make nothing out of the words before me. Failed the reading test! The principal then wrote on a card: 2 + 4 and handed that to my mother, who passed it to me. I wrote 6 on the card—and I was enrolled.

"There were no special classes for foreigners then, no English as a second language. I was thrust into first grade, with children half my age, in the hope that somehow, through necessity and osmosis, I would learn English. I would have given anything to be like the other children, the American children in the room. I was tall and skinny with long corkscrew curls bobbing unstylishly down my back. I wore a maroon velvet dress with a lace collar. I was terrified.

"I squeezed my legs under the tiny, immovable desk welded to the floor, eyes front, hands tightly clasped before me as in prayer. I fixed my attention on the teacher and began my education.

"On a chart over the blackboard was printed the English alphabet, each letter a different color. Even today *E* is forever orange to me, and *A* is always green.

"The first English I spoke that first day was 'Moo-woo-oom.' In order to go to the bathroom, I gathered, one had to raise an arm and make this sound, whereupon one was entitled to pick up the square wooden pass that hung by a rope near the door and, wearing it like a reproachful albatross around the neck, leave the room. This was a privilege granted to those who were unsuccessful in fulfilling what was required of them at a specified hour, in the cummunal march to pee.

"I raised a tentative hand and—on the edge of disaster—whispered a frantic 'Moo-woo—oom!' The teacher, Miss Murphy, understood. She put her arm around me and ignoring the wooden pass, led me out of the room, pointed in the direction of the toilet, and waited at the classroom door until I returned. Before we reentered the room, she hugged me, smiled, and said something. I didn't understand the words, but I understood the warm voice. It said I was accepted; it said I was special to her; it said all would be well. I was silent. Even had I known English, what words were there. . .to tell her I would remember her to this day?

"I soon learned that the password was 'May I leave the room?' and I grasped enough English to begin skipping and catching up with my age group.

"But that first day had already decided my future. It was my unforgettable Miss Murphy, who had put her arm around me and hugged me, who made me want to be a teacher, too."[3]

As a youngster, Kaufman "was allowed to read everything—Dostoyevsky, Tolstoy. . .whatever I read was finely filtered through my own innocence. . . .When I came to this country and learned English, a whole new wonderful world of literature opened up for me: *The Bobbsey Twins in School, The Bobbsey Twins in Camp, Anne of Green Gables*. I never knew such books existed.

"In my teens, I read contemporary authors, short stories with ironic endings (de Maupassant, O. Henry) and, to clear the air, my old favorite, Chekhov. 'How true, how true!' I used to pencil in the margins.

"*Cyrano de Bergerac* floored me at fifteen, but not when I was older. So did *The World's Illusion* and *Look Homeward,*

Angel. Other books survived adolescence. . . .They remained relevant.''[4]

"The turning point of my writing career was the publication of my book, *Up the Down Staircase*. Before that, I had found it difficult to be the grand-daughter of a great writer. The success of my book made me feel I had permission to be a writer too.

"I do not LIKE writing; in truth, I HATE writing, and would rather do anything else. But the joy comes when, almost in spite of myself, I come close to what I want to say. A sentence or an insight leaps from the page. I need to write alone, without guidance or suggestions from anyone, until the work is almost done.

"It is only in rewriting that—for me—the pleasures of my craft lie. But first I must get it all down on paper, no matter how careless it may be. Only then can I mold it, like so much clay.

"I write at home, at my desk, in my study, with my back to the view of the Manhattan skyline. But sheer physical comfort is not the answer. In the past, I have written on one knee, in a tiny bedroom. I suppose any place that is quiet will do (I have a low tolerance for noise or disturbance of any kind).

"It is difficult to say *when* I write, for I lack the discipline that I try to instill in my students. Most of the time I try to avoid writing by doing all kinds of things that are the equiv-alent to sharpening pencils. I write letters, answer the phone, clean out my closets—anything to avoid that confrontation with the typewriter. But when the writing is going well, I have been known to start early in the morning, and when I look up, the windows are dark! That is the kind of concentration that is devoutly to be wished for.

"I suppose when I say I don't like to write, I am referring to prose, for I love writing light verse, lyrics for musicals, skits and playlets. I have done lyrics for shows that were sheer joy to work on. One day I shall go back to my love—the theater."

Up the Down Staircase, the story of a young woman who teaches at an inner-city school, was a national best-seller for sixty-four weeks and number one in the nation for over five months, selling more than six million copies and translated into sixteen languages. In paperback it is in its forty-seventh printing. *Time* called it "easily the most popular novel about U.S. public schools in history."

Years after her successful novel, *McCall's* asked Kaufman to write an article about current schools—a postscript to *Up the Down Staircase*. "The situation has become much worse. I spent four months in some of the toughest high schools in New York. At times, I feared for my life. Even our faculty conferences were different: we used to discuss whether or not to teach Macbeth in the fifth or sixth term; today we are confronted by the problem of a fifteen-year-old girl who is pregnant, a boy who is a junkie. What I had described in my book

(From the movie "Up the Down Staircase," starring Sandy Dennis. Copyright © 1967 by Warner Bros., Pictures Inc.)

seemed a utopia compared to what I experienced in my later visits in our schools. I wrote that article and titled it 'Going Back Up the Down Staircase.'"

These problems begin long before a child enters school, according to Kaufman. "They begin with poverty, anger, prejudice. By the time a child enters school, it is often too late. In order to have better schools, we must have a better world. These are societal problems, not educational ones. Still, despite all this, inside each class there is that 'one child,' even if he is one in forty. He can be found, guided, salvaged. That is what the teaching profession is about."

Kaufman describes herself as first a teacher, and then as a writer. Education, according to Kaufman, "begins with the teacher. Plato didn't even have a room. Often teachers are the only ones who can instill a sense of worth in a child. We all remember the great teachers we had."

"I was a late bloomer. I was fifty-plus when I gathered the courage to scramble out of a deteriorated marriage and found myself for the first time entirely on my own. I was fifty-plus when I wrote my first novel....I was fifty-plus when I discovered a new career of public speaking. And I was fifty-plus when I formed a totally satisfying relationship with a man.

"Not that I spent my earlier years lolling on a chaise lounge, munching chocolates. I taught school, brought up two children, published an occasional story or light verse, but balancing for many years on the tightrope of a perilous marriage did not lend itself to creativity. Nor to independence. Nor to a sense of identity. I knew how to be a daughter, a wife, a mother; I did not know how to be *me*.

"Now I do. I have learned a simple, powerful lesson: I learned to say NO. What a heady, liberating sound that can be! I do not have to be loved by everyone; I can risk disapproval. I can trust my opinions. I have profited from my mistakes—and they were lulus! With each small success my confidence grew. And with my children's independence came my own. I no longer do what I *have* to do; I now do what I *want* to do.

"I am one of the lucky ones: I have options."[5]

Although Kaufman has always avoided politics, she accepted an invitation from the Soviet Embassy for December 8, 1987 as one of the "prominent Americans" to join Gorbachev and his wife, Raisa, for cultural exchanges, and during that same year participated in the Moscow International Forum for a Nuclear Free World as one of some thousand delegates from many countries at the invitation of the Soviet Union. Among those participating with Kaufman were Graham Greene, Daniel Ellsberg, Yoko Ono, Marina Vladi and Gregory Peck.

FOOTNOTE SOURCES

[1] Bella Ezersky "From Russia with 'Love, Etc.,'" *Theatre Collection* (Research Libraries, New York Public Library), January, 1980. Amended by Kaufman.
[2] Bel Kaufman: The Most Touching of All Gifts," *50 Plus,* December, 1985.
[3] B. Kaufman, "First Day of School," *Today's Education,* September/October, 1981.
[4] "Three Writers, Recalling Favorites, Urge Wide Choice of Literature," *New York Times Magazine,* May 29, 1977. Amended by Kaufman.
[5] B. Kaufman, "The Beauty of Being a Late Bloomer," *50 Plus,* June, 1986.

FOR MORE INFORMATION SEE:

America, February 6, 1965.
Time, February 12, 1965.
Commonweal, May 14, 1965.
New York Times, May 29, 1977.
Chicago Tribune Book World, October 28, 1979.
Washington Post Book World, November 11, 1979.
Arkansas Democrat, November 5, 1982.
Bel Kaufman, "From Russia with Hope," *50 Plus,* July, 1987.

KEATS, Ezra Jack   1916-1983

PERSONAL: Born March 11, 1916, in Brooklyn, N.Y.; died of a heart attack, May 6, 1983, in New York City; son of Benjamin (a waiter) and Augusta (Podgainy) Keats. *Education:* Attended Art Students League; studied painting with Jean Charlot. *Residence:* 444 East 82nd St., New York, N.Y. 10028.

CAREER: Worked as a muralist for the Works Progress Administration (W.P.A.) during the Depression; instructor, School of Visual Arts, New York City, 1947-48, and Workshop School, New York City, 1955-57; author and illustrator of books for children. Contributor of designs to the UNICEF series of holiday cards. *Exhibitions:* Associated American Artists Gallery, New York City, 1950, 1954. *Military service:* Camouflage expert in the U.S. Air Corps during World War II. *Member:* P.E.N., Author's Guild, Society of Illustrators.

AWARDS, HONORS: Caldecott Medal from the American Library Association, 1963, for *The Snowy Day; In a Spring Garden* was selected one of Library of Congress' Books of the Year, 1965; Venice Film Festival Award for Children's Film Shorts, 1967, for "The Snowy Day"; *The Little Drummer Boy* and *A Letter to Amy* were each selected one of Child Study Association of America's Children's Books of the Year, 1968, *Goggles,* 1969, *Hi, Cat!,* 1970, *Two Tickets to Freedom, The King's Fountain,* and *Apt. 3,* all 1971, *Pet Show!,* and *Over in the Meadow,* both 1972, *Dreams,* 1974, *Louie,* 1975, *Jennie's Hat,* and *Regards to the Man in the Moon,* both 1986, and *Apt. 3,* 1987; Caldecott Medal Honor Book, 1970, for *Goggles!; Boston Globe-Horn Book* Award for Illustration, 1970, for *Hi, Cat!; Apt. 3* and *The King's Fountain* were each selected one of *School Library Journal*'s Best Books, 1971; Brooklyn Art Books for Children citation, 1973, for *The Snowy Day;* Gold Venus Medallion from the Virgin Islands International Film Festival, 1977, for "Apt. 3"; Children's Choice from the International Reading Association and the Children's Book Council, 1979, for *The Trip;* Silver Medallion from the University of Southern Mississippi, 1980, for "Outstanding Service in the Field of Children's Literature."

WRITINGS:

ALL SELF-ILLUSTRATED

(With Pat Cherr) *My Dog Is Lost! or, Mi Perro Se Ha Perdido,* Crowell, 1960.
The Snowy Day (ALA Notable Book; *Horn Book* honor list), Viking, 1962, reissued, 1972.
Whistle for Willie (sequel to *The Snowy Day;* ALA Notable Book; *Horn Book* honor list), Viking, 1964.
(Reteller) *John Henry, an American Legend,* Pantheon Books, 1965.
Jennie's Hat, Harper, 1966.
(Compiler) *God Is in the Mountain* (adult), Holt, 1966.
Peter's Chair, Harper, 1967.
A Letter to Amy, Harper, 1968.

EZRA JACK KEATS

(Compiler) *Night* (adult; with photographs by Beverly Hall), Atheneum, 1969.

Goggles! (*Horn Book* honor list), Macmillan, 1969, reissued, 1984.

Hi, Cat!, Macmillan, 1970, 2nd edition, in press.

Apt. 3, Macmillan, 1971.

Pet Show!, Macmillan, 1972.

Skates!, F. Watts, 1973.

Psst! Doggie—, F. Watts, 1973.

Dreams, Macmillan, 1974.

Kitten for a Day, F. Watts, 1974.

Louie, Greenwillow, 1975.

The Trip, Greenwillow, 1978, large print edition, 1980.

Maggie and the Pirate, Four Winds, 1979.

Louie's Search, Four Winds, 1980.

Regards to the Man in the Moon, Four Winds, 1981.

Clementina's Cactus, Viking, 1982.

ILLUSTRATOR

Elisabeth C. Lansing, *Jubilant for Sure,* Crowell, 1954.

Eleanor Clymer, *Chester,* Dodd, 1954.

Frances Carpenter, *Wonder Tales of Dogs and Cats* (Junior Literary Guild selection), Doubleday, 1955.

Phyllis Whitney, *Mystery on the Isle of Skye,* Westminster, 1955.

Raymond Abrashkin and Jay Williams, *Danny Dunn and the Anti-Gravity Paint,* Whittlesey House, 1956.

E. C. Lansing, *Sure Thing for Shep,* Crowell, 1956.

George S. Albee, *Three Young Kings,* F. Watts, 1956.

J. Williams, *A Change of Climate: A More or Less Aimless and Amiable Account of Various Journeys and Encounters Abroad,* Random House, 1956.

R. Abrashkin and J. Williams, *Danny Dunn on a Desert Island,* Whittlesey House, 1957.

William McKellar, *Wee Joseph,* McGraw, 1957.

Tillie S. Pine and Joseph Levine, *The Indians Knew,* McGraw, 1957.

T. S. Pine and J. Levine, *The Pilgrims Knew,* McGraw, 1957.

Glenn Balch, *Little Hawk and the Free Horses* (Junior Literary Guild selection), Crowell, 1957.

T. S. Pine and J. Levine, *The Chinese Knew,* McGraw, 1958.

R. Abrashkin and J. Williams, *Danny Dunn and the Homework Machine,* Whittlesey House, 1958.

R. Abrashkin and J. Williams, *Danny Dunn and the Weather Machine,* McGraw, 1959.

G. Balch, *Brave Riders,* Crowell, 1959.

Dorothy C. Fisher, *And Long Remember: Some Great Americans Who Have Helped Me,* McGraw, 1959.

J. Williams, *The Tournament of Lions,* Walck, 1960.

Cora Cheney, *Peg-Legged Pirate of Sulu,* Knopf, 1960.

Irmengarde Eberle, *Grasses,* Walck, 1960.

Eleanor A. Murphey, *Nihal of Ceylon,* Crowell, 1960.

Herbert Best, *Desmond's First Case,* Viking, 1961.

Paul Showers, *In the Night,* Ambassador, 1961.

T. S. Pine and J. Levine, *The Eskimos Knew,* Whittlesey House, 1962.

Patricia M. Martin, *The Rice Bowl Pet,* Crowell, 1962.

Solveig P. Russell, *What Good Is a Tail?,* Bobbs-Merrill, 1962.

Ruth P. Collins, *The Flying Cow,* Walck, 1963.

R. Tooze, *Our Rice Village in Cambodia,* Viking, 1963.

Lucretia P. Hale, *The Peterkin Papers,* Doubleday, 1963.

Jim Can Swim, Knopf, 1963.

Ann Nolan Clark, *Tia Maria's Garden,* Viking, 1963.

Juliet Morgan Swenson, *Hawaii: A Book to Begin On* (Junior Literary Guild selection), Holt, 1963.

T. S. Pine and J. Levine, *The Egyptians Knew,* McGraw-Hill, 1964.

Maxine W. Kumin, *Speedy Digs Downside Up,* Putnam, 1964.

Ann McGovern, *Zoo, Where Are You?,* Harper, 1964.

John Keats, *The Naughty Boy: A Poem,* Viking, 1965.

Richard Lewis, editor, *In a Spring Garden* (*Horn Book* honor list), Dial, 1965, reissued, 1976.

Millicent E. Selsam, *How to Be a Nature Detective,* revised edition, Harper, 1966 (Keats was not associated with earlier edition).

Esther R. Hautzig, *In the Park: An Excursion in Four Languages,* Macmillan, 1968.

Katherine Davis, Henry Ohorati and Harry Simeone, *The Little Drummer Boy,* Macmillan, 1968, new edition, 1984.

Olive A. Wadsworth, *Over in the Meadow,* Four Winds Press, 1971.

Lloyd Alexander, *The King's Fountain,* Dutton, 1971.

Florence B. Freedman, *Two Tickets to Freedom: The True Story of Ellen and William Craft, Fugitive Slaves,* Simon & Schuster, 1971.

Myron Levoy, *Penny Tunes and Princesses,* Harper, 1972.

Also illustrator of *The Fire and the Gold.* Keats' work has been translated into sixteen languages, including French, Danish, Norwegian, Spanish, Italian, Portuguese, Turkish, German, Italian, Swedish, and Japanese. Contributor of illustrations to periodicals, including *Esquire, Colliers, Reader's Digest,* and *House Beautiful.*

ADAPTATIONS:

FILMS

"The Snowy Day" (animated film; VHS; Beta), Weston Woods, 1964.

"Whistle for Willic," Weston Woods, 1965.

"My Dog Is Lost," Bank Street College of Education, 1967.

"The Little Drummer Boy" (VHS; Beta), Weston Woods, 1970.

"Peter's Chair" (VHS; Beta), Weston Woods, 1971.

"Apt. 3," Weston Woods, 1977.

"Goggles" (VHS; Beta), Weston Woods.

"A Letter to Amy" (VHS; Beta), Weston Woods.

"In a Spring Garden," Weston Woods.

"The Trip" (VHS; Beta), Weston Woods.

FILMSTRIPS WITH CASSETTES

"The Snowy Day," Weston Woods, 1965.

"Whistle for Willie," Weston Woods, 1965.

"Peter's Chair," Weston Woods, 1967.

"In a Spring Garden," Weston Woods, 1967.

"John Henry," Guidance Associates, 1967.

"A Letter to Amy," Weston Woods, 1970.

"The Little Drummer Boy," Weston Woods, 1971.

"Goggles," Weston Woods, 1974.

"Apt. 3," Weston Woods, 1977.

"Maggie and the Pirate," Weston Woods, 1988.

"Hi, Cat!" (with teacher's guide), Miller-Brody Productions.

CASSETTES

"The Snowy Day" Live Oak Media, 1974, (with two puppets), Society for Visual Education, 1976, (read-along cassette), Random House.

"Whistle for Willie," Live Oak Media, 1975, (read-along cassette), Random House.

(From *John Henry, an American Legend* by Ezra Jack Keats. Illustrated by the author.)

(From *Peter's Chair* by Ezra Jack Keats. Illustrated by the author.)

"Hi, Cat!," Miller-Brody Productions.
"Goggles," Weston Woods.
"Peter's Chair," Weston Woods.
"A Letter to Amy," Weston Woods.
"Apt. 3," Weston Woods.
"In a Spring Garden," Weston Woods.
"The Little Drummer Boy," Weston Woods.
"Over in the Meadow," Scholastic.

VIDEOCASSETTES

"Smile for Auntie and Other Stories" (contains *The Snowy Day*), Weston Woods.
"The Snowy Day," Weston Woods.

PLAYS

(Also set and costume designer) "The Trip" (musical), first produced in New York City, at All-Children's Theater, October, 1983.

Apt. 3, God Is in the Mountain, Goggles!, Little Drummer Boy, My Dog Is Lost!, and *Tia Maria's Garden* have been adapted into Braille. *Goggles!, Over in the Meadow, Pet Show!, Tia Maria's Garden,* and *Whistle for Willie* have been adapted into Talking Books.

SIDELIGHTS: **March 11, 1916.** Born in Brooklyn, New York, where he grew up and attended public schools. His parents were Polish immigrants who settled in a poor, heavily populated section of Brooklyn. His father worked as a waiter in Greenwich Village, while his mother remained at home caring for Keats, his brother and sister. The children all showed an early inclination for the arts. Keats' older brother eventually became a portrait photographer, and his sister, a talented sculptor. While his father discouraged him from developing his artistic talents, his mother, on the other hand, delighted in Keats' drawings. "I think I started painting when I was about four years old. I really dedicated myself to what I did, avidly and lovingly. I drew on and colored in everything that came across my path, with the indulgent approval of my mother.

"We had this kitchen table—it was enamel, with two drawers, one for silverware, the other for bread. Anyway, I proceeded to draw on the top of it, all the things kids draw pretty much, a profile of a lady with long lashes and a lot of curls. . . .I filled up the entire table with pictures of little cottages, curly smoke coming out of the chimneys, men's profiles, and kids. I drew an Indian and a Chinese with straw hat and pigtails. . . .I finished, the entire area was covered with sketches, completely covered with them. My mother came in and I expected her to say, 'What have you been doing?' and 'Get that sponge and wash it off!' Instead she looked at me and said, 'Did you do that? Isn't it wonderful!' and she proceeded to look at each thing and clucked her tongue and said, 'Now isn't that nice!' Then she said, 'You know, it's so wonderful, it's a shame to wash it off!' So she got out the tablecloth which we used only on Friday nights and she covered the whole little mural and every time a neighbor would come in, she'd unveil it to show what I had done. They'd all say, 'Mmm, isn't that nice.' They couldn't say anything else, Mother was so proud."[1]

His father continued to discourage young Keats from becoming an artist, however, warning his son: "Never be an artist; you'll be a bum, you'll starve, you'll have a terrible life."[1]

Keats ignored his father's advice and continued to hide his paintings from him. "My father would come in and smell the paints and say, 'You've been painting. Get out and play ball and stop making a fool of yourself.' So I had to go out and play ball. . . .Then one day he came home and said, 'If you don't think artists starve, well, let me tell you. One man came in the other day and swapped me a tube of paint for a bowl of soup.' My father put down a brand-new tube of paint. I thought how lucky I was that the poor man had to make such a swap.

"The swap happened again and again, and one day my father brought home a package of brushes, very inexpensive brushes which no professional artist would have bought. It dawned on me that my father was buying this stuff for me and had a terrible conflict. He was proud of my painting and he wanted to supply me with paint, but at the same time he lived in real dread of my living a life like that of the artists he had seen."[1]

The supply of paint that his father gave him wasn't enough, however. He was always running out. His older brother suggested that he write to Clara Bow, the famous movie star, to ask for a box of paints. "So I grabbed an envelope and some lined paper and immediately sent off a letter to Hollywood. After a month of holding my breath, I received nothing more than a glossy picture of the 'IT' girl. She never had less 'IT' to me than at that moment.

(From the filmstrip "Goggles," produced by Weston Woods, 1974.)

"Then there was 'Daddy' Browning, the elderly millionaire who married young and pretty 'Peaches,' who later starred in the Peaches Browning case. I had seen his picture in the paper dispensing gifts to needy children. So I wrote to him, telling him I needed a painting set. . . .No answer; not even a picture of 'Peaches!'

"As a result of these disappointments, I began to trust less and less in bonanzas and started to improvise instead: stretching pieces of muslin over the rectangular ends of orange crates, using house paints and, occasionally, resorting to mercurochrome."[2]

"I lived in a very, very tough section of Brooklyn, in an old, beat-up tenement, and drawing was really a rather hazardous pursuit. I remember being intercepted once by some tough older neighborhood boys when I was about eight. I had a painting of mine under my arm. They closed in and pulled it out of my hands—I was really scared—and then a very strange thing happened. When they learned that I had done the painting, they began to treat me with great respect. From then on, when they'd see me, I'd be greeted with 'Hi, Doc!,' and I discovered that there was a place for me in my piece of the world.

"When I was about nine, I began to tell stories to the kids. All these little tough kids on my block would follow me around asking, 'Tell me a story, tell me a story.' I'd make them up as I'd go along—sort of a Pied Piper. I was ridiculed by my family when I read an early attempt at poetry. I continued to paint in a serious way, but the notion of writing my stories was put aside. I wanted approval very badly then, and so I just continued to paint.

"I taught myself to paint, using any kind of material I could find. Once I got some paint—just a few colors, two of which were blue and white—and I covered a board with my blue paint. I dipped my brush into the white paint and dabbed it onto the board, shook the brush a little and let it trail off. I stepped back and got the greatest thrill I can remember. I saw a little cloud floating across a blue sky. It was very real to me, and I'll always remember it. What a tremendous feeling of gratification, to have created something like this! Even to-day, when I look up and see a tiny cloud floating across the sky with little wispy ends trailing off, I think of that time."[1]

Keats' father continued to complain about his son's paintings, although he was impressed when Keats brought home a quarter that he had earned by drawing a sign for the neighborhood candy store. He told his son: "See, now you're using your head. You'll become a sign painter and you'll make a decent living, and you'll be a lot better off than these artists I see in the Village."[1]

His father became so impressed with his son's ability that he took him to the Metropolitan Museum in New York City. It was a day Keats would never forget: "My father thought that the most important paintings in the world would be those of important people. He showed me Gilbert Stuart's painting of George Washington and Andrew Jackson's portrait and all the colonial paintings. . . .It was all very nice and it was all really dull, and I was getting tired. Suddenly I looked down the length of the corridor and at the other end was an arched doorway which opened to another gallery, completely bathed in sunlight. Framed in that archway was Daumier's 'Third Class Carriage.' I never heard of Daumier and I knew nothing about his painting. . . .I felt a pounding in my heart and I just turned toward it and walked toward it as though hypnotized. As I got closer to it, it glowed more magnificently. . . ."[1]

When his father suffered a fatal coronary, Keats had "to identify him. As part of the procedure, the police asked me to look through his wallet. I found myself staring deep into his secret feelings. There in his wallet were worn and tattered newspaper clippings of the notices of the awards I had won. My silent admirer and supplier, he had been torn between his dread of my leading a life of hardship and his real pride in my work."[2]

Despite three scholarships he won to art schools, Keats was unable to attend. It was the late 1930s and the Depression forced him to abandon painting for awhile. At one point he supported his entire family by loading melons on a truck for $1.00 a day.

Later, he landed a position as a mural painter on W.P.A. (Works Progress Administration) projects. When World War II erupted, Keats became a member of the United States Air

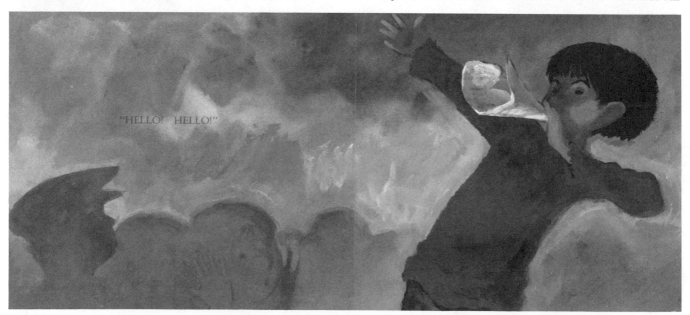

"HELLO! HELLO!"

(From *Louie* by Ezra Jack Keats. Illustrated by the author.)

One winter morning Peter woke up and looked out the window. Snow had fallen during the night. It covered everything as far as he could see.

(From *The Snowy Day* by Ezra Jack Keats. Illustrated by the author.)

Corps and served as a camouflage expert. After the war, he decided to become an illustrator.

In **1947,** he received his first illustration assignment for *Collier's* magazine. The following year he spent in Paris, and when he returned, his work was exhibited at the Associated American Artists Gallery in New York. A Doubleday editor asked him to do some covers after seeing the paintings. Another editor, after seeing his book jackets, asked him to illustrate some children's books.

His first commission was for *Jubilant for Sure,* a teenage novel by Elizabeth Lansing, which was set in the hills of Kentucky. "This was the real break. This was how I found my field, which fuses storytelling, children, and art.

"I wanted to do a good job, so I decided to go down and see the hill people in the Smokey Mountains to sketch them on location. One day I got a hitch on an ice truck. As we were bumping along, I saw a typical shack that had an old porch and a rocker. I asked the driver to stop and I hopped off.

"As I was sketching, I noticed a four-year-old girl with a head of golden curls standing on the right side of the porch. She looked very boldly and calmly at me and kept shifting over until she was directly in front of me. I included her in my drawing and then showed it to her. While we were talking, the child's mother came out. She liked the drawing and invited me to join them at lunch, which I did happily.

"When lunch was over, the family invited me to stay with them for a few days. Since I could see they were poor, I accepted their invitation but offered to pay my share of the expense. 'In that case,' the father said, 'the invitation is off!' So I accepted his condition and remained with them a whole week. They made my trip a fascinating excursion into another world. When the book was published, it was chosen as one of the fifty best children's books of the year and was exhibited in The Metropolitan Museum of Art."[3]

"For about ten years I illustrated other people's books. There were two things that troubled me at that time: one was that in many of the manuscripts I was given there was a peculiar quality of contrivance and rigid structure; the other was that I never got a story about Black people, Black children. I decided that if I ever did a book of my own it would be more of a happening—certainly not a structured thing, but an experience. My hero would be a Black child. I made many sketches and studies of Black children. . . .I wanted him to be in the book on his own, not through the benevolence of white children or anyone else."[1]

"The important thing is that the kids in a book have to be real—regardless of color. I don't like to emphasize the race thing, because what's really important is the honesty.

"The essential thing is that we see each other, 'see' as perceive, understand, discover.

"If we all could really see each other exactly as the other is, this would be a different world. But first I think we have to begin to see each other."[4]

In **1960,** *My Dog Is Lost,* written and illustrated by Keats and Pat Cherr, was published. It was followed by *The Snowy Day,* which was the first book that he wrote and illustrated without a collaborator. "In 1961 I used Peter in *The Snowy Day* which tells about the excitement I felt as a boy when I woke up to see snow outside the Brooklyn apartment where I grew up without a single picture book of my own. We were too darn poor, I just never saw a picture book. Really, it wasn't until I was about thirty-five that I discovered children's books."[4]

"Years ago, long before I ever thought of doing children's books, while looking through a magazine I came upon four candid photos of a little boy about three or four years old. His expressive face, his body attitudes, the very way he wore his clothes, totally captivated me. I clipped the strip of photos and stuck it on my studio wall, where it stayed for quite a while, and then it was put away.

"As the years went by, these pictures would find their way back to my walls offering me fresh pleasure at each encounter.

"In more recent years, while illustrating children's books, the desire to do my own story about this little boy began to germinate. Up he went again—this time above my drawing table. He was my model and inspiration. Finally I began work on

Peter thought, What will the boys say
when they see a girl at my party?
Suddenly there was a flash of lightning
and a roar of thunder!
A strong wind blew the letter out of his hand!

(From *A Letter to Amy* by Ezra Jack Keats. Illustrated by the author.)

The Snowy Day. When the book was finished and on the presses, I told Annis Duff, whose guidance and empathy have been immeasurable, about my long association with this little boy. How many years was it? I went over to *Life* magazine and had it checked. To my astonishment they informed me that I had found him twenty-two years ago!

The Snowy Day was a picture book done in collage, a favorite Keats' medium. "I had no idea as to how the book would be illustrated, except that I wanted to add a few bits of patterned paper to supplement the painting.

"As work progressed, one swatch of material suggested another, and before I realized it, each page was being handled in a style I had never worked in before. A rather strange sequence of events came into play. I worked—and waited. Then quite unexpectedly I would come across just the appropriate material for the page I was working on."[2]

"For instance, one day I visited my art supply shop looking for a sheet of off-white paper to use for the bed linen for the opening pages. Before I could make my request, the clerk said, 'We just received some wonderful Belgian canvas. I think you'll like to see it.' I hadn't painted on canvas for years, but there he was displaying a huge roll of canvas. It had just the right color and texture for the linen. I brought a narrow strip, leaving a puzzled clerk wondering what strange shape of picture I planned to paint.

"The creative efforts of people from many lands contributed to the materials in the book. Some of the papers used for the collage came from Japan, some from Italy, some from Sweden, many from our own country.

"The mother's dress is made of the kind of oilcloth used for lining cupboards. I made a big sheet of snow-texture by rolling white paint over wet inks on paper and achieved the effect of snow flakes by cutting patterns out of gum erasers, dipping them into paint, and then stamping them onto the pages. The gray background for the pages where Peter goes to sleep was made by spattering India ink with a toothbrush.

"Friends would enthusiastically discuss the things they did as children in the snow, others would suggest nuances of plot,

or a change of a word. All of us wanted so much to see little Peter march through these pages, experiencing, in the purity and innocence of childhood, the joys of a first snow.

"I can honestly say that Peter came into being because we wanted him; and I hope that, as the scriptures say, 'a little child shall lead them,' and that he will show in his own way the wisdom of a pure heart."[4]

"Collage is distinguished from other art forms in that its *harmonious fusion of independent shapes and colors* makes for a more unusual balance between illusion and reality. For instance, a pattern that has its own character, when used in combination with other patterns, becomes something else.

"Some of the pictures in *The Snowy Day* are examples of this. A decorative paper becomes a room; flat shapes of color and designs become buildings, snow, a pillow, pajamas on a boy, and so on. There is no shading on the pajamas or the linen to make them look solid, nor is there any delineation between the sleeve and the body. No definition of line or shading shows where the pillow meets the bed, nor is the edge of the bed cover defined. The viewer makes it round, gives it space, follows the implications. (In a few instances, for special reasons, more definition is introduced, such as in Peter's face.) If I were painting the sky behind the snow hill, I would try to design some interesting clouds on a blue sky. But here the patterned paper offered me a unique possibility.

"The edges of shapes are varied in several ways. Sharp edges are made by cutting; rough edges by tearing; soft edges by painting over them.

"The artist is unconcerned that the overlapping sheets of paper showing through, or the edges casting shadows, reveal an illustration to be composed of pasted paper and other materials. If anything, this obvious superimposition is an integral part of the character of the medium, as are, for instance, the thick impasto strokes in oil painting.

"There are also strange and unpredictable situations. What could be a minor disaster can turn out to be a pleasant surprise. Sometimes when all the materials have been cut out, composed, and are ready to paste, a careless movement of one's arm will sweep everything on the page into a frightful state—or into a new arrangement suggesting a composition one never would have thought of."[6]

Critics overwhelmingly agreed that *The Snowy Day* was an attractively illustrated read-aloud picture book. John Rowe Townsend said: "*The Snowy Day* comes closer than most books to reconciling the two viewpoints on 'pure' picture-book art and story-telling art: to look at it is to perceive and grant at once that pictures are indeed arrangements of colours, lines, shapes, and textures, and that a picture-book page can provide an aesthetic experience for the reader."[7]

In **1963** the book won a prestigious award. Its small black hero, Peter, appeared in subsequent Keats' books. "I really found myself when I produced *The Snowy Day* which won the Caldecott Award for the best children's book of the year."[3]

Using the same technique as he did in *The Snowy Day*, Keats' next book, *Whistle for Willie,* also had young Peter as its subject, but added a dachshund named Willie. "In *Whistle for Willie,* the sequel to *The Snowy Day,* Peter has been turning in circles and becomes dizzy. How to illustrate this? First there was the temptation to draw the often-used swirling ellipses around him. But to keep the illustration in the realm of collage, I decided to make the sky appear agitated by changing it from a solid to a marbleized pattern. On the next page I tilted the composition up, and on the following page I tilted it down. To increase the feeling of dizziness, I had the traffic lights appear to be floating about in mid-air!

"The ratio between the use of painting and drawing and the use of collage should be determined according to the judgment of the illustrator with every new book. Each new manuscript presents a challenge and an adventure; and I look forward to applying this technique in fresh and appropriate ways."[6]

Whistle for Willie was followed by *John Henry, an American Legend,* which retold the legend of the powerful Black American railroad worker. It used collage illustrations to enhance the tale. A young fan wrote: "I think your book *John Henry* is a beautiful book. I especially liked the part when John Henry was a little fat baby. The most exciting part was when there was a race and John Henry beat the steam drill. I felt sad, very sad, when John Henry died. Did he really die? Where did you find out the story of John Henry? Was John Henry married? What was his wife's name? Write to me, please."[8]

Keats responded: ". . .I would like to answer your questions as best I can.

"Yes, John Henry was a Negro. He was married and his wife's name was Polly Ann. I don't think he had any children, but I'm not sure.

"He was born about one hundred years ago. He was so big and strong, and also kind, that those who met him told their friends and children all about him. As the years went by, people wrote it down and sang songs about brave John Henry, and how he beat the machine, even at the cost of his life. He showed that there is nothing greater on earth than people.

"They still tell the stories and sing songs about him, and they always will, forever and ever."[8]

In **1966** Keats contributed five designs for UNICEF Christmas cards. He also produced a book for adults as well as for children, *God Is In the Mountain.* The book used only two colors for the illustrations. "I used one sheet for the black and one for the orange. Because I did not wish to intrude upon the religious experiences selected, I kept the elements simple to create an appropriate mood and background."[9]

Ezra Jack Keats at work. ■(Photograph courtesy of Weston Woods.)

(From the filmstrip ''Maggie and the Pirate,'' produced by Weston Woods, 1988.)

That same year, Keats returned to the style and manner of *The Snowy Day* in his book about a little girl, which was entitled *Jennie's Hat*. The source of the story, according to the author, comes from a remembered image. ''A picture of an old lady and man with a flock of birds circling around their heads stayed in my mind many years. Those birds seemed to be bringing this couple something. And so emerged the image of Jennie's bird friends, bringing her a shower of gifts to fulfill her heart's desire. . . .In addition to the painting, dried leaves, strips of fabrics, old valentines, postcards, lithographs and other memorabilia, cutout paper flowers, paper fans, bits of old wallpaper, and cutouts of background materials from my own books all became part of *Jennie's Hat*.''[9]

Ideas for his books came in the most unexpected places: ''I jot them down in a notebook; sometimes I take Polaroid shots in color of children's faces or lovely scenes. My problem is not to repeat myself as I move from book to book.''[3]

His twenty-two children's books have received many awards. *Goggles* was named a Caldecott Honor Book in 1970, and *Hi, Cat* won the *Boston Globe-Horn Book* Award the same year. Some of his books were also adapted into other media. ''Apt. 3'' received the Gold Venus Medallion, and, following the Japanese publication of *Skates,* a Tokyo roller-skating rink was built in his honor.

Keats once described the genesis of his stories, saying: ''I have an image of certain things happening—more of a visual image—and then I hear the characters talking to each other, and the story grows in counterpoint. Sometimes my emphasis is on the pictures and sometimes on the story. The pictures do pace the book, however. . . .I hang my illustrations on my studio wall in rows so that I can see them flow and move in sequence, like a ballet. I guess I'm the choreographer.''[11]

Keats died of a heart attack on **May 6, 1983** in New York City at the age of sixty-seven. In 1985 the Ezra Jack Keats Foundation established the Ezra Jack Keats Award, an international biennial award for promising illustrators. It is sponsored and administered by the United States Board on Books for Young People and UNICEF. An Ezra Jack Keats Medal, established by the Ezra Jack Keats Foundation and the University of Southern Mississippi, was given for the first time in 1986. The medal was designed by Keats specifically for the University of Southern Mississippi Medallion.

''All people want is the opportunity to be people. Let us open the book covers, these long-shut doors, to new and wonderful, true and inspiring books for all children; about all children—the tall and short, fat and thin, dark and light, beautiful and homely. Welcome!''[10]

FOOTNOTE SOURCES

[1]''A Conversation with Ezra Jack Keats,'' publicity folder, Macmillan, n.d.

[2]Esther Hautzig, ''Ezra Jack Keats,'' *Newbery and Caldecott Medal Books: 1956-1965*, edited by Lee Kingman, Horn Book, 1965.

[3]Erma Perry, ''The Gentle World of Ezra Jack Keats,'' *American Artist*, September, 1971.

[4]Margo Huston, ''Honesty Is Author's Policy for Children's Books,'' *Milwaukee Journal*, March 28, 1974.

[5]Ezra Jack Keats, ''Caldecott Award Acceptance,'' *Horn Book*, August, 1963.

[6]E. J. Keats, ''Collage,'' *Horn Book*, June, 1964.

[7]John Rowe Townsend, *Written for Children: An Outline of English Language Children's Literature*, revised edition, Lippincott, 1974.

[8]Florence B. Freedman, ''Ezra Jack Keats: Author and Illustrator,'' *Elementary English*, January, 1969.

[9]E. J. Keats, ''Ezra Jack Keats on Collage as an Illustrative Medium,'' *Publishers Weekly*, April 4, 1966.

[10]Selma G. Lanes, *Down the Rabbit Hole*, Atheneum, 1971.

[11]S. G. Lanes, ''Ezra Jack Keats: In Memoriam,'' *Horn Book*, September/October, 1984.

FOR MORE INFORMATION SEE:

Bertha Mahony Miller and others, compilers, *Illustrators of Children's Books, 1946-1956*, Horn Book, 1958.

Commonweal, November 16, 1962.

Saturday Review, December 15, 1962 (p. 27), November 9, 1963.

Horn Book, February, 1963 (p. 51), June, 1972, December, 1974 (p. 684).

A. Duff, ''Ezra Jack Keats: 1963 Caldecott Medal Winner,'' *Library Journal*, March 15, 1963.

Publishers Weekly, March 11, 1963, April 4, 1966, July 16, 1973.

Muriel Fuller, editor, *More Junior Authors*, H. W. Wilson, 1963.

L. Kingman and others, compilers, *Illustrators of Children's Books, 1957-1966*, Horn Book, 1968.

Lee Bennett Hopkins, *Books Are by People*, Citation Press, 1969.

Bettina Hurlimann, *Picture-Book World*, World, 1969.

Martha E. Ward and Dorothy A. Marquardt, *Authors of Books for Young People*, Scarecrow, 1971.

Miriam Hoffman and Eva Samuels, *Authors and Illustrators of Children's Books*, Bowker, 1972.

Contemporary American Illustrators of Children's Books, Rutgers University Art Gallery, 1974.

M. E. Ward and D. A. Marquardt, *Illustrators of Books for Young People*, Scarecrow, 1975.

Children's Literature Review, Volume 1, 1976.

Authors in the News, Volume 1, Gale, 1976.

L. Kingman and others, compilers, *Illustrators of Children's Books: 1967-1976*, Horn Book, 1978.

D. L. Kirkpatrick, *Twentieth-Century Children's Writers*, St. Martin's, 1978, 2nd edition, 1983.

Early Years, November, 1980.

Jim Roginski, compiler, *Newbery and Caldecott Medalist and Honor Book Winners*, Libraries Unlimited, 1982.

FILM

Jacqueline S. Weiss, ''Ezra Jack Keats'' (videocassette), Profiles in Literature, Temple University, 1970.

''Ezra Jack Keats,'' Weston Woods, 1971.

OBITUARIES

New York Times, May 7, 1983.

Publishers Weekly, May 20, 1983.

School Library Journal, August, 1983.

COLLECTIONS

De Grummond Collection at the University of Southern Mississippi.
Free Library of Philadelphia, Pennsylvania.
Gary Public Library, Gary, Indiana.
Gutman Library at Harvard University.
Iowa City Public Library, Iowa.
Kerlan Collection at the University of Minnesota.

He went into his house and put on his father's old hat to make himself feel more grown-up. He looked into the mirror to practice whistling. Still no whistle!

(From *Whistle for Willie* by Ezra Jack Keats. Illustrated by the author.)

Steven Kellogg with Angel Annie.

KELLOGG, Steven (Castle)　1941-

PERSONAL: Born October 26, 1941, in Norwalk, Conn.; son of Robert E. and Hilma Marie (Johnson) Kellogg; married Helen Hill, 1967; stepchildren: Pamela, Melanie, Kimberly, Laurie, Kevin, Colin. *Education:* Rhode Island School of Design, B.F.A., 1963; graduate study at American University. *Home:* Bennett's Bridge Rd., Sandy Hook, Conn. 06482. *Agent:* Sheldon Fogelman, 10 East 40th St., New York, N.Y. 10016.

CAREER: Author and illustrator of children's books; artist. American University, Washington, D.C., instructor in etching, 1966; has taught printmaking and painting.

AWARDS, HONORS: Matilda Who Told Lies and Was Burned to Death was chosen one of *New York Times* Best Illustrated Children's Books, 1970, *Can I Keep Him?*, 1971, and *There Was an Old Woman,* 1974; *Matilda Who Told Lies and Was Burned to Death* was chosen one of the American Institute of Graphic Arts Children's Books, 1970, and received the Art Books for Children citation from the Brooklyn Museum and the Brooklyn Public Library, 1973; *Can I Keep Him?* was chosen one of *School Library Journal*'s Best Books, 1971; *Can I Keep Him?* and *The Orchard Cat* were both included in the American Institute of Graphic Arts Book Show, 1971-72, *Pinkerton, Behave!*, 1980, and *A Rose for Pinkerton,* 1982; *Here Comes Tagalong* and *Can I Keep Him?* were each chosen one of Child Study Association of America's Children's Books of the Year, both 1971, *Come Here, Cat,* and *Abby,* both 1973, *The Mystery of the Missing Red Mitten,* 1974, *The Great Christmas Kidnapping Caper,* and *The Boy Who Was Followed Home,* both 1975, *The Most Delicious Camping Trip*

Ever, Much Bigger Than Martin, and *Gustav the Gourmet Giant,* 1976, *The Mysterious Tadpole,* 1977, *The Mystery of the Magic Green Ball,* 1978, *A Rose for Pinkerton,* 1981, *Tallyho, Pinkerton!,* 1982, *Paul Bunyan,* 1984, *How Much Is a Million,* and *Chicken Little,* both 1985, and *Best Friends,* 1986; Dutch Zilveren Griffel, 1974, for *Can I Keep Him?.*

The Mystery of the Missing Red Mitten was included in the Children's Book Showcase, 1975; *How the Witch Got Alf* was one of *New York Times* Outstanding Books of the Year, 1975; Christopher Award, 1976, for *How the Witch Got Alf;* Irma Simonton Black Award from Bank Street College of Education, 1978, for *The Mysterious Tadpole; The Mysterious Tadpole* was a Children's Choice of the International Reading Association, 1977, *Appelard and Liverwurst* and *There's an Elephant in the Garage,* both 1979, *The Day Jimmy's Boa Ate the Wash, Uproar on Hollercat Hill,* and *The Mystery of the Flying Orange Pumpkin,* all, 1980, *Ralph's Secret Weapon,* 1983, and *Jimmy's Boa Bounces Back,* 1984.

American Book Award Finalist, 1980, for *Pinkerton, Behave!;* Georgia Children's Picture Storybook Award from the University of Georgia College of Education, and Little Archer Award from the Department of Library Services at the University of Wisconsin-Oshkosh, both 1982, both for *Pinkerton, Behave!;* Parents' Choice Award for Literature from the Parents' Choice Foundation, 1982, for *Tallyho, Pinkerton!,* and 1986, for *Best Friends;* Michigan Young Reader's Award from the Michigan Council of Teachers of English, 1983, for *The Island of the Skog; Ralph's Secret Weapon* was selected one of New York Public Library's Children's Books, 1983; *Boston Globe-Horn Book* Award Illustration Honor Book, and selected one of American Library Association's Association for Library Service to Childrens' Notable Books, both 1985, both for *How Much Is a Million?; Iva Dunnit and the Big Wind* was exhibited at the Bologna International Children's Book Fair, 1985, *Pecos Bill,* 1987, and *Aster Aardvark's Alphabet Adventures,* 1988; David McCord Children's Literature Citation from the Framingham (Mass.) State College and the Nobscot Council of the International Reading Association, 1987, for ''Significant Contribution to Excellence in Books for Children''; Regina Medal from the Catholic Library Association, 1989.

WRITINGS:

JUVENILE; ALL SELF-ILLUSTRATED

The Wicked Kings of Bloon (Junior Literary Guild selection), Prentice-Hall, 1970.
Can I Keep Him? (Junior Literary Guild selection), Dial, 1971.
The Mystery Beast of Ostergeest, Dial, 1971.
The Orchard Cat, Dial, 1972.
Won't Somebody Play with Me?, Dial, 1972.
The Island of the Skog, Dial, 1973.
The Mystery of the Missing Red Mitten, Dial, 1974.
(Adapter) *There Was an Old Woman,* Parents Magazine Press, 1974.
Much Bigger Than Martin (Junior Literary Guild selection), Dial, 1976.
The Mysterious Tadpole (ALA Notable Book), Dial, 1977.
The Mystery of the Magic Green Ball (Junior Literary Guild selection), Dial, 1978.
Pinkerton, Behave! (Horn Book honor list; Junior Literary Guild selection), Dial, 1979.
The Mystery of the Flying Orange Pumpkin, Dial, 1980.
A Rose for Pinkerton (Junior Literary Guild selection), Dial, 1981.
The Mystery of the Stolen Blue Paint, Dial, 1982.
Tallyho, Pinkerton! (Junior Literary Guild selection), Dial, 1982.

(From *Pinkerton, Behave* by Steven Kellogg. Illustrated by the author.)

Ralph's Secret Weapon, Dial, 1983.

(Adapter) *Paul Bunyan: A Tall Tale* (Reading Rainbow selection), Morrow, 1984.

(Reteller) *Chicken Little,* Morrow, 1985.

Best Friends ("Reading Rainbow" selection), Dial, 1986.

(Adapter) *Pecos Bill,* Morrow, 1986.

Prehistoric Pinkerton, Dial, 1987.

Aster Aardvark's Alphabet Adventures ("Reading Rainbow" selection), Morrow, 1987.

Johnny Appleseed, Morrow, 1988.

ILLUSTRATOR

George Mendoza, *Gwot! Horribly Funny Hairticklers,* Harper, 1967.

James Copp, *Martha Matilda O'Toole,* Bradbury, 1969.

Eleanor B. Heady, *Brave Johnny O'Hare,* Parents Magazine Press, 1969.

Mary Rodgers, *The Rotten Book,* Harper, 1969.

Miriam Young, *Can't You Pretend?,* Putnam, 1970.

Hilaire Belloc, *Matilda Who Told Lies and Was Burned to Death,* Dial, 1970.

Ruth Loomis, *Mrs. Purdy's Children,* Dial, 1970.

Fred Rogers, *Mister Rogers' Songbook,* Random House, 1970.

Peggy Parish, *Granny and the Desperadoes,* Macmillan, 1970.

Anne Mallett, *Here Comes Tagalong,* Parents Magazine Press, 1971.

Jan Wahl, *Crabapple Night,* Holt, 1971.

Aileen Freidman, *The Castles of the Two Brothers,* Holt, 1972.

J. Wahl, *The Very Peculiar Tunnel,* Putnam, 1972.

Jeanette Franklin Caines, *Abby,* Harper, 1973.

Joan L. Nodset (pseudonym of Joan M. Lexau), *Come Here, Cat,* Harper, 1973.

Doris Herold Lund, *You Ought to See Herbert's House,* F. Watts, 1973.

Liesel Moak Skorpen, *Kisses and Fishes,* Harper, 1974.

Jean Van Leeuwen, *The Great Christmas Kidnaping Caper,* Dial, 1975.

Margaret Mahy, *The Boy Who Was Followed Home* (ALA Notable Book), F. Watts, 1975.

Cora Annett, *How the Witch Got Alf* (Junior Literary Guild selection), F. Watts, 1975.

Alice Bach, *The Smartest Bear and His Brother Oliver,* Harper, 1975.

H. Belloc, *Hilaire Belloc's "The Yak, the Python, the Frog"* (Junior Literary Guild selection), Parent Magazine Press, 1975.

Judith Choate, *Awful Alexander,* Doubleday, 1976.

For once, toward the close of day,
Matilda, growing tired of play,

And finding she was left alone,
Went tiptoe to the telephone

(From *Matilda Who Told Lies and Was Burned to Death* by Hilaire Belloc. Illustrated by Steven Kellogg.)

Lou Ann Bigge Gaeddert, *Gustav the Gourmet Giant,* Dial, 1976.
Edward Bangs, *Steven Kellogg's Yankee Doodle* (ALA Notable Book), Parents Magazine Press, 1976.
A. Bach, *The Most Delicious Camping Trip Ever,* Harper, 1976.
A. Bach, *Grouchy Uncle Otto,* Harper, 1977.
Carol Chapman, *Barney Bipple's Magic Dandelions* (Junior Literary Guild selection), Dutton, 1977, new edition, 1988.
A. Bach, *Millicent the Magnificent,* Harper, 1978.
Marilyn Singer, *The Pickle Plan,* Dutton, 1978.
Mercer Mayer, *Appelard and Liverwurst,* Four Winds, 1978.
Douglas F. Davis, *There's an Elephant in the Garage,* Dutton, 1979.
William Sleator, *Once, Said Darlene,* Dutton, 1979.
Susan Pearson, *Molly Moves Out,* Dial, 1979.
Julia Castiglia, *Jill the Pill,* Atheneum, 1979.
Jean Marzollo, *Uproar on Hollercat Hill,* Dial, 1980.
Trinka Hakes Noble, *The Day Jimmy's Boa Ate the Wash* (ALA Notable Book; Junior Literary Guild selection; "Reading Rainbow" selection), Dial, 1980.
Amy Ehrlich, *Leo, Zack and Emmie,* Dial, 1981.
M. Mayer, *Liverwurst Is Missing,* Four Winds, 1981.
Alan Benjamin, *A Change of Plans,* Four Winds, 1982.
Cathy Warren, *The Ten-Alarm Camp-Out* (Junior Literary Guild selection), Lothrop, 1983.
Jane Bayer, *A, My Name Is Alice* (Junior Literary Guild selection), Dial, 1984.
T. H. Noble, *Jimmy's Boa Bounces Back,* Dial, 1984.
David M. Schwartz, *How Much Is a Million?* (*Horn Book* honor list), Lothrop, 1985.
Carol Purdy, *Iva Dunnit and the Big Wind,* Dial, 1985.
A. Ehrlich, *Leo, Zack, and Emmie Together Again,* Dial, 1987.
T. H. Noble, *Jimmy's Boa and the Big Splash Birthday Bash,* Dial, 1989.
D. M. Schwartz, *If You Made a Million,* Lothrop, 1989.
Deborah Guarino, *Is Your Mama a Llama?,* Scholastic, 1989.

Contributor to periodicals, including *Family Circle,*

ADAPTATIONS:

"The Island of the Skog" (sound filmstrip), Weston Woods, 1976, (VHS and Beta videocassette), 1986.
"Yankee Doodle" (sound filmstrip), Weston Woods, 1976.
"The Mysterious Tadpole" (sound filmstrip; videocassette), Weston Woods, 1980.
"Pinkerton, Behave!" (sound filmstrip), Weston Woods, 1982.
"A Rose for Pinkerton" (sound filmstrip), Weston Woods, 1983.
"Tallyho, Pinkerton!" (sound filmstrip), Weston Woods, 1984.
"The Day Jimmy's Boa Ate the Wash" (cassette; filmstrip with cassette), Weston Woods, 1986.

WORK IN PROGRESS: Illustrations for Reeve Lindbergh's *The Day the Goose Got Loose,* for Dial; illustrations for Tom Paxton's *Englebert the Elephant,* for Morrow; illustrated retellings of the adventures of Mike Fink and of Casey Jones.

SIDELIGHTS: Born October 26, 1941, in Norwalk, Connecticut. "I grew up in a country town outside of New York City, where I spent hours every day walking in the woods. That's what I still like to do when I'm thinking about a story—go out walking with my Great Dane."[1]

"I have loved picture books ever since I was a child. The illustrations of Beatrix Potter and N. C. Wyeth were early favorites, and I always found any kind of animal story irresistible. I was an enthusiastic young artist as well, and I formulated pre-school plans to make drawing the center of my lifetime career.

"I used to dream up stories and illustrate them for my younger sisters, Patti and Martha. We called the activity 'Telling Stories on Paper.' I would sit between them with a stack of paper in my lap and a pencil in my hand, rattling off tales and scribbling illustrations to accompany them, and passing the pictures first to one of the girls and then to the other. I enormously enjoyed these story-telling sessions, and I usually persevered until my sisters were too restless to sit there any longer, or until they were buried under pieces of paper."[2]

"I'm an animal freak when it comes to illustrating. I think I drew my way through elementary school. And I always had projects I wanted to complete. One of those projects was to draw every animal and bird I could find in the encyclopedia, and then thumbtack the illustrations to my bedroom wall. I papered the wall almost completely, and I think to this day my parents will always remember that project. The walls were ruined by hundreds of thumbtack holes."[3]

"I had great hopes of becoming a naturalist-illustrator because I felt that the best of all possible worlds would be the combining of my love of drawing with my love of animals. . . .I dreamed of being invited to join a *National Geographic* expedition to draw animals in Africa!"[4]

"During the summers and after school when most kids were earning their spending money by mowing lawns and delivering newspapers, I worked in dog kennels. I used most of the money to buy art supplies and books. The artist materials I chose for my early pictures were charcoal pencils, crayons, watercolors, crow-quill pens, and India inks. The books I acquired for my own collection were tales of adventure and animal stories."

"My love of animals prompted me to do elaborate series of drawings with titles like: 'Every Known Breed of Dog,' or 'All the Great Cats of the World,' or 'The North American Birds of Prey.' I would use these pictures to wallpaper my room from floor to ceiling, so that I lived in a wonderful aviary-bestiary."[5]

"The majority of my school years were spent in Darien, Connecticut's public education system. I was fortunate to have had a number of teachers who encouraged my enthusiasm for drawing and writing. I was also lucky to have some wonderful friends, a number of whom are still friends today. Memories of various aspects of school and neighborhood relationships are an ongoing source of ideas for the books that I write and illustrate.

"Throughout junior and senior high school my determination to be an artist increased. When it was time for college I was fortunate to be accepted by Rhode Island School of Design [RISD], and to receive a full scholarship from Pitney Bowes Inc. which made my attendance possible. During my growing-up years I had become accustomed to being regarded as unique for my dedication to painting and drawing, so it was both exhilerating and somewhat overwhelming to begin college classes where I was surrounded by dozens and dozens of people with the same passion.

"I made some very special friends among them, and I learned an enormous amount in my classes. During those years I lived in the attic apartment of a spectacular wreck of an old Victorian house that had a beautiful, sweeping view of the city of Providence. It was the perfect spot for an art student! But the happiest thing that occurred during that period was the granting of a fellowship by the college that sent me to Italy for my senior year with two professors and a small group of fellow students.

It's *not* too windy and I'm *not* through painting! ■ (From *The Mystery of the Stolen Blue Paint* by Steven Kellogg. Illustrated by the author.)

"What a magical year that was! After an initial period at the school's Palazzo Cenci in Rome, each student was allowed to go to the city of his choice, and I selected Florence. I rented a tiny alcove above the bathroom in the Casa Guidi where the English poets Robert and Elizabeth Barrett Browning had once lived. My room was hardly big enough for a rodent, but I loved it! Every morning I studied the work of the Florentine Renaissance artists in the Uffizzi Museum. All I had to do was mention the name of one of those great artists and I was allowed to examine a portfolio of his original drawings for as long as I pleased! During the afternoons I made drawings of my own in the beautiful walled gardens and wooded hills around the city. I learned to speak Italian reasonably well, and the people I met were welcoming and generous. It was truly one of the happiest times of my life.

"I returned from Italy in time to graduate from RISD, and during the next few years I studied and, later, taught etching at American University in Washington. My etchings and acrylic paintings were exhibited at the Hinckley and Brohel Gallery. It was during that time that I began to write and illustrate children's books and to submit them to publishers. My first two stories were "The Orchard Rat" and "The True Skog," which were later published as *The Orchard Cat* and *The Island of the Skog.*

"Most of the books I've written and/or illustrated during my twenty-five years in this field have been dedicated to my wife, Helen, or to one of my six step-children, Pam, Melanie, Kim, Laurie, Kevin, or Colin. My kids are all grown up now, and the oldest three are married and have children of their own,

(From *The Orchard Cat* by Steven Kellogg. Illustrated by the author.)

so I have new names for the dedication pages of my books. My family has greatly enriched my life and my work, and I am very appreciative for all that we have shared.''

''The picture book is an art form that is designed specifically for children, but I feel that it can be appreciated and enjoyed by all ages. For centuries a distinguished tradition of illustrated books and manuscripts has existed, of which the picture book is a part. It is a synthesis of literature and the visual arts, and the relationship of the written word and the picture is its essence.

''An awareness of movement is extremely important in the conception of a picture book. My favorite illustrators delineate their characters so that animation is implied. The individual spreads are designed so that they crackle with graphic vitality. The characters seem to speak, cavort, and leap from the page

so energetically that their life and movement are totally convincing. The moving qualities of each picture are heightened by the placement of the turning pages within the unfolding narrative and by the conception of the book as a whole. It is here that one sees the relationship between the arts of picture book design and film-making, as both of them deal with the phenomenon of 'moving pictures.'

''No one will deny that language can be musical, and certainly visual images can suggest different forms of music by the feelings that they convey. The musical qualities of the pictures and the words can be orchestrated by the artist as he moves them across the pages of the book. Rhythms and harmonies can be established on some spreads, and atonal effects or dissonances can be introduced on others.

''There are limitless possibilities available to the artist who

The smallest is last. ■ (From *Much Bigger Than Martin* by Steven Kellogg. Illustrated by the author.)

sets up relationships and tensions between the illustrations and the text, allowing magical discoveries and subtle revelations to emerge in the areas between them. When this happens, there is an uncanny fusion between all the elements, and the dynamic new expression that is created introduces young readers to the world of art."[2]

Kellogg's studio is in his home, an old wooden farmhouse in Sandy Hook, Connecticut. "I have my own special place where I work. Upstairs in my house two little rooms were expanded into one larger room that was joined to an adjacent attic, and the result was a spacious and skylit studio that is perfectly suited to my requirements....If I get an idea while walking in the woods around my house, I go up there and start writing about it. The dog isn't allowed up there, the cats are not al-

lowed up there—so there are no distractions. It's very quiet. It overlooks the waterfall and it's a very peaceful place to work.

"I just try to let my mind drift and then, as the story starts to suggest a direction, I write and draw in response to that. I work for a few hours in the morning, usually almost all afternoon, and then sometimes, if a story is really going strongly and the illustrations are going very strongly, I work way into the night until very late.

"The special thing about the picture book is that it's a combination of both words and pictures, and the two of them work together to tell the story. I write with the illustration and with the words as well, and try to make the two of them dance together to tell the story. So they're both equally important to me when I'm putting one of my books together.

"I usually have just a small piece of an idea, or a little thought, or a little picture in my mind, and then I put that on the paper and try to let it grow in whatever way it wants to grow, to start to move. If something starts to happen, then I try to follow it and tune into the story. Sometimes I'll get an idea that seems to be an excellent ending, or a character that suggests the story. Often, it's a feeling that I want to share.

"One of the first books I wrote and illustrated, called *Can I Keep Him?*, has a character who's a little bit autobiographical. When I was a little boy I loved animals and had a great desire to have a pet. My parents weren't particularly fond of animals and didn't feel a need to have one in the house. I used to bring home stray animals and I'd even adopt the animals that were owned by my neighbours and had perfectly good homes. I remember that feeling—that yearning for a pet or something that I could love and share my home and life with. And that feeling became the book *Can I Keep Him?*

"My characters come from inside me, usually. They also come from fragments of things and people, and experiences that I've had. I just use lots of different pieces of things that seem right and put them all together to create a character.

"Some of the characters are lifted directly from life. Pinkerton was like that. I got Pinkerton as a puppy. . . , and he was a shock! He was wonderful, but he was so stubborn and perverse and crazy and impossible to train. Yet, somehow he was so innocent in the middle of all his destructive qualities that he was totally lovable and irresistible. I was so struck by him that I started. . .writing the Pinkerton books.

"The children in my books mostly come from the child within me. Also, I grew up in a neighbourhood with lots of children. It was like a huge family that was a street long. So the faces and the personalities of the children in my books are drawn from these memories.

"I always take notice of people around me to use in my stories. I feel like I'm always doing my homework. If I'm talking to children I'm always watching their expressions, the way they sit, their movements, and the way they mix with each other as they come into a room. I watch adults as well—teachers, librarians and adult friends. I'm constantly recording in my mind what I see, and then I use little pieces of that (if they fit) in my illustrations or a piece of writing.

"I don't think I could create a character I didn't really like. I would probably be bored and offended by it. But I think that villains can be lovable and exciting, and can make the story move more quickly. Dr. Kibble, for example, in the Pinkerton books, is so stuffy and bossy and awful, and yet I'm very fond of her.

"As I work on the story and illustrations, I sometimes become so obsessed with a certain part of the story that I'll work and work on that part. Usually it's a beginning or an ending that I work over and over.

"However, I always try to keep a picture of the whole book going as I work. Often at first the pictures might be very weak, while the text is strong. So I have to bring up the pictures so that the two become locked together in a complete kind of way. It's very important that the text doesn't crowd the pictures and try to do things that the pictures can do better. The words can do something very well, the pictures can do some-

thing very well, and together they can tell the story brilliantly if I can let each speak in its own particular way.

"Sometimes the story grows as if to a plan. As I'm working along, if I think of something a little further down the road that I think would be good, then I'll jump ahead and write that down so that when I come to the point when I think that it would work the best, then it's still there waiting for me.

"When I work on the illustrations, I work on a piece of paper which is the same size as the book page. I want the illustration to fit snugly and rightly on the page. I want to feel exactly what way the page is going to feel.

"My preliminary sketches are deliberately unformed, with no carefully drawn expressions or movements, because I want to save a real sense of discovery for the original illustration that I draw after my first draft. This is the one which will appear in the finished book, and hopefully it will appear fresh and alive.

"When I'm going to do the finished illustration, I work from my preliminary sketches. They tell me where I've decided to sit the illustrations in the story, but they leave me enough room to develop the illustration as I draw. That, in turn, can develop the story further, and so I keep working until I decide that it doesn't need shape any more—it fits right into place.

"The amount of time this takes can be very different. Some stories will come together in a couple of months. Some I've worked on for many years.

"I always have problems with each book as I'm writing it, and I think that this is healthy. It forces me to work harder, to think harder—to probe more deeply into my thoughts or my feelings or my experiences, or wherever the story is coming from, and find the real truth that I think is right for that book. If I try to create the book too quickly or too easily, I don't think that the book really has a chance to reflect my best efforts.

"I can tell that the book isn't working when the story or the pictures lose pace. The story starts to become heavy, and the words and pictures come more and more slowly. I can't think of the words, or the words and pictures don't tell the events and the feelings the way that I want the reader to see them.

"If that happens, and I can't work my way through it on the spot, then I stop and do something else. Usually I do something totally away from writing a book. It means it's time to get some exercise—to go outside, to go in the woods, or walk down the street.

"Often no one else can help me. It just takes time and effort. One story which I wrote had problems with the ending. I worked on it, put it away, and then worked on it some more, and kept doing this over nearly fifteen years. Suddenly it just came together last winter. Either I'd changed and grown enough, or I was just working in the right time and place, but I was able to write and draw my way through all the problems and the whole story came together.

"It also takes time and effort to discover when the writing and illustrations are finished. I think that when I was first writing books, I had to overwrite and overdraw in order to learn when I'd pushed too far. Gradually I've developed a certain instinct and can let the work speak to me and say: 'You've finished. Don't touch me again. I'm just right.'

When Alphonse became too big for his jar, Louis moved him to the sink. ■ (From *The Mysterious Tadpole* by Steven Kellogg. Illustrated by the author.)

"I constantly rewrite my books. This means that I change and correct what I've written, usually to try and make the story more concise, and to make the story and pictures work more smoothly together. I rewrite so that the text and the pictures tell their part of the story in their own way. I want the text and the pictures to dance in response to each other, because this is what makes the picture book special. It's something for the eye and something for the ear.

"Sometimes a good editor can be very helpful, especially if I'm stuck and can't go on writing. It needs to be someone who cares about the story, and cares about the way it turns out; who will read it and give me some sense of direction, so that I can work myself around whatever is the problem.

"The book that I'm working on can also become so important to me, and so much a part of me, that I forget about how other people are going to see the work, and an editor can help me there. I may not like to hear that the writing is bogged down and that it isn't communicating well, but I have to be able to trust that criticism from the editor and go back and work on the writing again.

"I also need to be my own editor, my own critic, my own judge of how the book is going.

"I love writing and drawing picture books. I love sharing the stories and characters. I feel compelled to do it. If I weren't doing it for my living, I'd be doing it in my spare time, and on the side, and on the sly! I consider myself very fortunate that my job is doing something that I absolutely love."[6]

Kellogg has retold the stories of Paul Bunyan, Pecos Bill, Johnny Appleseed, and Casey Jones. "I guess I like these characters because they are larger than life. To me, Paul Bunyan embodies the sense of adventure that created this country. And there's something very mystical and exciting about Babe, that great, benevolent blue ox—he's a very dream-like animal. In America we don't have the mythology that older cultures have, but Paul Bunyan is a real American folk hero."

He also writes from his personal experiences. In *Much Bigger Than Martin,* for instance, Kellogg describes the indignities suffered by his hero Henry at the hands of his older brother Martin. "When I was Henry's age I had many Martins in my family, my neighborhood, and my classes at school. Occasionally new ones still pop up and try to organize my adult life! But in my childhood, Martin-like behavior on the part of siblings, friends, and enemies became less of a problem as I realized that every Martin has a Martin in his own life who towers formidably over him, and it became clear to me that a person is only as insignificant as he feels.

"I thought it would be fun to deal with the situation in a picture book. I chose Henry to be the plucky hero who needs only to climb upon his stilts in order to defuse Martin's domineering schemes. And then there can be many days of happy comradeship, like the one when Martin has mounted the lower basketball hoop especially for Henry."[7]

Other ideas spring from the numerous dogs and cats raised in the Kellogg household, "The heroine of the sequel, *A Rose for Pinkerton,* is our senior cat, Secondhand Rose, an independent old grouch who was born a wild thing in the Catskill Mountains, and who has devoted her long life to harassing everyone in the world, including Pinkerton."[2]

Asked if he had a favorite book of those he has created, Kellogg commented: "That's like asking if you have a favorite child. Each child is different, each child has characteristics and traits that are unique. I feel that way about my books. But still, I think perhaps a book I illustrated a long time ago, *The Boy Who Was Followed Home* by Margaret Mahy, may be my favorite.

"I want my books to be enjoyable and emotionally rewarding. That's the primary role of picture books for children. I use humor a lot, too, because humor is one of the great elements of life. It's important to share humor with children, to help develop a sense of humor in each child.

"Hopefully, I bring to children a sense of fun, a sense of literature. Pictures can create a whole world, you can go into the picture and examine all objects, study expressions, touch the architecture. You can lose yourself in an illustration and at the same time, in many ways find yourself."[3]

"I'll never forget how important my first picture books were to me as a child—how I loved them, how many new ideas they gave me, and how they introduced me to the whole idea of art.

"So it makes me very happy to think that maybe my books are loved just as much by children today."[1]

The Castles of the Two Brothers was a preliminary selection for the Caldecott Medal, 1973, and *Steven Kellogg's Yankee Doodle* was suggested for the 1976 awards.

FOOTNOTE SOURCES

[1]"How a Picture Book Is Made" (filmstrip), Weston Woods, 1976. Amended by S. Kellogg.
[2]"Steven Kellogg," Publicity of Dial Books for Young Readers, n.d.
[3]"Steven Kellogg. . .Teachers' Co-conspirator," *Early Years,* January, 1986.
[4]"Steven Kellogg," *Illustrators of Children's Books: 1967-1976,* edited by Lee Kingman and others, Horn Book, 1978.
[5]*Junior Literary Guild,* September, 1979.
[6]Pamela Lloyd, *How Writers Write,* Methuen (Australia), 1987. Amended by S. Kellogg.
[7]*Junior Literary Guild,* March, 1976.

FOR MORE INFORMATION SEE:

Martha E. Ward and Dorothy A. Marquardt, *Illustrators of Books for Young People,* Scarecrow, 1975.
Doris de Montreville and Elizabeth D. Crawford, editors, *Fourth Book of Junior Authors and Illustrators,* H. W. Wilson, 1978.
Joel C. Thompson, "Kellogg's Great Dane Listens to the Beat of a Different Drummer," *Bridgeport Sunday Post* (Conn.), December 2, 1979 (p. B1).
Times Literary Supplement, July 18, 1980.
Deborah Mesce, "Childhood Memories Inspire State Author," *Hartford Courant* (Conn.), November 7, 1982.
Ursula Vils, "Teachers, Libraries and Pinkerton's Pop," *Los Angeles Times,* December 8, 1982.

KENNEDY, Brendan 1970-

PERSONAL: Born July 3, 1970, in Albany, N.Y.; son of William Joseph (a writer) and Dana (a business manager; maiden name, Sosa) Kennedy. *Education:* Trinity College, student.

WILLIAM and BRENDAN KENNEDY

Home: R.D. 3, Box 508, Averill Park, N.Y. 12018. *Agent:* Liz Darhansoff, 1220 Park Ave., New York, N.Y. 10128.

CAREER: Writer; student.

WRITINGS:

(With father, William Kennedy) *Charlie Malarkey and the Belly-Button Machine* (juvenile; illustrated by Glen Baxter), Atlantic Monthly Press, 1986.

WORK IN PROGRESS: A book entitled *Charlie Malarkey and the Bubblegum Trees.*

SIDELIGHTS: "My father and I wrote our book when I was five years old. It was rejected many times before Atlantic Monthly Press accepted it. It has now been published in Spain and will be published in England, Brazil, and elsewhere."

Brendan and William Kennedy's *Charlie Malarkey and the Belly-Button Machine* is a story about a boy who loses his belly-button and carries out a search for it. In a *Los Angeles Times Book Review* Kristiana Gregory described the story as "pure fun in a malarkey sort of way." *New York Times Book Review* critic Alice Miller Bregman commented on the father and son team: "Their effort is to be applauded: the writing is stylish, and it's clear testimony to the great affection that exists between them." Kennedy's father is the Pulitzer Prize-winning author of *Ironweed.*

FOR MORE INFORMATION SEE:

Los Angeles Times Book Review, October 26, 1986.
New York Times Book Review, November 2, 1986.

KENNEDY, William 1928-

PERSONAL: Born January 16, 1928, in Albany, N.Y.; son of William J. (a deputy sheriff) and Mary (a secretary; maiden name, McDonald) Kennedy; married Ana Daisy (Dana) Segarra (a former actress, singer, and dancer), January 31, 1957; children: Dana, Katherine, Brendan. *Education:* Siena College, B.A., 1949. *Agent:* Liz Darhansoff, 1220 Park Ave., New York, N.Y. 10028. *Office:* New York State Writers Institute, State University of New York at Albany, 1400 Washington Ave., Albany, N.Y. 12222.

CAREER: Post Star, Glen Falls, N.Y., assistant sports editor and columnist, 1949-50; *Times-Union,* Albany, N.Y., reporter, 1952-56, feature writer, 1963-70, film critic, 1968-70; *Puerto Rico World Journal,* San Juan, Puerto Rico, assistant managing editor and columnist, 1956; *Miami Herald,* Miami, Fla., reporter, 1957; correspondent for Time-Life in Puerto Rico, and reporter for *Dorvillier* (business newsletter) and Knight Newspapers, 1957-59; *San Juan Star,* San Juan, founding managing editor, 1959-61; writer, 1961—; book editor of *Look* magazine, 1971; State University of New York at Albany, lecturer, 1974-82, professor of English, 1983—.

Writer's Institute at Albany, founder, 1983, director, 1984—. Visiting professor of English, Cornell University, 1982-83. Co-founder, Cinema 750 (film society), Rensselaer, N.Y., 1968-70; organizing moderator for series of forums on the humanities, sponsored by National Endowment for the Humanities, New York State Library, and Albany Public Library. Panelist, New York State Council on the Arts, 1980-83. *Military service:* U.S. Army, 1950-52; served as sports editor and columnist for Army newspapers; became sergeant. *Member:* Writers Guild of America, P.E.N.

AWARDS, HONORS: Award for reporting from the Puerto Rican Civic Association (Miami, Fla.), 1957; Page One Award from the Newspaper Guild, 1965, for reporting; *Times-Union* won the New York State Publishers Award for Community Service, 1965, on the basis of several of Kennedy's articles on Albany's slums; NAACP Award, 1965, for reporting; Writer of the Year Award from the Friends of the Albany Public Library, 1975; D.H.L., Russell Sage College, 1980; National Endowment for the Arts fellowship, 1981; MacArthur Foundation fellowship, 1983; National Book Critics Circle Award for fiction, and one of *New York Times* Thirteen Best Books, both 1983, and received the Pulitzer Prize for fiction, 1984, all for *Ironweed;* New York State Governor's Arts Award, 1984; D.Litt., Siena College, 1984, and College of St. Rose, 1985; honored by the citizens of Albany and the State University of New York at Albany with a "William Kennedy's Albany" Celebration, September 6-9, 1984; Doctor of Arts and Humane Letters, Rensselaer Polytechnic Institute, 1987.

WRITINGS:

JUVENILE

(With son, Brendan Kennedy) *Charlie Malarkey and the Belly-Button Machine* (illustrated by Glen Baxter), Atlantic Monthly, 1986.

NOVELS

The Ink Truck, Dial, 1969, reissued, Viking, 1984.
Legs, Coward, 1975.
Billy Phelan's Greatest Game, Viking, 1978.
Ironweed, Viking, 1983.
Quinn's Book, Viking, 1988.

OTHER

(Contributor) *Gabriel Garcia Marquez* (criticism), Taurus Ediciones, 1982.
O Albany! An Urban Tapestry (nonfiction), Viking, 1983.

Also co-author with Francis Ford Coppola of screenplay "The Cotton Club," 1984; author of screenplay adaptation of "Ironweed," 1987, of unpublished novel *The Angels and the Sparrows,* and of monographs and brochures for New York State Department of Education, New York State University System, New York Governor's Conference on Libraries, Empire State College, Schenectady Museum, and New York State Library.

Contributor of short fiction to journals, including *San Juan Review, Epoch,* and *Harper's;* contributor of articles, interviews, and reviews to periodicals, including *New York Times Magazine, National Observer, New York Times Book Review, Washington Post Book World, New Republic,* and *Look.*

ADAPTATIONS:

"The Ink Truck" (cassette; includes *Legs, Billy Phelan's Greatest Game,* and *Ironweed*), American Audio Prose, 1984.
"Ironweed" (cassette), Books on Tape, 1986, (film), starring Jack Nicholson and Meryl Streep, Taft Barish, 1987.

WILLIAM KENNEDY

"Legs" (cassette), Books on Tape, 1986.
"Billy Phelan's Greatest Game" (cassette), Books on Tape, 1986.

WORK IN PROGRESS: A novel set in the mid-twentieth century in Albany.

SIDELIGHTS: **January 16, 1928.** Kennedy was born in Albany, New York. "I grew up in a very isolated pocket of Albany called the North End. . . .My father was involved in politics and wound up as deputy sheriff. He had been a gambler in his early life, a bad barber, worked in a foundry, sold pies. Oh, and he was an accountant. My mother worked all her life as a secretary. I'm just an only child—the only child in practically the whole family. It was that phenomenon that made me want to write my first novel—what happened to this family, why are there no kids."[1]

"[We were] Catholic working-class, Irish on all sides. We weren't poor but we never had much money. . . .I had a wonderful relationship with my father."[2]

"One of the great things about your life is [that] relationship. . .what else shapes you more than that? Even today, I keep discovering elements of my father in myself that I would not have suspected ever. I keep hearing phrases, representing values that were his, which he never really tried to impose on me but did in the same way that the church and the Democratic Party and the North End of Albany did—that matrix."[1]

As a child, Kennedy's idols were hustlers and baseball players. He hung out in pool halls, bowling alleys and was an avid movie goer. His father took him around to political clubs and gaming rooms. "Everyone was involved in some kind of gambling, including me when I was a kid. As soon as you were old enough to go to a candy store by yourself, you could play the punchboard. If you had an extra penny, you took a chance and you won something—a nickel, a dime, a quarter. Baseball pools were one of the biggest enterprises; I ran a football pool when I was in college. It was an accepted part of life. It was normal."[3]

An altar boy, he attended the Christian Brothers Academy in Albany and in the sixth grade began to play with a toy printing press. "I went on to think of a newspaper career without much knowledge of what it would involve—it was a kind of fantasy future that kids grow up with. My high school experiences were minimal, but they confirmed the direction I was taking because I was thinking about writing; I was valuing things like Poe's stories and *Our Town* as a sophomore, and also reading Dashiell Hammett and Raymond Chandler and Damon Runyon, understanding that Runyon was an incomparably comic writer. I was also finding the journalists in the daily paper to

be generally valuable citizens. That's where I decided I wanted to go, and I did go into journalism as a serious sideline as soon as I entered Siena College, a small school outside Albany, run by Franciscans. I didn't think much about literature then because it seemed beyond possibility, enormously desirable (in grammar school I used to collect literary classics in comic book form) but somebody else's province."[2] Kennedy became the editor of the Siena College newspaper.

Began writing fiction during his last two college years. "I didn't believe I would ever write serious fiction and be successful at it. I figured the best I'd ever wind up being was some kind of an O. Henry or a Runyon or a Mark Twain at his most casual."[4] With his bachelor's degree in English, Kennedy secured a job as a sportswriter for the Glens Falls, N.Y. *Post-Star.*

He was drafted into the army with the start of the Korean War. "Instead of being sent to Korea, where we thought we were

(Jacket illustration by Glen Baxter from *Charlie Malarkey and the Belly-Button Machine* by William and Brendan Kennedy.)

(From the movie "Ironweed," starring Meryl Streep and Jack Nicholson for which both received Academy Award nominations. Released by Tri-Star Pictures, Inc., 1987.)

heading, we went to Europe. We were the first division (the Fourth Infantry Division, which was Hemingway's, by the way) to be sent back to Europe after World War II. I had gotten enough taste of cosmopolitan life in Europe to believe that Albany was a backwater and would stifle me forever.

"When I came out of the army I knew I'd had enough sportswriting, even though I'd had a great time with it, and I went to work for the Albany *Times-Union* as a general assignment reporter. That meant I could write about anything, interview anybody—writers, entertainers, politicians, whatever. I covered the police beat early on and I loved it. The fact that so many dimensions of the world were opening up for me kept me here a while.

"I'd work on short stories on my days off, give all afternoon to it, and likewise in the late hours in the city room, when no news was breaking. I produced maybe thirty stories, none of which was ever taken for publication, but which all contributed to both my commitment and my apprenticeship in the use of language. The journalistic experience was a marvelous matrix, but a confusing one.

"But then I began to feel I was wasting my time in Albany, because I was working under some very limited editors."[2] "I felt I had probably outgrown Albany, the way you outgrow childhood."[5]

In **1956** Kennedy moved to Puerto Rico where he got a chance to help start the *Puerto Rico World Journal*. "I wound up being assistant managing editor in a matter of a few months. . . .That work was fun and it was good journalism, but the paper went under because of problems with distribution and advertising. Eventually I met my wife, Dana, married her within a month, went to Miami for about a year [worked at

the *Miami Herald*], and then moved back to Puerto Rico, where we lived very happily for another six years. In 1959 I wound up being a founder with [others] of another newspaper, the *San Juan Star*. It evolved into significant journalism, vastly different from the kind of thing that had driven me out of Albany."[2]

"[As a journalist] you were everything, everyplace. I loved it. But then the shine wore off. I didn't aspire to any higher job and I knew I wanted to be a writer."[1]

"I started to write about this expatriate life I had chosen for myself. Puerto Rico was certainly exotic enough as a setting. It was a Spanish-language community, full of both hostility and reverence for the United States, with all sorts of politics and beach bums to write about. But while I loved Puerto Rico, I found that I really didn't give a damn about it as a basis for my fiction because I wasn't Puerto Rican. I couldn't identify with the Puerto Rican mind because I couldn't read the language well enough. I felt I'd always be a second-class citizen in Puerto Rico because of the language barrier, that I could never possess the literature, could never possess the intellectual world of the scholars, or the political theorists. I'd written some short stories set in Puerto Rico with the beginnings of political contexts, but they were shallow, and I realized it was because I didn't know very much about the place. Finally I. . .started to write about Albany. And the transition was extraordinary. I found myself ranging through sixty years of the history of a family, the Phelan family—Francis Phelan was part of that first novel I began down there. I found that by focusing on these people and locations something happened to my imagination that freed me to invent very readily. With Puerto Rico I always felt I was a tourist. But I could understand the psychology of a wino in Albany, or a spinster, or a

Photograph by Margaret Bourke-White for Kennedy's Pulitzer Prize winner.

clandestinely married woman. I didn't know *why* I understood them, but I did. It became magical.''²

"It proved to me I really didn't need to go off to these exotic places. I felt like I didn't have to go anywhere else. It was really a young writer's education in discovering his own turf.''⁵ Kennedy decided to enroll in a writing workshop taught by Saul Bellow at the University of Puerto Rico. "He confirmed my belief that I had something to say. He was very, very encouraging, and helped me get an agent.''⁶

"Bellow talked about character. I stewed on that for years. He would never tell me precisely what that meant. He said: 'Talent goes a certain distance; the rest of the writer's life has to be carried forward by character.' For me, character has come to mean pursuit of the art—refusal to yield to failure.''⁷

Finished his first novel *The Angels and the Sparrows*. "It was once again one of those downbeat books that publishers say they can't use, but a success of a high order for me—that I could write a serious novel.''¹

"It went around to maybe twenty publishers and nobody took it on, but nevertheless that was when I decided I was a real writer. Oh, I wasn't a *real* writer—you're never a real writer until you publish something, right? 'Writer' is a sacred word. You can't use it until somebody consecrates you by putting you in print. But I was aspiring to something serious, and there were enough people taking me seriously that I felt confirmed that I had written something pretty good.''²

1963. Returned to Albany to care for his father. "My mother had died, he was alone, and he was really a stubborn Irishman, wouldn't pay attention to anybody. Well, we got him straight and then I decided I'd have to come back to keep him straight for a while. I didn't think I'd stay long but I was interested in my family's history, my neighborhood's history. And by inchworm accumulation of imaginative progress it became interesting to me.''¹

"Even before we moved back to Albany in 1963 I started taping conversations with my family. . . .I began to see patterns and structures among families and political relationships and the social dimensions in the gambling world and nighttown and the world of music. I was also coming to know the newspaper world, hanging out with reporters and editors who knew the old days of Albany and understood what it was like to cover all those gangsters in the Prohibition era when Albany was a wide-open city—and Albany *was* wide open for years. This all fertilized my imagination to the point where there was no dimensions of Albany I didn't want to understand.''²

Kennedy took a part-time job as a feature writer for the Albany *Times-Union*. "Send me anywhere. I'd do aything for $100. I refused to take a full-time job. I knew I'd never write fiction again.''¹

"I went for maybe six or seven years writing fiction the way a journalist would write it, transcending that now and again but still believing my fiction would be more or less a transcription of life. . .experience has loomed excessively large for writers of my generation, so much so that if you lacked it, your fiction seemed watery. But that's the journalistic trap of this age; for the writer needs to know that, essential as it may be, experience is only where fiction begins. What sets a good fiction writer apart from the journalistic guppies is that he, or she, understands that the truth comes up from below, that it develops from the perception of the significance of experience, and not from the experience itself.''²

1965. Nominated for a Pulitzer Prize for a series of articles he had written for the *Times-Union* on the city's slums.

1969. A strike at the newspaper inspired Kennedy's first published novel *The Ink Truck*. The book received warm reviews, but did not sell well. It is a surreal story of a man's bizarre leadership during a prolonged newspaper strike. "*The Ink Truck* is an effort to deny spiritual death access to the work area. It is this in theme and in fact. It is first a manic story, second a set of imposed and yet undiscovered meanings. It is, perhaps, a metaphor for commitment, a survival handbook for failures, a study in resistance, a comedy of metaphysical lust, a report on the willful pursuit of disaster. It is an effort to tell, in original style, a story that rides on a cushion of fetid and slightly flabby air, approximately six inches off the ground at all times. It is my hope that it will stand as an analgesic inspiration to all weird men of good will and rotten luck everywhere.''⁸

"*The Ink Truck*. . .grows out of the late 1960s and. . .absorbs a lot of the radical atmosphere of the time: the hippie movement, the drug movement, the sexual revolution, the crazy politics, all the death and assassination that was going on with Jack, and Bobby, and Martin Luther King, and so on. My book doesn't reflect these things directly, but they all helped me make the book what it is. I think its rebellion is not only in the wild style of writing and storytelling, but in the resistance to the social determinism that the naturalistic writers of the 1930s found so valuable. It seems to me vastly less important to castigate a society, which is easy, than it does to

(Jacket art: View of Albany, New York from Greenbush, 1851. From *Quinn's Book* by William Kennedy.)

demonstrate how the individual can survive its evils and perils, which is not easy.

"I was trying to talk about the world the way that book does—through surrealism, expressionism. . . .I was trying to leap out of realism because I felt the whole world of Dos Passos and O'Hara, a world I had once revered, was now dead for me. I knew I couldn't do that any longer, couldn't write another realistic line. I was trying to make sense of a new age in which, for me, Kafka was far more of a prophet than anybody with realistic politics."[2]

"I don't think you can talk about the life of the soul if you don't talk about the surrealistic, metaphysical elements. We think, we live, and we also dream and dreams are very logical and surrealistic and that's why I am a great lover of Luis Bunuel and Fellini. . . .They transcend realism and realism goes just so far and no further. . . .I want my people to go on. I want them to have that mystical element that I know exists in everybody's life. . . ."[9]

Although the mystical is inherent in Kennedy's work, and his roots are in Catholicism, he is "absolutely not interested in either Oriental philosophy or the formalities of the Catholic church. . . .I believe in the mystical relationship that exists among things. It has surfaced so many times in my life as to confirm my belief that it's worth writing about, thinking about, trying to figure it out. I don't believe in practicing mysticism as a religion, but I do know there are certain affinities and transferences of ideas and confluences of thoughts and inter-actions that are inexplicable in the ways we usually think or function. In *Ironweed* I'm interested in religion only insofar as I want to present anything you can imagine, including athe-ism and Catholicism, that would be on a man's mind in ex-treme situations where he's confronting the deepest part of his

own life. And that seems to me to be the *only* thing worth writing about. All the rest is so much gratuitous sociology or out-of-date philosophy or theology."[2]

1970. Left his part-time job at the *Times-Union* to devote all of his time to writing. "The feeling of looking into some-body's mind and soul by way of thcsc wild abstractions ap-pealled to me far more than did any kind of conventional reporting, and I think it may have come, in part, from the fact that I had discovered that I could go so far and no farther in journalism; and that was why I quit to write fiction. From then on it was a matter of deciding how to discover what was really going on inside my mind, inside your mind, and I wasn't ever able to go back to that mundane world of realism. . . .

"I didn't need that much money. I didn't aspire to Bestsell-erdom. I didn't aspire to big movie money or anything like that. I hoped for it. All I wanted to do was have a way of life and be able to write some fiction. And it was very, very dif-ficult and it got increasingly more difficult. The better I got the more difficult it became."[9]

"[In order to write] I need the sense of a specific world that is definable, like the Jazz Age, or the Depression, so that if I want to set a book in that time I know the thrust a character will have. I want to understand how an era affects the life of Albany, not in a sociological way—I couldn't give a damn less about that for fiction—but what was happening to people's emotional lives."[2]

Two new elements crept into his writing. "One was the dis-covery of realism and the other was the discovery of place. . . .I think if you leave out place you leave out one of the principal ingredients of fiction. I think we are what we are because of the place to some degree. We interact with it. We interact with

(From the movie "The Cotton Club," starring Richard Gere and Diane Lane. Produced by Orion Pictures, 1984.)

its mores, and this place is not like the next place. . .and you behave differently therefore. . . ."[9]

1975. *Legs,* a story about the infamous gangster, Jack "Legs" Diamond, who lived in Albany during the 20s and early 30s, was published. It took Kennedy nearly six years and eight drafts to complete it. "[After *The Ink Truck*]. . .I began to think of other dimensions of fiction and that I should write a political novel. I started to write about Dan O'Connell, the old Irish patriarch here, the boss of bosses here. . .and then I discovered Legs Diamond. . .Diamond just took over."[9]

"There were several reasons why I wanted to move into a new kind of statement, a new form, for my next book. In *The Ink Truck* I had been able to say what I wanted to say in a non-traditional way, yet still be true to the impetus for personal achievement in the world, and for political resistance. But I felt I couldn't go on writing this hyperbolic comedy which is always six inches off the ground. I needed to be grounded in reality, yet I didn't want to write a realistic novel. *Legs* is a consequence of that. . . .

"When I first started *Legs* I didn't give a damn about the real Jack Diamond because I was inventing everything. The first start was a free-floating ahistorical version in which Legs Diamond was going to be a mythical, generalized gangster whose name was just a designation that people would recognize. . . ."[2]

The first version didn't work, however, but "that notion of myth remained with me and became central to the final version of the book: the idea of how myth is created, an act which becomes a public fascination, and then is blown out of all proportion, so that the doer is given legendary status; then the legend is passed on, and becomes one of the defining myths of the age. That notion of myth is what I began with, and because of that I didn't give a damn about facts when I started the book. But the more I went into the book, the more respect I had for facts.

"I suppose I always had the sense of myself as a journalist looking over my shoulder at myself as a novelist, telling myself that you can't *do* this to a historical character. You don't abuse his history for the sake of myth, no matter how good your intentions are. I began to feel that it was very important not to be cavalier about his words and his life, so I wasn't. I then began to accumulate information so I could write that same mythic story, only this time using his particular facts as accurately as possible to build the myth. Once caught up in that desire, I began a period of intensive biographical research, and the farther I went, the more distance there was to go— new information presenting itself to me every day: more books, more magazines and newspapers, more people who knew Legs, or thought they did. And it became an endless process. It also became obsessive and then counterproductive, because I was a novelist; I wasn't supposed to be interested in writing history. But I became so fascinated with the history of the man and the age that I couldn't stop. I became a history junkie. . . .I was having such a great time in the library that I was turning into a mole. I hoarded my notes, was happy only under a microfilm machine.

"The reason my research finally stopped was that I knew it could go on forever. History had become very important to me because I had seen so many renderings of gangsters in so many different contexts—theater, magazines, movies, books, newspapers—that I felt were all wrong. I was convinced that my mission in *Legs* was to write a meticulously accurate historical gangster novel. Then I found out that that mission was not possible. There is no such animal. It could never be done because of the conflicting stories of who did what to whom, who paid for it, and who got killed because of it. I became aware that all this information was actually *preventing* me from writing the novel I wanted to write. . . .It's never the case that you ingest the information and then create a story *because* of the information. It's got to begin somewhere in your center—which is where Jack Diamond originally began in that first mythic version I wanted to write."[2]

1978. *Billy Phelan's Greatest Game* published. Based in part on an actual kidnapping, the book deals with Billy Phelan, a small-time gambler in the 30s, who became "caught up" in the kidnapping of the nephew of the city's political boss. "Basically, Billy Phelan is a political novel. It is all about the power of a few politicians to control everybody's life, right down into the lowly hustler on the street (Billy Phelan) who all he wants to do is play pool and cards and they can lock him out of every bar in town just by putting the word out. . .that despotism, that kind of life existed here and doesn't exist any more. . . ."[9]

"Billy didn't understand the way the world worked, even though he thought he did. *Billy Phelan* is about this curious misreading of his own extraordinary moral code that Billy has to deal with, come to grips with. Contrary to what those reviewers apparently thought, I had to reconstruct the city that was in order to show how Billy was enlightened by its singular power."[2] "The city of Albany of the 1930s and 40s was as much a character in Billy's life as Billy himself was. . . ."[9]

"[The novel is also] all about games. Just about every form of game you can imagine is being played out in that book.

This book is an attempt to strike a balance as to Albany's legend. ■ (From *O Albany!* by William Kennedy.)

But that notion of play, the way people live life as a game, has always been valuable to me."[2]

The novel sold very poorly. "When *Billy* first come out, I was looking for a way to make money. I didn't think I'd ever make money on books."[1]

Kennedy tried his hand at movie writing, got an agent and sold a script (unproduced). Even though he has always been a diligent movie watcher, and at one time worked as a movie critic for the *Times-Union,* he gave up scriptwriting as a career. "[I] was so broke that I even applied to write speeches for an oil company. They didn't even bother to reply."[10]

1983. Published *Ironweed.* Set in Albany during the 30s, the novel centers on Francis Phelan, an ex-baseball player, who returns home after abandoning his family for the life of a bum. "I thought that it was my best book. I felt that I really knew what I was doing in structuring that book and it was the best language I could bring to bear on the story. I also felt that I was more able to penetrate deeply into Francis Phelan's soul than I was in any other work. . . .I mean I had not quite tried this before. The other books were experimental in other ways. . . ."[9]

"By the time I'd gotten to *Ironweed* my realism was still there, but something else was going on. I'd realized that I didn't want to loosen that hold on reality, didn't want to let the fiction hover six inches off the ground. I still wanted the craziness of *The Ink Truck* but I wanted the craziness to emerge at the level of a more grounded significance. What I wanted to do in *Ironweed* was to take *the reality* of a man and try to move into his *soul.* You might think of Francis Phelan as always being aware of where he is, yet also always aware of all his history. Deeper inside he's aware of the obligations and evasions that go with his existence, and the kinds of conflicts that conscience generates. Then deeper still is his center, and there isn't any way he can *ever* articulate what is in there, and he knows this. That's the center of his soul, the ineffable element of his being. That's what I was trying to suggest—that we're enormously complex beings who can never know everything about ourselves. I know that's true about me. The center of Francis is the place I'd like to go to forever. It seems to me the only thing really worth writing about: the absolute center of somebody. Of course, it's very hard to get there; also to find somebody who has a center worth reaching.

"*Ironweed* wasn't researched, exactly. I hung out with a few winos, and I've been in saloons and watched them. Bums seem to me to have more interesting lives than most businessmen. I did a series of articles on them in Albany during the early '60s and there was one articulate bum whom I got to like. But that bit of journalism was really just an extension of my imagination, since I had already created Francis and the whole Phelan family in that first book I wrote that was never published. Francis of *Ironweed* was not the same character who was in *The Angels and the Sparrows.* The first man wasn't a ballplayer, for example—but he was the basis of Francis."[2]

After a series of disagreements, Kennedy separated from his publisher, Viking Press, after it had bought and was ready to publish *Ironweed.* He sent it out to various other publishers and collected thirteen rejections in all. His other novels were by now out of print. "The line I heard most frequently was that publishers would rather take the risk on a first novelist than on a fourth novelist with a bleak track record. I hardly think this the received wisdom of the ages—to reward the apprentice at the expense of the journeyman."[11]

Saul Bellow intervened in Kennedy's behalf with a letter to Viking: "These Albany novels will be memorable, a distin-

Kennedy in front of the state capitol in Albany.

guished group of books. That the author of *Billy Phelan* should have a manuscript kicking around looking for a publisher is disgraceful.''[3]

Viking published *Ironweed,* along with *Legs* and *Billy Phelan's Greatest Game* as an "Albany cycle." ". . .The notion of a cycle of novels has been mine for more years than I can remember. I chose the word because what I propose to write is an uncertain number of interrelated novels.''[12]

The publication of all three books was a major success. "When *Ironweed* came out, the good response to the other books was as if they never had been published before.''[13]

"What a coup that turned out to be. I couldn't imagine the kind of response the whole thing got when it was looked at as a body of work. Almost everybody reviewed all three books. It was amazing.''[6]

Ironweed sold more than 100,000 copies in the first two years, to a smashing critical success. "I am as much awash in critical magnanimity as I was bathed two years ago in insolvent obscurity. The nature of this new status is extreme pleasure, but also part of it is residual bewilderment at the causes of the previous condition. I was once deeply resentful at the rejection of *Ironweed*. . .but of course I am slowly coming out of that.''[14]

MacArthur Foundation of Chicago awarded Kennedy a tax-exempt, no-strings grant of $264,000 for "exceptional talent," to be paid out over a period of five years.

O Albany! An Urban Tapestry, published the same year, is a collection of essays on his home town, part history and part autobiography. "It is the task of this and other books I have written, and hope to write, to peer into the heart of this always shifting past, to be there when it ceases to be what it was, when it becomes what it must become under scrutiny, when it turns so magically, so inevitably, from then into now.''[15]

Making use of an additional grant made available under the MacArthur Foundation—$15,000 annually for five years—Kennedy created and is the director of the New York State Writers Institute at Albany. Its aim is to provide aspiring writers with workshops and lectures given by well-known authors. The governor of New York signed a bill that granted the Institute $100,000 a year in support.

The citizens of Albany and SUNY Albany joined forces to host a "William Kennedy's Albany" festival that lasted four days. "The end of anonymity. . .is pleasant enough, but it raises the new issue. . .: Who are you, now that you're not nobody? Prizes have come to me and to my work during the past two years, my books have been received with inordinate goodwill in this country and abroad, and even strangers seem to know me. . . .

"Very different from a few years back when only my children recognized me (and sometimes even they weren't sure who I had become) and the bank knew me only because of the absence of my mortgage payment.

"There is money on the table now and so the mortgage department recognizes me from the photo on my book jacket. People want to give me loans and bond deals and credit cards. I am a friend of lawyers and brokers, and to certain charitable and cultural organizations I look like an annuity.

"As a teacher it was beyond expectation that I would ever do much more than survive at subsistence level. I own only a bachelor's degree (at twenty-one I couldn't abide another lec-

ture). Now invitations come in five a day, to write, speak, teach or, when May comes, just to stand still and shimmer in the baccalaureated afternoon. I remember when all I wanted to do was make a few dollars to live on and talk literature to bright students. Now movies are there to write if I want that. People want me to write a play, a musical, a documentary film, a TV series, a history of their family, the story of their lives. Magazines want me to write about movies, books, the blues, baseball or myself.''[16]

". . .There's nothing I'd rather do tomorrow than go upstairs and play at my typewriter. Writing is the most satisfying game of all for me—you're matching your imagination against everybody else's. Is that a game or isn't it? I've always loved games, always considered myself a gambler—a rotten gambler—at most things. I could never win at craps. I was a pretty good poker player, and a fair pool player. I played bogie golf and got a hole-in-one one day. I was a good bowler—I bowled 299 once, just like Billy. I was a pretty good first baseman. I wasn't bad at any of the games I played. But the real game for me is writing. It's the pleasure principle at work at every imaginable level. What else is as great as creating a world out of nothing? You project yourself out into the beyond, to where you want to go, but you don't know how to get there. And everything after that is a quest for lucidity, a game of light and shadow.''[2]

"I'm writing *Billy Phelan* now, the [film] script. . . .I see my own work there and I'm juggling it. I'm taking essences out of it and reducing five, six pages in the book to three pages of dialogue. It's an enormous cut-back, but still you can find the nugget. . . .I guess maybe I know how to. . .find the word that moves the story forward.''[4]

Kennedy also completed film script adaptations for *Legs* and *Ironweed.*

1988. *Quinn's Book,* published. The book's an adolescent love story that turns into a historical odyssey set in Albany in the middle of the nineteenth century. It starts in 1849, progressing through the post-Civil War. . . .I've been working on it since about 1982, though with a great many interruptions, but at the moment I'm working on nothing else. . . .''[17] "[In the book]. . .I want to create a sense of modern consciousness, to see where my particular world came from.''[1]

Kennedy and his wife Dana, a former performer and native of Puerto Rico, live in a nineteenth-century farm house in an Albany suburb. They have two daughters, one son, a grandson born the evening Kennedy won the Pulitzer Prize for *Ironweed* and a granddaughter born two years later. Kennedy bought a two-story landmark building in downtown Albany. This former rooming-house, in which he has an office, is where Legs Diamond was murdered.

Kennedy and son, fourteen-year-old Brendan, co-authored *Charlie Malarkey and the Belly Button Machine.* It is designed for readers between the ages of six and ten and is illustrated by Glen Baxter.

FOOTNOTE SOURCES

[1]Curt Suplee, "William Kennedy," *Washington Post,* December 28, 1983.
[2]Larry McCaffery and Sinda Gregory, editors, *Alive and Writing,* University of Illinois Press, 1987. Amended by Kennedy.
[3]Margaret Croyden, "The Sudden Fame of William Kennedy," *New York Times Magazine,* August 26, 1984.

⁴David Thomson, "The Man Has Legs," *Film Comment*, March-April, 1985.

⁵Susan Chira, "Rogues of the Past Haunt an Author's Albany," *New York Times*, September 17, 1983.

⁶Joseph Barbato, "PW Interviews: William Kennedy," *Publishers Weekly*, December 9, 1983.

⁷Peter Prescott, "Having the Time of His Life," *Newsweek*, February 6, 1984.

⁸William Kennedy, "On *The Ink Truck*," *Library Journal*, October 1, 1969.

⁹Kay Bonetti, "William Kennedy," American Audio Prose Library, 1984.

¹⁰Harold Farber, "Albany Honoring a Native Literary Son for Four Days," *New York Times*, September 6, 1984.

¹¹John F. Baker and Madalynne Reuter, "NBCC Awards," *Publishers Weekly*, February 17, 1984.

¹²W. Kennedy, "Letters," *Newsweek*, March 19, 1984.

¹³Herbert Mitgang, "Inexhaustible Albany," *New York Times Book Review*, November 13, 1983.

¹⁴Evan Hunter, "Why Authors Are Singing the Mid-List Blues," *New York Times Book Review*, April 8, 1984.

¹⁵W. Kennedy, *O Albany!*, Viking, 1983.

¹⁶W. Kennedy, "How Winning the Pulitzer Has Changed One Writer's Life," *Life*, January, 1985.

¹⁷W. Kennedy, *Publishers Weekly*, January 3, 1986.

FOR MORE INFORMATION SEE:

Washington Post, October 5, 1969, May 18, 1975.

Best Sellers, October 15, 1969, August, 1975.

Observer, October 20, 1969.

New Republic, May 24, 1975, February 14, 1983.

Newsweek, June 23, 1975, May 8, 1978, January 31, 1983, February 6, 1984.

Contemporary Literary Criticism, Gale, Volume VI, 1976, Volume XXVIII, 1984.

Listener, May 6, 1976.

Book World, April 23, 1978.

Saturday Review, April 29, 1978, May 2, 1978.

Atlantic, June, 1978.

Commonweal, October 13, 1978, September 9, 1983.

Los Angeles Times Book Review, December 26, 1982, September 23, 1984.

New York Times, January 10, 1983, December 23, 1983, September 22, 1984.

Washington Post Book World, January 16, 1983, January 29, 1984, October 14, 1984.

New York Times Book Review, January 23, 1983, January 1, 1984, September 30, 1984, January 25, 1987 (p. 3).

Chicago Tribune, January 23, 1983.

Time, January 24, 1983, October 1, 1984.

Detroit News, January 30, 1983, February 26, 1984.

Village Voice Literary Supplement, February, 1983, October, 1984.

New Yorker, February 7, 1983.

W. J. Weatherby, "Cottoning-on to Coppola," *Guardian*, January 26, 1984.

America, March 17, 1984, May 19, 1984.

Globe and Mail (Toronto), September 1, 1984.

Times Literary Supplement, October 5, 1984.

People, December 24, 1984, January 18, 1988.

Publishers Weekly, May 31, 1985 (p. 30), July 5, 1985.

Nichols Loxley, "William Kennedy Comes of Age," *National Review*, August 9, 1985 (p. 46).

Current Biography Yearbook 1985, H. W. Wilson, 1986.

"Culture and Society," *Society*, September/October, 1986.

Jay Parini, "Man of *Ironweed*," *Horizon*, December, 1987 (p. 35).

"(Re)creating *Ironweed*," *American Film*, January-February, 1988 (p. 18).

Why do rats have long tails?

They can't remember short stories.

(From *Rat Race and Other Rodent Jokes* by Dave Ross and Dottie Kinzel. Illustrated by Dave Ross.)

KINZEL, Dorothy 1950-
(Dottie Kinzel)

PERSONAL: Born July 26, 1950, in Schenectady, N.Y.; daughter of Donald A. (a toolmaker) and Lois (a teacher; maiden name, Collier) Ross; married Paul Kinzel, Jr. (a truck driver), September 11, 1971; children: Paul J., III, Donald M. *Education:* Attended Mildred Elley Secretarial School. *Religion:* Protestant. *Home:* 133 Sanders Ave., Scotia, N.Y. 12302.

CAREER: General Electric, Schenectady, N.Y., secretary, 1969-73; Helping Hands Schools, Clifton Park, N.Y., secretary, 1981—.

WRITINGS:

UNDER NAME DOTTIE KINZEL

(With brother, Dave Ross) *Rat Race and Other Rodent Jokes* (illustrated by D. Ross), Morrow, 1983.

SIDELIGHTS: "It is very simple how I became an author. My brother, Dave Ross, is the author of many children's books. I have seen how he comes up with ideas, jokes and puns and was really anxious to try my hand at it. He was kind enough to work with me. It is such a thrill to have your name in print!

"I really lead a very normal life. I work full time, am married, and have two sons who keep me very busy."

KITZINGER, Sheila 1929-

PERSONAL: Born March 29, 1929, in Taunton, England; daughter of Alexander (a master tailor) and Clare (a midwife;

SHEILA KITZINGER

maiden name, Bond) Webster; married Uwe W. Kitzinger (a don at Oxford University), October 4, 1952; children: Celia, Nell, Tess, Polly, Jenny. *Education:* Ruskin College, Oxford, Diploma in Social Anthropology (with distinction), 1951; St. Hugh's College, Oxford, B.Litt., 1956. *Politics:* Labour. *Religion:* Quaker. *Home:* The Manor, Standlake, near Witney, Oxfordshire, England. *Agent:* Uwe Kitzinger, The Manor, Standlake, near Witney, Oxfordshire, England.

CAREER: University of Edinburgh, Edinburgh, Scotland, researcher on race relations in Britain, 1951-53; National Childbirth Trust, London, England, prenatal teacher and counselor, 1958—. Lecturer in England for Department of Education and Science, at universities and teacher training colleges, and to nurses and social workers; lecturer in United States for International Childbirth Association and American Society for Psychoprophylaxis in Obstetrics, 1972. *Member:* Institute of Health Educators. *Awards, honors:* Joost de Blank Award for research, 1972; *Boston Globe-Horn Book* Honor Book for Nonfiction, selected one of *School Library Journal*'s Best Books for Young Adults, and one of Child Study Association of America's Children's Books of the Year, all 1986, all for *Being Born.*

WRITINGS:

JUVENILE

Being Born (illustrated by Lennart Nilsson), Grosset, 1986.

OTHER

The Experience of Childbirth, Gollancz, 1962, Taplinger, 1972, 6th edition, Penguin (England), 1987.
Giving Birth: The Parents' Emotions in Childbirth, Gollancz, 1971, Taplinger, 1972, new edition published as *Giving*

Birth: How It Really Feels, Gollancz, 1987, Farrar, Straus, 1989.
(Editor) *Episiotomy: Physical and Emotional Aspects,* National Childbirth Trust, 1972.
Education and Counselling for Childbirth, Bailliere, 1977, Schocken, 1979.
Women as Mothers, Martin Robertson, 1978, Random House, 1979.
(Editor with John A. Davis) *The Place of Birth: A Study of the Environment in Which Birth Takes Place with Special Reference to Home Confinements,* Oxford University Press, 1978.
The Experience of Breastfeeding, Penguin (England), 1979, revised edition, Viking Penguin (U.S.), 1987.
Birth at Home, Penguin (U.S.), 1980.
The Complete Book of Pregnancy and Childbirth, Knopf, 1980, revised edition, 1989.
(With Rhiannon Walters) *Some Women's Experiences of Episiotomy,* National Childbirth Trust, 1981.
Birth over Thirty, Sheldon, 1982, Penguin (U.S.), 1985.
Woman's Experience of Sex: The Facts and Feelings of Female Sexuality at Every Stage of Life, Putnam, 1983.
(Editor with P. Simkin) *Episiotomy and the Second Stage of Labor,* Pennypress, 1984, 2nd edition, 1986.
A Celebration of Birth, Pennypress, 1986.
Freedom and Choice in Childbirth: Making Pregnancy Decisions and Birth Plans, Penguin (England), 1987, published in the United States as *Your Baby Your Way,* Pantheon, 1987.
Some Women's Experiences of Epidurals, National Childbirth Trust, 1987.
Breastfeeding Your Baby, Knopf, 1989.
The Crying Baby, Viking Penguin, 1989.

CONTRIBUTOR

Carol P. MacCormack, editor, *Ethnography of Fertility and Birth,* Academic Press, 1982.
Patrick D. Wall and Ronald Melzack, editors, *Textbook of Pain,* Churchill Livingstone, 1984.
Luke Zandere and Geoffrey Chamberlain, editors, *Pregnancy Care for the 1980s,* Royal Society of Medicine, 1984.
John Studd, editor, *The Management of Labour,* Blackwells Scientific Publications, 1985.
Murray Enkin, Marc Keirse and Iain Chalmers, editors, *Effective Care in Pregnancy and Childbirth,* Oxford University Press, 1988.

WORK IN PROGRESS: A book with her daughter Celia, a psychologist, entitled *Your Values and Your Child,* about the ways in which women communicate values to their small children, where they feel they failed, where they succeeded, and how their values differ from those their own mothers tried to communicate to them.

HOBBIES AND OTHER INTERESTS: Painting.

KLEIN, Norma 1938-1989

PERSONAL: Born May 13, 1938, in New York, N.Y.; died April 25, 1989 in Manhattan; daughter of Emanuel (a psychoanalyst) and Sadie (Frankel) Klein; married Erwin Fleissner (a biochemist), July 27, 1963; children: Jennifer Luise, Katherine Nicole. *Education:* Attended Cornell University, 1956-57; Barnard College, B.A. (cum laude), 1960; Columbia University, M.A., 1963. *Politics:* Democrat. *Home:* 27 West 96th St., New York, N.Y. 10025. *Agent:* Elaine Markson, 44 Greenwich Ave., New York, N.Y. 10011.

NORMA KLEIN

CAREER: Author of novels, short stories, and children's fiction. *Member:* Phi Beta Kappa. *Awards, honors: Girls Can Be Anything* was selected one of Child Study Association of America's Children's Books of the Year, 1973; *Media & Methods* Maxi Award for Paperback, 1975, and selected one of New York Public Library's Books for the Teen Age, 1980, both for *Sunshine; Love Is One of the Choices* was selected one of *School Library Journal*'s Best Books of the Year, 1978; O. Henry Award, 1983, for short story, "The Wrong Man."

WRITINGS:

JUVENILE

Girls Can Be Anything (Junior Literary Guild selection; illustrated by Roy Doty), Dutton, 1973.
If I Had It My Way (illustrated by Ray Cruz), Pantheon, 1974.
Dinosaur's Housewarming Party (Junior Literary Guild selection; illustrated by James Marshall), Crown, 1974.
Naomi in the Middle (illustrated by Leigh Grant), Dial, 1974.
A Train for Jane (illustrated by Miriam Schottland), Feminist Press, 1974.
Red Sky, Blue Trees, (illustrated by Pat Grant Porter), Pantheon, 1975.
Visiting Pamela (illustrated by Kay Chorao), Dial, 1979.

YOUNG ADULT NOVELS, EXCEPT AS INDICATED

Mom, the Wolf Man and Me, Pantheon, 1972.
It's Not What You Expect, Pantheon, 1973.
Confessions of an Only Child (illustrated by Richard Cuffari), Pantheon, 1974.
Taking Sides, Pantheon, 1974.
Coming to Life, Simon & Schuster, 1974.
What It's All About, Dial Press, 1975.
Hiding, Four Winds Press, 1976.
Girls Turn Wives, Simon & Schuster, 1976.
It's Okay If You Don't Love Me, Dial, 1977.
Love Is One of the Choices, Dial, 1978.

Tomboy (sequel to *Confessions of an Only Child*), Four Winds Press, 1978.
Breaking Up, Pantheon, 1980.
A Honey of a Chimp, Pantheon, 1980.
Robbie and the Leap Year Blues, Dial, 1981.
The Queen of the What Ifs, Fawcett, 1982.
Beginner's Love, Dial, 1982.
Baryshnikov's Nutcracker (adaptation of the *Nutcracker* Ballet; photographs by Ken Regan, Christopher Little, and Martha Swope), Putnam, 1983.
Bizou, Viking, 1983.
Snapshots, Dial, 1984.
Angel Face, Viking, 1984.
The Cheerleader, Knopf, 1985.
Family Secrets, Dial, 1985.
Give and Take, Viking, 1985.
Going Backwards, Scholastic, 1986.
Older Men, Dial, 1987.
My Life as a Body, Knopf, 1987.
Now That I Know, Bantam, 1988.
No More Saturday Nights, Knopf, 1988.
That's My Baby, Viking, 1988.
The World As It Is, Dutton, 1989.

ADULT NOVELS, EXCEPT AS INDICATED

Love and Other Euphemisms (novella and five short stories), Putnam, 1972.
Give Me One Good Reason, Putnam, 1973.
Domestic Arrangements, M. Evans, 1981.
Wives and Other Women, St. Martin's, 1982.
Sextet in A Minor (novella and short stories), St. Martin's, 1983.
The Swap, St. Martin's, 1983.
Lovers, Viking, 1984.
American Dreams, Dutton, 1987.

NOVELIZATIONS

Sunshine: A Novel (based on a television special written by Carol Sobieski), Holt, 1974.
The Sunshine Years (based on television series), Dell, 1975.
Sunshine Christmas (based on a screenplay by C. Sobieski), Futura, 1977.
French Postcards (based on screenplay of the same title), Fawcett, 1979.

Work has been anthologized in *Prize Stories: The O. Henry Awards,* 1963, and 1968, and *The Best American Short Stories of 1969,* 1969. Contributor of about sixty short stories to magazines, including *Sewanee Review, Mademoiselle, Cosmopolitan, Prairie Schooner,* and *Denver Quarterly.*

ADAPTATIONS:

"Mom, the Wolf Man and Me" (record or cassette), Caedmon, 1977, (film), Time-Life Productions, 1979.
"Confessions of an Only Child" (cassette), Caedmon, 1977.

WORK IN PROGRESS: Give Me a Yes (tentative title), a novel about a sixteen-year-old girl who is very close to her grandmother.

SIDELIGHTS: "I was born on May 13, 1938, in New York City and grew up on 88th Street between Park and Madison Avenue. By a strange coincidence, when my husband and I found our present apartment in 27 West 96th Street, my mother told me that it was the same building in which I had lived between the time I was born and when I was three when we moved to 88th. I suppose if I was more spiritually inclined, I would say I must have been drawn to that building for that

(From the movie "Mom, the Wolf Man and Me," starring Patty Duke Astin, David Birney and Danielle Brisebois. Produced by Time-Life Productions, 1979.)

reason. I loved the city as a child and therefore thought of it later as a wonderful place in which to raise children. But when I use the city as a background for my novels, I try to show the side of it I knew, not the extremes of wealth and poverty which have grown ever more acute in the heartless Reagan era, but simply middle class families, living in slightly shabby, bookish, rent-controlled apartments.

"I was very much influenced by the fact that both of the schools I attended, Dalton from age three to thirteen, Elizabeth Irwin for high school, were progressive schools, run in less extreme form somewhat along the lines of the famous English school, Summerhill. We called teachers by their first names, classes were small, the emphasis was on writing papers, not on cramming for exams. Even when you were very young, independent study was emphasized. At Dalton, for instance, you were given all the work assignments for a month ahead and could do them at your own pace. Unlike the English classes my daughters had, ours offered a chance to do a lot of creative writing as well as literary essays. I regret now that, when I applied to college, I decided I wanted a complete change and attended very rigid, conventional schools, (at least by contrast to Dalton and E.I.). I was at Cornell for my freshman year (1956-1957), and finished up at Barnard (1957-1960), but was miserable at both places and hated the style of education both offered which was filled with absurd do's and don'ts. You couldn't, for instance, take studio art at all, just art history. You could only study literature if you knew the language in which it was originally written. I wish now that I had gone to Antioch, as my younger daughter has, or to a college that emphasized the arts, like Bennington or Sarah Lawrence.

"Elizabeth Irwin was, in an educational sense, more conservative than Dalton and less imaginative. There were grades and exams, though the emphasis was still on a relaxed atmo-

sphere in which you studied because you were inspired to, not because you were forced. The parents of most of the students at E.I. were like my own, extremely liberal left-wing Jews. If you had parents who had voted for Adlai Stevenson, you were considered weirdly conservative; Eisenhower was beyond the pale. I thought then that the world was like the milieu in which I grew up, very understanding of differences between people, accepting of homosexuality or alternate life styles. When I began writing about this world, far from meaning to shock, I was simply describing what to me was 'real life.' I now realize that to many Americans this *is* shocking, though the kids who like my books often find it fascinating as well. Growing up in small, repressive communities, they look to my books, I think, as a glimpse of a wider, more rational, freer world which they hope to reach in adulthood.

"Few of the kids in my high school class dated. We were the class of 1956, conformity and repression were in vogue. Girls wore very full skirts with horsehair crinolines underneath. This was still an era of garter belts and padded bras. Since we had grown up in the city, virtually no one knew how to drive. Thus the whole car culture of America, so celebrated in movies like 'American Graffiti' was totally unknown to us; we took subways or buses.

"In addition, like most of my friends, I was completely unaware of popular music except for folk music like the ballads sung by Pete Seeger or social protest songs such as those sung by Paul Robeson, the famous black singer of that era. I assumed teenagers across America were singing 'I Ain't Gonna Study War No More,' or 'We Are the Peat Bog Soldiers.' In addition I listened to the same classical music I love today, went to chamber music concerts and the opera with my parents (my favorite opera then, as now, was 'The Marriage of Figaro,' not only for its exquisite music, but because it is one

I enjoy going places by myself in New York, especially when it's something unexpected. ■ (Cover illustration from *Mom, the Wolf Man and Me* by Norma Klein.)

of the few operas whose plot resembles that of a good realistic novel).

"My daughters, partly through their total immersion in rock music, are much more in touch with the contemporary culture of their time than I was of mine.

"Being the daughter of a Freudian psychoanalyst had a profound influence on me. Just as I inherited my parents' liberal political beliefs and their love of books and music, so I was raised in a home where Freud had replaced the God in whom my father had decided early on he didn't believe. My brother, Victor (who is sixteen months younger than I am), and I went to psychoanalysts even as children for problems which I would now consider simply a normal part of growing up: he wet his bed, I was afraid of the dark. We both voluntarily underwent psychoanalysis as adults. After my father died, in 1977 when I was forty, I began to question and ultimately reject much of psychoanalytic theory and practice. I believe Freud was an inspired thinker who developed some fascinating and important theories about human life such as the importance of early childhood sexuality, but I don't feel, from the evidence I've seen, that psychoanalysis, or 'talking' therapy, really helps people very much with their emotional problems, especially the kind of analysis my husband and I endured in which the patient rambles interminably on for close to a decade (or longer) and the therapist occasionally clears his throat and says, 'We'll continue next time.'

"Though I have rejected many of my father's beliefs, I am grateful to him for the immense support he gave me in my intellectual endeavors. Now I see that encouragement as deriving simply from the fact that he loved me and thought whatever I did—I loved painting and writing from the time I was very young—was wonderful. The effect this had on me was to make me feel that ultimately I would find people in the outside world who would be like my father, who would love my work. Like most self-created hypotheses, this has proved true, or to put it another way, I have an extraordinary amount of persistence in the face of rejection, based in part on the underlying thought that somewhere out there is that person, if only I can just hang in there long enough. My mother, a creative and talented person did not come into her own until after my father's death. In the past decade she blossomed and received her B.A. from Baruch College at the age of seventy-seven. She is still extremely active, writes, has friends of all ages, and travels (she went to China a few years ago).

"I think my daughters and their contemporaries are not only growing up in a world more hospitable to women, they also often have mothers who have had active professional lives throughout their childhood. Thus, they grow up with a sense that they, too, can achieve, though they often choose different fields than the ones in which their mothers excelled. It's interesting to me that though both my daughters are wonderful writers, thus far, they write mainly poetry or literary criticism, the two areas of writing I haven't explored.

"Since most of the women writers I admired while I was growing up, such as Jane Austen and Virginia Woolf, were either unmarried, or married and childless, I wasn't sure when I got married at the age of twenty-five that I wanted to have children. I felt then that if I had to choose between writing and children, I would choose writing. But as my marriage continued, like so many people who are happy in their marital choice, I gradually felt I *did* want children. By the time my daughters were born (Jen arrived when I was almost twenty-nine, Katie three and a half years later), this desire had grown to the point that I greeted their arrival with extreme delight, a delight which has only deepened over the years. Although I still love writing as much as ever, I feel being a parent has been an enormous joy to me.

"Until I entered college, painting was as important to me as writing. I've read nursery school reports which state that when I was three or four, I would immediately, upon coming to school, march over to the table where the poster paints and paper were kept and spend the morning happily immersed in an imaginary world, scarcely paying any attention to what was going on around me. That sensation, of being able to lose oneself in an imaginary world of art or writing, has remained central to my identity.

"There were two main reasons I chose writing rather than art as a profession. One was that Barnard, although it offered creative writing courses, did not 'believe' in studio art. I took several writing classes with writers such as George P. Elliott and Robert Pack (who now runs Breadloaf). Both were very encouraging to me. George, in particular, suggested I send my work out to literary magazines which I began doing when I was still a teenager. As fate would have it, the first story I sent out (I was nineteen), 'Ceremony of Innocence,' was accepted by a literary magazine, the *Grecourt Review*. I assumed from that experience that being accepted would be a matter of course. It wasn't. Some of my short stories were rejected as many as forty-five times and even today, as a much published writer, my work is still often rejected. I expect this will always be the case but, if acceptances are mixed in, it's a tolerable combination.

''I also found the process of submitting my work as a writer easier than what I had heard artists had to undergo. A writer can just slip his stories or novel into a book bag, send it out and suffer rejections privately; no one need know of them. An artist has to stand around while bored gallery owners browse through slides of their work. The thought of that terrified me. To this day I hate being in a room when someone is reading something I've written.

''Because my parents were not happy together, I didn't really believe in the possibility that two adult human beings could live together contentedly. Perhaps this is why some friends have commented that the short stories I wrote in my twenties are more bleak in tone than my novels. I feel marriage (I've now, as of 1988, been married twenty-five years), has softened and mellowed my feeling about life. Although I am an ardent feminist and deplore the macho ethic which dominates our society, I take pleasure in the fact that individual men, like my husband, can be exceptions to this rule. I believe my marriage was helped by the fact that my mother-in-law, though born at the turn of the century, got her Ph.D. and taught at the college level throughout her long and active life. Thus, my husband grew up with an example before him of a woman who was able to maintain loving and warm relationships with a husband and children while fulfilling herself intellectually. He accepted this as a given and I have never had to experience a

day without writing, unless I felt ready for a break between books.

''Although my books are frequently perceived as wildly daring by the children's book establishment, I feel I've led an almost tediously conventional life, which happens to have suited me. I've enjoyed having children, look forward eagerly to having grandchildren, and hope to be married to the same man for the rest of my life. Throughout their lives, I lived only five minutes away from my parents and I would love, though I know I can't count on, being that accessible to my daughters when they have families of their own. My brother, who married late and now has a four-year-old daughter, also lives near by. Family ties have always been crucial for me, and this may explain why they play such an important role in my books.

''From the age of nineteen, when my first short story was accepted, until the birth of my daughter, Jen in 1967, I devoted full time (except for the years from 1960-1963 when I was getting an M.A. in Slavic languages from Columbia), to writing short stories, several anthologized in *Prize Stories: The O. Henry Awards* and *The Best American Short Stories*. I had only limited success with the 'big' magazines: a few in *Mademoiselle* and *Cosmopolitan*. My list of rejections from the

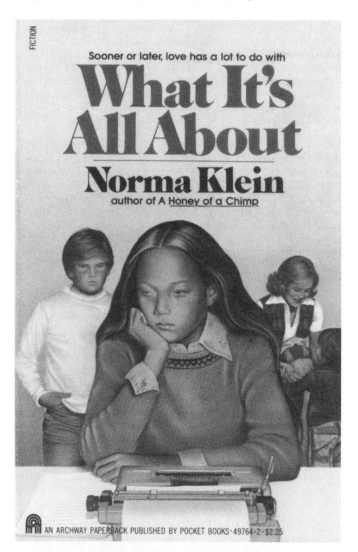

''Mom, what animals *do* you like?'' I asked. ■ (Cover illustration from *A Honey of a Chimp* by Norma Klein.)

(Cover illustration from *What It's All About* by Norma Klein.)

New Yorker (I've saved all of them), is equal to almost any living writer, I imagine.

"As I began reading picture books to my daughter, the idea entered my head that I might try writing and illustrating my own picture books. None of these manuscripts (*Girls Can Be Anything, Dinosaur's Housewarming Party*) were accepted until after the success of my first novel for 'middle-aged' (eight- to twelve-year-old) children, *Mom, the Wolf Man and Me*. Because the heroine, Brett, has an unmarried mother, *Mom* was forced into the young adult category where I strongly feel it does not belong. I wrote *Mom, the Wolf Man and Me* simply because a children's book agent to whom I submitted my picture book manuscripts felt there was more of a demand for books for middle-age readers. My only preparation was to read a few novels which had been published in the 60s, after the era in which I had been a child. Although some advances had been made, it was clear to me then (as, alas, it still is), that the level of writing in many of these books was inferior. 'Hey, I can do as well as that,' was my first, perhaps egotistical thought. I think, in fact, that I have.

"Like many writers who have an unexpected sudden success with a first book, I have now been able to analyze in retrospect what led to that success. I was lucky, I think, as were many of my contemporaries in the field like Judy Blume or Bob Cormier, in breaking in at a time when, due to the delayed influence of the 60s, openness and boldness were actually encouraged. Possibly a decade earlier, *Mom, the Wolf Man and Me* and certainly many of my later YA novels, would never have been published, or would have been published for adults. Censorship, which has become rife in the era of Reagan, was virtually unknown. I sailed forth, naively and happily, into a world I thought would greet my books for kids only with delight, certainly not with condemnation or outrage.

"Now, at the age of fifty, having been published as a children's book writer for sixteen years, I am less naive, sadder, wiser, but still undaunted. I want to write excellent, literary novels for teenagers. That, really, is my only goal. I loathe books that try to 'teach' or end with a moral lesson. My feeling is if you want to preach, become a preacher. Books should entertain, move, delight, not hammer the reader over the head. I still feel there are not enough fine, realistic novels for kids of any ages, and I now see that the few there are will always, to some extent, be under attack for doing precisely what they set out to do, describing the world as it is.

"Comparisons have been made and probably will continue to be made between my books for kids and Judy Blume's. Judy is a friend so it's almost as hard for me to be objective about her work as it is for me to be objective about mine, but I would say that, though both of us see similarities—humor, frankness, a colloquial narrative style—the differences are just as great. Basically Judy's forte, the area she has honed in on, is junior high, age ten to fourteen, where anxieties focus on getting a first bra, masturbating, being kissed at a spin the bottle party. I feel my own YA novels are much more akin to Salinger's *Catcher in the Rye*. They are about the last two years of high school or, increasingly, college and the anxieties are about what profession one will enter, how to evaluate one's parents as one approaches adulthood, what direction one's burgeoning sexuality will take. I don't think either set of anxieties is more important, they're just different.

"I also feel the world in which Judy's characters live is unlike the world of my heroes and heroines. Judy's characters usually grow up in the suburbs where a great effort is made to conform and fit in, to do what everyone else is doing when they are doing it. My heroes and heroines tend to grow up as I did, in

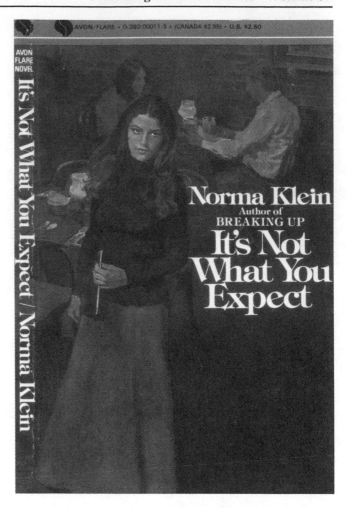

(Cover illustration from *It's Not What You Expect* by Norma Klein.)

Manhattan, in a world which cherishes and encourages individuality. My characters are usually intellectual, thoughtful, responsible and, occasionally, sexually active.

"To have sexual activity take place in a young adult novel is still to arouse total horror in the eyes of most children's book librarians and book reviewers. I think what bothers them most about my books is that there is no crime and punishment. That is, I don't see making love as a crime which must be punished by the book's end, either by a disastrous abortion which ages the heroine by several decades, or by an unwanted and miserable teenage marriage. I'm also, which perplexes and disturbs some, not writing about promiscuous kids or kids who are too careless or uninformed to use birth control. Somehow it's worse in the eyes of certain people in the field, to portray teenagers who are making love because, not only are they in love, but perhaps they are actually in tune with their sexual feelings and accept them joyfully.

"The advent of AIDS has, I am disturbed to notice, been greeted with barely concealed glee by a sizeable portion of the children's book world. Their thinking appears to be: great, now teenagers won't engage in sexual activity or think a sexual thought until the day they get married! It's a massive back swing to those ghastly Rosamund du Jardin romance novels of the 50s. The new version is 'Sweet Valley High' where the heroines are all white, well to do, sexy-looking and adored by a handsome boy who has no intent other than an occasional good night kiss. The dishonesty and hypocrisy of these books struck me even thirty years ago. To see it return is very sad.

"Luckily for me not all kids want to 'escape' into a fantasy never never world. Some actually love, as I did, books about real life, books which don't pull punches, which don't end happily but ambiguously, where heroes and heroines are allowed to be physically imperfect, where parents are sometimes cruel and erratic. When I reread my past books, I feel critical only of the extent to which I tried, usually unsuccessfully, to conform to what I was told were the 'rules' of the children's book world. In my more recent books like *My Life as a Body* or *Going Backwards* I've tried to be more muted, to create a tone of greyness, not black or white.

"Because my books are funny, some of my editors have found the element of tragedy at odds with the rest of the book, as, for example, the suicide of Jason's mother at the end of *Angel Face*. I don't see this as a discrepancy. I find life funny, I laugh a lot, but I also am increasingly aware of its darker sides, the way people so often suffer, or bring suffering upon themselves. In my early years as a children's book writer, I gave way to editors' demands and thus to some extent emasculated my books. Now I resist and, although my editor for *Angel Face* pressured me for a removal of the mother's suicide, I refused. My primary aim is to write the kinds of books I would have liked to read when I was in my teens, not the ones editors feel the 'average' (what an absurd term!) teenager wants to read.

"Unlike some of my writer friends, I never submit a partial manuscript or describe my ideas to my editors before I write the book. I prefer to have the months of writing a totally private time where I can focus my energies only on the book itself, not on the marketing problems with which editors have to concern themselves. One reason I've always had several different publishers for my YA novels is I don't want anyone to publish me half heartedly. If a particular editor doesn't like a particular book, there are no hard feelings. I simply publish it elsewhere, but feel free to return to the first editor on the next book. I've always been able to find editors who support me in what I'm trying to say. Jean Feiwel, Beverly Horowitz and Frances Foster are among those I now value highly; Phyllis Fogelman, Amy Ehrlich and Fabio Coen gave me a start when I was beginning my career.

"There are a lot of absurd 'rules' that are handed to writers of YA novels: don't make the book longer than 200 pages, always have a single narrator, usually first person, don't allow the adult characters to play a prominent part, just focus on teenage concerns, but downplay or avoid description of sexual feelings or actions. Phooey! I now include as many main characters as I want, make the book as long as it needs to be, allow the adult characters to be central, and include sexual thoughts and feelings, as well as actions, if I feel they are central to the book's purpose. Many of these rules are carryovers from an earlier time. For instance, in the beginning of this century, middle class kids often were raised mainly by servants and had little contact with, or knowledge of their parents as people. Hence the many English novels like *Mary Poppins* or those of E. Nesbit in which the nurse is a prominent character and is often an emotional substitute for the parent. To know one's parents intimately, as many kids do now, is not always to admire and respect them wholeheartedly. Therefore, the parents in my books are not, nor are they intended to be 'role models'; they are fallible, complex human beings, engaged in as difficult a struggle to live a meaningful life as are the teenage characters.

"I think I write well about sex, but my sex scenes are, as often as not, humorous and awkward. I don't incline toward the lyrical or the pornographic, but I try to show what sex is like between two often inexperienced, nervous teenagers. I

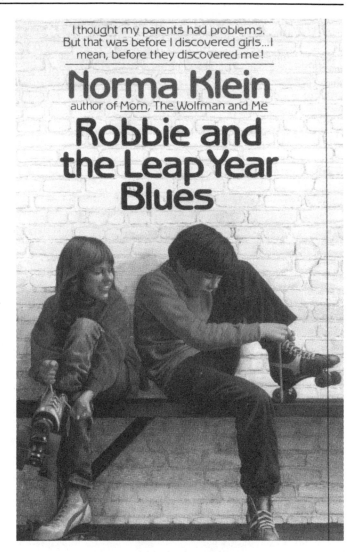

I thought my parents had problems. But that was before I discovered girls...I mean, before they discovered me!

Norma Klein
author of *Mom*, The Wolfman and Me

Robbie and the Leap Year Blues

(Cover illustration from *Robbie and the Leap Year Blues* by Norma Klein.)

have no fear that if I portray sex as an occasionally enjoyable activity, my readers, be they fourteen, twelve or eight will instantly rush out and 'do it,' thereby neglecting their piano lessons or hockey practice. Many of my readers are the way I was at their age, intellectually far ahead of their social development. These are the teenagers who can recite chapter and verse from *Lady Chatterley's,* but are still waiting for someone to ask them out.

"The term 'problem novel' came into existence because too many YA novels raised important and complex issues only to 'answer' them very superficially. I don't think I ever did that, though I was always prodded toward the conventional happy ending editors believe kids prefer. If I were to write some of these novels now, I would end them differently. Caroline in *Love Is One of the Choices* (a ghastly title; I will never again use love in a title), falls in love with and marries her high school science teacher and, at the end of the book, is expecting her first child. I meant to imply an unhappy future for Caroline in which she would become increasingly dissatisfied with her husband and ultimately divorce him. I wanted to end the book just as she is beginning to see that, in some sense, she has dug her own grave. But I left this so vague that many readers have written saying, 'What are you implying at the end?' This was not literary ambiguity, but failure of nerve.

"Similarly in *Breaking Up,* one of the few novels I've ever written from the point of view of a popular, pretty girl (since I know little of what it's like to be such a girl, I feel this is one of my less successful books), the heroine's father attempts to get sole custody of her after he learns his wife is engaged in an ongoing lesbian relationship. If I were to write the book now, I might well have the father succeed in his attempt and leave the reader a sense of horror at an action directly opposed to the heroine's own happiness.

"Recently I completed a novel in which there are flash forwards which tell what will happen, not only to the heroine, but to the boy she eventually marries and to all her best friends twenty-five years hence. 'My God,' said a friend, 'you've created a new unmarketable genre, a middle-age YA.' The paperback editor to whom it was submitted asked via my agent, 'But will the average thirteen-year-old girl be interested in these melancholy projections into the future?' I realized, by my indifference to that question, that I have never written for any audience except, possibly, myself at a given age or my daughters. I am writing about kids who are intellectually knowledgeable and sophisticated, but that doesn't mean that the kids who read my books are. I think all of us read partly to find out about people unlike ourselves. That's how we stretch our horizons, which is one of the important functions of reading. I've never conceived of my audience as 'average' because I don't think there is such a thing as an 'average' teenager any more than there is an 'average' adult. If one aims one's books at an average, one ends up with a stereotype.

"I have definitely been influenced by the fact that my daughters, who are now both in college, find the style and subject matter of most YA's, including some of mine, too young, simplistic, or lacking in complexity. I am trying, as it were, to capture their attention or the attention of young people like themselves who are also reading adult fiction, but would delight, as kids of my generation did, in books like *Catcher in the Rye,* which focus on teenage characters. This is an audience (sixteen to twenty-two year olds) which, thus far, publishers refuse to acknowledge. Kids are supposed to leap from S. E. Hinton to Joan Didion in one fell swoop.

"I also feel that many young people read 'ahead,' that good readers of eight or nine are often reading adult fiction and finding it fascinating, as I did. We all grow up at different rates, one reason why denying books to kids on the grounds that they are 'too young' to know about certain subjects is ridiculous. Just as kids mature at different ages sexually, some having love affairs at fourteen, others waiting until they are in their twenties, so people read, not according to a rigid set of guidelines, but according to their own personal tastes and preferences. Teenage readers, like adult readers, can have many different tastes simultaneously. Think only of the vast number of English professors who love murder mysteries, or the readers of literary fiction who are occasionally engrossed by best sellers. We need gourmet cuisine as much as we also like to indulge in a yen for junk food. A book reviewer once called me 'the thinking child's Judy Blume.' I would like to think that my books are not restricted to future intellectuals. I believe that teenage girls who are simultaneously reading romances may sometimes want a breath of real life so their teeth won't rot with too much sugar. Let's encourage diversity and not try to shove square pegs into round holes.

"In 1982 I published a novel, *Beginner's Love,* that represented a new departure for me in that the main character, Joel, was a teenage boy. Writers of YA fiction are often encouraged to write about girls on the grounds that girls are more likely to read fiction than boys. I'm sure there is some truth to this, just as women read more fiction than men, but I wanted to

(Cover illustration from *Snapshots* by Norma Klein.)

explore teenage life from a male point of view not only to interest male readers whose literary tastes might be more sophisticated than 'Bang, bang, you're dead,' but to reveal to young women some insights into the other sex. I've always had male friends, usually writers or editors, read these books carefully to make sure the male point of view seemed authentic or to point out any place where it wasn't.

"I suppose you could say that the teenage boys who people my novels incline toward being what our society perjoratively calls wimps. I myself love wimps since to me it is a term meaning a man who is sensitive, thoughtful, and rebellious against the macho posturing that is put forward as a male ideal in our society from birth onward. This doesn't mean that my male protagonists never hurt their girl friends or feel confused by sexual feelings, but, like my heroines, they are thinking human beings, trying to make sense of life as it unfolds before them. My most recent novel told from a male point of view is *No More Saturday Nights* in which eighteen-year-old Tim Weber takes his pregnant girl friend to court when he learns she is going to sell their baby for adoption and sues for sole custody which he gains, the result being that he sets off for Columbia on a scholarship with a six-week-old infant. A woman friend to whom I showed the book protested loudly: no teenage boy would ever, *ever* do such a foolish thing. The man to whom I showed it said, simply, 'I would have, at that age.' My mother, right after reading the book, saw a teenage boy walking down the street with a baby in a back pack, just like the cover of my book. Sometimes, life imitates art which imitates life, and so on.

"Most of my teenage characters are not only urban, but Jewish, and have a wry, Woody Allenish sensibility based on a mocking inner commentary on the world and oneself. Charles Goldberg in *Going Backwards* is a good example of this. Everyone I knew while I was growing up was Jewish and I thought this stance toward the world was universal. From twenty-five years of being married to a non-Jew who grew up in a small town in upstate New York, I have come to realize it isn't. We have gone back to my husband's home town (population 300) every summer and I feel now that I know it as well, if in a different way, than I know New York City. I feel able, through this knowledge, to write about boys like Tim in *No More Saturday Nights* or Spencer in *Give and Take* who are slightly more earnest, naive and straightforward than my urban Jewish heroes. The basics of growing up are the same, no matter what the size of the population or the ethnic group from which one derives, but I enjoy switching settings occasionally and attempting to see life through the eyes of young protagonists who are different than I was or am.

"Because I idealized my father when I was growing up, I tended to present in my early novels an idealized portrait of fathers or grandfathers such as the grandfather in *Mom, the Wolf Man and Me*, or the father in *Confessions of an Only Child* and *Tomboy*. I took the good traits of my father and husband and deftly air brushed out the bad or more troublesome ones. Now, rereading these books, I feel a bit impatient at some of these portrayals. It wasn't until after my father's death that I was able to begin writing about fathers who were more negative, sometimes even downright unpleasant. I see the beginnings of this trend in *Breaking Up* where the heroine's father, a lawyer, is manipulative and dishonest, attempting to destroy her bond with her mother which threatens his own domination of her. But the book which carries this darker side of fatherhood most vividly thus far is the father in *Older Men*, a doctor who 'adores' his daughter and has contempt for his wife whom he places against her will in a mental hospital. It might be hard for someone to see my father in both the grandfather in *Mom, the Wolf Man and Me* and the father in *Older Men*, but I think both represent different sides of his character. The father in *No More Saturday Nights* is based more on my father-in-law, a withdrawn, unsocial man who, in the course of the book, becomes more fully human through his experience as a grandfather.

"As the daughter of a psychoanalyst and as someone who spent the better part of her adult life, to little avail, on an analytic couch, I am interested in the emotional problems of teenagers which are clearly extreme, given the teenage suicide rate and rate of mental breakdown. To some people, disturbed by emotional disturbances in themselves or family, the very concept 'mental illness' is terrifying. They try to perceive such young people as beyond the pale, completely unlike their own hopefully perfect teenage sons or daughters. In [new book] 'Learning How to Fall,' I have portrayed a troubled teenage boy, Dustin, whose father has placed him in a mental hospital after he has had a psychotic episode. The book deals mainly with Dustin's first year after he gets out of the hospital (he is only there a few weeks) and how he tries to put his world together again. In fact, I don't think Dustin is any more disturbed than the characters in my other YA novels, and I hope that readers, in identifying with him, will have a greater understanding of what leads young people to go over the thin edge separating sanity from madness.

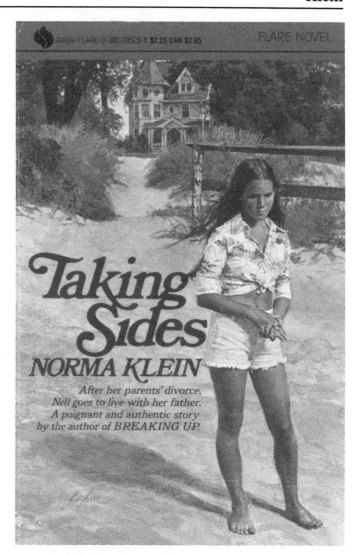

(Cover illustration by Gehm from *Taking Sides* by Norma Klein.)

"My work schedule has only varied slightly in the years since I began writing novels, around 1970. I type ten pages a day, five days a week, always allowing myself two days off each week, though these days may vary. I write from the beginning to the end, not skipping ahead to scenes in the middle or end of the book. I find that when I finally arrive at those scenes, they are quite different due to what has happened earlier. I usually write three novels a year, one in the fall, one in the winter and one in the spring. I enjoy the alternation of writing novels for adults, novels for kids in their early teens, and those in between late-high-school/early-college novels I described earlier. I think the ten-page-a-day schedule derived from the fact that I was originally a short story writer. It helped me to say to myself, 'You will never have to write a novel. You just have to write thirty ten-page scenes about the same characters which go in chronological order.' I like the six- to twelve-week gap between novels in which I can do what one friend describes as 'noodling around.' Noodling around can mean anything from writing an essay or book review to relabeling the spice jars or going out to see a movie at noon when the theatre is almost deserted. I've never been someone who holds with the view that writers are always writing. I think I spend far more time noodling around than I do writing and find it just as enjoyable an activity.

"When my daughters were growing up, the time I had to write was much more limited. They would be taken to the park by a babysitter in the morning and would return for lunch, a meal I liked to have with them. I knew, therefore, that I had to work quickly and efficiently in the morning hours. Since I'm a morning person, this suited me, but even now when I could work at any time of day or night for as long as I want, I find I still prefer the hours before noon.

"People sometimes ask why I write, and the answer to that question is, of course, complex, but essentially I think *I* write because I love the feeling I get when I am writing. For me it's as though, simply by going into my study and sitting in front of the typewriter, I am transported into a world peopled by human beings whom I will know much more intimately than I can ever know anyone in real life because I am simultaneously inside their heads and far outside, knowing things about them they themselves don't know. There is something indescribably thrilling about this. One aspect of sexuality is obviously the need to merge with another human being. Writing affords a way of actually doing this, of *becoming* another person.

"I still think of writing a novel as being like going on a trip. You have a general idea where you're going, but you don't know what will happen along the way, except that some of these experiences will be fascinating and by the end you will have learned a great deal and be, to some extent, a different person than you were before. Like most writers, I frequently have the experience, always delightful, that a character just marches into a book from somewhere unknown and begins saying and doing things which I listen to with total surprise and fascination. Just as the novel begins to slow down, such a character appears, as though waiting in the wings, though what 'the wings' are I don't really know, nor I think, does anyone.

"Writers sometimes worry about running out of ideas. I've never had this worry because, to the best of my knowledge, I've never had an idea. What I have are situations such as 'Write a novel about a teenage boy who gains sole custody of his son.' Once that sentence is written down, or even once it's a formed thought, the novel, in effect, exists. It's only a matter of going into my study and watching it unfold, perhaps in the way a sculptor feels the statue he is carving is *in* the piece of marble; he just has to take away the part that isn't the statue. The great thing about writing (and it's a good thing I enjoy it because I am totally devoid of marketable skills, never having had a 'real' job of any kind), is that all you need is time, a pad of paper and a typewriter or word processor if that happens to be your chosen method of writing. You can be waiting to cross the street and suddenly, for reasons known only to them, your characters appear and start 'writing' a crucial scene for you. Sometimes this is so interesting you forget to cross the street! I've been known to walk directly past close friends, stare right into their eyes and not see them, an experience, they tell me, which is distinctly unnerving.

"When people try to clobber me by saying, 'You write too fast,' or 'You'll never write anything good until you agonize more over your work,' I've learned to say, 'Poor Mozart. He wrote the Linz Symphony in just four days. Think what his music could have been like if he'd learned to slow down!' The fact is, I don't think either the method or speed with which a writer creates his world makes much difference. Great novels have been written with a quill pen and great novels assuredly will be written on word processors. Some writers allow their work to pour forth in a joyous stream while others spend two months putting in and taking out a comma. I've learned to live with my own method because, once I hand in the completed manuscript, I am eager and willing to make whatever changes my editor suggests. Quite often these suggestions lead to major

(Cover illustration from *Tomboy* by Norma Klein.)

rewritings of scenes, the removal of some, the addition of others. I have no sense that what I am writing is sacred. I only object to changes which do violence to my original intent.

"Having writer friends like Betty Miles, Bob Cormier and Steven Kroll has been, more than almost anything else, a help in getting through a life as a writer. It is wonderful to know that every single emotion you experience, in the course of writing and publishing a book, delight at its creation, incomprehension at its rejection, outrage at a hideous cover or poorly written jacket copy, is being experienced or has been experienced by virtually every writer you know. As they say, it goes with the territory. I once asked Norma Mazer (who in addition to being a fine writer and a good friend is the only other Norma I know) what she would say if God appeared before her and said, 'If you sign here I will guarantee that your future writing career will be identical to what has gone before, you will write neither better nor worse, will receive reviews as good but no better.' After a moment she said, 'I'd sign in a minute.' Adding that I would reserve the right to keep on complaining into eternity, I realized I felt exactly the same way."

FOR MORE INFORMATION SEE:

New York Times Book Review, September 24, 1972 (p. 8), October 15, 1972 (p. 31), June 3, 1973 (p. 8), May 5, 1974 (p. 16), September 29, 1974 (p. 8), November 3,

1974 (p. 48), April 25, 1976 (p. 49), May 1, 1977 (p. 10), March 25, 1979 (p. 28), July 13, 1980, December 30, 1984, August 24, 1986 (p.20).

School Library Journal, December, 1972 (p. 60), April, 1976 (p. 90), May, 1977 (p. 83), November, 1979 (p. 96), October, 1980 (p. 156), April, 1983 (p. 125), October, 1983 (p. 180), November, 1983 (p. 94).

Library Journal, December 15, 1972, November 15, 1974, February 15, 1976, April 15, 1977, November 15, 1978 (p. 2351), October 15, 1979 (p. 2236), June 1, 1982 (p. 1112).

Booklist, January 1, 1973 (p. 449), July 15, 1974 (p. 1254), November 1, 1975 (p. 369), November 1, 1976, December 15, 1979 (p. 595), June 15, 1982 (p. 1364), February 15, 1983 (p. 763), August, 1983 (p. 1448), October 15, 1983 (p. 360).

Horn Book, February, 1973 (p. 57), December, 1976 (p. 629).

Best Sellers, May 15, 1973 (p. 98), November 15, 1975, September, 1982 (p. 218).

Ms., January, 1974 (p. 36).

Top of the News, April, 1975 (p. 307); spring, 1985 (p. 248).

Margery Fisher, *Who's Who in Children's Books: A Treasury of the Familiar Characters of Childhood,* Holt, 1975.

Children's Literature Review, Volume II, Gale, 1976.

English Journal, May, 1976 (p. 90).

America, July 10, 1976 (p. 18).

Norma Klein, "Growing Up Human: The Case of Sexuality in Children's Books," *Children's Literature in Education,* summer, 1977.

Kliatt Young Adult Paperback Book Guide, winter, 1978 (p. 9).

D. L. Kirkpatrick, editor, *Twentieth-Century Children's Writers,* St. Martin's, 1978, 2nd edition, 1983.

Los Angeles Times Book Review, December 28, 1980, January 27, 1985.

Interracial Books for Children Bulletin, Volume XII, number 3, 1981 (p. 19).

Quill & Quire, October, 1981.

Voyager, October, 1981, October, 1983.

Voice of Youth Advocates, October, 1981 (p. 34), October, 1983 (p. 203).

Publishers Weekly, December 24, 1982 (p. 47), March 9, 1984 (p. 106); March 28, 1986 (p. 58), July 24, 1987 (p. 109).

Los Angeles Times, May 26, 1983.

Nation, June 11, 1983 (p. 738).

Sally Holmes Holtze, editor, *Fifth Book of Junior Authors and Illustrators,* H. W. Wilson, 1983.

Contemporary Literary Criticism, Volume XXX, Gale, 1984.

Lion and the Unicorn, Volume 10, 1986 (p. 18).

School Library Media Quarterly, spring, 1987 (p. 161).

COLLECTIONS

Kerlan Collection at the University of Minnesota.

LARSON, Gary   1950-

PERSONAL: Born August 14, 1950, in Tacoma, Wash.; son of Vern (an automobile dealer) and Doris (a secretary) Larson; married in September, 1988. *Education:* Attended Washington State University. *Office:* c/o Andrews, McMeel & Parker, 4400 Johnson Dr., Fairway, Kan. 66205.

CAREER: Cartoonist. Performed as a musician in a jazz duo, 1973-76; worked at a music store in Seattle, Wash., 1976-77; *Seattle Times,* cartoonist for weekly feature "Nature's Way," 1978-79; Humane Society, Seattle, animal abuse investigator, 1978-80; cartoonist for daily feature "The Far Side," syndi-

cated by Chronicle Features, San Francisco, Calif., 1979-84, syndicated by Universal Press Syndicate, Fairway, Kan., 1984—. *Exhibitions:* "The Far Side of Science," California Academy of Sciences, 1985, with subsequent tour. *Awards, honors:* National Cartoonists Society Award for best humor panel, 1986.

WRITINGS:

The Far Side, Andrews & McMeel, 1982.
Beyond the Far Side, Andrews, McMeel & Parker, 1983.
In Search of the Far Side, Andrews & McMeel, 1984.
Bride of the Far Side, Andrews & McMeel, 1985.
Valley of the Far Side, Andrews & McMeel, 1985.
It Came from the Far Side, Andrews, McMeel & Parker, 1985.
The Far Side Observer, Andrews & McMeel, 1987.
Hound of the Far Side, Andrews, McMeel & Parker, 1987.
Night of the Crash-Test Dummies, Andrews & McMeel, 1988.

CARTOON ANTHOLOGIES

The Far Side Gallery, Andrews, McMeel & Parker, 1980.
The Far Side Gallery 2, Andrews & McMeel, 1986.
The Far Side Gallery 3, Andrews & McMeel, 1988.

SIDELIGHTS: Born **August 14, 1950.** Larson grew up in Tacoma, Washington, along the shores of Puget Sound. His mother was a secretary for the American Plywood Association, his father was a Chrysler dealer, and his brother was a distant cousin to Count Dracula. "I was his lab for exploring various forms of torture. Since we were latchkey kids, every day from three to five-thirty became Survival Time."[1]

Brother Dan reduced his childhood to a ". . .sort of 'Theodore Cleaver Meets the Thing.'. . .I was plagued with an overactive imagination—compounded by the fact that we lived in a house with your standard, monster-infested basement. Occasionally, I would hear my father's command that never failed to horrify me: 'Go down to the basement, Gary, and bring up some firewood.' Death.

"And so down I'd go, certain I was about to become the leading character in a story that would be told around campfires for generations to come. ('Say, has anyone here heard "The Boy Who Went for Firewood"?')

"My task nearly completed, I would begin my quick ascent back to the world of the living. And then, as it had countless times before, it would happen. With an audible click, followed by sinister laughter, the lights would go off.

"Engulfed in blackness, I would scramble my way to the top of the stairs only to find the door held firmly shut. From the other side, where the light switch was controlled, I would hear my older brother's voice begin to chant: 'It's coming for you, Gary! It's coming! Do you hear it? Do you hear it breathing, Gary?'

"Unbeknownst to my parents the deep grooves in that side of the door were not caused by the dog."[2]

Although his older brother now works in a florist's supply shop, Larson still wakes "up at the proverbial bump in the night with my eyes wide-open. . . .Everyone has a bogeyman, don't they? For some people maybe it's a dirty rug with company coming over. Mine was something with fangs covered with hair."[3]

Oddly enough—for a boy whose childhood was laced with terror—the local swamp became his playground; creepy crawlies held no fear. He collected snakes, salamanders, lizards,

GARY LARSON. (Photograph courtesy of Nick Gunderson.)

frogs, tarantulas, iguanas, pigeons, small alligators, praying mantis, and one monkey; hunted tadpoles and newts in drainage ditches; and kept an eight-foot boa constrictor in his bedroom. His mother, seemingly impervious to her son's exploits, recalled in an interview: "A garter snake almost disappeared into the davenport one time. I caught it just as it was vanishing into the cushions. And another time a boa constrictor got wrapped in my sewing machine."[4]

Aided by the nefarious Dan, he regularly flooded the backyard to create swamps, hauled sand in the basement to duplicate the Mojave Desert complete with horned toads, and threw red ants in with black ants so he could play war correspondent.

"I was so intrigued by insects and things that crawled or flew— I could spend hours by myself in a vacant lot. I remember one time watching a bird snatch a dragonfly out of midair and thinking, 'Gee, life can come to an end—crunch!—just like that.'"[5]

"Is it a gene? Or environment? My favorite childhood book was 'Mr. Bear Squash You All Flat.' Mom read it to me over and over again. It was about this bear who sat on everyone's houses and squashed 'em flat. Finally, Mr. Bear sits on Mr. Porcupine's house. And Mr. Bear gets cured of his nasty habit. Fast. No one was *killed.* Mr. Bear didn't *kill* anyone. He just squashed their houses. And it wasn't like my mother came to me every night and said, 'Now, Gary—heh, heh, heh—it's time for another chapter of 'Mr. Bear Squash You All Flat'— heh, heh, heh.' She never did that. *Really.*"[6]

But she did notice, very early on, the cartoonist's innate sense of humor. She remembers waking him for the second day of kindergarten and hearing him say, "What again?"[7]

With the advent of school, his taste became more discriminating. "I started off reading Burroughs's Tarzan books and became fascinated with the jungle. It was the big rock python in the story of Mowgli that got me into snakes. When I was twelve, I bought and read *African Genesis.* It was way over my head, but I got it just because there was a gorilla on the cover."[8]

"I had an infatuation with animals in general. My friends would sit around and draw tanks and airplanes, and I used to envy them, because I could never draw them that well. But I could out do them when it came to whales and giraffes."[9]

1968. Attended Washington State University in Pullman. "I was a little wimp, five-foot-eight and 140 pounds in high school. Then I went to college at WSU. My first love was science, and I took all the zoology electives I could, but I majored in communications because I didn't want to teach."[1] He also wanted to avoid the dreaded physics.

"I was nuts not to get a biology degree, but. . .I didn't know what I'd do with a four-year degree in science. I hate to say it, but I was thinking at the time of going into advertising. I thought I could save the world from mundane commercials."[8]

1973-1976. "Young, stupid and right out of college," he formed a duo with a friend, Tom Howard, playing assorted lounges,

**"Well, the Parkers are dead.... You had to
encourage them to take thirds, didn't you?"**

(From *Valley of the Far Side* by Gary Larson. Illustrated by the author.)

**"You idiot! . . . Now this time wait for me to finish the first
'row, row, row your boat' BEFORE you come in!"**

(From *Bride of the Far Side* by Gary Larson. Illustrated by the author.)

hotels, steamers—and a cruise ship to Pago Pago: "We called ourselves Tom and Gary—a band as exciting as its name. I played banjo. I love music, but didn't particularly like the banjo. In fact, it's a bad instrument for a shy person—a torture instrument, because it just screams out for people to look at it, and I never wanted to be in the spotlight. As a professional musician, I was nauseous every night for three years."[1]

1976-1977. He found it easier to work behind the counter of a music store—at least, for a few months: "One morning I couldn't get the knot in my tie to go right, and I kind of freaked out. It wasn't the tie that bothered me, of course. It was just that I didn't like going to work. I've always considered music stores to be the graveyards of musicians."[9] ". . .So I took a few days off and drew a half-dozen cartoons."[10] A local magazine, *Pacific Search*—subsequentily titled, *Pacific Northwest*—bought all six for ninety dollars.

"I immediately quit my job. I thought I was a cartoonist. Wrong!"[9] For two months, he feverishly drew cartoons, while feverishly collecting rejection slips.

1978-1980. He then took a job as an animal cruelty inspector for the Seattle Humane Society. While driving his Plymouth Duster down a country road on the way to the job interview, he ran over a dog—a fact that's been gleefully reported by journalists all over the country as a living example of "Far Side" irony. "I want to make something very clear. I'm not at all *proud* of that incident. I was on my way to the interview and this bunch of mutts suddenly ran across the road. And I hit the last one in the bunch. I mean, he ran off afterwards, but I know I really thumped him. I think I thumped him pretty bad.

"People hear about that and they look at me like these kinds of things happen to me all the time. Like it's something I would find *amusing*. But being involved in it wasn't funny at all. Really. I mean, I'm the kind of person who will swerve off the road to avoid hitting a small *frog*. I mean, I'll swerve off the road and hit *humans* or something to avoid hitting a small frog."[6]

One day a reporter for the *Seattle Times* came to the shelter, investigating a case of Shetland "pony abuse." "The ponies' hooves were overgrown. If they aren't allowed to run around on hard surfaces, their hooves grow just like fingernails. Their hooves actually almost made a complete circle; they were like *skis*. The ponies were in an extreme amount of pain from the tendons in their legs."[9]

When the reporter arrived, "everything went wrong. It was a long, miserable rainy day. I got to know her a little bit, though, and mentioned my *Pacific Search* cartoons. She said I should show my portfolio to the *Times'* Jim King."[1] King bought. Larson now earned fifteen dollars every Saturday; the cartoon ran under the title "Nature's Way."

Larson's then girlfriend talked him into taking cartoons to the *San Francisco Chronicle*. The receptionist advised him not to get his hopes up "and I didn't. [She also said] the editor doesn't look at anything in front of the person who's displaying it, and he'd get back to me in a couple of days."[9] So he spent forty-eight hours wandering around the city. "I finally decided, who do I think I am anyway? So I went to get my cartoons back."[1] They handed him a syndication contract. ". . .I didn't understand anything in it after 'Dear Gary,' but I got that thing signed and mailed so fast!"[12]

The livestock would gather every morning, hoping for one of Farmer Dan's popular "airplane" rides.

(From *The Far Side Gallery 2* by Gary Larson. Illustrated by the author.)

Ironically, when Larson arrived home, he had a letter from the *Seattle Times* regretfully cancelling "Nature's Way," there had been too many complaints. "If that letter had arrived before I went to San Francisco, I probably would never have had the courage to go."[1]

January 1, 1980. Newly dubbed "The Far Side," the first panel appeared in the *San Francisco Chronicle.* "If I had struck out with the *Chronicle,* I would have given the whole thing up. My first month in syndication, I made about one hundred dollars. I thought it would be exciting if I ever got up to the level where I could pay my rent."[11]

"I lived in terror of cancellation. I was always being cancelled by newspapers, and I was horrified every time. All these *Nancy* readers would see this hideous thing and cry out. But the people on the news staffs enjoyed the strip. I think that's the single thing that saved me."[1]

Some of the cartoons were censored by syndicators, some never ran. "There was one where some dragon kids were at home alone with their parents gone, and they were up in their rooms lighting their sneezes. Another one—and I really didn't mean to ridicule the Shroud of Turin—it's a cartoon with a split image, one with the Shroud of Turin and the lower panel with a similar, striped short-sleeved shirt called the Shirt of Toledo."[1]

Another panel drew complaints from a considerable proportion of subscribers. It showed an enraged couple confronting a witch: "We hired you to babysit the kids, and you cooked and ate them BOTH?"

The editor of the *Fort Wayne News-Sentinel* (Ind.) tried to drop the strip because it played to the "humor of violence." Readers protested; the strip was reinstated. "Morbid humor is very valid, even healthy, as long as you don't do it gratuitously. There's more violence in Saturday morning cartoons."[11] "There have been some significant wars in cities between people who enjoy this kind of humor and those who don't."[13]

Success allowed Larson to move from a basement apartment to a two-bedroom suburban house. The original apartment was "about the size of a men's room" with a herpetarium coined by one journalist as a snake "Taj Mahal." It was a four-foot-high cabinet with five snake condos, each backlit with wood-chip flooring. The community consisted of a gray-banded Mexican king snake, a Florida king, a corn snake, and a black pine snake. There was also an unusual wall hanging—a molt shed by Phyllis, a fifteen-foot Burmese python: "I don't usually give names to my snakes. I'm in no way anthropomorphic about them, and they don't respond to names. But she was so big, it was kind of mandatory. Everyone wanted her to have one."[4]

One day, while feeding her dead rabbits, Phyllis gave him reason to pause. "I don't want to sound like Frank Buck. I don't want it to sound like some exciting adventure I had in the tropics of my bedroom...*but*...it confused me momentarily with the food and there we were. It was either she or I. I sold her to *another* fool."[14]

"That's the way snakes are. She was excited and had eaten one rabbit, and food was in the air. She could smell it, sense it and she was looking for some motion. It's a stimulus response kind of thing. I decided I didn't want to be a stimulus any longer."[4] Larson has since reduced his snake collection from a high of twenty: "I've cut back, I'm maturing. I'm down to four or five. . ."[14]

"General! Quick! Look! . . . Henderson is doing it again!"

(From *The Far Side Gallery* by Gary Larson. Illustrated by the author.)

On a drawing board that overlooks Union Bay, Larson now works in a second-floor studio in his Tudor-style house in suburban Seattle, surrounded by a papier-mache python, a stuffed wart-hog head, a framed shark jaw, and a fossilized mastodon tooth, given to him by his grandmother. Pets include several snakes and a carnivorous frog from Argentina. The frog's diet of mice is kept in his freezer: "Let's just say you don't automatically reach for the vanilla ice cream at my house."[11]

But the cartoonist seems uncomfortable with his comfortable life style: "Maybe it's my blue-collar background, but work meant to me that you come home covered with sweat. Now I just brush away the eraser shavings."[16] "I keep thinking someone's gonna show up and say, 'There's been a big mistake. The guy next door is supposed to be drawing the cartoon. Here's your shovel.'"[11]

The Far Side has become a regular feature in more than 700 newspapers, with six million books sold, and a feature film in the works. There are greeting cards, posters, coffee mugs, calendars, and t-shirts. Without Larson's permission, a bar in Seattle is called the Far Side Tavern. "At least they have good taste. At least it's not called the Garfield Bar and Grill."[3] "I've been swept along by the merchandising monster."[13]

The latest commercial venture involves animated advertising, thirty-second television commercials for DHL Worldwide Express, a courier service. "I never thought I'd link up with an advertiser, but finally one came through that would give me a lot of creative control. They won't prostitute the work—there won't be any characters with voices, for instance. But I

Lewis and Clark meet Sylvia and Rhonda.

(From *Beyond the Far Side* by Gary Larson. Illustrated by the author.)

don't know anything about animation, so it's going to be a hard thing for me to direct.''[1]

Celebrity, however, brings with it the usual problems. Not the least of which was the time he got hit with a cream pie at a book signing by a fan dressed in a rabbit suit. ''I felt bad for her—the crowd was kind of ugly about it, and she just didn't understand that I wouldn't like it. Then, one night I got surrounded by an autograph crowd, and a woman grabbed my hand and said, 'We're going' and led me into a car with a bunch of strangers. It turned out they had been befriended by the guy from my syndicate, but I felt almost hijacked. Nobody else would've been nervous, but I felt very claustrophobic. I quit doing book signing tours three years ago.''[1]

''It used to be simple. Draw the panels and send them out. Now it's too showbiz. I'm going to pull the plug, when necessary, to keep my sanity.''[11]

October 28, 1982. The nadir of his career—a day that will live in infamy—was brought on by ''cow tools.'' The cartoon showed a cow standing in front of a workbench displaying what looked to be a saw, a stone with a handle, a mound, and a stick with tines. The caption was ''COW TOOLS.'' And nobody got it.

''People wrote thousands of letters to their papers. Hundreds of them phoned me at home—my number was still listed— demanding to know what the cartoon meant. Radio talk show hosts were phoning me live. The *Spokane Spokesman-Review* put the cartoon on the front page with the caption, 'What does this mean?' The *Philadelphia Daily News* posted a fifty dollar reward for anyone in the newsroom who could explain it. All

I meant was I remembered learning in a WSU anthropology class that tools used to be the definition of man, but then they discovered that even birds made tools of a sort, so they had to revise the theory. I thought, what if cows made tools too— I knew they wouldn't be wonderful tools, so I made them crude and dumb-looking. It was a cartoon that did not work.''[1]

Larson issued a note of explanation, a sort of ''Apologia pro bovine sua'': ''Occasionally, between the time I first conceive a cartoon idea and the final product, something goes awry. Judging from the number of calls from puzzled readers (including my own mother), this happened with my recent 'cow tools' cartoon.

''The cartoon was meant as an exercise in silliness. I've never met a cow who could make tools, but if I had, I feel sure that its efforts would lack something in sophistication and would resemble the crude specimens shown in the cartoon.

''It is a joke that might have some success with anthropologists, but it obviously did not work as I intended and I regret that it has baffled so many readers.''[15]

The episode had one consolation. ''It was the first time that I had any inkling of how much this cartoon was being read.''[12]

''I realize that some of my cartoons go over people's heads. But if out of ten people, I think that one will bellylaugh and the other nine will be dumbfounded, I'll go for it. The one thing I try not to do is condescend to people. If you start doing cartoons that are too universal, you end up with something milked out and uninteresting. I'd rather be misunderstood.''[8]

''People try to look for deep meanings in my work. I want to say, 'They're just cartoons, folks. You laugh or you don't.' Gee, I sound shallow. But I don't react to current events or other stimuli. I don't read or watch TV to get ideas. My work is basically sitting down at the drawing table and getting silly.

''These are cartoons, not nuclear physics.''[7]

1984. Larson reluctantly left Chronicle Features for the larger Universal Syndicate. ''[It] was the hardest thing I have ever done in my life. . . .I spent many sleepless nights over it. But I started getting these amazing offers, and Chronicle was so small they just got left in the dust. When I saw the movie *Broadway Danny Rose,* God, it hit me hard. The guy at Chronicle Features was the Woody Allen character in that film to me. He discovers talent, and when they make it big—they leave. My attorney said when he told him I was going to Universal, it went down pretty hard.''[1]

December 1, 1985. Eleven thousand fans jammed an exhibit of 400 ''Far Side'' cartoons, sponsored by the California Academy of Sciences in San Francisco's Golden Gate Park. Even before the show opened, the Smithsonian Institution and the Los Angeles Museum of Natural History had signed up to host it. The exhibit, ''The Far Side of Science,'' ballooned to 600 cartoons for its crowded opening in Los Angeles in November, 1986. The Smithsonian drew an estimated two million. The road show has been ambling around the country ever since, with continuous bookings extending into 1989.

Since many of Larson's cartoons contain dinosaurs and wooly mammoths, he has become the pin-up of choice on lab refrigerators, file cabinets, and bunsen burners. Yellowed clippings grace the bulletin boards of biologists, botanists, anthropologists, herpetologists, ornithologists, mammalogists, and entomologists. ''I don't really analyze my work too much, but sometimes I can't help thinking, 'What's the point of this

"I just can't tell from here. ... That could either be our flock, another flock, or just a bunch of little m's"

(From *The Far Side Gallery 2* by Gary Larson. Illustrated by the author.)

cartoon?' Because I'm aware that scientists are reading. I get schizophrenic about who I'm drawing for.

"If you can't handle physics—attack it. It's not quite like me to ridicule. Even when I do something on the bold side, it's not mean or gratuitous. For me, the humor comes in being aware that the scientific world is something unto itself. It's in the white smocks and the microscopes. Anything that's set up to be very serious has comic potential when it all comes unraveled.

"You have to have some innate understanding of wildlife to do something that's truly silly. Even so, I don't get *too* hung up on accuracy. For example, I was drawing a cartoon with sharks in it and found myself wondering how many gill arches they had. A couple of years ago I would have looked it up. This time I just decided to guess."[8]

In Larson's cartoons, animals are guided by instinct; humans by social mores. He tends to deflate self-importance, ridiculing man's feelings of superiority over planetmates: "All we are is a species, like millions of others, a species that can go extinct, and probably will, at the rate things are going. I think it's dangerous to think otherwise, and that's one of the problems with the human race."[3]

Turning nature upside down, he roots for the animals: "When people ask me about my love for animals, it makes me think of puppies and kittens. My interests have always been from amoebas on up. I hope that's what comes through, a respect for life."[16]

"Look at it like this. There are so many animals on this planet that we're dependent on. Without them, we'd be history. But take us off the planet, and who suffers?. . .Okay, maybe dogs.

And then maybe just for a week. Until they figure things out. THE CATS ARE OURS!"[3]

"Mostly I think of animals as a vehicle for my own particular sense of humor. A lot of the time I end up exploring the weird prejudices we humans have toward some animals. If a real animal starts adding too many legs or too many eyes, it seems to become too alien for most of us to stand. But biologists instinctively look through that bias and are intrigued by the living organism, no matter what its shape is."[17]

Another recurrent theme reflects the vagaries of life: "Although we think we are in the driver's seat, we don't really know from one moment to the next what's going to happen to us. We might win the Pulitzer Prize one day and the next day we step off the curb and a sanitation truck runs over us."[18]

"It's wonderful that we live in a world in which there are things that can eat us. It keeps us from getting too cocky."[16]

Larson describes his work habits as "very chaotic. I sometimes find myself at the drawing board at very odd hours, but it's hard for me to do something that deals with humor in an assembly-line fashion. You can't say, 'I'm going to sit down at two o'clock and draw 'til five and run out these great things. It doesn't work that way. I think you have to capitalize on those moments when you're in the mood and you feel the juices flow."[10]

"I don't know where the ideas come from. I just sit down and let myself get silly. After that, I don't want to think about it. It is all smoke—and hard work. It's a pretty strange job, don't you think? I guess someone's gotta be sick for a living."[5]

"It's not in my personality to be assertive, and I sometimes think I've succumbed to the pressure. And the creative pressure is there all the time, too. After seven years, my career has become a little bit of a Frankenstein's monster. But every time I start to whine about it, my dad has the way to put me in my place. 'Well, kid,' he says, 'It sure beats workin' in a sawmill.' And I've got to admit, he's right."[1]

Major influences have been Don Martin of *Mad*, George Booth of the *New Yorker*, and B. Kliban's cat cartoons. "A great collision takes place on the comic pages because it's all there at once. 'The Far Side' juxtaposed with 'Nancy' definitely represents a conflict in styles of humor. But I think it's all valid—each of us has his readership. Humor is so subjective—there's nothing so universal that everyone will like and understand. If there were, it would have to be so washed out that it wouldn't be funny anymore. I enjoy humor that has nuances, that doesn't rely on blatant gags to succeed. I even dislike the word *gag*—it implies such a formula approach to humor.

"I think people expect me to be very bizarre, as if I had stepped out of one of my cartoons, and I think they're often disappointed. A recurring reaction when people meet me is, 'Gee, you look so normal.' I don't know if they expect me to have fangs or one eye like a Cyclops or what."[10] "I've never found the cartoon itself bizarre. I think *Nancy* is bizarre. I don't deny people the right to think it, but I look at 'The Love Boat,' and it has a laugh track, so evidently it's something that most people find funny. But I find 'The Love Boat' bizarre."[3]

In his spare time, Larson shoots baskets, plays guitar, and drives his Toyota pickup to Seattle's Woodland Park Zoo. He has also made several snake hunting expeditions to Mexico with his friend, Ernie Wagner, the reptile curator at the zoo and a rabid practical joker. With the help of other Ernie victims, Larson once filled Ernie's bathtub with hippopotamus manure. "Originally, we had thoughts of filling his house with live chickens. *Serious* thoughts. But we finally decided on the hippo manure. Fifty pounds. In the bathtub. I think it made quite an impression. Because Ernie's practical jokes had gotten to a level where it was clear to me that unless he was stopped, someone was gonna die.

"Don't get me wrong. My friend Ernie is a regular kind of guy. It's just that sometimes he scares me. I'm not sure if he knows that certain boundaries exist. I don't know if. . .Wait a minute. Retract everything I said about 'a regular kind of guy.' Ernie is not a regular kind of guy. He's capable of having normal *moments*. But he's not a regular kind of guy."

In 1978, Wagner asked Larson if he wanted to camp in the hills of central Mexico to hunt snakes. "I said, 'Sure.' Who wouldn't want to go to Mexico and hunt snakes?" Ernie had a jar of scorpions; Larson was terrified of scorpions. "[They were] large, black, and basically harmless. But if looks could kill, you'd take one look at them and you'd die. Early one morning, I was lying in my sleeping bag, all zipped up, halfway between sleep and wakefulness. Semi-conscious. Ernie walked over to me carrying his jar of whip scorpions and nonchalantly dumped them all into my sleeping bag. I was brought into full wakefulness by the sound of Ernie laughing hysterically. He was just standing there, laughing hysterically, holding the empty jar. I heard his laughter. And then I saw the jar, which I suddenly recognized as *the* jar, now vacant. And I realized what he had done. And I came out of that sleeping bag *real* fast. And I did not even *consider* the zipper. All of his jokes have the common theme of horror. That's how Ernie lets you know he likes you. (And remember, the scorpions weren't *poisonous* ones in there. That's what I mean by his normal moments.)"[6]

In a commencement speech to history majors at the University of California at Berkeley, Larson gave this advice: "My first

"Quit complaining and eat it! ... Number one, chicken soup is good for the flu—and number two, it's nobody we know."

(From *The Far Side Gallery 2* by Gary Larson. Illustrated by the author.)

Eventually, Stevie looked up: His mother was nowhere in sight, and this was certainly no longer the toy department.

(From *It Came from the Far Side* by Gary Larson. Illustrated by the author.)

controversial cartoon was of Santa Claus writing in his cookbook on the nine ways to serve venison." An editor encouraged him to ignore the hate mail. "His advice was to just keep doing it the way you're doing it. And I have. [By] listening to my own instincts. [I prefer] people who, despite their eccentricities, have shaped their lives around something they enjoy, something they are passionate about. In this 'yuppified' day and age, there's no substitute for doing something you enjoy. There are one hundred things worse than not hearing a different drummer and walking to the same beat that everyone else does."[19]

Beginning October 30, 1988, Larson took a hiatus from his immensely popular comic "The Far Side" to recharge those areas of his brain from which "The Far Side" comes each day, according to Universal Press Syndicate associate editor Jake Morrissey. Readers, meanwhile, will have to survive on a diet of reruns.

FOOTNOTE SOURCES

[1]Tim Appelo, "The Mischievous Mind of Gary Larson," *Pacific Northwest*, September, 1987.

[2]Frontispiece, *The Far Side Gallery*, Andrews, McMeel & Parker, 1980.

[3]Peter Richmond, "Creatures from the Black Cartoon," *Rolling Stone*, September 24, 1987.

[4]Nancy Shute, "Far Out!," *Chicago Tribune*, June 4, 1984.

[5]Mark A. Stein, "Far Out!," *Los Angeles Times*, December 9, 1985.

[6]Dan Geringer, "A Cartoonist on the Wild Side," *Philadelphia Daily News*, September 18, 1984.

[7]Mei-Mei Chan, "The Mind behind 'The Far Side'," *USA Today*, October 24, 1984.

[8]Sheridan Warrick, "'The Far Side' of Science," *Pacific Discovery*, October-December, 1985.

[9]Robert Cross, "Larson Draws a Winner from the 'Far Side' of Humor," *Chicago Tribune*, January 5, 1983.

[10]Charles Solomon, "Near Side of a 'Normal' Artist," *Los Angeles Times*, December 1, 1984.

[11]"Looney 'Toonist Gary Larson Takes Millions for a Daily Walk on 'The Far Side,'" *People*, February 4, 1985.

[12]Beaufort Cranford, "Not So Far Out," *Detroit News*, November 20, 1984.

[13]Lisa Kinoshita, "A View from the 'Far Side'. . . ," *Saturday Review*, November/December, 1984.

[14]Richard Harrington, "The Bizarre Side," *Washington Post*, June 16, 1983.

[15]Press release, *Chronicle Features*, n.d.

[16]James Kelly, "All Creatures Weird and Funny," *Time*, December 1, 1986.

[17]David Perlman, "Cartoonist's Animal Weirdos" *San Francisco Chronicle*, December 1, 1985.

[18]Tim Gaffney, "The Woody Allens of Cartooning: Offbeat, Sophisticated Humor," *San Francisco Chronicle*, February 3, 1982.

[19]Edward Iwata, "Cartoonist's Advice to the Graduates," *San Francisco Chronicle*, May 13, 1985.

FOR MORE INFORMATION SEE:

Clarence Petersen, "Far-Out 'Far Side' Comes to Tempo," *Chicago Tribune*, November 22, 1981.

Clifford A. Ridley, "A Cartoonist Is Cowed by Own Far-Out Humor," *Detroit News*, November 9, 1982.

Honolulu Advertiser & Star-Bulletin, June 15, 1983.

Michael Robertson, "The Woody Allen of Cartoonists," *San Francisco Chronicle*, October 11, 1983.

Nancy Shute, "Scientists Meet Their Alter Ego on the 'Far Side,'" *Smithsonian*, April, 1984.

Carol Krucoff, "Why Does Everybody Think I Must Be Far Out?," *Washington Post*, June 10, 1984.

Publishers Weekly, September 21, 1984.

People, October 1, 1984, June 18, 1985, June 21, 1985.

Eileen Lanzafama, "Life on the 'Far Side,'" *National Wildlife*, October/November, 1984.

Reader's Digest, July, 1985.

"'Far Side' Graces Many a Lab Wall," *Minneapolis Star and Tribune*, December 13, 1985.

Carrie Dolan, "The 'Far Side's' Gary Larson," *Seventeen*, April, 1986.

Charles Solomon, "'Far Side' Exhibit," *Los Angeles Times*, November 19, 1986.

C. Petersen, "Effing the Ineffable 'Far Side,'" *Chicago Tribune*, February 24, 1987.

Smithsonian, April, 1987.

"'Far Side' Is a Natural for Smithsonian," *St. Louis Post-Dispatch*, April 23, 1987.

"Who's the King of Comics?" *Sacramento Bee*, April 23, 1987.

Jon Greer, "DHL 'Far Side' Ad Campaign," *San Francisco Chronicle*, August 20, 1987.

C. Petersen, "Shameless Plug for a Neighbor," *Chicago Tribune*, September 3, 1987.

"Taking a Break from 'The Far Side,'" *Newsweek*, October 10, 1988.

LEIBOLD, Jay 1957-

PERSONAL: Born October 15, 1957, in Denver, Colo.; son of James Edward (a doctor) and Angela (a designer; maiden name, Montavon) Leibold. *Education:* Williams College, B.A., 1980. *Home:* 46 Albion, San Francisco, Calif. 94103.

JAY LEIBOLD

CAREER: Farrar, Straus & Giroux (publisher), New York, N.Y., editorial assistant, 1981-82; writer, 1982—; *Fiction Network,* San Francisco, Calif., senior editor, 1988—.

WRITINGS:

"CHOOSE YOUR OWN ADVENTURE" SERIES; NOVELS FOR YOUNG PEOPLE

Sabotage, Bantam, 1984.
Spy for George Washington, Bantam, 1985.
Grand Canyon Odyssey, Bantam, 1985.
The Antimatter Formula, Bantam, 1986.
Beyond the Great Wall, Bantam, 1987.
Secret of the Ninja, Bantam, 1987.

Also author of a collection of short stories for Hard Press, 1988. Contributor of stories and reviews to magazines and newspapers.

SIDELIGHTS: "The 'Choose Your Own Adventure' series has given me a chance to earn a living as a writer and time to work on other kinds of fiction."

LEVINE, Sarah 1970-

PERSONAL: Born March 9, 1970, in Pittsburgh, Pa.; daughter of Jonathan (a human relations executive) and Abby (an editor and author; maiden name, Bernstein) Levine. *Education:* Attended high school in Evanston, Ill. *Home:* 9509 Ridgeway Ave., Evanston, Ill. 60203.

CAREER: Writer.

WRITINGS:

(With mother, Abby Levine) *Sometimes I Wish I Were Mindy* (juvenile; *My Weekly Reader* selection; illustrated by Blanche Sims), A. Whitman, 1986.

LOEB, Jeffrey 1946-

PERSONAL: Original name, Jeffrey Lob; surname legally changed in 1986; born June 6, 1946, in New York, N.Y.; son of Erich (an insurance broker) and Dorothea (a preschool teacher; maiden name, Meyer) Lob; married Catherine Snyder (an occupational therapist), July 19, 1981; children: Jeremy, Carolyn. *Education:* Attended Union College, Schenectady, N.Y.; 1964-66; Antioch College, B.A., 1969; graduate study at Boston University, 1972-74. *Home:* 35 Brooks St., Maynard, Mass. 01754. *Office:* Hole in the Sock, P.O. Box 119, Maynard, Mass. 01754.

CAREER: Teacher at Glenwood Elementary School, Short Hills, N.J., and Millburn Junior High School, Millburn, N.J.; composer and musical manager in Maynard, Mass., 1976—; Hole in the Sock Productions, Maynard, co-founder and co-director, 1982—. Producer of "Zoom," for WGBH-TV, and "Spider's Web," for GBH-FM Radio. *Member:* International Television Association, National Teachers' Association, Massachusetts Association of Educational Media.

WRITINGS:

JUVENILE

(Editor with Eric H. Arnold) *Lights Out! Kids Talk about Summer Camp* (illustrated by True Kelley), Little, Brown, 1985.
I'm Telling! Kids Talk about Brothers and Sisters (illustrated by G. Brian Karas), Little, Brown, 1987.

Contributor to newsletters.

WORK IN PROGRESS: A book on "rites of passage."

SIDELIGHTS: "The children's book projects are a logical spinoff of my music and my activities as a media teacher and audio producer. Hole in the Sock Productions incorporates the diversity of skills and interests which I have held for many years, and our upcoming projects—radio drama in the schools, a pilot radio program on adolescence for the major National Public Radio station in Boston, and a third book—also reflect the development of these interests."

MacKINNON GROOMER, Vera 1915-

PERSONAL: Born August 5, 1915, in Corvallis, Ore.; daughter of John Fredrick (a farmer) and Danella (a medical receptionist; maiden name, Lamar) MacKinnon; married Clyde C. Groomer (a retired clergyman), October 2, 1938; children: Yvonne McClure, Danella Kotrba. *Education:* Attended San Mateo College, 1956-67, and Loma Linda University, 1944-46. *Politics:* Republican. *Religion:* Seventh-Day Adventist. *Home and office:* 4820 Gull Rd., Lansing, Mich. 48917.

CAREER: Central California Conference of Seventh-Day Adventists, San Jose, Calif., child evangelism coordinator, 1962-69; Michigan Conference of Seventh-Day Adventists, Lansing, Mich., child evangelism director and coordinator, 1969-

I have to dust every Saturday. ■ (From *Sometimes I Wish I Were Mindy* by Abby Levine and Sarah Levine. Illustrated by Blanche Sims.)

83; author, 1951—. Seminar leader; certified lead consultant for Calling and Caring Ministries. *Awards, honors:* Certificate of Achievement from the Southern Publishing Association, 1978, 1979 (two), and 1980.

WRITINGS:

Illustrating Sabbath Songs for Tiny Tots, Pacific Press, Book 1, 1966, Book 2, 1967.
Teaching That Communicates (illustrated by Hazel Todd), Visual Aid Press, 1972.
Kind Kristy (illustrated by Harry Baerg), Review & Herald, 1979.
Obedience Brings Happiness (illustrated by Ronnie Hester), Review & Herald, 1979.

Quiet Because (illustrated by R. Hester), Review & Herald, 1979.
Good Friends Again (illustrated by R. Hester), Review & Herald, 1980.
Growing Stronger (illustrated by R. Hester), Review & Herald, 1980.
Talking to My Friend Jesus (illustrated by R. Hester), Review & Herald, 1980.
Dibe Yazahi (illustrated by Brenda Basler), Review & Herald, 1980.

Also author of numerous articles in denominational journals, and of several stories (illustrated in color on felt) printed by B. J. K. Triplet and World Wide Visual.

VERA MacKINNON GROOMER

WORK IN PROGRESS: A story, "Reaching the Handicapped Child," to be illustrated in color felt, for B. J. K. Triplet.

SIDELIGHTS: "I was born in Corvallis, Oregon. We were a family of six, four children and parents. Later, my parents added two foster children; there were four girls and two boys. My father farmed, sometimes large and other times smaller acreage in Colorado where I spent most of my childhood years. We had lots of wildlife to enjoy. Our farm was joined on three sides by forest about six miles from a small village which provided our big trip once a week. Other than our church, our social life was limited and we spent time in the forest observing and studying as well as making friends with things in nature.

"Later we moved to California close to a college when all the children needed more education. Our home was within walking distance of Loma Linda University, La Sierra Campus.

"After marriage, my husband, who was in pastoral work and later in an administrative position, and I traveled extensively throughout the United States, holding seminars and workshops, demonstrating materials and training workers to give better religious instruction to the children of the church. This traveling and visiting many National Parks and various places of interest has given me a background for the stories I have written. Most of them have centered around nature or have been religious.

"I developed an interest in young children in my early teens. My three-year-old cousins would spend hours listening to my make-believe and real stories. From this I began to work with the young children in our church. The need for more material inspired my writing of children's religious material. This included many stories, poems, verses and program outlines published by the General Conference of Seventh-Day Adventist, Sabbath School Department in Washington, D. C. To make

these more effective several felt companies produced felt illustrations to accompany the stories.

"Having raised two daughters and three grandaughters I had a perfect laboratory for my writing. I still have as my aim to bring to young children, material that will build better character. I would like them to experience the happiness of living that can be possible in a world where they see much of the opposite."

HOBBIES AND OTHER INTERESTS: Flower arranging, ceramic painting.

MANNETTI, Lisa 1953-
(L. A. Kane)

PERSONAL: Born January 9, 1953, in White Plains, N. Y.; daughter of Armand J. (in sales) and Anne (a public health director; maiden name, Luongo) Mannetti; married Terence L. Kane (an engineer), September 9, 1978. *Education:* Fairfield University, B.A., 1975; Fordham University, M.A., 1981, doctoral study, 1983-84. *Home:* Wappingers Falls, N.Y. 12590.

CAREER: New York, New York City, editorial assistant, 1975-76; *More,* New York City, editorial assistant, 1976-77; Walter Panas High School, Shrub Oak, N.Y., substitute English teacher, 1977-81; author, 1981—. *Member:* National Writers Union. *Awards, honors: Iran and Iraq* was selected one of Child Study Association of America's Children's Books of the Year, 1986.

LISA MANNETTI

WRITINGS:

JUVENILE

Equality, F. Watts, 1985.
Iran and Iraq: Nations at War, F. Watts, 1986.

WORK IN PROGRESS: A novel set in nineteenth-century England.

SIDELIGHTS: "I began writing when I was eight years old; I had already fallen in love with reading (my favorite book was Bronte's *Jane Eyre*). I'm certain my early attempts were an outgrowth of my fascination with the printed word. Not long after we acquired a typewriter, since everyone else in the family could type, I decided I would learn, too. And when I was ten I began writing a novel. I distinctly remember (in addition to knowing it was not very good), it was about twins named Linda and Pam. It had sixty-three chapters, because it was sixty-three pages long when I left off writing it.

"I continued writing through my adolescence. I worked on the school newspaper, wrote for the literary magazine, and was the editor of the yearbook. These were small triumphs, but were no less encouraging. During my teens, I also became fascinated by antiques and old houses.

"At Fairfield, I majored in English. One of my professors taught a course entitled 'Development of the Novel' so well, and with so much enthusiasm, he cemented my life-long adoration of the eighteenth and nineteenth centuries, which then became the precise area of my specialty in graduate school, and still continues to hold my interest.

"For my fictional works, research consists of any scrap of information I can pounce on, including visits to historic houses, conversations, and oddments in addition to more traditional sources—period novels, books on costume, manners, etc.

"For my non-fiction works I relied on textbooks, newspaper accounts, and magazine articles.

"I enjoy my life as a writer tremendously. Although there may not be rewards in the form of bonuses, promotions, or pay-raises, there is the everyday satisfaction in doing something I really love: learning new things, pursuing in depth interests I may have, a well-crafted sentence, or a finely-tuned character.

"There are frustrations, but knowing they occur with any occupation helps me maintain a sense of optimism. More importantly, each day there is the literal excitement of beginning with a blank page: the chance to create anew."

HOBBIES AND OTHER INTERESTS: Theater, sculpting, gardening.

MANNING-SANDERS, Ruth   1895(?)-1988

OBITUARY NOTICE—See sketch in *SATA* Volume 15. Born in 1895 (one source says c. 1888), in Swansea, Wales; died at her home on October 12, 1988, in Penzance, Cornwall, England. Editor and author. Manning-Sanders was best known for folk and fairy tales that she retold for children, including the Cornish collection *Peter and the Piskies*, and the French collection *Jonnikin and the Flying Basket*. She also wrote original works for young people such as *Mystery at Penmarth*, and *Hedgehog and Puppy Dog Tales*, and edited a number of anthologies. Before concentrating on children's books in the late

1930s, Manning-Sanders wrote several books for adults, including *The Pedlar and Other Poems*, and the novel *The Twelve Saints*. The two years she spent with a traveling carnival inspired her study *The English Circus*. Her children's book, *A Bundle of Ballads* was awarded the Kate Greenaway Medal in 1959. Her last work, *A Cauldron of Witches*, was published in 1988.

FOR MORE INFORMATION SEE:

Twentieth-Century Children's Writers, 2nd edition, St. Martin's, 1983.

OBITUARIES

Times (London), October 13, 1988.

MANSON, Beverlie   1945-

PERSONAL: Born June 10, 1945, in Manchester, England; daughter of Lewis (a fashion designer) and Betty (Meggitt) Manson; married Eric Jacobs (divorced); married Roger William Taylor (in business), February 16, 1981; children: (first marriage) Emma, Daniel. *Education:* Manchester College of Art, Fellow Chartered Society of Designers (FCSD), 1965. *Home:* 11 Southwood Ave., London N.6, England. *Agent:* Pat Curren, 34-30 78th St., Apt. 3E, Jackson Heights, N.Y. 11372.

CAREER: Stowe and Boroden, Manchester, England, fashion artist, 1966-68; World Distributors (publisher), Manchester, book illustrator, 1968-69; free-lance writer and illustrator, 1969—. *Member:* Society of Industrial Artists and Designers (fellow).

WRITINGS:

JUVENILE; SELF-ILLUSTRATED

Favorite Fairy Stories, Hamlyn, 1978.
The Fairies' Alphabet Book, Doubleday, 1982.
Fairy ABC, Doubleday, 1982.
The Fairies' Nighttime Book, Doubleday, 1983.

BEVERLIE MANSON

ILLUSTRATOR

My Little Book of Birthdays, Tyndall Mitchell, 1969.
The Storybook Annual, Purnell, 1970.
Lornie Leete-Hodge, *The Big Golden Book of Fairy Tales,*
    Golden Press, 1981.
Fairy Poems for the Very Young, Doubleday, 1982.
Mimi Khalvati, *I Know a Place,* Dent, 1985.
Kenneth Williams, *I Only Have to Close My Eyes,* Dent, 1986.
Fay Marden, *The Almond Blossom Fairy,* Peter Bedrick, 1987.

Also illustrator of greeting cards and textiles.

WORK IN PROGRESS: Children's books.

SIDELIGHTS: "I want my future books to be more like my
book *I Only Have to Close My Eyes.* The subject matter is
quite unusual and the illustrations are rich, lavish, and fantastic.

"I think that my books now reflect that I do not take life
seriously. I try to make books that make people smile, and
even giggle, a little. What is also very important is that my
pictures have so much going on that the child will spend a
long time finding new things."

FOR MORE INFORMATION SEE:

Vineyard Gazette, November 18, 1983.
Richmond Times, November 20, 1983.
Potomac News, December 7, 1983.

MARKLE, Sandra L(ee) 1946-

PERSONAL: Born November 10, 1946, in Fostoria, Ohio;
daughter of Robert (a general foreman) and Dorothy (a secretary; maiden name, Sauler) Haldeman; married William
Markle (a programmer/analyst), August 10, 1968; children:
Scott, Holly. *Education:* Bowling Green State University, B.S.
(magna cum laude), 1968; graduate study at Ohio University,
1970-71, and University of North Carolina, Asheville, 1973-
74. *Home and office:* 535 Spindlewick Dr., Dunwoody, Ga.
30338.

CAREER: Teacher at elementary schools in Woodville, Ohio,
1968-69, Athens, Ohio, 1969-71, and Asheville, N.C., 1971-
79; Chapel Hill Middle School, Douglasville, Ga., science
teacher, 1979-80; full-time writer, 1980—. Presents teacher
workshops and science programs for children; presented "Science Shop," a series on WLOS-TV, Asheville, N.C., and
"Ms. Whiz," a series on WANX-TV, Atlanta, Ga.; science
consultant to *Instructor* and Corporation for Public Broadcasting.

WRITINGS:

JUVENILE

Primary Science Sampler, Learning Works, 1980.
Science Sampler, Learning Works, 1980.
Computer Tutor: An Introduction to Computers (illustrated by
    Bev Armstrong), Learning Works, 1981.
Computer Tutor Junior (illustrated by B. Armstrong), Learn-
    ing Works, 1982.

SANDRA L. MARKLE

Weather/Electricity/Environmental Investigations, Learning Works, 1982.

Kids' Computer Capers: Investigations for Beginners (illustrated by Stella Ormai), Lothrop, 1983.

Exploring Winter (self-illustrated), Atheneum, 1984.

The Programmer's Guide to the Galaxy (illustrated by S. Ormai), Lothrop, 1984.

(With husband, William Markle) *In Search of Graphics: Adventures in Computer Art,* Lothrop, 1984.

Digging Deeper: Investigations into Rocks, Shocks, Quakes, and Other Earthy Matters, Lothrop, 1987.

Exploring Summer: A Season of Science Activities, Puzzlers, and Games (self-illustrated), Atheneum, 1987.

Science Mini-Mysteries, Atheneum, 1988.

Author of "Natural Wonder Notebook," a monthly column in *Instructor,* and "The Learning Center," a monthly column in *Teaching and Computers.* Contributor to magazines, including *Cricket, Highlights for Children, Jack and Jill, Ranger Rick, 3-2-1 Contact,* and *Learning.* Contributing editor, *Teaching and Computers,* 1983—.

WORK IN PROGRESS: A series of magazine feature articles for *Peanut.*

MARTYR, Paula (Jane)   1960-
(Paula Jane Lawford)

PERSONAL: Born March 9, 1960, in Romford, England; daughter of John (a charity worker abroad) and Jennifer (Fox) Lawford; married Andrew Martyr (a telecommunications engineer and writer), November 19, 1983; children: Jonathan. *Education:* Reigate School of Art, Diploma, 1981. *Home:* 17 Aragon Ave., Thames Ditton, Surrey KT7 0P4, England. *Agent:* c/o Hamish Hamilton Ltd., Garden House, 57-59 Long Acre, London WC2E 9JZ, England.

CAREER: Illustrator of children's books.

ILLUSTRATOR:

JUVENILE

Shelia Lavelle, *Fetch the Slipper,* Hamish Hamilton, 1989.
Andrew Martyr, *The Magic Hiccup,* Hamish Hamilton, 1989.

JUVENILE; UNDER NAME PAULA JANE LAWFORD; ALL WRITTEN BY HUSBAND, ANDREW MARTYR, EXCEPT AS NOTED

Willisk's Tooth, Hamish Hamilton, 1985, David & Charles, 1988.

Winston's Ice Cream Caper, Hamish Hamilton, 1986, David & Charles, 1988.

Patch the Pirate Cat, Hamish Hamilton, 1987, David & Charles, 1988.

Margaret Stuart Barry, *Diz and the Big Fat Burglar,* Hamish Hamilton, 1987.

Beeswax the Bad, Hamish Hamilton, 1988.

WORK IN PROGRESS: An educational series of eighteen reading books by Julia Jarmen, to be published by Ginn.

SIDELIGHTS: "I think I was probably born holding a pencil, no piece of paper is ever without a doodle or a scribble. I had one ambition at school—l wanted to become an illustrator of children's books.

"I went to art school in 1976, where, after a foundation course I was guided into graphic design and advertising. I left college

PAULA MARTYR

five years later realising that graphic design wasn't really for me.

"It was about this time that I met my husband. Together we created *Willisk's Tooth,* which to my surprise and joy was eventually published by Hamish Hamilton. I suppose to date our most successful books have been about cats. *Beeswax the Bad,* a story in rhyme, was great fun to illustrate, especially with my two fat cats for reference!

"We now have a small son, Jonathan, to whom we have dedicated *The Magic Hiccup.* It is about an angelic baby bear who is the apple of his parents' eye, that is until he hiccups and turns them into frogs!

"We hope to continue producing children's books and hope that the children who read them enjoy them as much as we enjoyed creating them."

McCLINTOCK, Barbara   1955-

PERSONAL: Born May 6, 1955, in Flemington, N.J.; daughter of Earl Irving (a photographer) and JoAnn (a teacher and shop owner; maiden name, Herigstad) McClintock; married Lawrence DiFiori (an illustrator), April 14, 1982; children: Larson Alan. *Education:* Attended Jamestown College, 1973-75, and Art Student's League, 1985. *Address:* c/o David Godine, Publishers, Horticultural Hall, 300 Massachussetts Ave.,

Barbara McClintock and son, Larson Alan.

Boston, Mass. 02115. *Office:* P.O. Box 60, Cold Spring, N.Y. 10516.

CAREER: Illustrator, 1975—. *Exhibitions:* Master Eagle Gallery, 1976; Jamestown Art Center (one-man show), N.D., 1980; Garrison Art Center, N.Y., 1987. *Awards, honors:* Selected one of *Ms.* magazine's three favorite illustrators, 1983; International Children's Reader Award, 1986, for *The Revolt of the Teddy Bears.*

WRITINGS:

SELF-ILLUSTRATED

(Reteller), *The Little Red Hen,* Random House, 1979.
Down at Fraggle Rock (coloring book), Holt, 1984.
The Heartaches of a French Cat, Godine, 1989.

ILLUSTRATOR

Elizabeth Winthrop, *Potbellied Possums,* Holiday House, 1977.
David Young, *Marooned in Fraggle Rock,* Holt, 1984.
Louise Gikow, *What's a Fraggle?,* Holt, 1984.
L. Gikow, *The Legend of the Doozer Who Didn't,* Holt, 1984.
James Duffy, *The Revolt of the Teddy Bears: A May Gray Mystery,* Crown, 1985.
H. B. Gilmour, *Why Wembley Fraggle Couldn't Sleep,* Holt, 1985.
Stephanie Calmenson, *Waggleby of Fraggle Rock,* Holt, 1985.
J. Duffy, *The Christmas Gang: A May Gray Mystery,* Scribner, 1989.

SIDELIGHTS: "One of my earliest memories is of drawing huge red and yellow circles as I sat on the floor. I have always drawn. As a child, I wasn't interested in drawing flowers in vases and that sort of thing, I drew cartoons. I almost always drew anthropomorphised animals, usually cats. I loved making my characters dance, jump and run. I drew characters on cardboard, cut them out, and played with them for hours on end. I copied cartoon characters from comic books and animated Saturday morning cartoons constantly. By the time I was in second grade, I had developed a callous on the index finger of my drawing hand from holding pencils and crayons!

"Visual images have always made a very profound impression on me. I remember that while in kindergarten, an art teacher did a drawing of Little Red Riding Hood and the wolf in pastels for our class. I fell in love with the rich red of the hood and the deep browns and greys of the wolf; and I desperately pleaded with my teacher that I be given the wonderful picture to take home with me. Luckily, she complied!

"My parents ran a small photography studio in Clinton, New Jersey, so I had the great fortune of living in an artistic setting with parents who operated on a free-lance basis. My father was the photographer—portraits were his specialty—and I used to love watching him at work, ducking under the cloth of his bellows camera as my mother combed the hair, straightened the collars, and poised the hands of the customers in front of the studio backdrop. My mother retouched photos in the back of the studio shop, and colored black and white portraits with oil paints. My father, the family 'alchemist,' did all of the developing work in the darkroom. I remember how thrilling it was when I was deemed old enough to stay in the darkroom with him as he developed a picture (the door had to stay shut for quite some time). Watching the ghostly image of the print emerging as the paper was placed in various chemical baths was magical.

"I drew and wrote comic books and cartoon panels and strips in alarming volume. I copied the Hanna-Barbera character Top Cat and his gang constantly. When I was seven, I asked my sister what sort of artist I should be. She said, 'A children's book illustrator, of course!' and so began my career!

"My grandfather was an international business man and he always brought wonderful toys and dolls home with him for my sister and me. That is where my fascination for European settings originated.

"When I was eight, my parents divorced and my sister and I moved with my mother near her father in North Dakota. I was devastated and as solace, I turned to music. I started playing the violin in the fourth grade, and was faced with the dilemma of choosing between a career in music or art in college. I thought that since I'd always drawn, that's what I should continue to do.

"So, how to proceed? How should I go about getting involved in children's books? I decided, with the encouragement of my art professor, to call Maurice Sendak and ask him what I should do. I found his number through Ridgefield, Connecticut information and called him. Mr. Sendak was so helpful, kind and supportive. He told me how to put together a dummy book and suggested I move to New York.

"I flew to New York that summer. I took a bus from Newark Airport to Port Authority bus terminal, called the YWCA and found a hotel room. By the end of the week I'd found an apartment, in a month I'd found an agent, and in several months I had my first book. I was extremely lucky. It was very, very hard for the first several years.

"I met my husband at a Graphic Artists Guild meeting. He is also an illustrator, and I feel that we share a unique, visual

Gertrude ate almost anything. . . .And for desert, she ate garbage. ■ (From *Potbellied Possums* by Elizabeth Winthrop. Illustrated by Barbara McClintock.)

language. We have a young son and we are anxiously awaiting his getting old enough to assist us in the studio!

"I have travelled throughout Europe, staying in Paris for a month sketching and doing research for *The Revolt of the Teddy Bears,* and for *The Heartaches of a French Cat,* a forty-eight page, wordless book that I have loosely based on stories by P. J. Stahl and Honore de Balzac.

"I use a flexible dip-pen and Pelican ink for most of my drawings. I use watercolor as my coloring medium.

"I love nineteenth-century illustration and painting. Perhaps my biggest influences are the artists Grandville, Daumier, Delacroix, Gericaults, Dore, and the English illustrators Rowlandson, Leech, Phiz, and Cruikshank (and need I mention Caldecott!). Moving into other centuries, Callot, Tiepolo, Ronald Searle and Edward Ardizzone are big favorites and influences.

"To anyone who wants to learn to draw, the best way is to draw! And the more you do, the better you will be! I used to carry a sketchbook with me at all times and I drew from life. I filled up a sketchbook a week with subway riders, people waiting in line at the grocery store and theater, and people in restaurants. I also copied drawings of the mentors listed above. Making pictures is hard work, but the most pleasurable and rewarding work I can think of!"

MORRISON, Toni 1931-

PERSONAL: Born Chloe Anthony Wofford, February 18, 1931, in Lorain, Ohio; daughter of George and Ramah (Willis) Wof-

TONI MORRISON

ford; married Harold Morrison (divorced); children: Harold Ford, Slade. *Education:* Howard University, B.A., 1953; Cornell University, M.A., 1955.

CAREER: Texas Southern University, Houston, instructor in English, 1955-57; Howard University, Washington, D.C., instructor in English, 1957-64; writer, 1965—; Random House, Syracuse, N.Y., and New York City, senior editor, 1965-83; State University of New York at Purchase, Purchase, N. Y., instructor in Afro-American literature and creative writing, 1969-70; visiting professor, Yale University, New Haven, Conn., 1975-77; visiting lecturer, Bard College, 1979-1980. Appointed by President Carter to the National Council on the Arts, 1980. *Member:* Schomburg Commission for the Preservation of Black Culture (co-chairman), New York African American Institute (advisory board), Queens College Corporate Advisory Board, American Academy of Arts and Letters, Helsinki Watch Committee, Center for the Study of Southern Culture (national advisory board), Author's League, Writer's Guild of America, Dramatist's Guild of America, New York Public Library (board of trustees).

AWARDS, HONORS: National Book Award finalist for fiction, 1975, for *Sula,* and 1988, for *Beloved;* Cleveland Arts Prize in Literature, 1978; National Book Critics Circle Award for fiction, 1978, for *Song of Solomon;* American Academy and Institute of Arts and Letters Award, 1978; New York Public Library's Books for the Teen Age, 1980 and 1981, for *Song of Solomon,* and 1982, for *Tar Baby;* New York State Governor's Arts Award, 1986; City College of New York Langston Hughes Festival Award, 1986; Washington College Literary Art Award, 1987; Anisfield Wolf Book Award, 1987; Pulitzer Prize for fiction, and National Book Critics Circle Award nomination, both 1988, both for *Beloved;* Melcher Book

Award, 1988; Robert Kennedy Book Award, 1988; Peggy V. Helmerich Distinguished Author Award, 1988; City of New York Mayor's Award of Honor for Art and Culture, 1988; honorary degrees from the University of Pennsylvania, College of Saint Rose, Spelman College, University of Massachusetts at Amherst, Bard College, Barnard College, Morgan State University, Oberlin College, Dartmouth College, Wesleyan University, Georgetown University, Bryn Mawr College, Columbia University, and Yale University.

WRITINGS:

College Reading Skills, Knopf, 1965.
The Bluest Eye, Holt, 1969.
Sula, Knopf, 1973.
(Editor) *The Black Book,* Random House, 1974.
Song of Solomon, Knopf, 1977.
Tar Baby, Knopf, 1981.
Beloved, Knopf, 1987.

Contributor to periodicals, including *New York Times Magazine, New York Times Book Review, Black World,* and *Mademoiselle.*

ADAPTATIONS:

"Song of Solomon" (cassette), Random House, 1985.

WORK IN PROGRESS: "*Beloved* is part of a much longer work. It is an examination of the obligations toward oneself and the obligations one has toward others."

SIDELIGHTS: **February 18, 1931.** Morrison was born and raised in Lorain, Ohio. "Only *The Bluest Eye,* my first book, is set in Lorain. In the others I was more interested in mood than in geography. . . .[However], no matter what I write, I begin there. I may abandon this focus at some point, but for now it's the matrix for me."[1]

"I never lived in a black neighborhood. Poor neighborhoods, yes, black neighborhoods, no. People in small Midwestern towns came from everywhere. There were Germans, Irish, Afro-Americans, Eastern Europeans, Italians, Greeks. In a sense, we were integrated. We all went to the same school. However, uncrossed ethnic and religious lines existed—Czech social clubs, Italian social clubs, groups attached to particular churches. Blacks were frequently barred from various spots in town, including one of the municipal parks that had a lake for swimming. So we went to another, prettier lake, a secret place that only black people knew about. We followed a path and there, hidden beyond some tall shrubs, was an exquisite, unspoiled beach.

"I always thought that there was something wrong with adults who kept black people out of certain settings. I never saw their actions and attitudes as having anything to do with me personally. It never engendered in me an absence of self-esteem. I went to school with some very stupid white kids—there were bright and dull kids of all ethnicities, of course—so I never held their race in awe. I also happened to like the company I kept in our places. In the movie theatre, I preferred to sit on the left side with my friends where blacks were permitted.

"This is not to say that groups of black children were always left peacefully alone. There was a certain corner that black elementary-school girls would avoid because white teen-age boys would throw rocks at us and call us names. Even then, I thought, 'How weak they must be—fourteen-year-old boys, attacking six-year-old girls half their size.' I felt enormous contempt for them. But I also felt physical fear—their rocks *connected!*—and a good deal of perplexity. The name I most

(Cover illustration from *Tar Baby* by Toni Morrison.)

remember is 'Ethiopian.' I had never heard the word before. I asked my mother what it meant, but she was more concerned with protecting us and teaching us how to defend ourselves from violence. We were to avoid fights, but if that was impossible we were instructed to fight back.

"Even in church, there was a general acceptance that the world was wicked. But no one confused that acceptance with allowing himself to be beaten. There was a lot of very stern and instructive love in the black community. Kids had to get strong fast in order to survive, in order for the community to survive. We were taught that as individuals we had value, irrespective of what the future might hold for us. Black parents were painfully aware that they could not guarantee our future.

"All black adults felt responsible for all black children. You could be walking down the street and a strange lady would come up to you and tell you to pull up your socks. I sometimes felt suffocated by what I considered their meddlesome ways, but I knew we were watched over and absolutely safe. There was no such thing as babysitters or daycare. In addition to our mothers, we all had aunts and grandmothers and women from the neighborhood taking care of us."[2]

Morrison traces her strength to an age of black grandmothers, whom she calls "the liberated women of the world, who could shroud the dead, nudge African violets into bloom, make beautiful biscuits, plow; they could hold you in their arms, honey, and you'd think you were in heaven."[3]

"My community was important not only in terms of my personal happiness and moral development, but in terms of my

Haunted by Their Nightmares

BELOVED

By Toni Morrison.
275 pp. New York: Alfred A. Knopf. $18.95.

By Margaret Atwood

"**B**ELOVED" is Toni Morrison's fifth novel, and another triumph. Indeed, Ms. Morrison's versatility and technical and emotional range appear to know no bounds. If there were any doubts about her stature as a pre-eminent American novelist, of her own or any other generation, "Beloved" will put them to rest. In three words or less, it's a hair-raiser.

In "Beloved," Ms. Morrison turns away from the contemporary scene that has been her concern of late. This new novel is set after the end of the Civil War, during the period of so-called Reconstruction, when a great deal of random violence was let loose upon blacks, both the slaves freed by Emancipation and others who had been given or had bought their freedom earlier. But there are flashbacks to a more distant period, when slavery was still a going concern in the South and the seeds for the bizarre and calamitous events of the novel were sown. The setting is similarly divided: the countryside near Cincinnati, where the central characters have ended up, and a slave-holding plantation in Kentucky, ironically named Sweet Home, from which they fled 18 years before the novel opens.

There are many stories and voices in this novel, but the central one belongs to Sethe, a woman in her mid-30's, who

Continued on page 49

Margaret Atwood is the author of "The Handmaid's Tale," "Bluebeard's Egg" and the forthcoming "Selected Poems II."

(Detail art by David Shannon from *The New York Times Book Review* cover, September 13, 1987.)

education as well. There were blacks in Ohio going back to the Underground Railroad. There was an active black press, black journalists and historians. We learned history and stories and songs. I could feel the trauma suffered in those songs and on some level understood that the songs helped my people survive the trauma. I was an excellent student with little effort. As a matter of fact, I was the only kid in town who already knew how to read prior to entering the first grade, but was always conscious that most of the curriculum had little to do with me. In science class, we were taught that blacks were inherently less intelligent than whites, in the face of classrooms full of dull white children and bright blacks. This sort of thing was not limited to my small town in Ohio. The eleventh edition of the *Encyclopedia Britannica* gave what was widely accepted to be the 'scientific explanation' for the inferiority of black intelligence: that the soft spot on infants' heads closed more slowly in blacks than in whites. Now this is poppycock, but by no means the only red herring in the history of science. The entire western scientific tradition is loaded with racist bias. Generations of schoolchildren have been taught rank bigotry under the guise of 'empirical evidence.'

"Our classes in the humanities tended to simply ignore the contributions of black people to world culture. In junior high or high school I again encountered the word *Ethiopian,* but in a very different context. I was reading a translation of a Greek tragedy in which Ethiopia is referred to as the land of the gods. Now we all knew that the Greeks—not the ones next door, of course, but the ones in the books—had created a perfect, el-

egant civilization, and so if they said the Ethiopians were gods. . . .Well, you can see that between Pericles and the kids on the corner, I was *confused*! The teacher never thought to relate the Ethiopians, as mentioned in the play we were studying, to contemporary Africa or Afro-Americans.

"The deficiencies of our schools notwithstanding, it was important to my family and to myself that I do well. Both my parents set great store in education. In school I absorbed a great deal of information which I placed in the realm of a personal history that was not really mine. I was aware that what we studied was somebody else's reality, not mine. I also was made aware that one could learn skills with which to manipulate the reality we were taught, as well as to investigate other realities, namely black reality.

"The process by which one becomes educated and the process by which one becomes an adult are two entirely different things. This is particularly true for Afro-Americans because schools are not willing to teach that which will help black youngsters grow into fully functioning citizens. In all societies it is believed that the business of schools is to produce good citizens. This is legitimate business. But the notion of good citizenship varies. As a student I was conscious that 'good citizenship' meant a disassociation with the realities of black history and black culture. This was done simply by virtue of the absence of black history and culture from our curriculum. Now there are certain decisions pertaining to work—raising children and voting habits, for example—that one cannot make without sufficient information. Afro-Americans must make a special effort to find alternate sources of information.

"I entered Howard University with high hopes. But that, too, was disappointing. I took courses from Alan Locke and Sterling Brown. So I did have the opportunity to read literature written by blacks, but far less than I had hoped for. The bulk of the Howard English curriculum consisted of Shakespeare, Melville, Hawthorne and so on."[2]

Morrison became active in the Howard University Players and, as part of a student-faculty repertory company, toured the South. Her grandparents, who had emigrated from Alabama to Ohio in 1912, had told her wondrous stories of this archetypal land. Her first-hand impressions of the South, along with the Apocrypha she had absorbed as a child, would play a powerful part years later in *Song of Solomon*.

In 1955 she received an M.A. from Cornell. Her master's thesis was on the theme of suicide in the works of William Faulkner and Virginia Woolf. "Needless to say, there was very little black literature studied at Cornell while I was there. Perhaps I was attracted to Faulkner because at least in his world there is the presence of blacks."[2]

Morrison taught undergraduate English at Texas Southern University in Houston before returning to Washington, D.C. as a

Sula was a heavy brown with large quiet eyes, one of which featured a birthmark...shaped something like a stemmed rose. ■ (Cover illustration from *Sula* by Toni Morrison.)

member of the Howard University English Department. During these years she met and married Harold Morrison, a Jamaican architect, and gave birth to two sons, Harold Ford and Slade.

"I never wanted to be a writer, but I was always an avid reader of fiction. I really began writing myself when I drifted into a writer's group while teaching at Howard University in 1962. There were about ten of us who got together once a month, and the only rule was that you couldn't come unless you brought something to read. The others were mostly poets. . . .Anyway, I brought all that old junk I'd written in high school. Then one day I didn't have anything to bring, so I wrote a little story about a black girl who wanted blue eyes. It was written hurriedly and probably not very well, but I read it and some liked it."[4]

In 1964 she separated from her husband and returned to her parents' home in Lorain, Ohio for a year or so. She then accepted a job as a textbook editor with a subsidiary of Random House in Syracuse, New York and went back to the story she had shown her writing group in Washington, working on it evenings after her two young sons were asleep.

"I wrote *The Bluest Eye* after a period of depression, but the words 'lonely, depressed, melancholy' don't really mean the obvious. They simply represent a different state. It's an unbusy state, when I am more aware of myself than of others. The best words for making that state clear to other people are those words. It's not necessarily an unhappy feeling; it's just a different one. I think now I know better what that state is. Sometimes when I'm in mourning, for example, after my father died, there's a period when I'm not fighting day-to-day battles, a period when I can't fight or don't fight, and I am very passive, like a vessel. When I'm in this state, I can hear things . . . .I've never had sense enough to deliberately put myself in a situation like that before. At that time I had to be put into it. Now I know how to bring it about without going through the actual event."[1]

In *The Bluest Eye*, Morrison juxtaposes increasingly typographically distorted versions of an excerpt from the Dick-and-Jane basic reader with a story centering on three black girls in a Midwestern town. The novel is an exploration of the devastation that may be wreaked on the self-esteem of a black child who has not the resources to deal with life in a dominant, often bigoted culture. Pecola, who had been raped by her father, and who is routinely shunted by a mother who favors the white children of her employer, yearns to have blue eyes. Says Claudia, one of the other characters in the book: "She seemed to fold into herself, like a pleated wing. Her pain antagonized me. I wanted to open her up, crisp her edges, ram a stick down that hunched and curving spine, force her to stand erect and spit the misery out on the streets. But she held it where it could lap up into her eyes."[5]

"Pecola took the contempt that other people had shown her all her life and turned it inward. She took that self-contempt and turned it into a world she could live in. What else can be expected of a child who grows up hearing, 'You're nothing, you're nothing?' She slipped through with no one to speak for her and unable to speak for herself. There has been an understandable emphasis in black literature on the triumphs of the race. I wanted to speak about Pecola, whom others would rather forget because it is so painful. But the lame and the halt have a rightful place in our literature, and should not be banished."[2]

By the time *The Bluest Eye* was published, Morrison had moved to New York to work as an editor in Random House's Trade

At 3:00 p.m. on Wednesday the 18th of February, 1931, I will take off from Mercy and fly away on my own wings. ■ (Cover illustration from *Song of Solomon* by Toni Morrison.)

Division. Her authors included Muhammad Ali, Angela Davis, Toni Cade Bambara, Gayl Jones and Henry Dumas. "I really didn't start reading literature written by blacks until the late 1960s and 1970s when I was living in New York. A lot of the work I encountered as an editor was absolutely thrilling, life-changing material. It was very important to me to find excellent black writers and to participate in the development of the canon."[2]

1973. *Sula* published. "I began to write my second book. . .because of my preoccupation with a picture of a woman and the way in which I heard her name pronounced. Her name was Hannah, and I think she was a friend of my mother's. I don't remember seeing her very much, but what I do remember is the color around her—a kind of violet, a suffusion of something violet—and her eyes, which appeared to be half closed. But what I remember most is how the women said her name: how they said 'Hannah Peace' and smiled to themselves, and there was some secret about her that they knew, which they didn't talk about, at least not in my hearing, but it seemed *loaded* in the way in which they said her name. And I suspected that she was a little bit of an outlaw but that they approved of her in some way."[6]

"In *Sula,* I wanted to explore what was forgivable and what was unforgivable in the world of women. Sula taking Nel's husband is a grave thing. For years Nel lives with the thought that she has a marriage, a family, a life with the man she loves and then one day it is over. Sula has taken Jude without even loving him. Now a woman without a man is serious business: she has no father for her children, she has to make all the decisions alone, she has got to figure out a way to support herself and her kids. Today it might not seem so dire, but back in the 1940s when the book is set, it was *serious.*"[2]

Other dark, disturbing things happen in *Sula.* Eva Peace kills her son, Plum, because he has become a drug addict and she makes the decision that life as an addict is not worth living. "You say the scene is shocking, and so it is. But what is shocking is *not* that she kills her son, but that she likes him. She is not abusive nor psychopathic nor even particularly violent. But there is an arrogance in her love that is indefensible. Her love is very dictatorial. It simply was not her decision to make whether Plum should live or die. Yet she does decide, and while Plum is so 'out of it,' he doesn't even know the decision is in the balance."[2]

"When I wrote *Sula,* I knew I was going to write a book about good and evil and about friendship. . . .Friendship between women is special, different, and has never been depicted as the major focus of a novel before *Sula.* Nobody ever talked about friendship between women unless it was homosexual, and there is no homosexuality in *Sula.* Relationships between women were always written about as though they were subordinate to some other roles they're playing. This is not true of men. It seemed to me that black women have friends in the old-fashioned sense of the word; perhaps this isn't just true for black people, but it seemed so to me. I was half-way through the book before I realized that friendship in literary terms is a rather contemporary idea. So when I was making up people in *Sula,* it was inevitable I would focus on black women, not out of ignorance of any other kind of people, but because they are of compelling interest to me."[1]

The critical reception of *Sula* caused some controversy. Jerry H. Bryant of the *Nation* stated, "Writers like Toni Morrison, like Ed Bullins and Alice Walker are slowly, subtly making our old buildings unsafe. There is something ominous in the chilling detachment with which they view their characters. It is not that their viewpoint is amoral—we are asked for judgment. It's that the characters we judge lie so far outside the guidelines by which we have always made our judgments. . . .The feeling I get. . .is not so much that of the familiar literary viewpoint of moral complexity as that of a calm sardonic irony over the possibility of ever sorting out the good from the bad. This feeling gives *Sula* a portentousness that makes it perhaps an inadvertent prophet, whose prophecy is that all our old assumptions about morality are disintegrating before a peculiarly black assault against them."[7] "*Our* assumptions? He means white assumptions. Then yes, I hope those assumptions are under 'assault,' as he puts it,"[2] adds Morrison.

"Critics generally don't associate black people with ideas. They see marginal people; they just see another story about black folks. They regard the whole thing as sociologically interesting perhaps but very parochial. There's a notion out in the land that there are black people or Indians or some other marginal group, and if you write about the world from that point of view, somehow it is considered lesser. It's racist, of course. The fact that I chose to write about black people means black people are my sole stimulation. We are people, not aliens. We live, we love, and we die."

"It is not only certain white writers who have objected to the absence of white characters in my books. Some black critics and readers have expressed disappointment that I don't deal

March 30, 1981 / $1.25 ®

Newsweek

Black Magic

Novelist Toni Morrison

Newsweek **heralded the publication of** *Tar Baby*. ■ (Cover photograph by Richard Avedon from *Newsweek*, March 30, 1981.)

with the successful, assimilated black middle class. They have said that in ignoring the triumphs of that milieu I neglect a political responsibility. However, I do not regard that as my political or artistic mission. The much more important political point in my books is precisely that the characters are black. In my books, the world is black. The existence of the white world is felt, some of the effects of the white world are felt, but the white world itself is absent."[2]

That many of her characters are outcasts is one way in which the white world manifests itself in Morrison's books. "There are several levels of the pariah figure working in my writing. The civilization of black people that lives apart from but in juxtaposition to other civilizations is a pariah relationship. In fact, the concept of the black in this country is almost always one of the pariah. But a community contains pariahs within it that are very useful for the conscience of that community.

"When I was writing about good and evil [in *Sula*], I really wasn't writing about them in western terms. It was interesting to me that black people at one time seemed not to respond to evil in the ways other people did, but that they thought evil had a natural place in the universe; they did not wish to eradicate it. They just wished to protect themselves from it, maybe even to manipulate it, but they never wanted to kill it. They thought evil was just another aspect of life. The ways black people dealt with evil accounted in my mind for how they responded to a lot of other things. It's like a double-edged sword. It accounts for one of the reasons it's difficult for them to organize long-term political wars against another people. It accounts for their generosity and acceptance of all sorts of things. It's because they're not terrified by evil, by difference. Evil is not an alien force; it's just a different force. That's the evil I was describing in *Sula*. . . .

"A woman who wrote a paper on *Sula* said she thought Sula's community was very unnurturing for her. That's very strange to me because I found that community to be very nurturing for Sula. There was no other place in the world she could have lived without being harmed. Whatever they think about Sula, however strange she is to them, however different, they won't harm her. Medallion is a sustaining environment even for a woman who is very different. Nobody's going to lynch her or call the police. They call her bad names and try to protect themselves from her evil; that's all. . . .

"I wrote *Sula* and *The Bluest Eye* because they were books I had wanted to read. No one had written them yet, so I wrote them."[1]

"Looking back on my early work, I can isolate technical things I would now handle differently. In *The Bluest Eye,* for example, I had some difficulty establishing and maintaining the proper tone. At the end of that book, the voice is definitely an adult voice. If I were writing that book now, I would know how to maintain that special voice that is neither child nor adult. Only occasionally was I able to strike that 'chord.' I could not sustain it. I wanted a sort of Greek chorus at the close of *The Bluest Eye*, but did not achieve it to my complete satisfaction. The voice is too obviously adult and I think perhaps too close to the story's events."[2]

1974. *The Black Book,* edited by Morrison, was published by Random House. A compilation of newspaper clippings, recipes, photographs, patent office records, excerpts from slave narratives, advertisements and other memorabilia, *The Black Book* has been likened to a scrapbook spanning three-hundred years of black life in the United States. The project, conceived by Morrison, would prove crucial to her artistic work. Not only did it give her access to parts of black history that would

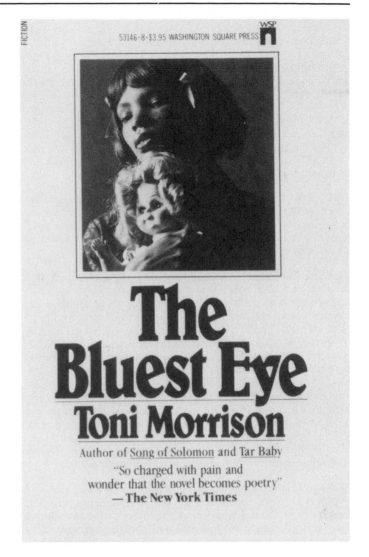

Each night, without fail she prayed for blue eyes. ■ (Cover illustration from *The Bluest Eye* by Toni Morrison.)

figure prominently in her subsequent novels but led her to articulate a fictional strategy she calls literary archeology, a blend of history, autobiography and imagination.

". . .On the basis of some information and a little bit of guesswork you journey to a site to see what remains were left behind and to reconstruct the world that these remains imply. What makes it fiction is the nature of the imaginative act: my reliance on the image—on the remains—in addition to recollection, to yield up a kind of a truth. By 'image,' of course, I don't mean 'symbol;' I simply mean 'picture' and the feelings that accompany the picture. . . .

"I can't tell you how I felt when my father died. But I was able to write *Song of Solomon* and imagine, not him, and not his specific interior life, but the world that he inhabited and the private or interior life of the people in it. And I can't tell you how I felt reading to my grandmother while she was turning over and over in her bed (because she was dying, and she was not comfortable), but I could try to reconstruct the world that she lived in. And I have suspected, more often than not, that I *know* more than my grandfather and my great-grandmother did, but I also know that I'm no wiser than they were. And whenever I have tried earnestly to diminish their vision and prove to myself that I know more, and when I have tried to speculate on their interior life and match it up with my own, I have been overwhelmed every time by the richness of theirs compared to my own. Like Frederick Douglass talking about his grandmother, and James Baldwin talking about his father, and Simone de Beauvoir talking about her mother, these people are my access to me; they are my entrance into my own interior life. Which is why the images that float around them—the remains, so to speak, at the archeological site—surface first, and they surface so vividly and so compellingly that I acknowledge them as my route to a reconstruction of a world, to an exploration of an interior life that was not written and to the revelation of a kind of truth.''[6]

1977. *Song of Solomon* published to critical and popular acclaim. It won the National Book Critics Circle Award for the best novel of 1977 and was the first fictional work by a black writer to be named a Book-of-the-Month-Club Main Selection since *Native Son* was chosen in 1940.

''I wrote *Song of Solomon* shortly after my father died, in a state of profound grief. In my earlier books, the main characters were women and while in *Solomon* there are three extremely strong females, I wanted the world of this novel to be predominantly male. Usually my books come to me by way of theme; this time I wanted to explore the meaning of betrayal. I also wanted to deal with a large time-span, covering several generations and the distances (physical, emotional, historical) they traveled. I needed a loose, meandering, expansive structure that would encompass the way I wanted time to work. In addition, I was thinking about flight and the significance of soaring in our folklore. A seminal tale deals with a plantation of African-born slaves in America who fly back to freedom in Africa. The whole sense of leaving, soaring, flying, adventure seemed more natural to men than to women.''[2]

''Now if you are a middle-class white man or a rich man and you decide to go paint in Tahiti, that is considered heroic. If a black man decides to do anything, it is called abandoning his family. Ulysses left his wife and son for twenty years— and he wasn't alone, either, he was with Circe a good part of the time. Nobody calls Ulysses 'an irresponsible character.' No, he is a mythic hero. All those white men who in the nineteenth century left their homes in Boston to 'go west'— they, too, are cultural icons. Not so the black man who goes off to find something better (than slavery, for example). The black man is 'running away.' There's a double standard. Criticism of that stripe says much more about the critic than about the book in question.''[2]

With *Song of Solomon* Morrison became an undeniably major writer. The book became a paperback best-seller. In addition to the National Book Critics Circle Award, she was given an award by the American Academy and Institute of Arts and Letters. In 1980, President Carter named her to the National Council on the Arts. In 1981, she was elected to the American Academy and Institute of Arts and Letters. That same year, the publication of her fourth novel, *Tar Baby* occasioned a *Newsweek* cover story.

''In *Tar Baby* I wanted a closed environment, like that of a hothouse. I wanted violence but no blood. And there could be no escape, for the people are already imprisoned by their attitudes.''[2]

Tar Baby is the first Morrison novel to have major white characters. The settings in the book include small, all-black Southern towns, Paris, New York and a dizzyingly lush island in the Caribbean. As in earlier works, Morrison uses myth, this time the story of Brer Rabbit and the Tar Baby. Jadine, a beautiful young black model, is the 'tar baby' in this work.

Having been raised by an aunt and uncle who are longtime house servants of Valerian and Margaret Street and educated on Street's generous funds, Jadine feels she is falling through the cracks between her black heritage and the white world she has taken by storm. In an effort to reintegrate herself with her people, she has a torrid but abortive love affair with Son Green, a poor black man who has stowed away on the Street's pleasure boat and then stolen into their house.

Tar Baby received mixed notices, with a number of critics objecting to what they referred to as Morrison's overwrought language and use of the pathetic fallacy. Some critics felt that Morrison's sense of place was less sure in this than in her other books. However, the book was also praised, especially in Europe, as a daring novel of ideas dealing with the difficult themes of race relations, cultural identity, and the various corruptions of power.

1987. *Beloved* was hailed as Morrison's magnum opus. ''The effect of this book has been like no other. Magnum opus, I don't know. *Beloved* is part of a much longer work. Every book I write is 'unlike anything I have written previously' because I set myself new technical and artistic challenges with every work. In *Beloved* I wanted to look at the ways in which slavery affected women specifically, particularly the ways in which it affected the manner and the extent to which a slave woman could be a mother.

''You will notice that in *Beloved* breasts are nowhere mentioned as errogenous zones or as erotic enticements. Breasts are *food/sustenance,* the means by which a woman keeps her children alive. When Paul D. comes back to Sethe the two tell each other of their past in an amorous interlude that eventually will lead to consummation. Sethe tells him of a brutal beating she received and Paul D. focusses on the tree-shaped scar on her back. But the worst thing, Sethe tries to make him comprehend, is that the white boys maliciously took her milk so she couldn't nurse her baby.''[2]

> '''They used cowhide on you?'
> 'And they took my milk.'
> 'They beat you and you was pregnant?'
> 'And they took my milk!' ''[8]

''The point was to find the one thing that would express all the degradation, rage, bestiality and heartbreak of slavery. For Sethe, it was the white boys taking her milk. For the men, it was perhaps the bit they were forced to wear in their mouths.

''My story of Sethe is based on a true one, one of many such accounts incidentally. In my readings of slave narratives and related materials I came across a lot of documentation of women who killed children born to them by white masters or who killed their black children as a way of freeing them from slavery. Sethe is based on a young woman who ran away from her plantation, was caught and then returned to her owner. She killed one of her children so that he would not live as she was forced to live. Her owner then shipped her downriver—downriver was Mississippi, a land of untold horrors. Apparently she jumped ship with her remaining child in her arms, drowning the two of them.

''Now a woman killing her child is fearsome. But look at the ways in which slavery victimized women. Women could be punished twice—they could be worked to death *and* raped. As mothers, they had absolutely no control over their children's lives. Their children could be taken away from them at a moment's notice, as they frequently were. The character of Baby Suggs in *Beloved* knew very well that she couldn't really afford to love her sons. In the sense that we think of, her children weren't *hers* at all.

"It is easy to lose sight of the fact that being a slave was a very complicated life. Not only were you totally at the mercy of whoever owned you, but there were all sorts of subtle local codes. The slaves had to do very modern, in fact post-modern, things with their intelligence in order to figure it all out. This was no 'ordinary crime.' I had to dig very deep to even get close to Sethe's motives.

"Sethe's killing Beloved is different from Eva Peace killing Plum. Unlike Eva, Sethe is not judging her child. Rather, Sethe is making a judgment of the society in which she finds herself captive. One can understand that she didn't want her child to be a slave, to never smell a flower without having to realize that it *belongs to the master*. Sethe is claiming her role as a parent, claiming the autonomy, the freedom she needs to protect her children and give them some dignity. Still, this is a fearsome thing, for the exercising of Sethe's freedom means death for her child. I wanted to judge Sethe and yet I could not. How could I? I was not born a slave. And yet I felt that judgment had to be passed. The only one who rightfully could judge Sethe was the child, Beloved. And so the history becomes a palpable presence."[2]

Morrison's "literary archeology" was the means by which she was able to make history palpable in *Beloved*.

Beloved was nominated for the 1988 National Book Award. When the book did not win, publications like the *New York Times* ran stories expressing astonishment and even doubt as to the worth of the award and the state of the publishing industry. Fifty major black writers wrote an open letter in the *New York Times Book Review* protesting "the oversight and harmful whimsy" of denying Morrison the NBA, and thanking her for the example of her work and life. The controversy was largely dissipated by the novel's garnering the 1988 Pulitzer Prize for Fiction. When asked by the *New York Times* how she felt about receiving the award, Morrison said, "I think I know what I feel. It's true that I had no doubt about the value of the book and that it was really worth serious recognition. But I had dark thoughts about whether the book's merits would be allowed to be the only consideration of the Pulitzer committee. The book had begun to take on a responsibility, an extra-literary responsibility, that it was never designed for."[9]

Writers remember. "You know, they straightened out the Mississippi River in places, to make room for houses and livable acreage. Occasionally the river floods these places. 'Floods' is the word they use, but in fact it is not flooding; it is remembering. Remembering where it used to be. All water has a perfect memory and is forever trying to get back to where it was. Writers are like that; remembering where we were, what valley we ran through, what the banks were like, the light that was there and the route back to our original place. It is emotional memory—what the nerves and the skin remember as well as how it appeared. And a rush of imagination is our 'flooding. . .' Like water, I remember where I was before I was 'straightened out.'"[6]

FOOTNOTE SOURCES

[1]Claudia Tate, editor, *Black Women Writers at Work*, Continuum, 1983.
[2]Based on an interview by Marguerite Feitlowitz for *Something about the Author*.
[3]Curt Davis, "Toni Morrison and Her Wild 'Sula,'" *People*, March 18, 1974.
[4]Mel Watkins, "Talk with Toni Morrison," *New York Times Book Review*, September 11, 1977 (p. 48).

[5]Toni Morrison, *The Bluest Eye*, Pocket Books, 1970.
[6]T. Morrison, "The Site of Memory," *Inventing the Truth*, edited by William Zinsser, Houghton, 1987.
[7]Jerry H. Bryant, "Something Ominous Here," *Nation*, July 6, 1974 (p. 23).
[8]T. Morrison, *Beloved*, Knopf, 1987.
[9]Dennis Hevesi, "Toni Morrison's Novel 'Beloved' Wins the Pulitzer Prize in Fiction," *New York Times*, April 1, 1988.

FOR MORE INFORMATION SEE:

New York Times, November 13, 1970 (p. 35), April 1, 1988 (p. B5).
Newsweek, November 30, 1970, January 7, 1974 (p. 63), March 30, 1981 (p. 52).
New York Times Book Review, December 30, 1973 (p. 3), September 11, 1977 (p. 1), March 29, 1981 (p. 1), September 13, 1987 (p. 1), January 24, 1988 (p. 36).
New York Post, January 26, 1974 (p. 35).
Washington Post, February 3, 1974 (p. 3), March 6, 1974 (p. B1), September 30, 1977 (p. C1).
Black World, June, 1974 (p.51).
Studies in Black Literature, number 6, 1976 (p. 21).
Village Voice, August 29, 1977 (p. 41), July 1-7, 1981 (p. 40).
First World, winter, 1977 (p. 34).
Black Scholar, March, 1978 (p. 47).
Black American Literature Forum, summer, 1978 (p. 56).
New York Times Magazine, May 20, 1979 (p. 40).
Obsidian, spring/summer, 1979 (p. 142).
Black American Literature Forum, winter, 1979 (pp. 123, 126, 130).
Roseann P. Bell and others, editors, *Sturdy Black Bridges: Visions of Black Women in Literature*, Doubleday, 1979 (p. 251).
Anne Z. Mickelson, *Reaching Out: Sensitivity and Order in Recent American Fiction by Women*, Scarecrow, 1979.
Barbara Christian, *Black Women Novelists: The Development of a Tradition, 1892-1976*, Greenwood, 1980.
American Literature, January, 1981 (p. 541).
New Republic, March 21, 1981 (pp. 25, 29).
Washington Post Book World, March 22, 1981 (p. 1).
Atlantic, April, 1981 (p. 119).
Vogue, April, 1981 (p. 288).
New York, April 13, 1981 (p. 42).
Nation, May 2, 1981 (p. 529).
Ebony, November, 1984 (p. 59).
Publishers Weekly, August 21, 1987.
Judith Thurman, "A House Divided," *New Yorker*, November 2, 1987 (p. 175).

MOSLEY, Francis 1957-

PERSONAL: Born July 24, 1957, in Eastwood, England; son of Eric and Moira (Brown) Mosley. *Education:* Sussex University, England, B.Sc., 1979; attended Brighton Polytechnic, England, 1979-82. *Home:* 8 Lamb St., London E1, England. *Office:* 45 Charlotte Rd., London EC2, England.

CAREER: Author and illustrator of books for children, 1982—. *Member:* Greenpeace, Friends of the Earth.

WRITINGS:

ALL SELF-ILLUSTRATED

Animal Numbers, Patrick Hardy, 1984.
The Clever Apple Pie, Deutsch, 1986.
The Dinosaur Eggs, Barron, 1988.

There was an awkward moment when he was balancing on tiptoe with nothing to hold on to. ■ (From *The Rich Kid* by Bill Gillham. Illustrated by Francis Mosley.)

Nessie Goes to Mars, Collins, 1988.
Nessie Goes on Holiday, Collins, 1988.
Tim and Emily Meet Nessie, Collins, 1988.
Nessie Goes to Hollywood, Collins, 1988
Jason and the Golden Fleece, Deutsch, 1989.

ILLUSTRATOR

Bill Gillham, *Home before Long*, Deutsch, 1983.
B. Gillham, *The Rich Kid*, Deutsch, 1984.

SIDELIGHTS: "*The Clever Apple Pie* is a picture book version of a traditional Scottish folk tale called 'The Wee Bannoch' which is a variation on the story of 'The Gingerbread Man.' What appealed to me is the idea of a pie coming to life. Children seem keen to invest all sorts of inanimate things (particularly toys) with life and the power of speech. I suppose this is because they imagine everything to be just like themselves until it is proven otherwise.

"*The Dinosaur Eggs* is a simple tale of three dinosaurs hatching into the present day and finding willing foster parents. I like to draw amusing or ridiculous things and I think children like to look at amusing and ridiculous things. At least I hope so."

MOSS, Elaine (Dora) 1924-

PERSONAL: Born March 8, 1924, in London, England; daughter of Percy and Maude (Simmons) Levy; married John Moss,

October 5, 1950; children: two daughters. *Education:* Bedford College B.A., 1944; University of London Institute of Education, Diploma of Education, 1945, Chartered Librarian, 1947. *Politics:* Liberal. *Religion:* Jewish. *Home:* 7 St. Anne's Close, London N6 6AR, England.

CAREER: Stoatley Rough Schools, Haslemere, Surrey, England, teacher, 1945-47; Bedford College, University of London, assistant librarian, 1947-50; publisher's reader for children's books, 1955-80; *Spectator*, London, England, director of children's book reviews, 1960-65; children's book critic, 1960—; writer, 1963—. *Awards, honors:* Eleanor Farjeon Award from the Children's Book Circle, 1977, for "distinguished services to children's books."

WRITINGS:

Twirly (illustrated by Haro), Constable, 1963, American edition (illustrated by Shan Ellentuck), Coward, 1965.
The Wait and See Book (illustrated by Sally Ford), Constable, 1964.
Polar (illustrated by Jeannie Baker), Dutton, 1975.

"PETER PIPERS" SERIES

Peter Pipers, Berridge Johnson, 1984.
The Peter Pipers at the Fair, Berridge Johnson, 1984.
The Peter Pipers at the Wildlife Park, Berridge Johnson, 1984.
The Peter Pipers Birthday Party, Berridge Johnson, 1984.
The Peter Pipers in the Garden, Berridge Johnson, 1984.

OTHER

(Selector) *Reading for Enjoyment with Two to Five Year Olds*, Children's Booknews, 1970, third edition, 1977.
(Selector) *Paperbacks for Children: Two to Eleven*, National Book League, 1973.
The Audience for Children's Books, Library of Congress, 1978.
Part of the Pattern: A Personal Journey through the World of Children's Books, 1960-1985, Greenwillow, 1986.

EDITOR

Gulliver's Travels (illustrated by Hans Baltzer), Constable, 1961, Duell, Sloan & Pearce, 1963.
Helen Waddell, *The Story of Saul the King* (illustrated by Doreen Roberts), Constable, 1966.
One Hundred Books for Children 1966-67, 2nd edition, National Book League, 1968.
From Morn to Midnight (children's verse; illustrated by Satomi Ichikawa), Crowell, 1977.
Picture Books for Young People: Nine to Thirteen, Thimble, 1981, revised edition, 1985.
(Editorial advisor) *The Good Book Guide to Children's Books* (illustrated by Quentin Blake), Penguin, 1983, new edition, 1986.

Editor of *Children's Books of the Year*, a joint publication of the National Book League and the British Council, 1970-1979. Contributor of articles and reviews to periodicals, including *Children's Book News, Times Educational Supplement, Guardian, Signal*, and *Times Literary Supplement*.

WORK IN PROGRESS: Various lectures, including keynote speech for the International Board on Books for Young People Congress in Williamsburg, Virginia, in 1990.

SIDELIGHTS: Moss' life has been filled with books; over the years she has been an author, editor and critic of books for children. She has been employed as a children's book reviewer, has written several books for children, and has edited several books on reading material for children. From 1970 to

ELAINE MOSS

1979 Moss was an editor of the National Book League and British Council's *Children's Books of the Year*. "After serving my apprenticeship as teacher, librarian, publisher's reader, and mother (the last was the most important by far), I did start my more public life in children's books as a newspaper critic for the *Times* (London). But with the parlous state of adult knowledge about children's books at that time—and it still exists now—newspapers hardly seemed to be the place for serious discussions of children's book trade issues or for academic criticism. Yet both began to creep into that *Times* page. Surely, the space that is given to children's books should be used positively to help parents and teachers get a grasp of the basic principles of choosing with children the books they will enjoy.

"So I began to ask myself what the *Times* page was doing, and why. Who was reading what was written? What was the effect? Were the hordes of children out there a lot better off because of it? Or were they, possibly, marginally worse off because of the widening gap between the critics' choice of books and what real children want to read? Did these children get books? If so, what—and how? If not, why not? With questions like these assailing me, I couldn't settle for the quiet (well, relatively quiet) life of the so-called quality press critic. I began to look at aspects of the children's book world, to learn by experience, and to use what I discovered as an integral part of what I wrote: the historian in me, I now suppose, thirsting for field work.

"The first step was to leave the *Times,* a prestigious newspaper, and take over an occasional column in the *Sunday Mir-*

ror, which is anything and everything *but*. Here was a massive audience—and massively indifferent, if some people were to be believed. Certainly you write for readers of a tabloid quite differently from the way you write for readers of the *Times*. It is really very easy to write about books for the quality press, for you are mainly talking to people of your own background and education about something that should be of automatic interest, even if it isn't always so.

"But for the *Sunday Mirror* you have to think about hooking your readership, stimulating people, and sending them off not to a bookshop but, in all probability, to one of a large chain of stationers and booksellers. . .where they will find the right books for their families. You have to write simple but arresting prose; there is no room for convoluted subsidiary clauses in an opening sentence that mustn't exceed nine words. And, above all, you have to guard against disappointment and disillusion on the part of the book-seeker, for the first steps in using books with children are hard and people are easily discouraged. . . .

"It was at this period, in 1973, that by great good fortune I was invited by a group of social workers and teachers in London's Dockland to help set up a children's book stall in the Saturday market in Whitechapel High Street. There was no bookshop in that vast area, nowhere children could even see new books, let alone buy them. With that stall we proved, through blazing summers and perishing rainy winters, that if the right books are easily accessible and you are prepared regularly on Saturdays to stand around between the eels and the cauliflowers, you make friends, influence people, and sell books. . . .And you learn the value of knowing what's inside a book if you want to sell it.

"At this time I had already embarked upon the ten-year marathon of _Children's Books of the Year,_ so I knew what was inside the books. No 'real' critic, I fancy, would have taken on that job. I didn't actually take it on, though; it just happened. For some years the National Book League had chosen annually what it called '500 Children's Books' for a traveling exhibition. The choice could be arbitrary and haphazard because there was no annotated catalog through which the selectors had to justify their choices or balance their selections. When I was called upon to assist the NBL in the choice of fiction (three weeks in which to choose two hundred titles), I began to ask awkward questions to which I received very dusty answers. Finally, someone said in exasperation, 'Well, if you want to be responsible for the whole selection _and_ write an annotated catalog, go ahead!' That, they thought, would silence me. Instead, it opened the way for me eventually to turn the '500 Children's Books' touring exhibition into the catalog and exhibition which came to be known in 1970 as _Children's Books of the Year._"[1]

During her years with _Children's Books of the Year,_ Moss ". . .was presented with a now-or-never opportunity to get a worm's eye view of children and books. Would I like to be the Inner London Education Authority's first chartered librarian in a primary school—just one day a week, as an experiment? I have to confess that, like the proverbial fools, I rushed in. Why else, I asked myself, looking for a pattern as always, had I qualified in my twenties both as a teacher and as a librarian?"[1]

For six years Moss was the librarian at Fleet Primary School and found time to continue her other activities, including writing and editing books for children. No wonder that she was awarded the Eleanor Farjeon Award in 1977 for "distinguished services to children's books."

FOOTNOTE SOURCES

[1]Elaine Moss, "Critical Decisions: Reflections on the Changing Role of a Children's Book Reviewer," _Horn Book,_ April, 1984.

NATHANSON, Laura Walther 1941-
(J. K. Thorpe)

PERSONAL: Born January 3, 1941, in Lakewood, Ohio; daughter of Roy Paul (a manual laborer) and Sara (a teacher; maiden name, Cadwell) Walther; married John Gliedman, June 17, 1962 (divorced, 1969); married Charles Nathanson (a professor of sociology), June 27, 1972; children: Sara. _Education:_ Radcliffe College, B.A. (magna cum laude), 1963; Tufts University, M.D., 1970. _Politics:_ Democrat. _Religion:_ Unitarian-Universalist. _Office:_ El Camino Pediatrics, 475 El Camino Real, Suite B 105, Encinitas, Calif. 92024.

CAREER: Children's Hospital, Detroit, Mich., fellow in neonatology, 1974-76, emergency room physician, 1976-77; private practice in pediatrics in Littleton, N.H., 1977-80; El Camino Pediatrics, Encinitas, Calif., pediatrician in group practice, 1980—. _Member:_ American Academy of Pediatrics (fellow), Physicians for Social Responsibility, California Medical Society. _Awards, Honors: The Trouble with Wednesdays_ was chosen one of Child Study Association of America's Children's Book of the Year, 1987.

WRITINGS:

The Trouble with Wednesdays (juvenile), Putnam, 1986.

Author of mystery stories, under pseudonym J. K. Thorpe.

WORK IN PROGRESS: Fiction for and about children; stories.

SIDELIGHTS: "My medical work-week is a steady fifty-eight hours, except for every fourth weekend when I take calls. I write on a Macintosh Plus computer."

NORDSTROM, Ursula 1910-1988

OBITUARY NOTICE—See sketch in _SATA_ Volume 3: Born February 1, 1910, in New York, N.Y.; died of ovarian cancer, October 11, 1988, in New Milford, Conn. Editor and author. Nordstrom was an editor and executive at Harper & Row for most of her life, specializing in children's books. Hailed as an innovator in young people's literature, she spurned the moralistic teachings of earlier works in favor of characters and situations that reflected the experiences of her young audience. She once remarked: "We don't publish books for adults; we do them for children, and sometimes it's a problem to get books through adults to the children. The important thing is for our writers to have the fresh, original view of things that children have."

Nordstrom joined Harper & Row in 1936 and became director of children's books during the 1940s. In 1960 she became the company's first female vice-president, rising to senior vice-president and publisher seven years later. Though withdrawing from the publisher's post in 1973, she remained associated with Harper until 1979 as a senior editor in charge of her own line of books. Throughout her forty-three year association with Harper, Nordstrom launched the careers of many artists and authors, as well as several editors in the children's book field, among them Charlotte Zolotow of Harper and Susan Hirschman of Greenwillow. The first book that Nordstrom edited was E. B. White's _Stuart Little._ In 1952, when White presented her with the only copy of _Charlotte's Web,_ Nordstrom was overwhelmed. "I didn't dare take a chance on losing the manuscript on the train home," she said. "So I sat down and began to read." In 1963 she published Maurice Sendak's _Where the Wild Things Are_ after other publishers had rejected it. In addition to White and Sendak, Nordstrom published books by Ruth Krauss, Shel Silverstein, Tomi Ungerer, Laura Ingalls Wilder, M. E. Kerr, Louise Fitzhugh, Garth Williams, and others.

She wrote the children's book _The Secret Language,_ believed to have been based on her own experiences at boarding school. It was selected one of American Library Association's Notable Children's Books in 1960.

FOR MORE INFORMATION SEE:

Clare D. Kinsman, editor, _Contemporary Authors,_ Volume 13-16R, Gale, 1975.

OBITUARIES

New York Times, October 12, 1988.
Washington Post; October 14, 1988.
Los Angeles Times, October 14, 1988.
Chicago Tribune, October 16, 1988.
Publishers Weekly, October 29, 1988.
School Library Journal, November, 1988.

ORMAI, Stella

PERSONAL: Married. *Education:* Rhode Island School of Design, B.F.A. *Home:* 449 Morris Ave., Providence, R.I. 02906.

CAREER: Illustrator of children's books. *Awards, honors:* Don Freeman Memorial Grant from the Society of Children's Book Writers, 1980; *Heartbeats: Your Body, Your Heart* was chosen an Outstanding Science Trade Book for Children from the National Science Teachers Association and the Children's Book Council, 1983, and *Soap Bubble Magic* and *Shadow Magic,* 1985.

ILLUSTRATOR:

JUVENILE

Norma Q. Hare, *Mystery at Mouse House,* Garrard, 1980.
Alvin Silverstein and Virginia B. Silverstein, *Heartbeats: Your Body, Your Heart,* Lippincott, 1983.
Vicki Cobb and Kathy Darling, *Bet You Can! Science Possibilities to Fool You,* Avon, 1983.
Susan D. Lipscomb and Margaret A. Zuanick, *BASIC Beginnings,* Avon, 1983.
Sandra Markle, *Kid's Computer Capers: Investigations for Beginners,* Lothrop, 1983.
S. Markle, *The Programmer's Guide to the Galaxy,* Lothrop, 1984.
Jacqueline Briggs Martin, *Bizzy Bones and Uncle Ezra,* Lothrop, 1984.
Lee Bennett Hopkins, editor, *Creatures: Poems,* Harcourt, 1985.
Seymour Simon, *Soap Bubble Magic,* Lothrop, 1985.
S. Simon, *Shadow Magic,* Lothrop, 1985.
J. B. Martin, *Bizzy Bones and Moosemouse,* Lothrop, 1986.
Barbara Lucas, *Sleeping Over,* Macmillan, 1986.
B. Lucas, *A Close Call,* Macmillan, 1986.
B. Lucas, *Home Is Best,* Macmillan, 1986.
Nancy W. Carlstrom, *The Moon Came Too* (Junior Literary Guild selection), Macmillan, 1987.

SIDELIGHTS: As a child Ormai spent many summers exploring the countryside near her grandfather's farm. Her life-long love of nature which developed in those early years along with her interest in children's fantasy have inspired her work as an illustrator.

HOBBIES AND OTHER INTERESTS: Collecting children's books.

PERSKE, Robert 1927-

PERSONAL: Born October 16, 1927, in Denver, Colo.; son of Paul Frederick (a municipal and state government official) and Elva (a housewife; maiden name, Laveck) Perske; married Martha Packard (an artist), February 26, 1970; children: Richard, Ann, Dawn, Lee, Marc. *Education:* Attended University of Colorado, 1946-48; Westmar College, B.A., 1950; Garrett-Evangelical Seminary, B.D., 1955. *Home and office:* 159 Hollow Tree Ridge Rd., Darien, Conn. 06820.

CAREER: Ordained United Methodist minister, 1955; pastor of United Methodist churches in Genoa, Colo., 1952-55, Sterling, Colo., 1955-59, and Espanola, N.M., 1959-60; Kansas Neurological Institute, Topeka, psychiatric chaplain, 1960-70; Greater Omaha Association for Retarded Citizens, Omaha, Neb., executive director, 1970-74; Accreditation Council for Services for the Mentally Retarded and Other Disabled, Chicago, Ill., accreditation surveyor, 1974-76; Random House, Inc., New York, N.Y., director of joint project (with U.S.

Robert Perske and Tillie

Department of Health, Education and Welfare) on persons with handicaps, 1976-78; free-lance writer, 1978—. Fellow at Menninger Foundation, 1963-64, staff affiliate in department of education, 1964-70; writer for and consultant to the President's Committee on Mental Retardation. *Member:* American Association on Mental Deficiency (fellow), Association for Retarded Citizens, Association for the Severely Handicapped, Connecticut Association for Retarded Citizens (president, 1980-81).

AWARDS, HONORS: Distinguished Service Award from the Sterling Junior Chamber of Commerce (Colo.), 1958, and the Greater Omaha Association for Retarded Citizens, 1975; Rosemary Dybwad International Award from the Association for Retarded Citizens, 1968, for research in Sweden and Denmark; Book Award from the Printing Industries of America, 1974, for *New Directions for Parents of Persons Who Are Retarded;* Book Award from the American Medical Writers Association, 1978, for editing *Mealtimes for Severely and Profoundly Handicapped Persons;* National Media Award from One to One, 1981, for *New Life in the Neighborhood.*

WRITINGS:

OF INTEREST TO YOUNG ADULTS

Show Me No Mercy: A Compelling Story of Remarkable Courage, Abingdon, 1984.
Don't Stop the Music, Abingdon, 1986.

OTHER

(Contributor) Robert Noland, editor, *Counselling Parents of the Mentally Retarded,* C. C. Thomas, 1968.

(Contributor) Wolf Wolfensburger, editor, *The Principle of Normalization in Human Services*, National Institute on Mental Retardation, 1972.

New Directions for Parents of Persons Who Are Retarded, Abingdon, 1973.

(Contributor) Carolyn Cherington and Gunnar Dybwad, editors, *New Neighbors: The Retarded Citizen in Search of a Home*, President's Committee on Mental Retardation, 1974.

(Contributor) Ray Nathan and Henry Cobb, editors, *Mental Retardation: The Century of Decision*, President's Committee on Mental Retardation, 1976.

(Chief editor) *Mealtimes for Severely and Profoundly Handicapped Persons*, University Park Press, 1977.

Listen Please, Canadian Association for the Mentally Retarded, 1978.

Mental Retardation, the Leading Edge: Service Programs That Work, President's Committee on Mental Retardation, 1978.

New Life in the Neighborhood: How Persons with Retardation and Other Disabilities Can Help Make a Good Community Better, Abingdon, 1980.

Hope for the Families: New Directions for Parents of Persons with Retardation or Other Disabilities, Abingdon, 1981.

Circles of Friends: People with Disabilities and Their Friends Enrich the Lives of One Another, Abingdon, 1988.

Contributor of articles to professional journals.

SIDELIGHTS: "I try to build bridges between ordinary citizens and persons with handicaps. I try to chase myths about handicapping conditions, cast fresh light on awkward human situations with these people, and inspire my audience to value and make healthy connections with them.

"My writing career, which began at age forty-six, draws on better than twenty years of personal experiences with persons who have handicaps—as a pastor, a professional in institutions, a director of a community agency, and an accreditation surveyor.

"I believe that the more a civilization understands, values, and relates healthily with its members who have severe handicapping conditions, the more advanced that civilization can become."

HOBBIES AND OTHER INTERESTS: Regenerating soil for flower beds from other people's leaves.

PORTE, Barbara Ann
(Barbara Ann Porte-Thomas)

PERSONAL: Daughter of a pharmacist and a lawyer. *Education:* Attended Iowa State University; Michigan State University, B.S.; Palmer Graduate Library School, Long Island University, M.S. *Address:* P. O. Box 786, Mineola, N.Y. 11501.

CAREER: Nassau Library System, Uniondale, N.Y., children's services specialist, 1974-86; author of books for children. *Awards, honors: Harry's Visit* was named one of New York Public Library's Children's Books, 1983; *Harry's Mom* was selected one of Child Study Association of America's Children's Books of the Year, 1986.

WRITINGS:

JUVENILE

Harry's Visit (ALA Notable Book; Junior Literary Guild selection; illustrated by Yossi Abolafia), Greenwillow, 1983, large print edition, 1983.

BARBARA ANN PORTE

Jesse's Ghost and Other Stories, Greenwillow, 1983.

Harry's Dog (ALA Notable Book; Junior Literary Guild selection; illustrated by Y. Abolafia), Greenwillow, 1984, large print edition, 1984.

Harry's Mom (ALA Notable Book; illustrated by Y. Abolafia), Greenwillow, 1985.

The Kidnapping of Aunt Elizabeth, Greenwillow, 1985.

I Only Made Up the Roses, Greenwillow, 1987.

Harry in Trouble (illustrated by Y. Abolafia), Greenwillow, 1989.

The Take-Along Dog (illustrated by Emily A. McCully), Greenwillow, 1989.

Ruthann and Her Pig (illustrated by Sucie Stevenson), Orchard Books, 1989.

Jesse's Ghost and Other Stories is available as a Talking Book from the Library of Congress. Contributor of stories and poems to literary magazines, including *Earth's Daughters, Women: A Journal of Liberation, Lake Superior Review, Confrontation, San Jose Studies, Karamu,* and *Green's.*

ADAPTATIONS:

"Harry's Dog" (cassette), Random House.

WORK IN PROGRESS: An adult novel under name Barbara Ann Porte-Thomas, entitled *Mirra Durante; Fat Fanny and Beanpole Bertha.*

SIDELIGHTS: Porte was raised in New York City. "'Whatever you do,' our mother said, 'don't call attention to yourselves.' 'If you can't say something nice,' our father said, 'don't say anything at all.' And with depressing regularity, both of them, speaking to me and my two sisters, said, 'You needn't tell everything you know. In fact,' they'd add, 'you needn't tell anything you know.'

"Given these strictures, conversation wasn't easy. We made things up. We whispered stories to each other. 'Sssh, she'll hear,' we warned, and meant of course our lawyer mother would, with her courtroom mind. Our father didn't mind. He was a pharmacist who after all spent all his life just making up things.

"At the time, I planned to be an ornithologist, zoologist, or farmer. 'No pets,' our mother said, so we hid the animals we found—dogs and cats and wounded birds. 'Do you hear something mewing?' our mother was forever asking. 'Not me,' I'd answer, 'Do you?' I'd ask my sister, 'Who me?' she'd say and shake her head. She heard nothing either. She got a goat when she grew up to eat the grass. Instead, it ate her trees. 'See,' our mother told her, 'I was right.'

"But it was our father who was right. 'Read something every day and write something every day,' he told us every day, 'no matter what else you do with your lives.' And we did, and we do.

"All three of us are grown up now, or so it seems. We go to work, sometimes to school, and look after all the cats and children. And we warn the children: 'Sssh, you needn't tell everything you know.' In fact, we add, 'you needn't tell *anything* you know.' They make up things. But all of us know, every day of our lives, what the truth is: just getting by is the hard part; the stories and books are the stronghold."

FOR MORE INFORMATION SEE:

School Library Journal, December, 1987 (p. 41).

REICHERT, Edwin C(lark)   1909-1988

OBITUARY NOTICE: Born April 4, 1909, in Duluth, Minn.; died July 7, 1988, in Lake Forest, Ill. Educator, administrator, consultant, and author. A specialist in educational administration and psychology, Reichert was the author of popular children's books featured in the "Book Elf" and "Time to Read" series. Reichert held various teaching and supervisory posts in Minnesota and Wisconsin school districts before becoming superintendent of schools in Highland Park, Illinois, in 1944. In 1946 he became head of the education department at Lake Forest College, remaining there until his retirement in 1974. Additionally, Reichert was a consultant to a children's program, "Clown Alley," on WBBM-TV during the 1960s. Among Reicher's books are *My Truck Book, Space Ship to the Moon, Freight Train,* and *Becky's Friends.*

FOR MORE INFORMATION SEE:

Letters in Education, 2nd edition, Bowker, 1974.

OBITUARIES

Chicago Tribune, July 14, 1988.

ROCHE, P(atricia) K.   1935-

PERSONAL: Born June 15, 1935, in Brooklyn, N.Y.; married John Roche (a lawyer); children: Janet, Keith. *Education:* St.

P. K. ROCHE

John's University, B.A.; New York University, M.A.; also studied at New School for Social Research. *Home:* Brooklyn, N. Y., and Huntington, N.Y.

CAREER: Author and illustrator of children's books, 1976—. Has also worked as a copy writer for WCBN-FM, Cambridge, Mass., for a university agricultural research project, as an assistant to the head of a graduate school of business, and with an engineering firm. *Awards, honors: Dollhouse Magic* was named a Children's Choice by the International Reading Association and the Children's Book Council, and an *American Bookseller* Pick of the Lists, both 1977; *Dollhouse Magic* was selected one of Child Study Association of America's Children's Books of the Year, 1977, *Good-bye, Arnold!* 1979, *Webster and Arnold and the Giant Box,* 1980, *Plaid Bear and the Rude Rabbit Gang,* 1982, and *Jump All the Morning,* 1985; *Good-bye, Arnold!* was included in the American Institute of Graphic Arts Book Show, 1980.

WRITINGS:

JUVENILE; ALL SELF-ILLUSTRATED, EXCEPT AS NOTED

Dollhouse Magic: How to Make and Find Simple Dollhouse Furniture (Junior Literary Guild selection; illustrated by Richard Cuffari and with photographs by John Knott), Dial, 1977.
Good-bye, Arnold! (Junior Literary Guild selection), Dial, 1979.
Webster and Arnold and the Giant Box (sequel to *Good-bye Arnold!;* Junior Literary Guild selection), Dial, 1980.
Plaid Bear and the Rude Rabbit Gang, Dial, 1982.
(Selector) *Jump All the Morning: A Child's Day in Verse,* Viking, 1984.
(Selector) *At Christmas Be Merry,* Viking, 1986.
Webster and Arnold Go Camping, Viking, 1988.

ADAPTATIONS:

"Webster and Arnold and the Giant Box" (read-along cassette), Random House.

WORK IN PROGRESS: A story about how Webster and Arnold spend a boring indoor day; a kind of Cinderella story; another story.

SIDELIGHTS: "As a tall, thin, nearsighted child growing up in Brooklyn during the time the Brooklyn Dodgers played at Ebbetts Field, baseball dominated my childhood. With friends I went to ballgames, scoring each one carefully. I memorized batting averages, read baseball biographies, drew ballplayers, and—one memorable day—sat on the fender of pitcher Carl Furillo's car as it edged slowly out of an Ebbetts Field parking lot. I was hoping for an autograph which I did not get.

"But, alas, at home my family had no interest in baseball whatsoever. When I listened to ballgames on the radio, my mother would kindly ask me what 'round' they were up to, rather than inning. At home we read a lot: books and three newspapers a day came into the house. My first independent piece of reading was a 'Moon Mullins' comic strip. On Fridays, I waited for *Saturday Evening Post* and *Collier's* magazines to arrive so that I could read the cartoons in the back. To this day I read most magazines backwards, still looking for the cartoons. My sister and I both wrote and drew a lot when we were children. Our parents were encouraging and, although we weren't rich, we had paper, pencils, occasional large boxes of Crayolas, and our parents' pride in what we did. As for reading, my mother, who worked full time from the time I was eight, regularly bought a book for me on her paydays. None that I can remember were about baseball.

"Shortly before my great interest in baseball began and before my sister, who is eight years older than I, blossomed into a popular teenager, she both wrote and illustrated several stories for children. She would then read these aloud to small neighborhood children clustered in admiration on our front steps, while I, the younger sibling, lurked in the background. My wonderful sister has grown up to be a successful businesswoman and part-time artist. I, in a triumph of late-blooming sibling rivalry and earlier rejection of baseball, have grown up to do what my sister did so well as a very young teenager: write and illustrate children's books.

"More immediately, my family's love and support have much enriched me. I would probably not have found my way to this career had it not been for having my own children, especially my son. He made me think a lot about childhood in trying to better understand him. Because of my children, memories of my own childhood returned with great clarity and, with them, all the early feelings. Without my husband's strong encouragement, I doubt that I would have persevered at something for which I felt so unprepared.

"About *Dollhouse Magic:* First, because of general klutziness, I have never considered myself a craftsperson. The ideas for *Dollhouse Magic* initially came from the furniture which my daughter and I made for her dollhouse (which was a bookcase). Later, new ideas came and came. I went nowhere without a small stack of index cards. It became a time of seeing the world in small. I tried to write the book so that a child, with only occasional adult help, could have the fun and satisfaction of independently making or finding really pretty dollhouse furniture. I look on *Dollhouse Magic* as only a beginning for its readers because children have so many good ideas of their own.

"The idea for *Good-bye, Arnold!* came in part from the distinctly Webster and Arnold goings-on in our own house. But some of the feelings are also from my own childhood. One of the most exciting things for me about *Good-bye, Arnold!* is that I not only wrote but illustrated it. . . .When I began writing stories, I realized that I could also 'see' them but was frustrated by being unable to draw them. I sought a solution in a properly New York-y way: I took a course at the New School.

"The course was in children's book illustration and was taught by Uri Shulevitz, a very fine and caring author-illustrator himself. Almost everyone in the class had some formal art background and drew quite well. I, on the other hand, had not drawn much since I was a child. However, early on, Uri assured me that anyone could learn to draw—it just took working at. I continued to study with Uri in his advanced workshop, working on general drawing, composition, pen and ink, watercolor, and color separation—I look on Uri as a one-man art school. And I love to draw."

Webster and Arnold and the Giant Box is a sequel to *Good-bye, Arnold!* "The immediate idea came one day as I was walking down our block and saw a group of children noisily occupied with an empty refrigerator box. Like Proust and his crumb of madeleine—in a more modest cardboard variation!—seeing the box brought back memories of the many boxes that friends and I had played with when we were little. Refrigerator boxes were of course the best kind, the giants of them all. In thinking about box play, I also realized how similar my own and my children's play has been. The two most outstanding similarities have to do with box appearance and rules. None of us ever bothered to change the box physically. However, although we neither painted it nor cut windows into it, the box easily became all sorts of buildings, vehicles, or sometimes, a quiet, secret place. Of greater importance to us were the RULES. Our box games, so flexible in what the box could be, curiously had none of that freedom for the players. A lot of hard negotiating went on as to who would be what, and what that character would do, or even better, what that character would allow *others* to do. It all came down to pecking order. On this—if not on box decoration—we were willing to spend quantities of time.

"Our boxes, mine and my children's, usually would not have lasted for more than a day's hard play. When the box began to sag, we often liked to take turns being rolled inside it—a hot, dark, and jolting ride, but very exciting. This sort of thing led quickly to the final stage of the game, which occurred sometime before dinner. First, the box had to be properly flattened by judicious jumping. It then became a wonderful, bumpy slide—bumpy because it was leaned against someone's front steps. All of this led to wondering what Webster and Arnold would do with their own giant box. Plenty, of course. Hooray for giant boxes!

"*Plaid Bear and the Rude Rabbit Gang* came about because I wanted to write an adventure story with unconventional villains. And what more unconventional villains than. . .rabbits! For the main characters I decided to have four friends, two of whom—Plaid Bear and Rod Panda—are based on my children's favorite childhood stuffed toys. Old and worn though they are, I drew them young and new. The other two characters—Sarah Mouse and Amanda Chicken—are from the little toys that were used in *Dollhouse Magic*. Our beagle Ben was the model for both Finn Doggo and the judge. One way or another, he has made an appearance in three more of my books. Our currently twenty-pound cat was included, too, as a small grey-striped kitten. In a way, *Plaid Bear and the Rude Rabbit Gang* was a family book, using family toys and family pets. Also, had it not been for my son, who was about eleven at the time, I wouldn't have known that bagpipes were historically used to frighten the enemy—a major part of *Plaid Bear*'s deep, dark plot. Yes, definitely a family book.

"*Jump All the Morning* and *At Christmas Be Merry* are companion books, done in the same style and sharing some of the same characters. This is how they came to be. When I begin writing, I like to go to the public library. Most often I use the Donnell Branch's Central Children's Reference Room in New

Higher than a house,
Higher than a tree;
Oh, whatever can that be? ■ (From *Jump All the Morning: A Child's Day in Verse*, selected by P. K. Roche. Illustrated by the author.)

York City, which not only has helpful librarians, but also has a superb collection of children's books and a sprinkling of study carrels in which to work.

"It was at Donnell one day when my writing was far from flowing, that I came upon and began to read with much enjoyment the Opie collection of nursery rhymes. From there I went on to children's poetry in general. I thought I wasn't working. Certainly I was no longer thinking of my own writing, but I began to think that it would be interesting to try to tell a story within a collection of poems. While the idea of a child's day came quickly enough, I also wanted to tell a real story along with the ordinary doings of the day. I wanted to find the characters' names in the poetry as well. Finding the right poems became like a game.

"For a poetry research method, I remembered and took some advice that Helen Plotz, the distinguished poetry anthologist, had given several years ago. When asked how she went about her research, she modestly answered that she began at A. I read hundreds of poems and rhymes and did research in early versions of Mother Goose before the story of Joan and Tommy

and the latter's lost dog became *Jump All the Morning*. Although the book can be read as a collection of some favorite and some less well-known poems and rhymes, I like the idea that even a very young child can follow in the pictures the story of how Tommy lost and found his little dog. The characters are toy rabbits, other toys, and animals, which I loved drawing.

"While reading poetry for *Jump All the Morning*, I came upon beautiful Christmas poems by e. e. cummings, Eleanor Farjeon, and others. I began to make note of these poems with the idea of telling a simple story of a family's Christmas preparations and of the day itself. This idea became *At Christmas Be Merry*, for which I drew a family of teddy bears. The bear children are Johnny and Mary, who are named in the poems. Although the poems can be read singly, there is again, as in *Jump All the Morning*, a story which very young children can follow in the pictures. This time it is of an unusual present wished for and received.

"I did the first rough drawings during one hot, steamy July. Although I played Christmas carols and thought cold thoughts, perspiration dripped and my hand stuck to the paper. But from the very beginning I loved this book. In cooler weather, the illustrations evolved into highly detailed finished pieces of artwork. Both *Jump All the Morning* and *At Christmas Be Merry* were done in watercolor, using tiny triple 'o' brushes and colored inks—the former book in pastel tones and the latter in what I thought of as bright jewel-like colors. For both of these books, I worked under a magnifying glass, which seemed especially right for all the glowing details of Christmas. However, after finishing the jacket of *At Christmas Be Merry*, which has on it almost sixteen hundred tiny holly leaves (each delicately shaded in blue!) and thousands of tinier holly berries, I decided that my next book would be much different. Resolutely, I packed away my magnifying glass.

"The book that came next began long ago. *Webster and Arnold Go Camping* is my most elderly story. It began its life many years ago as a silly, but scary story that Webster told to Arnold about a teeny tiny ghost dog and a great big enormous chicken. Every so often, I'd come across it and laugh, but the story didn't stand alone and I didn't know with what it went. Eventually I thought of my own children and their fears and bravery on a dark night's backyard camping trip. So, too, Webster and Arnold and *their* fears and scary stories! (Plus very little sleep, an early rising, and a happy ending.) How-

ever, I first wrote the story in an easy-to-read form. Several more years passed before, rewritten, *Wester and Arnold Go Camping* became a story picture book with chapters. When I talk to classes of very young children, I like to put the development of a book in terms of their experience, but this one probably began when their parents were teenagers!

"Drawing *Webster and Arnold Go Camping* was a joy—except for the tent. I couldn't seem to draw one. I had lots of picture references for tents, but they were all so fancy and modern, and large enough to throw family reunions in. They didn't look like our old pup tent. One day my dear, patient, supportive husband dug out the original family tent and put it up in our yard. It had holes in it that something far larger than moths had made (monsters, maybe?), and it sagged no matter what. It looked just right. I took two dozen pictures of it with our five-year-old neighbor and our cat in and out of it, and. . .finally, I could draw a tent! After that, everything else was easy and fun to do—in colored pencils and no magnifying glass. I was especially proud of the large size of the great big enormous chicken and of the dinosaur that strode across the width of a double page. Truly sizable accomplishments for me!

"Sometimes I've been asked what I'd like to be doing in five years or ten and what else I'd like to do—write a novel for

I shake-shake,
Shake-shake,
Shake the package well.

But what there is
Inside of it,
Shaking will not tell.

(From *At Christmas Be Merry*, verses selected by P. K. Roche. Illustrated by the author.)

adults has been one frequent suggestion. What I love doing and hope to continue doing is just what I am doing now: writing and illustrating children's books. I feel it is a privilege to do this. Besides being able to do what I love, where else would I find a job with such fine working conditions?

"Even when I'm beginning a project and go to the library to write, I'm not there for more than a few hours at a time. Although I've tried sitting and writing from nine until five, little has come of it. My work day is different. Until I begin the art work for a book, my day consists of a few hours for writing, but also often includes walks in the city, visits to museums, to the zoo, a few hours of sketching children at play, pets at rest, clouds, flowers, anything I please. In some way it's all work. It's also how my best ideas come.

"Once I begin a book's art work, I stay at home much more. After many years, I finally have the luxury of a room of my own in which to work. I do a lot of my drawing late at night, especially the finished art. Although I have always liked the special quiet of the night, I first began working this way when my children were little, beginning work after they went to bed.

"In some ways, writing and illustrating is lonely work, but again, unique job that it is, where else could I have such freedom as to what I do and how I do it? Where else could my work companions be a dog, a cat, two guinea pigs who whistle when the refrigerator door is opened and warble when petted, two baby hooded rats (saved from being snake food), and a rabbit who sits by me and nudges my foot when she wants to be petted? When I am very involved in some aspect of a story or a drawing, sometimes everything else around me is blotted out, even my rabbit's soft nudges. This kind of intense focusing—while difficult to describe—is deeply satisfying. And it's all part of my job.

"Recently on television I saw a famous children's writer surrounded by a circle of young children sitting at his feet. He advised them, seriously I believe, that they shouldn't attempt to write, for they were too young and lacked experience. He then stressed the perfection that writing involves. Had I had such advice when young, I'd probably not have put pencil to paper and might now be out making donuts on an assembly line.

"Few writers begin with a perfect story; few illustrators begin with a perfect drawing. My stories begin handwritten in notebooks and are written and rewritten until they feel right. My early pencil sketches for a story are often small and smudgy. They're no beauties, but they're a beginning. There are always mistakes. I look on mistakes as something to learn from and then go on—sometimes to something much better than if there had been no mistake to begin with. Along with not worrying about mistakes, I also think it's important to try to work every day."

RODD, Kathleen Tennant 1912-1988 (Kylie Tennant)

PERSONAL: Born March 12, 1912, in Manly, New South Wales, Australia; died February 28, 1988, in Sydney, Australia; daughter of Thomas Walter and Kathleen (Tolhurst) Tennant; married Lewis Charles Rodd (a teacher), November 21, 1932 (died, 1979); children: Benison, John Laurence (died, 1978). *Education:* Attended Brighton College, and University of Sydney, 1931. *Religion:* Church of England. *Residence:* New South Wales, Australia. *Agent:* Judy Barry, 25 Yarranabbe Rd., Darling Point, Sydney, New South Wales, Australia.

Kylie Tennant, 1950.

CAREER: Writer, 1935-88; Macmillan Ltd., Melbourne, Australia, literary adviser and editor, 1959-69. Member of board, Australian Aborigines Co-operatives Ltd.; lecturer for Commonwealth Literary Fund, 1957-58, member of advisory board, 1960-72. Has made appearances on Australian television and radio. *Member:* Australian Fellowship of Writers (life patron), Australian Journalists' Association, Australian Society of Authors. *Awards, honors:* S. H. Prior Memorial Prize for Best Australian Novel, 1935, for *Tiburon*, and 1941, for *The Battlers;* Gold Medal from the Australian Literary Society, 1941, for *The Battlers;* Commonwealth Literary Fund Fellow, 1951; Commonwealth Jubilee Stage Play Award, 1952, for *Tether a Dragon;* Children's Books of the Year Award from the Australian Children's Book Council, 1960, for *All the Proud Tribesmen;* Officer, Order of Australia, 1980.

WRITINGS:

ALL UNDER NAME KYLIE TENNANT

Tiburon (novel), Endeavor Press, 1935, Angus & Robertson, 1973.

Foveaux (novel), Gollancz, 1939.

The Battlers (novel), Macmillan, 1941, new edition, Angus & Robertson, 1973.

Ride on, Stranger (novel), Macmillan, 1943, new edition, 1965.

Time Enough Later (novel), Macmillan, 1943.

Lost Haven (novel), Macmillan, 1946, new edition, 1965.

John o' the Forest and Other Plays (juvenile), Macmillan, 1950.

Tether a Dragon (play), Associated General Publications, 1952.

Australia: Her Story: Notes on a Nation (history), St. Martin's, 1953, revised edition, Pan, 1971.

The Joyful Condemned (novel), St. Martin's, 1953, new edition published as *Tell Morning This*, Angus & Robertson, 1967.

Long John Silver: The Story of the Film (juvenile fiction), Associated General Publications, 1954.

The Bells of the City and Other Plays (juvenile), Macmillan, 1955.

The Honey Flow (novel), St. Martin's, 1956, reissued, Angus & Robertson, 1973.

The Development of the Australian Novel, Commonwealth Literary Fund, 1958.

The Bushranger's Christmas Eve and Other Plays (juvenile), Macmillan (Australia), 1959.

Speak You So Gently (travel), Gollancz, 1959.

All the Proud Tribesmen (juvenile fiction; illustrated by Clem Seale), Macmillan (London), 1959, St. Martin's, 1960, new edition, Macmillan, 1983.

Trail Blazers of the Air (juvenile fiction), Macmillan (Australia), 1965, St. Martin's, 1966.

Ma Jones and the Little White Cannibals (short stories), St. Martin's, 1967.

Evatt: Politics and Justice (biography), Angus & Robertson, 1970.

The Man on the Headland (biography), Angus & Robertson (Australia), 1971, (London), 1973.

Tantavallon, Macmillan (Australia and London), 1983.

The Missing Heir: The Autobiography of Kylie Tennant, Macmillan (Australia), 1986.

EDITOR

Great Stories of Australia, 1-7, St. Martin's, 1963-66.
Summer's Tales I, St. Martin's, 1964.
Summer's Tales II, St. Martin's, 1965.

Critic for *Sydney Morning Herald*, 1953-88. Editor with husband L. C. Rodd, *The Australian Essay*, 1968.

SIDELIGHTS: Rodd was born **March 12, 1912,** in Manly, New South Wales, Australia. Her father, Thomas Walter Tennant, was the son of a Scottish doctor, once a Presbyterian missionary to China, who had emmigrated to Australia around 1870, but continued to remind his son, Thomas, that he was heir to a Scottish clan. Thomas became known as ''The Parent'' to his wife and two daughters. ''The Tennant Clan, the Glenconners, were the curse of my childhood: rich, aristocratic, owning a castle and various mansions, they led the 'Parent' to contrast his own circumstances of suburban anonymity in a second-class country on the backside of the world. 'You have to have influence,' he would repeat. 'If you don't know the score where are you?' Underneath this not unusual layer of discontent he was an average Australian with the Australian's naive generosity, curiosity and interest in everything whether it concerned him or not. He had a capacity for enjoyment and good fellowship; he made friends easily and busied himself with his friends' affairs. He had an extraordinary charm when he cared to exercise it. If there was a scheme for money-making, however fantastic, he was into it. He had money in shares. At one time he even owned the fourth part of a race horse but it never won when the owners were told it would. 'My leg must have been the one that wasn't running,' the 'Parent' said.

'''I wish I had all the money your father has sunk in gold mines,' my mother would say. 'And inventions.'

''My parents had married far too young. She was eighteen and he just twenty-three. At that time my mother's father, Frank Tolhurst, had a large house overlooking North Steyne at Manly. He was a prosperous builder, and the house had a tennis court. My uncle had a sailing boat. It was a hospitable house where everyone sang at the piano. Grandpa had a splendid tenor, my aunt Beryl was a contralto, mother sang soprano. They danced, they gave dinners and musical evenings. The 'Parent' was entranced by the pretty blonde elder daughter, Kathie Tolhurst.

I have often heard my mother describe life at The Gumtrees on a rocky eminence with the surf rolling below, the magnificent view of the coastal headlands, and outside the gate a stone statue put up where the first kangaroo was killed by Captain Phillip's men when he landed at Manly. This, in some later flurry of sentimentality, commemorated a murderous beginning that continues to this day.

''Anyway, handsome young Thomas Tennant had no more chance than that first kangaroo. At the time he had a secure job with Lysaght's, he was building up a carrying business for himself with teams of Clydesdales and he owned a block of land, inherited from his father over towards Harbord beyond North Steyne.

''There should have been set up some marriage board to test incompatibility. Neither Katherine Tolhurst nor Thomas Walter Tennant would have passed. Alarms should have been sounded in the streets to warn them. Instead the Tolhursts moved happily to their new house—Lauderdale above Fairlight. Grandpa Tolhurst built his daughter a house called Narbethong on the rise of land behind Lauderdale. Orange blossoms, my red-headed young aunt Beryl as bridesmaid, white satin, costly wedding presents of silver and china, a three-tiered iced cake with a sailing skiff on the top and the motto: 'God sends the wind to fill the sails,' which Tom Tennant claimed was his family crest, all these signalised a wedding that should never have taken place. My mother treasured the little silver-painted skiff from her wedding cake for many years when the lustre had worn off everything else.

''It looked, then, as though the future was set fair for them. After a year the 'Parent' was brooding. Why had his wife not

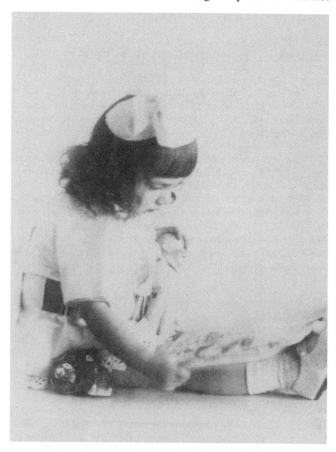

Kylie at three years old. ■ (From *The Missing Heir: The Autobiography of Kylie Tennant.*)

produced a son? Did she not realise it was her duty to carry on the Tennant name? This naturally aroused resentment in an idealistic young girl who had looked forward to a romantic and continuing dream; the 'Parent' being expected to equal that deference, courtesy and affection with which Grandpa Tolhurst treated his womenfolk.

"She was just twenty when I was born. A daughter! What the hell use was a daughter? Where was his son? The heir? He lamented dramatically and went on lamenting. Two years later she bore my sister Dorothy. By this time my mother's attitude to her husband was tinged by disillusion. My sister was adorable, cuddly, with a blue mark on her lip which caused anxiety. Not even the 'Parent' could resist her. He enjoyed his second daughter, petted her, but did not cease his vocal dramatics, telling everyone of his great tragedy. He had grown up with a widowed mother and two sisters. Now he had a wife and two daughters. 'I always wanted a son, not a lot of women.'

"He had not reckoned with my mother, who had a far firmer character than his. She set her face against any further childbearing. There was nothing a husband could do. So many women of my mother's generation had their own means, handed down for generations, of protecting themselves from unwanted offspring. Had the 'Parent' been just a little less selfish, arrogant, overbearing towards her, he could possibly have had a flock of sons, but he had spoilt his chances.

"My family discovered that I could learn anything. At the age of two I was set to recite 'The Night Before Christmas'—which I knew by heart—before a circle of adults and my Uncle Toss, who married my aunt Beryl, laughed so immoderately that he fell off his chair when I came to the words 'He had a white beard and a little round belly which shook when he laughed like a bowl full of jelly.' I hated him with a cold hatred which endured. He was laughing at the precise diction I had copied from my grandmother.

"What upset the women about me was that I was left-handed. Spoons were always being snatched from my good left hand and transferred to my right. Later, at school I was taught to write with my right hand. So I now draw with my left hand and wrote with my right, all because before people owned toilet paper it was taboo to use the left hand—which was used for toilet purposes—for food which was taken with the right. Maybe there was some other less logical reason. Excrement was associated with the Evil One so the left hand was the Hand of the Devil. Extraordinary how the two lobes of the brain have been distinguished. Being ambidexterous didn't worry me but anything that did not conform to the ordinary worried my mother and grandmother. What grandmother said was gospel. She imposed her will. Also I was undersized. Very active and precocious but undersized. Not a big fat handsome baby like my sister."[1]

1914. "I was two years old when I can remember running in the dusk to meet my grandfather and being given The Book; my first book. It was read to me and I burst into tears at the pathos of the story, which was *Mamie and Her Little Wog* by May Gibbs. Mamie was a small girl and she and her dog Wog were lost. By this time the family dreaded any display of emotion on my part. Owing to my successful expanding of an outsize pair of lungs and the practice I had put into breathing, my voice was enormous in comparison to my body."[1]

By the age of four, Rodd was her parents' darling. "I was their doll, to be dressed in little pleated skirts. My hair was curled every night and the curl-rags hurt. My sallow skin was improved with rouge and lipstick, which I rubbed off when I had the chance. I was supposed to be 'cute.' I was saved in

my self-respect by learning to read at the age of four. I followed my grandmother around, reading aloud to her. I despised children's books. At five I abandoned *Dombey and Son* when Florence grew up; I started on *Alan Quartermain,* a book by Rider Haggard, which won my approval because of all the fighting. Umslopagaas the Zulu was my favorite character. I liked pirates but anything with a great deal of bloodshed would do. For my Christmas present I demanded and received a bound *Chums* annual. Plenty of gore."[1]

The family moved to a new address at Condamine Street, in Manly, where her parents argued a great deal and decided to divorce. "One of the great rows in Condamine Street was over our schooling. I was to go from the dear little dame school at the top of our street to the public school where the neighbouring children went in a tram to Manly. On the first day there I did not mind the asphalt playground and its yelling hordes but when introduced to the classroom I broke into screams and sobs. The teacher had to send me out to sit in the playground all day. The next day was no better.

"'What is the matter with her?' one teacher asked another.

"'We don't know.'

"I had found I was in a gaol. The door was shut, the windows were too high up for a tiny girl to climb out. I did not know until then that I was claustrophobic. I couldn't even have pronounced the word. I just lost my breath and screamed.

"My mother took me away and introduced me to the private school, Brighton College, where she had spent her school years. 'I only sat in the back seat and dreamed out the window,' she admitted. Also she had carved her initials K.T. so deeply into a desk that I was occasionally called up and had to explain that it was not K.T. for Kylie Tennant but Katherine Tolhurst. 'My mother,' I said simply. That desk was always following me around—not in the kindergarten which had French windows and doors always open. I was very happy to be there after the public school. My father was furious. At the public school the education was free. At a private school you had to pay for it. Thereafter he took his revenge by owing the school fees, refusing to pay for textbooks or uniforms. No wonder my mother ran into debt or had to cajole him when he grumbled. As a boy he had finished his education at Shore, a private school, because Australian snobbery still takes children from public schools to 'finish' them at private school just so that they can claim the accolade later. My mother's view was that public school children were rough and 'common.' Girls must have beautiful manners.

"The 'Parent's' attention had been attracted to the fact that I wrote little stories. He proudly marched me down to visit my dear Aunt Arbie who had married Uncle Stan, a journalist. 'Shut her up in a room,' he proclaimed, 'and she'll write something.' The experiment was promptly tried. 'Write,' he commanded. As all the windows were shut I scribbled feverishly (some mush) in order to get out. Uncle Stan was duly impressed. The 'Parent', from that time, never ceased to boast of my queer habit."[1]

Soon, Rodd and her mother and sister moved into Rosedale with the Tolhurst grandparents. Rodd continued her scribbling. "While we were at Rosedale waiting for the divorce that never happened we missed a term at school and were kept home because Grandma was convinced the 'Parent' would steal us away. I produced my first newspaper, writing it out by hand. This was a pleasant time of leisure but I found the newspaper became so popular that my hand ached from writing out copies so I gave it up.

The prefects of Brighton College. Kylie Tennant is in the middle, back row.

"...I would climb up to the roof and write doggerel or encourage a family of mice who lived under the back doorstep. The dog gave me away by sniffing there and Grandpa massacred the poor mice. My relatives were impressed by my doggerel. Mother sent it to a poetical magazine which reported 'child's verse of more than usual promise' which I thought sickening. Grandpa gave me a subscription to the Manly School of Arts Library. There was no children's section and the fat librarian detested me as I never read the ladylike fiction which I considered slushy. I started at A for astronomy. (I still scan any new discoveries in astronomy.) I liked travel books. I developed a fondness for the *roman policier;* detectives with bowler hats and dandruff on their collars, who would trace a railway ticket until they unearthed the body. I demanded the right to go into the city library on Saturday morning where, starting at A, I discovered archeology and anthropology. I then read straight through three volumes of Frazer's *Golden Bough*. I chanced on Freud's *Interpretation of Dreams,* and read anything I could find that he wrote. I pronounced his famous name like some obscure disease (Frood) because, of course, I never met anyone who could discuss his work with me. My ambition was to go to the Gobi Desert and dig up ancient cities. I reckoned that anywhere people had been living for centuries would turn into deserts and the Gobi sounded promising.

"My father was in the process of coaxing his family back and, hearing—no doubt from my mother—that I was writing 'poems,' rang up Rosedale to say that a magazine called the *Farmer and Grazier* wished to publish my verse. As the 'Parent' was, at this time, the advertising manager of his firm this was a very good move on the part of the editor. Several little pieces of my doggerel with the requested agricultural motif duly ap-

peared in this worthy journal with a hideous photograph of me looking nervous in white socks. I was losing my front teeth at the time and had to have them pulled out under anaesthetic as the second teeth refused to come through while the first were hanging on grimly. 'Kylie Tennant, age 11' was written under the hideous photograph.

"The 'Parent' was able to boast to Uncle Stan. I detested writing this silly stuff and after three lots refused to do any more. I have always been able to judge mediocrity because it makes me sick on my stomach."[1]

Rodd was bright, but a poor student. "My brains only lit up when I advanced to Upper School. I could mop up necessary facts and dates the night before the exam and forget them happily two days later. In third class we had started on Latin and algebra when we had never heard of them. I detested both. The mathematics teacher gave up on me when I was wending my erratic way through primary school. The headmistress always set us sums for detention. I got a psychic block when I was expected to calculate 14 pounds of potatoes at 2.10 1/2 a pound. I had to be let go when darkness fell or I would have been there yet.

"I was always brought forward to read aloud in sewing class. I had the same petticoat (unfinished) follow me from class to class like my mother's desk. It had ancient bloodstains from needlepricks around the hem. I couldn't draw—with the correct shading—left-handed again. Instead I made wicked little sketches. They were not appreciated. Years later I coached a red-headed boy in geometry and Latin. When he went back to school he was way ahead of the class. The geography mistress

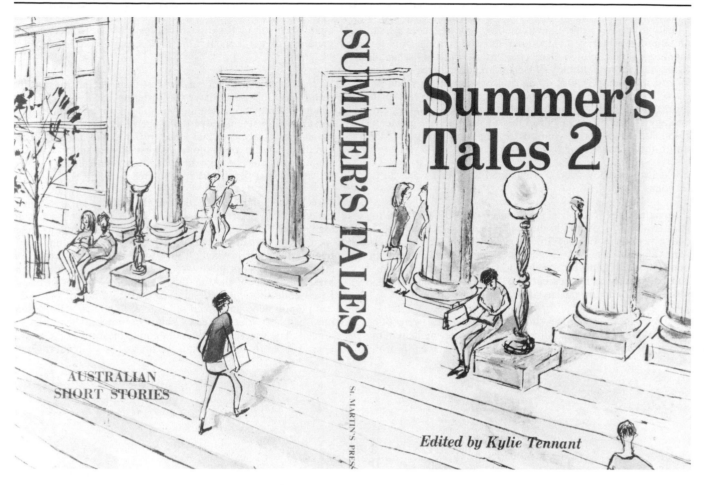

(Jacket illustration by Arthur Brocksopp from *Summer's Tales 2*, edited by Kylie Tennant.)

was right to suspect that I never learnt anything at all in a reasonable way. . . .

"Above all I never did anything in the right way. This has always amazed people. 'But you do things the *hard* way,' they would exclaim. It had never occurred to me that there was an easier way of going about whatever I was engaged on. I fully expected to make a mess of it and was very surprised when, by a miracle, it proved a great success."[1]

At the age of sixteen, Rodd went to work for the Australian Broadcasting Company. For two years, working at various jobs, assisting the Hello Man, Uncle Frank, The Farmyard Fire, Uncle Jim, Aunt Willa and Auntie Goodie: all of ABC radio fame.

Meanwhile she was plotting how to run away from home. On one attempt, a friend "after promising to escort me to the train, sneaked to my father, who came pouncing down and hauled me home in a taxi. Next morning I dropped my suitcase over the front verandah and jumped after it. It was my eighteenth birthday.

". . .There is a consensus of opinion among my friends that Kylie—while a dear girl, of course—has not enough nous to come in out of the wet. Or, as one said, 'Too damn green to burn.' With this opinion I am at times inclined to agree. It is nevertheless irritating that throughout my life I no sooner escape from whoever owns me than some other proprietor pops up to tell me what to do. Not that I take any notice; but my life has this background of admonition, criticism (often affectionate), orders (disregarded) and helpful suggestions for my improvement.

"To this chorus I have managed to raise a family, nurse people through illnesses, undertake journeys, write books, run houses and try to be in two places at once.

"Nobody save an idiot, these helpful persons point out, would desert a good job to journey to Melbourne, a city they had never seen, with their poor meagre savings, in what was to be the darkest days of the financial Depression. It may have been fugue, it may have been crazy, but there was an excellent outcome to this flight into what could have been disaster: I developed my sense of humour."[1]

Rodd intended to work as a journalist but during the Depression ended up working in a kiosk selling candy and magazines. She was finally persuaded to return home.

In **1931** she announced to her family that she was ". . .going to the university to get my BA. They seemed relieved. My Tennant grandmother announced that she would pay my fees for the first term. My old headmistress offered me a place, free, to study for the matric. I had three months to prepare for matriculation and do a year's work. I did it. My mother, on the last lap, decided that I should have a coach and dug up a funny little man from a local coaching college who fitted in to the maxim of my current suitor that whenever I appeared 'strange characters popped up out of the woodwork.' The suitor attributed this to a strain of insanity in myself. This coach of mine was later arrested for impersonating a young woman in an exam. Having decided she wouldn't get through, he handsomely offered to do the exam for her.

"I passed even Latin and mathematics myself. My old maths teacher couldn't believe it. She said she thought it must be a mistake when she saw the results in the paper.

"I had got myself a part-time job selling typewriters as a result of entering a literary competition the typewriting firm was running. I didn't sell too many typewriters but used the sample typewriter for my old ploy of penetrating any place I thought looked interesting. I was doing honours psychology and because I started late I needed a partner for experiments. I informed Professor Martin that a student who was doing Psychology II had offered to drop this to become my partner in Honours I. 'Well, bring your boyfriend along,' Professor Martin grinned, 'and let me have a look at him.'

"'He isn't my boy friend,' I snapped. 'He just wants to do Honours I.'

"Lewis Charles Rodd was graciously allowed to become my partner and I discovered in the experiments on hearing that he had a hearing deficiency in his right ear. His eyesight—he wore glasses—was not as good as mine either. He got top marks in everything he attempted. I was near the bottom. I had only taken economics because he advised it and it was a mistake. Economics and myself were incompatible.''[1]

Although she had another suitor, she and Rodd were often together. ''. . .He was full of good advice, offering help in my university studies. From that time, much to the anguish of my established suitor, Rodd went wherever I was. He became the secretary of the Labour Education League and I was press secretary.

"I had to find a better paying job than freelancing for the yellow press. Just as they were offering me a staff job and announced they were sending me out on police rounds I quit and took a job at a big advertising agency that Professor Martin found me. This meant that I had to transfer to a night course and drop honours psychology. My established suitor was very happy about this because he thought it would mean I would see less of that pernicious fellow, Rodd.

"I explained sadly to Roddy that there had been a sad misunderstanding between myself and my editors, over a certain assignment. They had been on the track of a Macquarie Street specialist who had been telling patients they had syphilis and treating them for it when all they were suffering from was an attack of nerves, or guilt. Would I, the editor asked, present myself as a patient and trap this scoundrel? 'You bet I would,' I said enthusiastically. I had once gone to a doctor because I had painful acne and asked if I had 'sigh-phillis.' He assured me I had not. 'But you can catch it from public lavatories,' I argued. The gruesome posters in public lavatories on Circular Quay set out in sinister detail the horrors of venereal disease.

KYLIE TENNANT RODD. (Photograph by A. T. Bolton.)

I had been warned by my mother when a child *never* to use public lavatories. This warning had been passed down from mother to daughter ever since the first settler landed, when public hygiene was non-existent.

"The angry objections of my established suitor—of whose jealousy and conformity I was beginning to tire—caused me to seek another interview with my editors. 'I was wondering,' I told them, 'whether it would be a drawback on this latest job that I am *virgo intacta?* A friend of mine tells me it would.' The editors were dumbfounded. They had never for a minute dreamt I had such a drawback and immediately told me I had lost the assignment. I was very dejected. I confided to Roddy that I had once again been found unworthy—and why.

"'The fools!' he exploded. 'Didn't they realise that you were ideal to catch this fraud?' He seemed to me the only person who had any common sense. I beamed on him. Here, I thought, was the only man for my money.

"Unfortunely he was being shipped away to the farthest school in the state the Office of Education could find for him: Coonabarabran—which means in Aboriginal 'where the cows sit down.' They didn't give him any notice. They just told him to report there. They could do that in those days. Head Office had found out that the man who was conducting the campaign to have flag-saluting in the school abolished was L. C. Rodd. It was a campaign that was causing a lot of trouble and of course it lapsed when Roddy was removed. . . ."[1]

Around this time Rodd began two life-long habits: political action and long-distance walking. In 1932 she walked to the northern swamps of Australia when "Roddy" asked her to come visit him. "I had, before Roddy was sent off to Coonabarabran, told him that I intended to take a long walk and needed to buy some trousers. In those days slacks for women were not sold yet and jeans were still in the far future. Roddy accompanied me down to Paddy's Market onc night after lectures and was measured by the man on the clothing stall. 'What size is he?' I asked. 'A four.' 'And what size would I be?' He measured me with his eye. 'You'd be a perfect four, miss.' 'Right,' I said. 'Wrap those trousers up.' I could always get shirts, a coat and a felt hat—the uniform for the road. These would not show the dirt of campfires. I had a knapsack and my sister's ski-ing boots. These managed to rip the skin off my feet so it was fortunate I took a pair of sandshoes with me. I wore the sandshoes more than I did the boots. Later I'd start out in the boots to walk a hundred miles or so and end up in the sandshoes. I hated to be licked but I finally threw those damned boots away. I can only pass on the wisdom of the road, if anyone is still walking it: look after your feet.

"My poor 'Parent' was, by this time, quite resigned. He even drove me to the foot of the Blue Mountains when I set off on my six-hundred-mile walk to Coonabarabran. Six hundred miles always seemed to me just a good distance. The car ride gave the 'Parent' the opportunity for one more recitative, prophecying my doom. My murdered body would be found, he felt, before very long. Turning off south, he presented me with ten shillings to take me on my way. I went off whistling cheerfully."[1] She camped with tramps, ate in soup kitchens, took lifts from strangers and learned to jump trains.

On **November 21, 1932** she and Lewis Charles Rodd were married in Coonabarabran. "Marriage is like turning a corner and coming on an undiscovered landscape. It is even more complicated if you shift from a city to what is, for you, unknown territory in the scrub. I was so ignorant that I did not know that when strangers said 'G'day' in passing, you were supposed to reply 'G'day.' A country girl I knew later went

through King's Cross courteously saying 'G'day' to everyone she passed, and was hurt by their not returning her greeting. In Coonabarabran, people commented unfavourably on my manners for the first couple of months. However, by the time Christmas came I was learning—but not much.

"Coonabarabran was a sheep town in the Warrumbungles, with cedar trees down the main street, a cafe kept by two Greek brothers who were our great friends, a small church where we were married, a school where my husband taught— and a conviction that Coonabarabran was the hub of the universe. It was a two-pub town—pretty big."[1]

Roddy had thought about becoming an Anglican priest and Rodd, knowing how important the church was to him, joined the church in Coonabarabran. "I must admit I made a poor Anglican. When I had told Good Ole Bill I wished to join his church he said incredulously: 'Are you sure?' But I had been through the book of words and adjusted to their interpretations. Kneeling I considered an Oriental posture rightly rejected by my Scottish ancestors. I agreed with the man who said that instead of praising the Lord we should be offering him sympathy. Roddy's Christ Church St Laurence reminded me of the saying that 'the Roman Catholics can go through a whole Mass while the High Church of England is changing its robes.' I had to keep reminding myself that tolerance is the most necessary of all religious qualities. I never got the hang of the High Church liturgy and I crossed myself politely when everyone else did.

"I am an inveterate sleeper-through-sermons, sitting erect, eyes shut, a pious expression from ear to ear, waking as soon as the preacher says: 'And lastly. . . .' I became a suburban Christian out of solidarity with the human race, thousands of years of it. I used to tell people I was a Communist and they would flinch. Now I say I am a suburban Christian and they flinch. Fun!

"Of course, in the first years of our marriage, we were, like so many young Australians of our generation, saving up to go to Europe. Australia was a backwater of backwaters. I was forced to send all my earlier books to England to be published because, as Ken Prior told me, they were 'such a bad advertisement for Australia.'

"In those days if you wrote about Australian society as it was, nobody wanted to know about it. I was determined that they were going to know about it. I became so interested in forcing my readers to see the seamier side of our society in the form of fiction that for some years the idea of 'going overseas' was buried in a weight of work. . . .

". . .In the 1930s. . .we stirred up quite a little action where we were. Anyone who held left liberal views was a Red— which was like being a witch in medieval Europe. We were Reds. Our colouration faded with the years until Roddy even refused to vote for the local Labor candidate if he didn't think he was any good, or even to vote at all. . . ."[1]

Rodd was beginning to write short stories for the *Bulletin* because she was too far away from publishing houses. ". . .I. . .loved inertia and only worked when I had built up a huge load of guilt for not working. I liked going around filling up notebooks but when the actual sweat was on and I had to pound a typewriter and turn out a book, I was like all other writers. I'd do anything else as an excuse not to write. Roddy kept me in line, holding out his hand firmly for the chapter when he came home from school. I turned out a chapter a day. Roddy read it and criticised it.

Tennant on the set of the television series "Ride On Stranger."

"So I wrote short stories and the first three or four were so awful that they came back promptly with caustic comment. Roddy had read my first novel, which I had written before I married him. He then threw it in the creek. He fished it out again, saying we mustn't pollute the water, and we took it home and burnt it. I was relieved because I didn't think much of it either."[1]

During the Depression, Rodd, her husband, and a Mrs. McLean collected donations for the poorest families and delivered them. "...Mrs McLean got into the front seat with the driver, I perched on top of the bags, and we set off for tiny holdings away from the road that only Mrs McLean could find. I never knew before that lean families with children as shy as bush animals were living in humpies with mud floors, saplings supporting leaky iron roofs. In one place the kitchen table was wooden slabs set on timber supports driven into the earth floor.

"This was the unknown poverty which hides away. The eyes of those children when they saw the fruit—peaches, plums, apricots, oranges! They never came into town. They hadn't any means of getting there. Their meagre supplies would be delivered to a roadside box, and they had to tramp to the box. My respect for the stout Mrs McLeans of country towns was fixed forever. From that day onwards, I knew that in any country town, where I might be, there would be one Mrs McLean, shrewd, knowing everyone, stout, unhurried. She was the woman I always sought out for a friend.

"When we moved to Canowindra...the 'Parent' carefully cut out a notice that the *Bulletin* was offering a prize for a novel—the S. H. Prior Memorial Prize—and posted through to me. He wrote on it: 'Get cracking.'

"This struck Roddy as an excellent idea. I began typing *Tiburon* which had in it all that I had seen and observed of

conditions of the unemployed in Canowindra and Coonabarabran, and on the many walks I had taken through the midwest."[1]

1935. *Tiburon* won the S. H. Prior Memorial Prize. "...One person who did not care for the tone of the book was Ken Prior, editor of the *Bulletin,* who told me as I autographed his copy that *Tiburon* was 'a bad advertisement for Australia.' In those days, perhaps in these days also, writing was considered a branch of publicity—national publicity, if you like. *Tiburon* suggested that something had gone wrong somewhere and that was not the impression a patriot would wish to give in the shining circles of omnipotence in London."[1]

Writing the book was Rodd's attempt to do something to improve the plight of the itinerant workers. "I was to the left of the Communist Party. My detestation of violence took the form of a demand for action to improve conditions *now*. Coming from a suburban background from Sydney, the conditions under which the country poor and the itinerant workers lived struck me as astonishing. They were accepted by those who lived under them because they had always been like that.

"When I walked twenty-five miles to interview the Shire Council and plead for a water tank to be placed beside a shed on the stock route where the travelling workers camped, the Shire clerk demanded: 'What's wrong with drinking the creek water? I've drunk it.'

"'There's a dead horse in it,' I told him. He seemed to think people should draw their water from above the dead horse, but I got my water tank. Their astonishment that anyone, particularly a young woman, a schoolteacher's wife living in a hotel, should be concerned with the conditions under which 'bagmen' lived was extreme. The explanation was that I was a Red. . . ."[1]

1939. Moved back to Sydney where her husband taught at a suburban boys' school. Published *Foveaux*, about life in Surrey Hills, the slum area where her husband grew up and in which they lived together for a while on their return to Sydney.

1940. Rodd began research on a new book. She camped and picked cherries and peas with other migrant workers, encountering dust storms and drunken Aborigines. "When we were living in a small suburban house in Dulwich Hill handy to Roddy's school in 1940 I wrote *The Battlers*. Roddy went to stay with his mother while I was away getting the material, and we then moved to this small house, built on what was once a tennis court and almost buried under nasturtiums, morning glory and trees.

"I wanted to go out on the roads by cart because the people on the roads who had turnouts' (sulkies, carts, vans) did not mix with lesser persons who used feet or bicycles to go from dole station to dole station.

"I was indebted to the Nicholson family of Roddy's step-sister Bray for practical help in finding a half-draught horse and buying an old laundry cart. I had no experience of horses—a disadvantage which Roddy, as ignorant as myself of horses, waved away. Anyone he felt who could drive a car could drive a horse. The Nicholsons, on the other hand, who knew all about horses because they had a thriving dairy and milk run at Ryde, thought that to send out someone who had never driven a horse, harnessed a horse, groomed or fed a horse, was a dubious proposition. They were both right—Roddy in airly dismissing all difficulties, Bray's charming family in recognising them."[1]

Finally, while she worked as a waitress to make a little money, her horse, Violet, died. "It was in Leeton that I unfortunately managed to strangle poor Violet. I had been lent a stable and I had also been shown a new knot for tethering horses by an old drover. Tying this new knot I produced a slip knot and, leaving Violet tied up in the stable to await the return of the man in charge, I hurried back to serve dinner at the boarding house. In the morning one of the breakfasters looked at me sadly and said: 'Your horse is dead.'

"'Nonsense,' I replied, laughing heartily. I thought he was 'having me on.' But it turned out to be true. Violet had pulled back on my new knot and strangled herself. I mourned her terrible end, killed by my incompetence. I had meant to sell the horse and cart at Leeton. Now I sold the cart and went home to my husband who had not realised that my researches would take so much time."[1]

1941. Rodd published *The Battlers*, which won the Australian Literary Society's Gold Medal and the S. H. Prior Memorial Prize. Next, the Rodds moved to Laurieton, where they stayed eleven years.

1943. Rodd published *Time Enough Later* and *Ride on, Stranger*, which years later became popular as an Australian television series.

1949. She began work on a new novel published as *The Joyful Condemned* (published in 1967 in its entirety as *Tell Morning This*). For this work about life in jail, she insisted on more research. "...I began to think that conscientious objectors and young girls picked up for living with servicemen—people who weren't robbers or burglars—were having a thin time of it. My fatal curiosity, my go-and-find-out urge stirred and smouldered. Roddy could help in the holidays but he would have to make our living as headmaster of the Laurieton school while I investigated in Sydney.

"I chose the title from a book by Lord Dunsany: 'And ever at the heels of regal night whispers arose saying: "Tell morning this."' I took a job in a delinquents' home where the splendid headmistress was a Christian Socialist, one of our friends. I proved almost too successful in uncovering minor lapses and a threatened breakout. I later worked in a jam factory where the word would go around: 'The Fleet's in' and there would be noticeable absenteeism next day.

"I lived in strange houses and semi-brothels. I made the acquaintance of prostitutes, criminals, warders. When we drew up my list, Roddy said thoughtfully: 'And I think you should do a week in gaol.' The suggestion did not appeal to me as I am a claustrophobiac. I become uneasy if there is not a door or window open. Thinking it over, I realised he was right as usual. You cannot describe what you have not experienced at first hand. Roddy and I began our campaign by taking the head of the Vice Squad out to lunch.'"[1]

She found it difficult to get arrested until she had disguised herself and dyed her hair. Even then, she had to be obscene to a policeman before he would arrest her. "I was placed in a cell by myself overnight and then moved to the remand ward, which was a big dormitory. When I arrived the inmates eyed me suspiciously. When I left two ladies connected with nightclubs and a recent murder kissed me on the cheek and called me 'love.'

"What I noticed, settling in comfortably and making friends, was that a number of mattress workers were physically not very good specimens. They all had something wrong with them—poor eyesight, bow legs, bad teeth, skin troubles, weak bladder. They probably took up mattress work from an early fear that they were unattractive.

"There was a wide range and sampling. They taught me to sing their cheerful bawdy songs after lights out. . . .

"I always think it is a great tribute to the human spirit that people will sing in gaols, detention homes, hospitals and armies. Wherever they are you can judge them by what they sing and learn new songs from each other. . . .

"Anyway nobody decided to prosecute me for public mischief. I always contended I was not a well-known novelist. I was a *notorious* novelist. Many people cannot remember anything about me except that I once spent a week in gaol. I always believe that innocent, middle-class people should go to gaol. They would tear the walls down. Now there are outcries that the conditions in gaol are too luxurious and lax and too many people are escaping. Don't you believe it. Gaols are run by the worst crims and some of them are so savage that not only the warders but also their fellow criminals are afraid of them. Just the other day a man hanged himself in his cell and some of the men arrested with him, who had been held for many months without trial, were allowed to go out, under guard, to his funeral. I suppose they count that as a reform."[1]

Gave birth to her first child, Benison, a daughter.

September 26, 1951. A son, John Laurence "Bim," was born. "Before Bim was even conceived I was aware of a spirit with wings of flame pleading with me and I welcomed this being. After he was conceived I was aware of the history of an Indian who had camped as a hawker in the bush and was murdered there.

"While I was in labour I was aware of this radiance and joy. Bim was born smiling and hungry, seemingly relieved to have a human body again. . . .Aboriginal women, when they wish for a child, will go to the sacred place of the ancestors and summon a spirit. Because men had so long exclusively claimed the role of doctor no woman is likely to tell such a person how a mother communicates with a child before it is born and while she is supplying the body it will later use. Even a bird listens to the chicken in the shell before it breaks free of the constricting shell and her warm feathers. She will croon to it.''[1]

1953. Prompted by the 'Parent', Rodd wrote a popular history of Australia titled *Australia: Her Story: Notes on a Nation.* ''. . .It was deliberately written for people who knew nothing of Australian history. Popularising was not then the great industry it is today. Real historians shudder if they have ever heard of *Australia: Her Story;* but there is a good deal of snobbery among historians. I revised *Australia: Her Story* later to bring it up as far as the fifties but refused to do more work on it after that. The book would have been too large for my simple public. While I was writing it I was writing plays for Roddy's children (three little books of them were published by Macmillan and they are still being acted in schools); teaching them to handle a puppet theatre; teaching sewing; running the school residence; getting meals for visitors; raising vegetables; and seeing to the two horses. I taught in the school if any teacher fell ill. I was also the star of the first-aid class. This simple boast is justified as we were thirty-five miles from the nearest doctor and when anyone had an accident the trail of blood would lead to my back door. . . .''[1]

1956-1966. While researching *The Honey Flow,* a book about migrating apiarists, or beekeepers, Rodd managed to keep busy with their new house in Hunter's Hill. ''. . .The house came with a substantial mortgage and henceforth it was my aim to pay off the interest on that mortgage as I had an extreme horror of debt. I slaved at every hack job that came my way, writing anything from a libretto for a musical comedy to a book made out of a film. I continued writing little plays for Roddy's school, articles for the school magazine, radio talks.

''. . .In between I helped with the school, if Roddy fell ill, ran the house, provided meals and was a worthy suburban matron. Of course I could not attend morning teas or charity functions but I was popular because I was the only woman with a truck which could be requisitioned for Meals on Wheels or carting turf to make a lawn somewhere.

''Over the years I became more and more tired. Every night the children demanded a story and I supplied it before they went to sleep, every day I got them off to school with their father and then—I ran. I had so much to do. I wrote while they were at school.

'''What was the colour of your hair before it was grey?' Bim asked.

'''I really don't remember, darling,' I replied. 'A sort of mouse, I think.'

''This was, then, the settled end of my endeavours: I was a hard-working journalist paying off a mortgage on a suburban house with two children and a garage. My mother, I reflected, had fared better. She didn't have to write books.''[1]

Rodd was prolific during these years, writing juvenile plays and novels and editing several collections of Australian short stories. She also served on the advisory board of the Commonwealth Literary Fund.

Misfortune became commonplace during this period of her life. Roddy, who had suffered depressions before, made several attempts at suicide. Finally, he threw himself under a train, surviving with a fractured skull but losing an arm and a foot.

Bim, who was the pride and hope of the family, the heir apparent, began using drugs and was diagnosed as schizophrenic. ''While at the university he and a fellow student had an affair; she became pregnant. I made her an allowance and threatened Bim with mayhem if he didn't stand by her. He wouldn't marry her because she insisted he become a Roman Catholic. It was no use my bringing her home to live because Roddy was going through a bad spell. She passed her exams and had the child three days later. I went to see her in hospital and tried to adopt Bim's son. She was adamant. The child must be adopted by Catholic parents and have a good Catholic upbringing.

''As they were not legally married Bim had no claim on the child.''[1]

This was Rodd's only grandchild, whom she later referred to as ''The Missing Heir.'' Like his father, Bim repeatedly tried suicide.

1976. Rodd decided a change of scene would help the family, so she moved to a farm called Cliffview Orchard in the Blue Mountains above Sydney. The same year cancer claimed a breast. '''Well, now I am an Amazon.' I told my visitors. 'The Amazons used to cut off one breast from their warriors. I have forgotten which it was—for a captain who used a sword. It was the opposite one for a common Amazon who fought with a long speer. I'm probably a common Amazon.' There was no question of my having a recurrence of this blighting disease from which all my family die—and so many others in the population. I had too many responsibilities.''[1]

1978. Bim was pushed out a window by derelicts selling him drugs, and he died in the hospital on June 3rd.

The next year, Roddy died of cancer at their farm. ''. . .Benison and I nursed him for seven weeks. She had moved in with me from the small house, Hillside, we owned the other side of Blackheath. She had a job as an occupational therapist at a hospital but gave it up to manage the farm. This farm was cleared in 1912 and has never made a profit in all that time. I do the light jobs, jam-making for the stall at the gate, feeding the workers, washing, cleaning, paying the bills. We have honey, ducks, goats, turkeys, fruit trees, berries of all kinds. Benison is building up the trade in ducks and jams. You look out from our old sprawling farmhouse, over the barns and the fowl pens, to a smiling orchard which has just survived the five-year drought. People come and lean over our gate to admire wistfully our farm and envy us. We have been here ten years now and work seven days a week. Friends, well-wishers and people writing theses and bringing their tape-recorders pour in and out. A farm should be there to provide work and food.''[1]

''After my son and husband had died I found it rather ironical that. . .I should be offered the Order of Australia. I had already turned down, twice, being made an OBE [Order of the British Empire]. For an old revolutionary there was something faintly ridiculous about symbolically joining the Establishment. Then I thought how the 'Parent' would enjoy going to Government House and basking in glory. My sister might as well come too. Roddy would have refused to go and Benison had to mind the farm. So I accepted the Order of Australia.

''The 'Parent' had a wonderful time at Government House at the presentation. There was a fountain and a band and crowds of elderly has-beens, like myself, tottering forward to be presented with what looked like the Order of the Golden Cabbage. . . ."[1]

1983. Rodd published *Tantavallon*. In June, the 'Parent' died.

"After Roddy and Bim had died I spent time, effort and money trying to trace Bim's son. I joined an organisation which asked for greater rights for the relatives of adopted children. I wrote to the (then) Child Welfare Department and they stonewalled me. I suppose it is just and reasonable that adoptive parents should not be annoyed by claims or interference from the bereft. When Bim's son—I call him Michael—is eighteen years old he will be at liberty to seek out his origins and trace his natural parents if he so desires. But not before. He must be eleven years old now so it is not likely I will ever see him.

"The terrible fear was that the adopting parents might find, as people do when they take a kitten or a puppy, that it is nothing but a pest when it grows older. Many adopting parents return the child to a state home if any defect develops. I brushed from me the thought of Michael, desolate and defective, limping or brain-damaged, in some state home. We could give him a good life on the farm, Benison and I, even if he were half-witted or crippled. Benison is waiting for Michael to turn eighteen and will share the farm with him faithfully if he should ever seek her out. He is the Missing Heir. Benison is nobody's heir. She is my partner, a legal share-farmer entitled to half the profit of an orchard that has never made a profit. She is with me, a survivor on this wild, beloved place, where the fowls have one leg longer than the other from trying to find a level place to stand, and our chief product is instant squalor. Not much of an inheritance for the Missing Heir, although people flow in and out the gate, saying 'How lovely this place is. How lucky you are!'

"Then I reflect that the country is rich in my heirs: 'All those girls called Kylie, who bear my name! (Maybe they won't be so happy about it after this revelation of all my muddled stupidities.) There are all those scribbling children who are frowning and exultant over their first buddings of prose and verse. What shall I leave them? The power to smile crookedly at life? Not to fear anything and laugh at disaster? The power to make their own unique pattern on chaos? Warm friends—I have so many—and the kindness and generosity of poor people; the ferocity of the hunter and fighter; and the almost-Irish courtesy to the guest. My ghost to guard them. No: more potent than all, I will leave them the impulse to make fools of themselves.'"[1]

February 28, 1988. Two weeks before her seventy-sixth birthday, Rodd died in Sydney.

FOOTNOTE SOURCES

[1]Kylie Tennant, *The Missing Heir: The Autobiography of Kylie Tennant,* Macmillan (Australia), 1986.

FOR MORE INFORMATION SEE:

New York Times, November 8, 1941.
Listener, March 23, 1943.
Colin Roderick, *An Introduction to Australian Fiction,* Angus & Robertson, 1950.
Dorothy Auchterlonie, "The Novels of Kylie Tennant," *Meanjin Quarterly* (Australia), number 4, 1953.
T. Inglis Moore, "The Tragi-Comedies of Kylie Tennant," *Southerly* (Australia), number 1, 1957.
Margaret Dick, *The Novels of Kylie Tennant,* Rigby, 1966.
T. Inglis Moore, *Social Patterns in Australian Literature,* Angus & Robertson, 1971.
John Wakeman, editor, *World Authors: 1950-1970,* H. W. Wilson, 1975.
Martha E. Ward and Dorothy A. Marquardt, *Authors of Books for Young People,* supplement to the 2nd edition, Scarecrow, 1979.
William H. Wilde, Joy Hooten and Barry Andrews, editors, *The Oxford Companion to Australian Literature,* Oxford University Press, 1985.
James Vinson and Daniel L. Kirkpatrick, editors, *Contemporary Novelists,* 4th edition, St. Martin's Press, 1986.

OBITUARIES

Times (London), March 10, 1988.

COLLECTIONS

Australian National Library, Canberra.

RODDY, Lee 1921-
(Rachel Banner)

PERSONAL: Surname rhymes with "body"; born August 22, 1921, in Marion County, Ill.; son of Thomas Lee (a laborer) and Neva D. (a homemaker; maiden name, Gordon) Roddy; married Cicely Price (an author), October 17, 1947; children: Steven L., Susan D. Roddy de Haas. *Education:* Los Angeles City College, A.A., 1945. *Politics:* Republican. *Religion:* Protestant. *Home:* 18007 Jayhawk Dr., Penn Valley, Calif. 95946. *Agent:* Linda Allen Agency, 2881 Jackston St., San Francisco, Calif. 94115. *Office:* Roddy Publications, P. O. Box 700, Penn Valley, Calif. 95946.

LEE RODDY

CAREER: National Broadcasting Company, and Blue Network (now American Broadcasting Company), Hollywood, Calif., started as part-time page boy, became advertising and radio drama writer, 1942-47; KTRB Radio, Modesto, Calif., commercial manager, 1947-55; sales manager and general manager for various radio stations, Los Angeles, Calif, 1955-60; sales representative, Orange County, Calif., 1955-62; *Turlock Daily Journal,* Turlock, Calif., reporter and columnist, 1963, editor of weekly newspapers, 1967-72; *Modesto Bee,* Modesto, Calif., reporter and feature writer, 1963; *Kula,* Honolulu, Hawaii, sales manager, 1963-66; Waikiki Beach Press, Honolulu, advertising manager, 1963-66; Roddy Publications, Ceres, Calif., owner, 1969—; Regional Times Publishers, Inc., Ceres, part-owner, corporation vice-president, editor, and publisher, 1972-74; promotion director for an advertising agency, Los Angeles, 1975-76; full-time freelance writer, 1976-77, 1980—; Schick Sunn Classic Pictures, Inc., Salt Lake City, Utah, staff writer, 1977-79; author and speaker, 1974-76, 1980—.

Professional speaker; lecturer in fiction for *Writer's Digest,* 1980-81. Founding director and vice-president of Codemakers, Inc., Milpitas, Calif., 1982-85, Achievers R*, Roseville, Calif., 1982-86, Orcom, Inc., Millbrae, Calif., 1982-85, and Adam II Productions, Inc., Millbrae, 1983-86. Consultant to government agencies, corporations, and educational institutions.

MEMBER: Radio Writers Guild, Writers Guild of America West, Authors Guild, Authors League of America, National Speakers Association (Northern California). *Awards, honors:* Silver Angel Award for Excellence in Quality Moral Media from Religion in Media, 1986, for *The Hair-Pulling Bear Dog, The City Bear's Adventures, Dooger, the Grasshopper Hound,* and *The Ghost Dog of Stoney Ridge.*

WRITINGS:

JUVENILE

Robert E. Lee, Gallant Christian Soldier (biography), Mott Media, 1977.
The Taming of Cheetah (fiction), Victor Books, 1979.
Search for the Avenger (historical fiction), Accent Books, 1980.

"D. J. DILLON ADVENTURE" SERIES; JUVENILE FICTION

The Hair-Pulling Bear Dog, Victor Books, 1985.
The City Bear's Adventures, Victor Books, 1985.
Dooger, the Grasshopper Hound, Victor Books, 1985.
The Ghost Dog of Stoney Ridge, Victor Books, 1985.
Mad Dog of Lobo Mountain, Victor Books, 1986.
The Legend of the White Raccoon, Victor Books, 1986.
The Mystery of the Black Hole Mine, Victor Books, 1987.
The Ghost of the Moaning Mansion, Victor Books, 1987.
The Hermit of Mad River, Victor Books, 1988.
Escape from the Raging Rapids, Victor Books, 1989.

"THE LADD FAMILY ADVENTURE" SERIES; JUVENILE FICTION

Secret of the Shark Pit, Focus on the Family, 1988.
The Legend of Fire, Focus on the Family, 1988.
Mystery of the Blue Lagoon, Focus on the Family, 1989.

"AN AMERICAN ADVENTURE" SERIES; YOUNG ADULT

The Overland Escape, Bethany House, 1989.
The Desperate Search, Bethany House, 1989.

ADULT; NONFICTION, EXCEPT AS NOTED

(With Paul G. Peppin) *The Family Necessary Book,* Fleming Revell, 1975.
(Ghostwriter) Charles E. Sellier, Jr. and David Balsiger, *The Lincoln Conspiracy,* Schick Sunn Classic Books, 1977.

(Ghostwriter) C. E. Sellier, Jr., *The Life and Times of Grizzly Adams* (novel), Shick Sunn Classic Books, 1977.
(With George B. Derkatch) *Word of Fire,* W.C.M., 1977.
(With C. E. Sellier, Jr.) *In Search of Historic Jesus,* Bantam, 1979.
Jesus, Fleming Revell, 1979.
Intimate Portraits of Women in the Bible, Christian Herald, 1980.
The Mystery of Aloha House (novel), David Cook, 1981.
Love's Far Horizon (novel), David Cook, 1981.
On Wings of Love, T. Nelson, 1981.
(Contributor) *Writing to Inspire* (anthology), Writers Digest, 1982.
(With Steve Douglass) *Making the Most of Your Mind,* Here's Life, 1983.
(With wife, Cicely Roddy, under joint pseudonym Rachel Banner) *The Impatient Blossom* (novel), Simon & Schuster, 1985.

Ghostwriter. Wrote video scripts for the State of California, and short film scripts. Author of "Roddy's Ramblings," a daily column in *Turlock Journal,* 1967-70. Roddy's children's books have been translated into Norwegian and Finnish. Contributor to periodicals, including *Saturday Evening Post, Christian Science Monitor, Denver Post, Seattle Times, Honolulu Advertiser, Honolulu Beach Press, Paradise of the Pacific,* and trade journals.

ADAPTATIONS:

"The Life and Times of Grizzly Adams" (motion picture), Sunn Classic, 1974, (televison series), NBC-TV, 1978-80.
"The Lincoln Conspiracy" (motion picture), Sunn Classic, 1977.
"Word of Fire" (motion picture), 1978.
"In Search of Historic Jesus" (motion picture), Schick Sunn Classic, 1979.
"Jesus" (motion picture), 1979.

WORK IN PROGRESS: A third young adult novel in "An American Adventure" series; a proposed new series for readers aged eight to twelve, "The Adventures of Mudhole Muldoon"; "a non-fiction book and companion tapes based on my fifteen years of teaching people how to write and sell their first novel."

SIDELIGHTS: "A shoe with a five-and-one-half inch cork sole made me a writer. I was born sick and crippled. My left leg was five-and-one-half inches shorter than the right. I was confined to a bed or chair until surgeries at age ten corrected my handicap.

"I began school in Dixon, Illinois, where President Ronald Reagan had gone. In July, 1930, I moved with my parents to California where I completed my education.

"During my earliest years, I couldn't run and play with other kids, so I read. My parents were very poor, so my reading material was mostly newspapers and 'dime novels' given us. Out of this grew a desire to write. I always loved to read action adventure and suspense stories, so that's what I primarily write today. Kids and teachers seem to love my novels. So far, I've not seen a single negative review of my books in any periodical.

"I grew up with a shortage of everything except poverty. Born in a rural farm house and reared on small California ranches, I'm the oldest of ten children, all living. Through childhood reading, I developed a love of adventure that was never fulfilled as a boy because of my handicap. However, I always

(Cover illustration from *Mad Dog of Lobo Mountain* by Lee Roddy. Illustrated by Myron Sahlberg.)

made notes of stories I heard, and now have many pounds of aging material that helps enhance the adventures of my fictional characters.

"My love of reading as a child caused me to try writing. My first short stories and articles were published when I was about fourteen years old. I won my first public speaking contest when I was fifteen. I have wanted to be an author as long as I can remember, but I was not aware of a desire to be a lecturer until 1972.

"After high school, I attended a nearby junior college where I studied journalism and radio broadcasting. My ambition then was to someday write for the movies. So, when I was about twenty-two, I left the rural area to try breaking into the motion picture industry as a screen writer. However, with no experience beyond writing for the school paper, I didn't get anywhere with the studios. That turned out to be a break, because I got into radio drama. That taught me dialogue writing while completing my college education.

"As a page boy at NBC and the old Blue Network (now ABC) in Hollywood, I was associated with all the great radio stars. Only Bob Hope remains of those famous people. I once turned down a chance to write a sketch for one of Hope's guests; an action that still causes me painful regret.

"I never stopped trying to write during the years that I supported my wife and family in a variety of executive positions.

I changed jobs often, always trying to hit that elusive goal of making my living as a writer. I became a cub reporter on a daily newspaper when I was forty. I consider that the best training possible. I also wrote a daily newspaper column prior to selling my first book.

"I had been writing for thirty-eight years before selling my first book in 1974. Since giving my first lecture in 1973, I've taught all over the United States and into Canada. My career has also taken me to Europe, the Orient and Mexico. I consider myself an inspirational or motivational speaker offering proven, practical principles to success in any field.

"My current interest is in teaching seminars/workshops in colleges, at private conferences, etc., on how to write and sell novels. My highly-effective system is based on what I learned that totally turned my writing life around. I'm also interested in strengthening the family, so have some seminar and book ideas along that line.

"When my first book contract was signed, I had eleven completed but unsold fiction and non-fiction books on hand. However, many of my stories, articles and newspaper works had been published prior to 1974.

"Since then, I've written, ghosted, co-authored or collaborated on forty-two books. Of those, thirteen have been book club selections, award-winners, best-sellers, motion pictures and a television series. I have been offered contracts for six more novels and recently turned down four other contracts.

(Cover illustration by Myron Sahlberg from *The Mystery of the Black Hole Mine* by Lee Roddy.)

"Originally, I did not plan to write inspirational books, nor did I plan to author juvenile and young adult novels. However, in 1974 I made what I called a 'peaceful marriage' to write juveniles above all. It still took about ten years for that to click, but it finally did.

"My fiction and non-fiction works all reflect my own strong traditional moral and spiritual family values. My clean, non-violent, character-building juvenile and young adult novels seemed to hit the market just as there was a demand for such works. The result was that my first series for readers ages eight-to-twelve sold more that 100,000 copies in a relatively short time. The first two novels in my second series for 'middlers' sold about 50,000 copies in three months. I hope my third series for young adults will do very well, too.

"I present 'Author's Day' programs in public and private schools with very satisfactory results. Parents, faculty and students are enthusiastic about the type of high adventures I write, each with a subtle message about right values inculcated in the drama. These programs keep me in close contact with the type of kids about whom I write, and I learn what they like. Then I try to write to meet that need.

"The most-often asked questions are: (1) 'Where do you get your ideas?' (2) 'How long does it take to write a book?' and (3) 'Do you draw your own cover illustrations?' The answers: (1) Ideas are everywhere, so I have about one hundred concepts on paper for possible future books. (2) It takes about ninety days to complete a novel from idea to mailing the finished manuscript, although twice I've written six books in twelve months. (3) I'm no artist, so the publisher contracts for an outside illustrator on all my titles.

"I consider myself very fortunate because I always knew what I wanted to do in life and, even though it took a long time to achieve that, for the past several years I've made a very good living as an author. Combine that with my wonderful family, living where I want, and having a clear vision of what I still want to accomplish, I expect to continue making my timed goals. Then someday I can say, 'I'm satisfied with life.' So, in a way, I'm even grateful that a five-and-one-half inch cork-sole shoe made me an author."

RUSSELL, Paul (Gary) 1942-

PERSONAL: Born December 27, 1942, in Toronto, Canada; son of Frank (a lithographer) and Norma (Gauvin) Russell. *Education:* University of Toronto, B.A. (with honors), 1964, M.A., 1965; attended Courtauld Institute, University of London, 1962-63, and Sir John Cass College, London, 1965-66. *Home:* 460 Palmerston Blvd., Toronto, Ontario, Canada M6G 2P1.

CAREER: Writer, director. Canadian Broadcasting Corporation (CBC), Toronto, Canada, national editor and adjudicator for "Reach for the Top," 1971-88; Paulus Productions, Toronto, Canada, president, producer and writer, 1973—; Mediavision, Toronto, story editor for "Behind the Scenes," 1975; Columbia Pictures Television, Toronto, Canada, and Boston, Mass., adjudicator for "The New Quiz Kids," 1977-79; Scene II Productions, Toronto, and San Francisco, Calif., producer and director of "Fitness and Lifestyle," and "Stress," 1981. Created the board game "Travelon" for Kenley-Taylor Marketing, 1985; Muskoka Theatre Festival, Gravenhurst, Ontario, co-director with Robert Jeffrey of musical "Robin for Good," 1985. Curator, Hart House Collection, University of Toronto, 1963-64; assistant curator, Stratford Festival exhi-

PAUL RUSSELL

bitions, 1964-65; lecturer, 1969-70; education supervisor, Ontario Educational Communications Authority (TV Ontario), Toronto, 1970-74. Exhibition director, "Ten Decades, Ten Artists," Stratford Art Gallery, 1967, "Art Nouveau" Travelling Display, Toronto, 1968, "Sculpture—New Directions," Hart House, Toronto, 1969; co-ordinator and author of catalogue introduction, "Canada at the Edinburgh Festival," 1968; exhibition co-ordinator and writer, "The Great Lakes Region," Museumobile Program, National Museum of Canada, 1977-78; exhibition writer, "Two Rivers Theme," Canadian Pavilion, Louisiana Expo, 1984.

MEMBER: Arts and Letters Club (Toronto). *Awards, honors:* International Emmy nomination, 1974, for nature series "Untamed World"; Gold Award from the New York Film and Television Festival, 1981, for educational film series "Stress."

WRITINGS:

Brantford: Sketches of a Town, Glenhyrst Arts Council, 1966.
(With Barry Lord) *Ten Decades, 1867-1967, Ten Painters*, The Gallery, 1967.
The Great Canadian Quiz Book (illustrated by Roy Condy), Gage, 1977.
(With Robert Jeffrey) *Trivia: Inconsequential but Irresistible Facts about Canada*, Gage, 1980.
(With R. Jeffrey) *The Canadian Royal Tour: Their Royal Highnesses, the Prince and Princess of Wales*, Methuen, 1983.
(Contributor) *The Arts in Ontario*, Government of Ontario Publications, 1983.
(With R. Jeffrey) *Toronto's Top Ten*, Methuen, 1984.

(Picture editor) *Illustrated Guide to the Canadian Establishment,* Methuen, 1984.
Pope John Paul II: The 1984 Canadian Tour, Methuen, 1984.
(With R. Jeffrey) *The Queen on Moose Handbook* (illustrated by Charles Pachter), Methuen, 1985.

"THE BEAUTY OF CANADA" SERIES

The Beauty of Ontario, Methuen, 1982.
The Beauty of Quebec, Methuen, 1983.
The Beauty of the Maritimes, Methuen, 1983.
The Beauty of British Columbia, Methuen, 1984.

TELEVISION

(And director) "Landmarks" (architectural series), TV Ontario, 1971-74.
"The Magic Circle" ("Images of Canada" series), CBC, 1973.
"Elements of the Unknown: The Sea," Mediavision (Toronto), 1974.
(And producer) "The Untamed World" (nature series), CTV/Metromedia (Toronto/Los Angeles), 1974-77.
"Lorne Greene's Last of the Wild" (nature series), syndicated and broadcast on NBC-TV and CBS-TV, 1974-76, 1976.
"Untamed Frontier" (nature series), TV Toronto, 1976.
(And director) "The Maya, Children of Time" (special), Ziggurat Productions (Toronto), 1979.
(And producer) "Dentistry," Scene II Productions (Toronto), 1979.
(And director) "Medical Malpractice," Scene II Productions, 1980-83.
(And director) "Primary Nursing," Scene II Productions, 1980.
(And producer and director) "Stress," Scene II Productions, 1981.

Free-lance critic and contributor to *Globe and Mail, Toronto Star, Arts Magazine, City and Country Home, Select Homes, Society of Decorative Arts Bulletin, Maclean's* and *Time.* Contributor to *The Arts in Ontario.* Assistant editor, *Arts Canada,* 1966-67; contributing editor, *Toronto Life,* 1969-71.

WORK IN PROGRESS: The Loewen Legacy, a family biography in five books; "POW," a drama for theatrical production; *Louis Janetta's Fifty Years at the Royal York Hotel* to be published by McClelland & Stewart.

SIDELIGHTS: "Drawing and painting, developing a visual sense, have been my chief interests since childhood. I studied oil painting at a young age and sold canvases for small amounts to family friends.

"At university the academic element compounded my interest in art and the refined detail of a painting or a building acquired new significance. The Courtauld Institute in London reinforced this historicism in lecture series such as that on 'Neopolitan Baroque Staircases' by Sir Antony Blunt, then director of the school.

"My career took a right-angled turn after a few years of art criticism and journalism when I began writing for a high school quiz show 'Reach for the Top,' televised by the Canadian Broadcasting Corporation. Television was fun—so were the students. I stayed with the show writing and adjudicating the competitions. The program became an educational institution in Canada and led to a contract with 'The New Quiz Kids' for Columbia Pictures Television.

"'Reach' meant that it was important to keep in touch with students on a regular basis, to gage interest levels in general information areas and keep track of changing curricula at the schools.

"After some years with 'Reach,' it seemed logical to write for the audience that I had become comfortable with through the television show, and so there were books on trivia and essay books on Canadian achievements.

"It's always stimulating when students arrive at the studio year after year to see, in spite of the change in dress or haircut or latest all-important crusade, that the confidence, eagerness, vitality and vulnerability are a constant in every generation.

"My current interest is biography, continuing an extensive series of five books on the military, clerical and investment careers of Canada's Loewen family, and co-writing with maitre d' Louis Janetta, his real-life "Hotel" story, recounting fifty years with the Royal York, Toronto's 'grande dame' of the hotel world.''

SCHULKE, Flip (Phelps Graeme) 1930-

PERSONAL: Born June 24, 1930, in St. Paul, Minn.; son of Walter Edward and Elizabeth (Kalman) Schulke; married Marlene Phyllis Wallner, August 7, 1950 (divorced); married Pau-

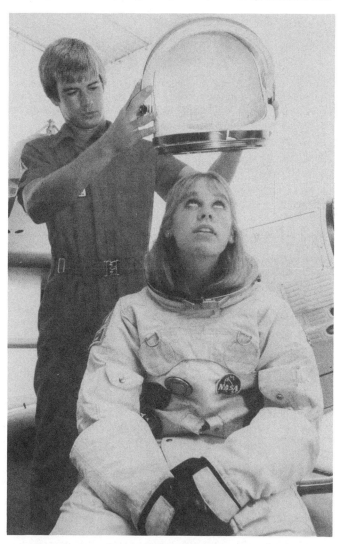

Space Camp trainee, Dacia Jessick, looks up apprehensively as her space helmet is lowered into place for the first time. ■ (From *Your Future in Space* by Flip and Debra Schulke. Photograph by the authors.)

line Kay Gillham (divorced); married Debra Streuber (divorced); children: (first marriage) Robin, Paul, Lisa, Maria. *Education:* Macalester College, B.A., 1953. *Politics:* Democrat. *Religion:* Roman Catholic. *Home:* P.O. Box 570669, Miami, Fla. 33257. *Agent:* Robert Dukas, 9 West 29th St., New York, N.Y. 10001.

CAREER: Photojournalist. University of Miami, Coral Gables, Fla., photographer, 1953-57; Black Star Publishing Co., New York, N.Y., staff photographer, beginning 1957. Owner of Flip Schulke Enterprises, Inc., 1950-51; contract photographer for *Life* magazine, 1965-69. *Military service:* U.S. Army, 1950-51. *Member:* National Press Photographers Association, American Society of Magazine Photographers, Academy of Underwater Photographers. *Awards, honors: Martin Luther King, Jr.* was selected one of New York Public Library's Books for the Teen Age, 1980, 1981, and 1982.

WRITINGS:

(Editor) *Martin Luther King, Jr.: A Documentary, Montgomery to Memphis,* Norton, 1976.
Underwater Photography for Everyone, Prentice-Hall, 1978.
King Remembered, Norton, 1986.
(Contributor) *A Day in the Life of America,* Collins, 1986.

ILLUSTRATOR

(With Debra Schulke, Penelope McPhee and Raymond McPhee), *Your Future in Space,* Crown, 1986.

WORK IN PROGRESS: Updated second edition of *Underwater Photography for Everyone;* a book about Grand Prix auto racing in the fifties and sixties for auto enthusiasts; a book on the Russian cosmonauts.

SIDELIGHTS: "All the books I work on are books I generate—all the research material is mine, and I find the writer for the text."

Underwater Photography for Everyone has been published in Germany.

FOR MORE INFORMATION SEE:

Popular Photography, September, 1980.
New York Times Book Review, November 9, 1986.

SKARMETA, Antonio 1940-

PERSONAL: Born November 7, 1940, in Antofagasta, Chile; son of Antonio (a bookkeeper) and Magdalena (a housewife; maiden name, Vranicic) Skarmeta; married Cecilia Boisier (a painter), August 1, 1964 (divorced, 1983); children: Beltran, Gabriel. *Education:* University of Chile, Professor of Philosophy, 1963; Columbia University, M.A., 1966. *Politics:* Independent. *Religion:* Catholic. *Home:* Goethestrasse 37-38, 1000 Berlin 12, West Germany. *Agent:* Carmen Balcells, Diagonal 580, Barcelona 21, Spain.

CAREER: University of Chile, Santiago, professor of philosophy, letters and Spanish-American literature, 1967-73; Catholic University, Santiago, professor, 1971-73; Academy of Cinema and Television, West Berlin, West Germany, professor, 1978-81; free-lance writer, 1980—; Washington University, St. Louis, Mo., distinguished professor of Romance Languages, 1988—. Writing workshop director, Santiago, 1970. Lecturer. *Member:* Society of Writers of Chile, P.E.N. (West Germany), Center for the Defense of Chilean Culture (West Germany; founding member).

AWARDS, HONORS: Casa de las Americas de la Habana Prize (Cuba), 1969, for *Desnudo en el tejado;* Prize from the Festival of Prague, 1973, for film, "La victoria"; Berlin Artists Program Grant, 1975; Bandeja de Oro (German Cinematic Prize), 1976, for "Reina la tranquilidad en el pais," and 1980, for "La insurreccion"; Prize for Major Film of the Year, 1976, for "Reina la tranquilidad en el pais"; Prize from the European Broadcasting Union, 1977, for radio drama, "La busqueda," and 1987, for "Nupcias"; Prize from the Festival of Strassburg, 1980, for film, "Desde lejos veo este pais"; Prix Italia Honorable Mention, 1980, for radio drama, "La Composicion," and 1983, for "Ardiente paciencia"; *Chileno!* was named one of New York Public Library's Books for the Teen Age, 1980, 1981, and 1982; Grand Prize from the Festival de Cine Iberoamericano (France), and Grand Prize from the Festival de Cine Hispanoamericano (Spain), both 1983, both for film "Ardiente paciencia"; Georges Sadoul Prize, 1983; Prize from the Minister of Culture of the Federal Republic of Aleman, 1983; Special Prize from the Festival de Cine de Salsomaggiore (Italy), 1983; Prize from the Festival de Cine de Bordeaux (France), 1985; Guggenheim Fellowship for Literature, 1986; named Chevalier of the Order of Arts and Letters by the Minister of Culture of France, 1987.

WRITINGS:

El entusiasmo (title means "Enthusiasm"; short stories), Zig-Zag, 1967.
(Contributor) Rodgrigo Quijada (compiler), *Cronicas de Chile* (title means "Chilean Chronicles"), Editorial J. Alvarez, 1968.
Desnudo en el tejado (title means "Naked on the Roof"; short stories), Casa de las Americas (Cuba), 1969.
El ciclista del San Cristobal (title means "The Cyclist from San Cristobal"; short stories), Quimantu (Chile), 1973.
Tiro libre (title means "Free Shot"; short stories), Siglo Veintiuno (Argentina), 1973.
Novios y solitarios (title means "Together and Alone"; short stories), Editorial Losada, 1975.
Sone que la nieve ardia (novel), Planeta, 1975, translated from the Spanish by Malcolm Coad, published as *I Dreamt the Snow Was Burning,* Readers International, 1985.
(Editor) *Joven narrativa chilena despues del golpe* (title means "Young Chilean Writers after the Coup"; anthology), American Hispanist, 1976.
No paso nada (young adult), Pomaire (Spain), 1978, translated from the Spanish by Hortense Carpentier, published as *Chileno!,* Morrow, 1979.
Tres cuentistas: Reme Marques, Antonio Skarmeta, Luis Britto Garcia (title means "Three Short Story Writers"), Casa de las Americas, 1979.
La insurreccion (novel), Ediciones del Norte (U.S.), 1980, translated from the Spanish by Paula Sharp, published as *The Insurrection,* Ediciones del Norte, 1983.
Ardiente paciencia (novel), Editorial Sudamericana (Argentina), 1985, published as *Burning Patience,* Pantheon, 1987.
No paso nada y otros relatos (title means "Nothing Happened"; illustrated by Federico Ayma), Pehuen, 1985.

Contributor of short stories to American and European magazines.

FILM SCRIPTS

"La victoria" (title means "The Victory"), 1973.
"Reina la tranquilidad en el pais" (title means "Peace Rules over the Country"), 1975.
"Desde lejos veo este pais" (title means "I See This Country from Afar"; in German with English subtitles), 1978.

ANTONIO SKARMETA

(Also director and writer of music) "Permiso de residencia" (title means "Resident Visa"), SFB/Common Films, 1979.

"La huella del desaparecido," 1980, published as *Footprint of the Vanished*, Henschel Verlag, 1982.

"El regalo" (title means "The Present"), 1981.

(And director) "Ardiente paciencia" (title means "Ardent Patience"), ZDF, 1983.

(And director) "Despedida en Berlin" (title means "Farewell in Berlin"), ZDF, 1985.

(And director) "Si vivieramos juntos" (title means "If We Lived Together"), WDR/Vietinghoff Film-Production, 1987.

(And director) "Matilda y Neruda," ZDF/Santiago Films, 1988.

Also author of film scripts "Su Ultima Oportunidad," "La Herida," and "El Ciclista del San Cristobal."

RADIO DRAMAS

"La busqueda" (title means "The Search"), SWF/SFB/WDR, 1976.

"No paso nada," SFB/SWF, 1977.

"La Mancha" (title means "The Blot"), SWF, 1978.

"La composicion," SWF/SFB, 1979, published under title *The Composition*, Henschel Verlag, 1982.

"Muertos Mientras Tanto" (title means "Dead. Temporarily"), SWF/SFB/WDR, 1981.

"Ardiente paciencia," SWF/SFB/Bayerischer Rundfunk, 1982.

"Nupcias," SWF/SFB, 1986.

"Match-Ball," Radio Bremen/Sender Freies Berlin, 1988.

PLAYS

Ardiente paciencia (two-act drama), first produced in Berlin, at Bat Theater, June, 1983), Verlag der Autoren (Germany), 1983 (also included in anthology *Contemporary Drama of Latin America*, PAJ Publications, 1987.

EDITOR

Joven Narrativa Chilena despues del Golpe, American Hispanist, 1976.

Zeit der Durre, Zeit des Regens, Pctcr Hammer Verlag, 1983.

Translator of English texts into Spanish, including *An American Dream* by Norman Mailer, 1968; *The Pyramid* by William Golding, 1968; *Typee* by Herman Melville, 1968; *The Graduate,* and *Love Roger* both by Charles Webb, both 1969; *Visions of Gerard* by Jack Kerouac, 1969; and *The Last Tycoon* by F. Scott Fitzgerald, 1969, all published by Zig-Zag.

Co-founder and animator of the television program, "Libro Abierto," dedicated to the popularization of literature, 1971-73. Contributor of numerous articles and essays to anthologies and periodicals in many countries, including *Review, Nueva Sociedad, Revista de Bellas Artes, American Hispanist, Casa de las Americas, Cuadernos Universitarios, Araucaria, Die Horen, Mapocho, Revista Chilena de Literatura*, and *Mexico en la Cultura*. Skarmeta's works have been published in Spanish, Italian, French, German, Russian, Dutch, Danish, Bulgarian, Swedish, Slovene, Portuguese, Turkish, and Czech.

ADAPTATIONS:

"La insurreccion" (film; title means "The Insurrection"; in Spanish with English subtitles), 1980.

"Pequena revancha" (film; based on "La composicion"), Venezuela, 1985.

"A las arenas," 1987.

SIDELIGHTS: Skarmeta was born in Antofagasta, Chile on November 7, 1940. His grandparents were Yugoslav immigrants.

"Astonished by the wondrous world," he began writing as a child, but had the good sense not to publish until the age of

(From *La Insurreccion* by Antonio Skarmeta. Illustrated by Mark Spencer.)

twenty-seven. During his youth, what he most loved was "the physical act of writing, comparable in intensity only to erotic excitement." According to his avowals at that time, he was more interested in *living* like a writer than being considered one. His family moved frequently during his formative years. Today he says, "Having travelled from place to place as a child, I was well-prepared for the life of an exile after the 1973 military coup in Chile."

In 1958, he entered the University of Chile as a student of literature, theatre arts, and philosophy, studies which were often interrupted to "thumb" his way throughout Latin America and the United States in search of the adventure he found missing in formal lecture halls. On these journeys, he earned his living as a juggler and puppeteer. He drew on these vagabond odysseys for his first book of short stories, *Enthusiasm.*

At the age of eleven, in Buenos Aires, when his father was unemployed, Skarmeta became the family provider for a few months by virtue of his job selling fruit. "In 1951 I missed not being able to buy a bicycle, but the pride I felt holding a job and being a student at the same time gave me a great sense of security. Morally, my parents found it difficult to cope with their budding literary genius who prowled the streets at all hours of the night getting to know 'interesting people.'"

While a student at the University of Chile, Skarmeta directed theatrical works for the Faculty of Philosophy and Letters. In

spite of youthful confusion and the usual fatal love affairs, Skarmeta completed his studies and graduated in 1963 as Professor of Philosophy. He then went to New York to do his graduate work and received his Masters in literature from Columbia University in 1966.

On returning home, he taught contemporary Latin American literature at the University of Chile and writing technique at the Catholic University's School of Journalism. For the publisher Zig-Zag, he translated into Spanish novels by Norman Mailer, F. Scott Fitzgerald, Herman Melville, and Jack Kerouac, and he directed experimental theatre productions of works by Calderon de la Barca, Ionesco, Garcia Lorca, Jasudowicz, and Saroyan.

In 1969, his book of short stories, *Naked on the Roof,* won the most prestigious award in Latin American literature, the Casa de las Americas de la Habana Prize. His stories began to be translated in several countries.

In 1970, the Allende government began its move toward socialism through peaceful and legal means. Skarmeta was then active as a teacher and writer, participating in university reforms, initiating programs dedicated to exposing television audiences to literature, and continued his efforts to attain and express the political process of the Unidad Popular which was ended abruptly in 1973 by General Pinochet's military junta. Those experiences inspired a book of short stories, *Free Shot,* and a novel, *I Dreamt the Snow was Burning,* which he completed while living in Buenos Aires in 1974.

During this same period in Buenos Aires, Skarmeta worked on a screenplay, "Peace Rules over the Country," which was filmed in Portugal in 1975. "Only in a country that had freed itself of fascism could one make a movie about fascism in other countries. It was a strange phenomenon to enlist the Setubal Division of the Portuguese Army to portray a fascist Latin-American army in our film, when that same Division had, in reality, fought against fascism in Portugal. Those were soldiers less addicted to firing weapons than to receiving pink carnations from the hands of young girls, even though they were battle-hardened troops."

In 1975, Skarmeta received a grant under the Berlin Artists Program and has lived in that city with his family ever since. There he has written new film and radio scripts, short stories, songs, and essays. As a founding member of the Center for the Defense of Chilean Culture in Germany, he has promoted democratic cultural activities in Chile and has coordinated the work of Latin-American artists in exile.

From 1978 to 1981 Skarmeta taught film writing at the West Berlin Academy of Cinema and Television. He has travelled to many Latin-American artistic conferences and has given seminars and lectures about his work at American and European universities. In 1979 he spent time in Nicaragua and wrote, "Insurrection," a screenplay dealing with the overthrow of the Somoza regime. His most recent international participation was in the Conference on Latin American Literature at the Wilson Center in Washington, D.C. He is presently a professor of romance languages at Washington University in Missouri.

FOR MORE INFORMATION SEE:

Del cuerpo a las palabras: la narrativa de Antonio Skarmeta,
    Ediciones LAR (Madrid), 1983.

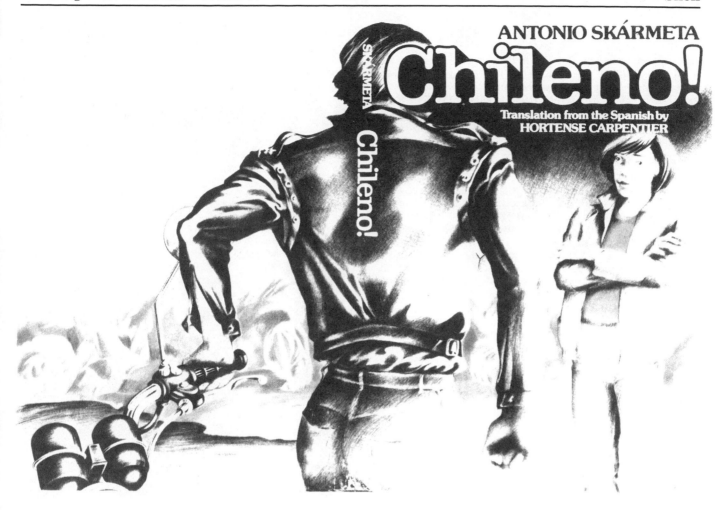

I backed off a little and looked at him. ■ (From *Chileno!* by Antonio Skarmeta. Jacket illustration by Maria Horvath.)

Constanza Lira, *Skarmeta: la inteligencia de los sentidos,* Dante (Chile), 1985.

SNELL, Nigel (Edward Creagh)   1936-

PERSONAL: Born November 9, 1936, in Hampstead, London, England; son of William Edward (a physician) and Yvonne (Brown) Snell; married Gillian Lola Etherton, June 18, 1960; children: Hony Charlotte Creagh, Justin William Creagh. *Education:* Attended Central School of Art and Design, 1955-58. *Religion:* Church of England. *Home:* Hambleden near Henley-on-Thames, Oxfordshire, England.

CAREER: Impress Graphics (advertising company), London, England, principal, 1966—; author and illustrator of books for children. Art director for advertising agencies in London. *Member:* Society of Industrial Artists and Designers.

WRITINGS:

SELF-ILLUSTRATED CHILDREN'S BOOKS

Johnny Gets Some Glasses, Hamish Hamilton, 1978.
Lucy Loses Her Tonsils, Hamish Hamilton, 1978.
Peter Gets a Hearing Aid, Hamish Hamilton, 1979.
Tom Visits the Dentist, Hamish Hamilton, 1979.
David's First Day at School, Hamish Hamilton, 1981.
Jane Has Asthma, Hamish Hamilton, 1981.
Kate Visits the Doctor, Hamish Hamilton, 1981.
Sally Moves House, Hamish Hamilton, 1981.

Clare's New Baby Brother, Hamish Hamilton, 1982.
Danny Is Afraid of the Dark, Hamish Hamilton, 1982.
Julie Stays the Night, Hamish Hamilton, 1982.
Paul Gets Lost, Hamish Hamilton, 1982.
Sam's New Dad, Hamish Hamilton, 1983.
Ann Visits the Speech Therapist, Hamish Hamilton, 1983.
Jenny Learns to Swim, Hamish Hamilton, 1983.
Nigel Feels Lonely, Hamish Hamilton, 1983.
Tasting and Smelling, Hamish Hamilton, 1983.
Hearing, Hamish Hamilton, 1983.
Touching, Hamish Hamilton, 1983.
Seeing, Hamish Hamilton, 1983.
Steve Is Adopted, Hamish Hamilton, 1985.
Jamie Meets a Stranger, Hamish Hamilton, 1986.
What Do You Say. . .?, Hamish Hamilton, 1986.
A Bird in Hand: A Child's Guide to Sayings, Hamish Hamilton, 1987.

WORK IN PROGRESS: Children's books on wildlife preservation and conservation.

SIDELIGHTS: "The idea behind my books is to bring some humor into situations that frighten children, and hopefully to relieve their fear. I am also interested in wildlife and in many forms of sport and outdoor activity, and I take part in as many as possible."

HOBBIES AND OTHER INTERESTS: Garden landscape design, painting, sports, outdoor activities.

STOCKHAM, Peter (Alan) 1928-

PERSONAL: Born July 7, 1928, in Birmingham, England; son of Linneaus William (a salesman) and Ivy (a housewife; maiden name, Imms) Stockham; married Anne Mallock Hadley (a bookshop director), January 11, 1958; children: Penelope Ruth, Joanna Mary. *Education:* University of Keele, B.A. (with honors), 1956. *Home:* Hertsfordshire and London. *Office:* 16 Cecil Court, London, WC2N 4HE.

CAREER: Dillon's University Bookshop Ltd., London, England, assistant, 1956-67, chief executive, 1967-75; Peter Stockham Ltd., London, and Lichfield, Staffordshire, chief executive, 1975—; Images Booksellers, London, managing director, 1976—. Member of board of directors, John Hopkins University Press Ltd., London, 1969—; library committee chairman, Mark Longman Library, London, 1974-76; honorary chairman, British Library National Bibliography Research Fund, 1975-80; consultant to Ironbridge Gorge Museum Trading Co., 1980-81. *Member:* National Book League (honorary treasurer, 1970-76), Bibliographical Society (London), American Bibliographical Society, Wynken de Worde Society, Society of Bookmen, Booksellers Association, Staffordshire Record Society, St. Albans Archaeological Society, Royal Archaeological Institute. *Awards, honors:* Houblon Norman Research Grant, 1963, for study of the economics and history of publishing and bookselling.

WRITINGS:

EDITOR

(With Anne Stockham), *Jack and Jill, and Old Dame Gill,* Images, 1968.
Old Mother Hubbard, Astu Studios, 1984.

EDITOR AND AUTHOR OF INTRODUCTION

Chapbook Riddles: Reprints of Six Rare and Charming Early Juveniles, Dover, 1974.
Chapbook ABC's: Reprints of Five Rare and Charming Early Juveniles, Dover, 1974.
The Mother's Picture Alphabet (illustrated by Henry Anelay), Dover, 1974.
Little Book of Early American Crafts and Trades, Dover, 1976.

EDITOR AND AUTHOR OF NOTES

The House That Jack Built, Scolar Press, 1978.
Punctuation Personified, Scolar Press, 1978.
Old Aunt Elspa's ABC, Scolar Press, 1978.
The Life and Death of an Apple Pie, Scolar Press, 1978.
Walter Crane: Flora's Feast, Windward Press, 1982.

NONFICTION

British Local History, Bibliography, Dillon, 1963.
University Bookselling, Hutchinson, 1965.
Publishers Catalogue: A Standard for Essential in Content and Format, Booksellers Association, 1972, revised edition, 1987.

Also editor of facsimile editions and reprints of chapbooks and eighteenth and nineteenth century children's books. Contributor to literary journals and magazines, including *Bookseller, British Book News,* and *British Journal of Aesthetics.*

WORK IN PROGRESS: A history of children's book illustration; a history of chapbooks and broadsides; a history of children's book publishing in England.

SIDELIGHTS: "My interest in children's literature stems from two main interests; that of book illustration, and in particular

PETER STOCKHAM

the clear simple illustration of the chapbook, and of many eighteenth- and nineteenth-century children's illustrated books. Secondly, I am interested in the growth of literacy, which includes how children and the poor and illiterate of past centuries have come to achieve satisfaction and mental growth through the book.

"I am fascinated by the low status that, up to now, the children's book has had in our culture. This is particularly remarkable when one thinks of the real place that children's books have in most of our lives. As children we read these books and have them read to us. As parents, as aunts and uncles, we again have a continued acquaintance with children's books. As we grow older and become grandparents and godparents we again have a contact with children's books, and yet this literature, which is more real to us than the latest novel, appears not to have an adult acceptance, nor is its role acknowledged in our own mental development, particularly as an adult. I am reminded of this daily as I am a specialist seller of new and antiquarian children's books.

"Many of my enquiries in a day are by adults wanting to secure the books (often insufficiently remembered, certainly bibliographically) that they remember from their own childhood. This is to satisfy two different needs. One is to reread the books, usually fiction, but in the case of boys in particular, fact books are wanted that the customer read as a child. The other need is for a copy of the book that gave them great pleasure as a child so that they can reread it to their children, or their nieces and nephews, or sometimes to pass on this

(From *The Mother's Picture Alphabet*. Introduction by Peter Stockham. Illustrated by Henry Anelay.)

pleasure to an adult friend. I am surprised at the number of people who want to be reminded of the book that they remember as a physical object. They are not satisfied, many of them, with a modern reprint. They want the sensuous pleasure of the original they remember—the old paper and binding, the illustrations printed on heavy art paper, the book often printed on very thick, card-like paper. And as I myself collect the books loved by children in the past, I can understand this very real pleasure.

"I have tried to encourage the reproduction in facsimile of many of the children's books of the past, but this has to be done very carefully, and in a marketing sense requires very real skills in making new so that a new generation can understand and appreciate the old. That is also why I place such a high premium on the skills of publishing, confirmed by such pioneer histories as Barbara Bader's *American Picturebooks from Noah's Ark to the Beast Within* (Macmillan, 1976), for which there is sadly no English equivalent, a subject on which I have been working for many years.

"My own editing for publishers such as Dover and Scolar Press has been very much concerned with filling in this historical background, particularly with accurate facsimile of colour and black and white illustration, for which both publishers are noted. I also like to 'make new' by adding general and bibliographical notes and introductions which stress the continuing interest and tradition of such books. My ambition is to find a publisher willing to expand this work on a large scale

before much of this tradition is lost by lack of republication. I know both as a bookseller and a publisher some of the economic problems of making available the best of the past, but I believe that this is one of our greatest current challenges, and modern marketing ideas present many possible solutions. It is sad that so many so-called classics, and many of the very attractive illustrated books from the past, are no longer in print, and it is my continual ambition to rectify this."

HOBBIES AND OTHER INTERESTS: Bibliography and the history of books, local history, bookbinding, looking at old churches and old buildings, collecting African art and English and foreign folk art, writing, reading, enjoying the countryside.

SUMMERS, James L(evingston)　1910-1973

PERSONAL: Born September 11, 1910, in Oshkosh, Wis.; died October 26, 1973 in Atascadero, Calif.; son of Levingston Lee (a teacher) and Anna Louise (Pratt) Summers; married Vera Mae Elmquist (a teacher), June 4, 1932; children: Julia Anne (Mrs. Michael Marcus), Richard Lee. *Education:* Attended Chaffey College, 1928, University of Wisconsin, 1928-30; University of California, Los Angeles, A.B., 1939, Secondary Teaching Credential, 1940; graduate studies at University of Southern California. *Politics:* Democrat. *Religion:* Episcopalian. *Home and office:* 5280 Olmeda Ave., Box 564, Atascadero, Calif. 93422. *Agent:* McIntosh & Otis, Inc., 18 East 41st St., New York, N.Y. 10017.

CAREER: Industrial Laboratory Supply Co., Los Angeles, Calif., owner, 1940-42; teacher of industrial arts at high schools, Lone Pine, Calif., and Barstow, Calif., 1942-46; high school

JAMES L. SUMMERS

teacher of U.S. history, Paso Robles, Calif., 1948-54; full-time writer, primarily for young people, 1954—. *Member:* California Writer's Club, Phi Delta Kappa, Masons. *Awards, honors: New York Herald Tribune* Children's Spring Book Festival Honor Book, 1953, for *Girl Trouble;* Prize from the Bureau for Intercultural Education, for "Boy in the Mirror."

WRITINGS:

Open Season, Doubleday, 1951.
Girl Trouble, Westminster, 1953.
Prom Trouble (Junior Literary Guild selection), Westminster, 1954.
Operation ABC, Westminster, 1955.
Off the Beam, Westminster, 1956.
Trouble on the Run, Westminster, 1956.
Ring around Her Finger, Westminster, 1957.
Sons of Montezuma, Westminster, 1957.
The Wonderful Time, Westminster, 1958.
Wait for Private Black, Westminster, 1958.
Heartbreak Hot Rod (Junior Literary Guild selection), Doubleday, 1958.
The Limit of Love, Westminster, 1959.
Tougher Than You Think, Westminster, 1959.
This Random Sky, Westminster, 1960.
Trouble on Hogback Hill, Westminster, 1960.
Gift Horse (Junior Literary Guild selection), Westminster, 1961.
The Karting Crowd (Junior Literary Guild selection), Westminster, 1961.
Muscle Boy, Westminster, 1962.
The Shelter Trap, Westminster, 1962.
The Trouble with Being in Love, Westminster, 1963.
Tiger Terwilliger (Junior Literary Guild selection), Westminster, 1963.
The Cardiff Giants, Westminster, 1964.
The Amazing Mr. Tenterhook (Junior Literary Guild selection), Westminster, 1964.
Wild Buggy Jordan, McKay, Westminster, 1965.
Senior Dropout (Junior Literary Guild selection), Westminster, 1965.
The Long Ride Home, Westminster, 1966.
Cumash Summer, McKay, 1967.
The Shelter Trap, Pflaum, 1967.
The Lucky Suzuki, McKay, 1968.
The Iron Doors Between, Westminster, 1968.
You Can't Make It by Bus, Westminster, 1969.
Don't Come Back a Stranger, Westminster, 1970.
Change of Focus, Westminster, 1972.

Contributor of short stories to *Southwest Review* and to other literary journals.

SIDELIGHTS: After receiving his A.B. degree from the University of California at Los Angeles, Summers decided to teach. "I had different jobs, interesting ones—lemons, radios, neon signs, and vacuum cleaners. All the time I was writing poetry. Finally I decided to teach. While teaching I...met a lot of young people...They have all taught me a great deal, and so I decided to write about them." He has since written many short stories and books for young people.

Summers was once asked by a friend if he had ever ridden a horse that couldn't swim. "I said I hadn't, not adding that whenever I rode a horse, I didn't bring up such complicated questions with him, preferring to stick with simpler issues. The [friend] went on to tell of a stream crossing he had made in which his mount insisted upon walking across on the bottom instead of swimming. The animal's behavior surprised him, he said. From this anecdote it occurred to me that, despite the vast equine literature already extant, the full nature of horses

Being second-string fullback on a team that barely had a first string was an honor. ■ (From *Tiger Terwilliger* by James L. Summers. Illustrated by Richard Horwitz.)

is yet to be entirely explored. Besides, from my own experience I knew that not every rider is master of his horse; often it is exactly the opposite. Frequently the horse is a 'people expert,' quite capable of superb 'boymanship.' Out of this concept rose the idea for my book, *Gift Horse.*"

Senior Dropout contains autobiographical material. "Like its hero, I came to Milwaukee from California, a year or two after my mother died, to attend my senior year in high school. There was a real girl something like Hermine but of course not she at all. I didn't drop out of school as Lon did; but the feeling of the story is quite true, and I did live in that strange and wonderful old house.

"Naturally everything in the story is entirely fiction and no actual people are described, but I did go to work in a factory something like the one Lon found. Although the Milwaukee Chamber of Commerce sent me a large sheaf of material that enabled me to update my memory of the city, the spirit of it is out of my own boyhood.

"My theme is that the potential dropout needs plenty of the sort of help I had. He needs to be encouraged to see his education through just as far as he can go.

"My juvenile writing has all been undertaken with the most serious literary intent and I find the work to be exacting. When I work on my books I do almost nothing else, preferring a sustained effort to other techniques of writing."

FOR MORE INFORMATION SEE:

Muriel Fuller, editor, *More Junior Authors,* H. W. Wilson, 1963.
Horn Book, October, 1968.
Dorothy A. Marquardt and Martha E. Ward, *Authors of Books for Young People,* 2nd edition, Scarecrow, 1971.
Library Journal, October 15, 1972.
Alleen Pace Nilsen and Kenneth L. Donelson, *Literature for Today's Young Adults,* 2nd edition, Scott, Foresman, 1985.

SWEAT, Lynn   1934-

PERSONAL: Born May 27, 1934, in Alexandria, La.; son of Charles M. (a welder) and Oueda (a homemaker; maiden name, White) Sweat; married Elynor Glynn (a teacher), April 6, 1956; children: Brian, Susan, Linda, John. *Education:* Lamar University, B.S., 1956. *Religion:* Protestant. *Home:* 17 Goodhill Rd., Weston, Conn. 06883. *Office:* Publisher's Graphics, 251 Greenwood Ave., Bethel, Conn. 06801.

CAREER: Beaumont Enterprise & Journal, Beaumont, Tex., staff artist, 1956-59; KFDM-TV, Beaumont, artist and cameraman, 1959; Continental Can Co., Beaumont, artist, 1959-60; Macmillan Publishing, New York, N.Y., assistant art director, 1960-64; Altman, Stoller Advertising, New York, N.Y., staff artist; free-lance illustrator, 1964—. *Exhibitions:* Roko Gallery, New York, 1973; Fairfield Library, Conn., 1986; Rose Farm Gallery, Conn., 1988. *Awards, honors:* Award of Excellence from the Society of Illustrators, 1970, for a promotional book, ''Birds without Words''; *The Rub Book* was selected one of Child Study Association of America's Children's Books of the Year, 1968, *Granny, the Baby, and the Big Gray Thing,* 1972, *The Garden Is Doing Fine,* 1975, and *Let's Celebrate: Holiday Decorations You Can Make,* and *Good Work, Amelia Bedelia,* both 1976; Golden Kite Award from

LYNN SWEAT

the Society of Children's Book Writers, 1975, for *The Garden Is Doing Fine;* Garden State Children's Book Award from the New Jersey Library Association, 1980, for *Teach Us, Amelia Bedelia;* Children's Choice from the International Reading Association and the Children's Book Council, 1982, and Garden State Children's Book Award, 1988, both for *Amelia Bedelia and the Baby.*

WRITINGS:

SELF-ILLUSTRATED

Cluck, the Captain's Chicken, Macmillan, 1966.
The Wonderful Hunting Dog, Macmillan, 1973.
Vacation and Holiday Fun, Childrens Press, 1987.

ILLUSTRATOR

James E. Seidelman and Grace Mintoyne, *The Rub Book,* Macmillan, 1968.
J. E. Seidelman and G. Mintonye, *Creating with Wood,* Macmillan, 1969.
Peggy Parish, *Costumes to Make,* Macmillan, 1970.
Hal Hellman, *Energy and Inertia,* Evans, 1970.
John S. Marr, *The Good Drug and the Bad Drug,* Evans, 1970.
J. S. Marr, *A Breath of Air and a Breath of Smoke,* Evans, 1971.
H. Hellman, *The Lever and the Pulley,* Evans, 1971.
P. Parish, *Sheet Magic: Games, Toys and Gifts from Old Sheets,* Macmillan, 1971.
P. Parish, *Granny, the Baby, and the Big Gray Thing,* Macmillan, 1972.
Seymour Simon, *Science Projects in Ecology,* Holiday House, 1972.
J. S. Marr, *The Food You Eat,* Evans, 1973.
S. Simon, *Projects with Plants,* F. Watts, 1973.
Kay Nation and Bob Nation, *Meters, Liters, and Kilos: Understanding the Metric System,* Hawthorn, 1974.
Carol Farley, *The Garden Is Doing Fine* (Junior Literary Guild selection), Atheneum, 1975.
Norma Johnston, *Of Time and of Seasons,* Atheneum, 1975.
P. Parish, *Let's Celebrate: Holiday Decorations You Can Make,* Greenwillow, 1976.
P. Parish, *Beginning Mobiles,* Macmillan, 1979.
Wesley Porter, *Dragons of Peking,* F. Watts, 1979.
W. Porter, *First Winter, First Summer,* F. Watts, 1979.
W. Porter, *The Magic Kettle,* F. Watts, 1979.
David Eastman, *What Is a Fish?,* Troll Associates, 1982.
P. Parish, *The Cat's Burglar,* Greenwillow, 1983.
Caroline Arnold, *Maps and Globes: Fun, Facts, and Activities,* F. Watts, 1984.
Seth McEvoy and Laurie Smith, *The Electronic Hurricane,* Dell, 1985.
S. McEvoy and L. Smith, *The Magnetic Ghost of Shadow Island,* Dell, 1985.
S. McEvoy and L. Smith, *Revenge of the Raster Gang,* Dell, 1985.
S. McEvoy and L. Smith, *Save the Venturians!,* Dell, 1985.
C. Arnold, *Bodies of Water: Fun, Facts, and Activities,* F. Watts, 1985.
C. Arnold, *Land Masses: Fun, Facts, and Activities,* F. Watts, 1985.
Laurence Santrey, *Rivers,* Troll Associates, 1985.
Keith Brandt, *Sound,* Troll Associates, 1985.
K. Brandt, *Sun,* Troll Associates, 1985.
Rose Greydanus, *Let's Get a Pet,* Troll Associates, 1985.
Elin McCoy, *Secret Spaces, Imaginary Places: Creating Your Own Worlds for Play,* Macmillan, 1986.
Ginny O'Donnell, *Hide-and-Seek Birthday,* Bantam, 1987.

She found the powder.
And Amelia Bedelia used it. ■ (From *Amelia Bedelia and the Baby* by Peggy Parish. Illustrated by Lynn Sweat.)

"AMELIA BEDELIA" SERIES; ALL WRITTEN BY PEGGY PARISH

Good Work, Amelia Bedelia, Greenwillow, 1976.
Teach Us, Amelia Bedelia, Greenwillow, 1977.
Amelia Bedelia Helps Out, Greenwillow, 1979.
Amelia Bedelia and the Baby, Greenwillow, 1981.
Amelia Bedelia Goes Camping, Greenwillow, 1985.
Merry Christmas, Amelia Bedelia, Greenwillow, 1986.
Amelia Bedelia's Family Album, Greenwillow, 1988.

SIDELIGHTS: "My childhood was spent on the coast of Texas. My first memories are those of being close to nature, dragon-flies, turtles, frogs, ducks, wild geese, birds, and clouds. I always had a love for pencils, crayons and libraries. After I graduated from high school, my interest in art led me to study commercial illustration in college.

"I am best known for the 'Amelia Bedelia' series which I have done in collaboration with Peggy Parish. I am the illustrator, Peggy is the author. I have worked on over forty children's books usually in collaboration. *Cluck, the Captain's Chicken* and *The Wonderful Hunting Dog* are two that I wrote and illustrated.

"I have worked as a commercial illustrator in addition to devoting much of my time to painting. As time has gone on I have gone into fine arts more and more, so that illustration has become a secondary part of my life as an artist."

FOR MORE INFORMATION SEE:

Idea (Japan), September, 1968.
Dorothy A. Marquardt and Martha Ward, *Illustrators of Books for Young People*, Scarecrow, 1975.

SZUDEK, Agnes S(usan) P(hilomena) (Mary McCaffrey)

PERSONAL: Surname is pronouced shoe-deck; born November 28, in Scotland; daughter of Hugh (in mathematics) and Mary (McCaffrey) Hughes-Meechan; married Major Przemyslaw Andrjei Richter Szudek (a military writer), 1961; children: Victor Alexander, Andrew Casimir. *Education:* Montessori Training Centre, Richmond, Yorkshire, England, diploma; attended Maria Assumpta Training College, London, England, Jean Boothway Dancing School, Kettering, England, and Guildhall School of Music and Drama, London. *Home:* 42 Hillyard St., Stockwell, London SW9 0NL, England. *Agent:* Murray Pollinger, 4 Garrick St., London WC2E 9BH, England.

CAREER: Teacher at several schools in Northamptonshire, England; St. Peter and Paul's School, Islington, head of infant department; free-lance writer, 1972—. *Member:* Society of Authors, National Book League, Arts Club, Authors' Lending Rights Society. *Awards, honors:* Polish Gold Cross of Merit, 1980, for *Stories from Poland* and *The Amber Mountain and Other Folk Stories; Victoria Plumb* was selected a Childrens' Book of the Year by the National Book League, 1978, and *Victoria and the Parrots Gang,* 1979.

WRITINGS:

Stories from Poland (illustrated by John Mousedale), British Broadcasting Corp., 1972.
The Amber Mountain and Other Folk Stories (illustrated by Jan Pienkowski), Hutchinson, 1976.
(Contributor) *Humblepuppy* (illustrated by Ron Maris), Bodley Head, 1978.
Victoria Plumb (illustrated by Gillian Gaze), Hutchinson, 1978.
Victoria and the Parrots Gang (illustrated by L. Graham-Yooll), Hutchinson, 1979.
Specs Forever (illustrated by Susan Sansome), Hamish Hamilton, 1981.
(Contributor) Frank Muir, *Big Dipper* (illustrated by Jacqueline Sinclair), Heinemann, 1981.
The Trumpeter of Krakov and Other Stories from Poland, Granada, 1982.

AGNES S. P. SZUDEK

I've Got Frogs! (illustrated by Laszlo Acs), Hamish Hamilton, 1988.
Flicker of Light, Ginn, 1989.
Up, Up and Away, Ginn, 1990.

UNDER PSEUDONYM MARY McCAFFREY

The Mighty Muddle (illustrated by Colin McNaughton), Eel Pie, 1981.
Smoke-Drift to Heaven, Abelard, 1981.
One Way to Rome, Abelard, 1982.
My Brother Ange (illustrated by Denise Saldutti), Crowell, 1982.
Night of the Tiger, Abelard, 1983.

TELEVISION

"Nothing but Noise," for "Play School," BBC-TV, 1976.

RADIO

"Mr. McPot Stories," for "Listen with Mother," BBC Radio, 1982-83.

Specs Forever has been published in Welsh and Danish. Contributor to *Brownie Annual, Guide Annual, Cricket* and *Child Education.*

ADAPTATIONS:

"Stories from Poland," for "Jackanory," BBC-TV, 1972.
"The Black Goat and Other Stories," for "Jackanory," BBC-TV, 1972.
"Gavel and King Hobnail and Other Stories," for "Jackanory," BBC-TV, 1982.
"The Trumpeter of Krakow," BBC-TV, 1982.

WORK IN PROGRESS: I'll Remember Eddie, a novel about a disgruntled boy who finds an enriching friendship with a disabled child.

SIDELIGHTS: "Rememberances of my own childhood, children, and my two sons have motivated my stories which are all rooted in fact.

"I was born in Scotland but brought up in England in the beautiful east-midlands county of Norhthamptonshire. My education was at the Ursuline Convent School in Kettering ten miles away, a school which my friends and I adored. We wept buckets when it was time to leave. From there I went north to Richmond, Yorkshire to take a diploma in the Montessori Method of teaching because I was too young to go to college. I subsequently trained as a teacher at college in Kensington Square, London and began my teaching career.

"My childhood was very happy with strict but loving parents, and two brothers, Thomas, the elder, and Hugh, the younger. We were very literary minded, never without an armful of books wherever we went. My mother influenced our reading greatly, taking us regularly to an ancient bookshop in Northampton owned by an old man with a long black coat, a long grey beard and red skull-cap. There were dusty wooden floorboards over which we clattered to reach a small counter at the far end. It was all very dim. The ceiling was lost high in darkness and I always imagined it led up to another world filled with writers from the past. Our visits to this shop (now long since demolished) have remained so clearly in my mind that I have written a short story about it, 'A Book from What's-His-Name.' From there I have some treasured Charles Dickens novels published in 1844, etc. with illustrations by Cruikshank, Cattermole, etc.

"Our home was on the road to Rockingham Village one mile away which is overlooked by the magnificent Rockingham Castle complete with battlements and with a view over five counties. It was originally built by William the Conqueror in the eleventh century. Here I used to play among the battlements and the rose gardens with a friend whose aunt worked at the castle. In our teens my brother Thomas and I loved to take a picnic and sit in the old churchyard of the castle, he writing poems, I stories, and we both sketched and painted. The tiny church was a hallowed resting place for knights and ladies and from where we could take brass rubbings.

"Our other great thrill was to go over to Naseby where the Battle of Naseby took place in 1645 between the Cavaliers and the Roundheads. A stone column marks the field of battle and here my brother and I would sit in silence for hours, eyes closed, trying to transport ourselves back to those Cromwellian days. Sometimes we believed it worked.

"Also in our teens we started to write an operetta about pirates, Thomas the words, I the music, but he went to university before we had time to finish it. We were a very self-sufficient family, inventive, with masses of activities based on rudimentary materials provided by our parents. At one time, ages seven and nine, we started a bank, taking deposits from various adults, doing the whole thing, making bank books, etc. I recall a serious complaint from my father objecting to our high interest rates! We combined this with a post office, designing our own stamps, drawing sheets of them and labouriously perforating them with pins.

"I am always amazed when I hear of young people being bored because there is nothing to do. My brothers and I never had enough hours in the day.

"When I was fourteen I became church organist and being so small (or the electric organ so big), I could not reach the foot pedals. But I loved it all, especially playing for weddings.

"Although I became a schoolteacher my lifelong ambition was to be an actress. My father forbade it saying, 'We don't do that kind of thing in our family.' And, since I came from a long line of educationalists, I joined on the line. But I also acted in amateur dramatics from the age of twelve and later went to the Guildhall School of Music and Drama in London. Still my father disapproved and the fates seemed to be on his side with several near-misses in the film world.

"Bowing to my father I returned to teaching and used my skills and training with stories, plays, poems and songs written for school productions. But, to tell the truth the bite from the acting bug has never healed. Never will! There is nothing I like more than a 'live' audience. For this reason my visits to schools, libraries, and bookshops to give talks and story sessions have been a great joy to me and, of course, holding handwork afternoons, etc. in my home.

"In 1962 I married Major P. A. Szudek who is Polish from Warsaw and a military writer. With him I have travelled in Europe, the Middle East and have lived in Far East Malaysia. We have two sons, Victor Alexander and Andrew Casimir. Andrew wants to be a writer. I think he will, having written a children's novel at the age of ten. He is now at Cambridge.

"My favourite character is Victoria Plumb about whom I have written two volumes of short stories, each selected as a Childrens Book of the Year by the National Book League. Her creation was tied up very much with my own tomboy youth. She is a modern, zany young girl who finds her own way of coping with her rapidly changing environment. My greatest

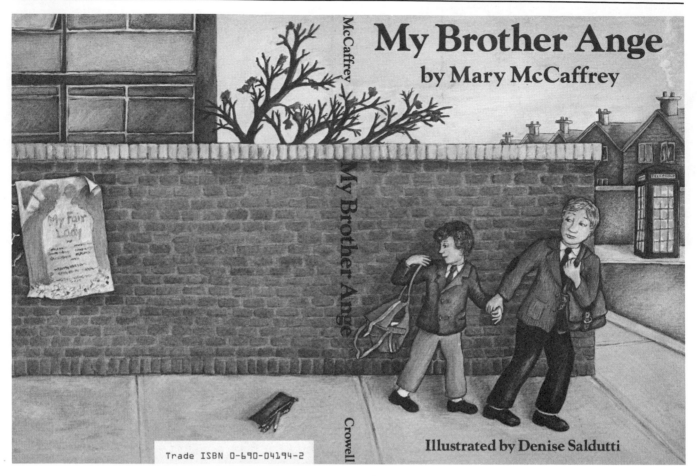

"Come on, Ange," he said. "Let's go." ■ (Jacket illustration by Denise Saldutti from *My Brother Ange* by Mary McCaffrey.)

regret is that a third collection of stories has not been published since confusion over another Victoria Plum, a fairy which appeared on the market.

"*The Mighty Muddle* was inspired by the bedroom of one of my sons. *My Brother Ange* combines a local danger area by a school and the road accident of my older brother when he was seven years old. *One Way to Rome* was inspired by a proposed visit to Rome with my mother in the year that she died. The visit never made was achieved only in the book.

"My connections with the United States were very close during my childhood. I was always dressed American style with beautiful dresses and accessories sent by my uncles from New York. Unfortunately since the death of my parents I have lost touch with my American relatives. The pseudonym Mary McCaffrey was my mother's name. She in turn was named after her aunt, Mary McCaffrey, a New Yorker and philanthropist whose married name was McGovern. One day I may find the other members of my family in Chicago, New York and Orange County. I hope so. Oh, and, of course, I should love to have another book published in the United States.

"The preceeding is a far-from-complete account of my life which has fashioned me into the person and, therefore, the writer I am. The encouragement to be resourceful, inventive and independent, and above all, book-loving have been the best gifts my parents could have given me. I hope to go on writing, singing, dancing, painting, playing my piano, etc. etc. etc. until my last gasp."

HOBBIES AND OTHER INTERESTS: Cooking Malaysian and Chinese food, books, china, porcelain, flowers, eighteenth-century French decor.

THOMPSON, Stith   1885-1976

PERSONAL: Born March 7, 1885, near Bloomfield, Ky.; died January 10, 1976, in Columbus, Ind.; son of John Warden (a farmer) and Eliza (McClaskey) Thompson; married Louise Faust, June 14, 1918; children: Dorothy Cosette (Mrs. Robert L. Letsinger), Marguerite Frances (Mrs. David G. Hays). *Education:* Attended Butler College, 1903-05; University of Wisconsin, B.A., 1909; University of California, Berkeley, M.A., 1912; Harvard University, Ph.D., 1914. *Religion:* Unitarian Universalist. *Residence:* Bloomington, Ind.

CAREER: Teacher in secondary schools in Springfield, Ky., 1905-07; Lincoln High School, Portland, Ore., English teacher, 1909-11; University of Texas at Austin, instructor in English, 1914-18; Colorado College, Colorado Springs, professor of English, 1918-20; University of Maine, Orono, associate professor of English, 1920-21; Indiana University of Bloomington, associate professor, 1921-29, professor of English, 1929-30, professor of English and Folklore, 1939-53, Distinguished Service Professor of English and Folklore, 1953-55, professor emeritus, 1955-76, dean of Graduate School, 1947-50, director of doctoral program in folklore, 1949-55. Lecturer in South America and technical advisor to Ministry of Education, Venezuela, on the establishment of a service of folklore investi-

STITH THOMPSON

gations, 1947; visiting Fulbright professor, University of Oslo, 1951-52; lecturer in South America under the auspices of the U.S. Department of State, 1960-61; visiting professor at University of Texas, University of Kansas, Northwestern University, University of California at Los Angeles, and University of Hawaii. U.S. delegate to International Folklore Congress, Paris, 1937; organizer of Folklore Institutes of America, Indiana University, 1942, 1946, 1950, and 1954; official in various international folklore meetings.

MEMBER: International Commission of Folk Arts and Folklore (past vice-president), Medieval Academy of America, American Philosophical Society, Modern Language Association of America, American Folklore Society (president, 1936-39), Norwegian Academy of Science (fellow), Danish Academy of Letters and Science (fellow), Gustav Adolphs Akademi fuer Folklivsorskning, Societe finnoe-ougrienne (Helsinki); honorary member of folklore societies in various foreign countries and member of many state folklore societies; Delta Tau Delta, Phi Beta Kappa. *Awards, honors:* Litt.D., University of North Carolina, 1946, and University of Kentucky, 1958; L.H.D., Indiana Central College, 1953; Guggenheim fellow, 1956-57; Dr. Phil. honoris causa, Christian Albrecht University (Kiel), 1959, and Colorado College, 1965.

WRITINGS:

The Ideal of Social Reconstruction in Tolstoy's "What Shall We Do Then?," University of California Press, 1912.
(Editor) *Round the Levee,* Texas Folklore Society, 1916, reissued, Southern Methodist University Press, 1975.

(With J. F. Royster) *Manual and Notebook for English Composition,* Scott, 1917.
(Translator with Cosette Faust Newton) *Old English Poems,* Scott, 1918, reissued, Richard West, 1976.
(With J. F. Royster) *Practice Sheets for English Composition,* Scott, 1918.
(With J. F. Royster) *Guide to Composition,* Scott, 1919.
European Tales among the North American Indians, Colorado College, 1919.
(With A. Aarne) *The Types of the Folktale,* Finnish Academy of Sciences, 1928, 2nd edition, 1961.
Tales of the North American Indians, Harvard University Press, 1929, reissued, Indiana University Press, 1966.
(Editor with Curtis H. Page) *British Poets of the Nineteenth Century,* B.H. Sanborne, 1929, reissued, Books for Libraries, 1972.
The Motif-Index of Folk-Literature: A Classification of Narrative Elements in Folk-Tales, Ballads, Myths, Fables, Mediaeval Romances, Exempla, Fabliaux, Jest-Books, and Local Legends, six volumes, Finnish Academy of Sciences, 1932-37, revised and enlarged edition, Indiana University Press, 1955-58.
(With Henry S. Canby and others) *English Composition in Theory and Practice,* Macmillan, 1933.
(With Malcolm McLeod) *New Handbook of English,* Nelson, 1936.
(With H. H. Carter) *Remedial Exercises in English Composition,* Heath, 1937.
Our Heritage of World Literature, Cordon, 1938, new edition (with John Gassner), Dryden Press, 1942.
(With B. D. N. Grebanier) *English Literature and Its Backgrounds,* Volume I, Cordon, 1939, Volume II, 1940.
The Folktale, Dryden Press, 1946, reissued, AMS Press, 1979.
(Editor) *Four Symposia on Folklore,* Indiana University Press, 1953, reissued Greenwood Press, 1976.
(With Jonas Balys) *The Oral Tales of India,* Indiana University Press, 1958, reissued, Greenwood Press, 1976.
(With Warren E. Roberts) *Types of Indic Folktales,* Finnish Academy of Sciences, 1960.
Shipley, Mitchell, annd Thompson Families: Notes Based in Part on Researches of Kate A. Thompson, [Bloomington], 1964, Lost Cause Press, 1972.
Second Wind: A Sequel after Ten Years to Folklorist's Progress, [Bloomington], 1966.
(Editor) *One Hundred Favorite Folk Tales,* Indiana University Press, 1968.
(With Hari S. Upadhyaya) *Reminiscences of an Octogenarian Folklorist,* [Tokyo], 1968.
Story-Telling to Story-Writing, University of Belgrade, 1969.

Managing editor, *Texas Review,* 1917-18. Contributor of articles on the teaching of English and on folklore to periodicals, including *Texas Review, Publications of the Modern Language Association, Journal of American Folklore, English Journal, American Anthropologist, Southern Folklore Quarterly, American Scholar* and *Western Folklore.*

SIDELIGHTS: Born **March 7, 1885** in Nelson County, Kentucky, the son of John Warden Thompson and Eliza McCloskey. "The mixture of peoples which produce the family into which I was born in Kentucky in 1885 contained almost every element of our colonial population. Always following the main line of movement and settlement these people all converged on the counties of the southern Kentucky Bluegrass before the year 1800. They were all in America before 1750. . . .

"Though I can remember a few things from 1889, it was only with the year 1890 that my recollections cease to be blurred. . . . Almost a half mile from the road was the very modest house, a low, rambling story-and-a-half structure, always too small for the uses to which it was put. But it was a good farm, with excellent land at the front and gradually sloping back on long ridges to Mayes Creek. . . .

"As I look back on these earliest years it is surprising what important things are forgotten, what trivialities are remembered: the wading and 'going a-washing' in Mayes Creek; the playing with the young Negro boys; the hours of watching Uncle George Knox who had once belonged to the family while he did jobs of carpentering and talked with his picturesque stutter; the Sunday afternoon visit of Uncle Nathan, who also had belonged to the family but who was well-to-do and maintained his own carriage and was received as an honored guest; harvest and reaping time and the attempts of the poor little rabbits to escape; and the most exciting time of the year in the fields, the coming of the thresher. The very first threshing engine that came to our place was still drawn by oxen, but the next year a traction engine was used and gave Mother's driving horse a good scare. And there was hog-killing time, with the rendering of lard and the making of sausage and the hanging of hams and sides of meat in the smokehouse and the meeting of the neighbors at the beef company where we each brought back our share of beef and added variety to the menu; riding on the wagon full of wheat or on the wool sacks; apple-picking and cider-making, nutting, and picking blackberries; the delicious smell of spring flowers and the joy of wading in the spring freshets; and finally the mystery and sadness of death. Twice I saw my little sisters go into convulsions and cry themselves to death, and I saw my mother's sister who came to our house to die and heard the superstitious comments of the Negroes about her."[1]

Thompson had fond memories of a simple country education. "Since this is the account of a scholar, school would seem to be very important. For the first three or four years he went to the country school at Pleasant Grove. I suppose there were thirty or forty pupils under one teacher. These were not graded, but except for our first teacher I think we had excellent instruction. We used the old McGuffey Readers and I got my first feeling for poetry there. As for geography, I learned much from the cards that came in our Arbuckle's coffee. I can still remember maps of South American countries, and when a few years ago we were in Bolivia and Peru, I could hardly look on these maps without recalling the smell of those packages and coffee. When after about three years we transferred to the town school I could read rather well, I knew the geography of the United States and of a good part of the world, could spell excellently, and though I hated to do it, could perform arithmetic problems without much trouble."[1]

When his father suffered financial setbacks, Thompson was forced to work while in high school. In addition to a paper route, he worked at the shipping room at Bobbs Merrill, where he caught glimpses of famous authors. "Though often weary, I think I was never rebellious about working after school and on Saturdays. Many of my friends were doing the same thing and I have no doubt that it taught me some things and also kept me out of a certain amount of mischief. But I had no leisure; I had to struggle for opportunity to satisfy my growing intellectual interests, and my social life was very limited."[1]

He enrolled in The Manual Training High School, but "it was clear enough after a while that my interests lay in quite another direction. Consequently, although it meant making up considerable work, I shifted midway to the regular high school course. I did not realize it at that time, but I am sure now that this was one of the important decisions of my life. At least I had learned that it was not with my hands that the future was to be carved out."[1]

1903. Graduated from high school and entered Butler College where he pursued his love of literature. "By the summer of 1905 I had finished two years of college and was twenty years old. I had worked at various jobs during these two years—newspaper reporting, selling college scholarships, and most of all looking up genealogical records for various people. But I began to feel a sense of frustration and an urge to get some kind of regular job that would make a living."[1]

1905-1907. Taught high school in Springfield, Kentucky.

1907-1909. Continued his education at University of Wisconsin, majoring in English and studying Latin, Greek, French and German. "During my two years at Wisconsin I earned my board by washing dishes or waiting table or otherwise spending at least four hours a day. Thus I had very little time for the usual social life of the university. It was obviously impossible to be active in my university fraternity, but I took every opportunity to go to the theater and to hear lecturers who came to the university. Socially the most important thing was association with some very promising students."[1]

1909-1911. Taught at Lincoln High School in Portland, Oregon, and his first summer there he and a friend worked in a lumber camp. "Normally this was a camp of fifty to a hundred men. We tried it for a night or two in the bunkhouse but the air was too foul and we built us a small leanto in the woods and slept there during the whole summer. It was the dry season and not once did it rain during the three months we were there.

"Our camp was in the Blue Mountains at about three thousand feet elevation and we had extremes of temperature. Usually we found ice in the morning, and by early afternoon it was hard to work with any clothes on. We would start off loaded down with sweaters and then have to carry these for the rest of the day. Tracks were laid at the creek bottoms and the great pine and fir trees were cut from the hillsides."[1]

While there he learned to speak Norwegian from a group of men from Norway who couldn't speak English. This proved to be an important addition to the languages he could speak, for he later became a visiting professor in Norway. Also, he began to form an interest in folklore. "On one or two occasions the men gathered around and heard an Irishman named Duffy tell tales about Paul Bunyan. This, it will be remembered was the summer of 1910 and was before Paul Bunyan had been taken up by professional folklorists and lumber company publishers. This fact was to be important years later. . . .

"I had my guitar sent up from Portland and would often play in the evenings.

"In after years we always looked back on this summer at the lumber camp with nostalgia. I am certain that it was good for us physically, and for a folklorist who was going to have to deal with lumberjack songs and tales in later years it was very well to know at first hand what in 1910 the lumberjacks of eastern Oregon told and sang."[1]

1911-1912. Completed a masters degree in English and folk literature at the University of California at San Francisco. He won a Bonnheim Fellowship the following year for further work at Harvard.

1912-1914. Completed his Ph.D. at Harvard, writing his thesis on "European Tales Among North American Indians." He went to Europe after graduating, the first of many such trips. "Not much about this summer in Europe would interest anyone who has made the trip himself. But it must be remembered that I took this at the end of an intensive study of English

(From *One Hundred Favorite Folk Tales,* edited by Stith Thompson. Illustrated by Franz Altschuler.)

literature and that I was to see places which I had long ago visited in imagination. It was a profound spiritual experience for me, and I visited with energy and enthusiasm which I have never done since.''[1]

September, 1914-1918. Taught composition and literature at the University of Texas, during which time he published *The Notebook for English Composition,* an accompanying manual, and *The Guide to Composition.* He was active in the Unitarian Church and in campus activities. He roomed in the home of John Lomax, who, with his son Alan, became famous for their folksong collecting.

In **1915** he met Louise Faust and dated her for a while. ''The next year she went out to West Texas and taught school, riding horseback and living a wild cowboy life. We exchanged some letters and another year rolled by.''[1] Then World War I broke out, but Thompson was too tall and too thin to be drafted.

June, 1918. Married Louise Faust in a double ceremony with her sister. He received an offer to teach at Colorado College, so he resigned from Texas and moved to Colorado Springs in late summer.

1920-1921. Moved to Orono, Maine to teach at the University of Maine. ''The University of Maine in those days was an

entirely new kind of environment for both of us. The institution itself was attractive enough in a woods of pine and birch and mostly with brick buildings. But almost a mile of open country separated it and the town. The University was on an island in the Penobscot River. The other side of the island from the main Penobscot and really a part of that river was the Stillwater, a very deep and rapid stream. Four miles north of the University was Old Town with its settlement of Penobscot Indians. Our own village of Orono was in many ways typical of New England villages—some neat white churches and some dignified old places, a paper pulp factory, and a general feeling of timelessness. I remember seeing a map of the village in the barbershop and being able to recognize every building in the map and only later realizing that the map was dated 1835.''[1]

1921. Moved to Bloomington, Indiana to teach at Indiana University. ''I had a theory that no one should stay longer than four years at any university and get into a rut. At Bloomington I was to stay thirty-four.

''Though Indiana University in 1921 was not a fourth the size of the present institution, it was an extremely pleasant place. The great central woods were there as they are today, surrounded on three sides by the older group of buildings. I still remember my delight with the beauty of it all and my feeling of the contrast between it and the University of Maine.''[1]

March 17, 1922. Daughter Dorothy born. Thompson published *European Tales Among North American Indians* and began studying the cello.

Summer, 1924. Began his motif-index, creating a classification of motifs in folktales that would become his life's work. ''The scholars of the generation around 1900 were increasingly aware of the importance of the narratives of such peoples as the Africans or the American Indians. By what seems to me now as mere good fortune, I early became interested in making some comparison between the tales of the American Indians and the Europeans. My studies at that time had to do with the actual clear-cut borrowings of whole tales on the part of the American Indians from the European settlers. Later, when I tried to study the less obvious parallels, the hundreds of small items I had run across that seemed familiar to the student of European folklore, I was faced by the problem of their arrangement. I saw that no one had ever brought together the narrative motifs of peoples in all parts of the world and in all types of social and industrial development so that they could be compared. It was because of this specific need that I began a classification of motifs which they could be brought together for easy study. This was essentially the beginning of the work which grew into the *Motif-Index of Folk-Literature.*

''. . .We can generally say that motifs have to do with things— with gods and demigods, with heavenly bodies, insofar as their description is not purely astronomical; the origin of animals and their habits, when these differ from the teachings of zoological departments; queer and unusual animals, again not found in the zoological handbook; forbidden things of all kinds, normally not mentioned in the codes of law; magic objects; various manifestations of the dead or of marvelous creatures, ogres and the like; monstrous people; unusual pieces of luck; unusual social practices; and the like. Or it may be that a simple action of some kind is told because it has a humorous point, or because it is marvelous to listen to. And many motifs are nothing more than a reflection of a whole world of belief which forms a background of narrative.''[2]

1925-1926. Compiled *Tales of the North American Indians.* In August, 1926, he left for a year in Europe with wife Louise and her mother and Dorothy. While in Copenhagen he met the famous folklorist Kaarle Krohn. Later in the trip, while visiting Krohn's home in Finland, he agreed to revise and complete the work of Antti Aarne, a student of Krohn's who had died while making an important survey of folktale types. "As the time came close for me to leave, Krohn talked to me a good deal about my future plans. One day he told me that he was counting on me very particularly to carry on the cause of folktale research in my generation. And some time later he told me how when he was a young student having just finished his doctor's degree in 1883, he had made a trip to Weimar to visit the Ducal Librarian, Reinhold Kohler. Kohler was certainly the most famous student of the folktale in the period of the 1870's and 80's. On the day Krohn was to leave, Kohler called him in and talked to him. He said in effect, 'Dr. Krohn, I am now an old man. I have spent many years working on the folktale but now I can do very little more. It is to you that I look for carrying on these researches in your generation.' And then Krohn turned to me and he said, 'I hope you remember what I said to you yesterday.' It can well be imagined that the confidence he expressed has stayed with me all through the years."[1]

April 15, 1930. Daughter Marguerite (Rita) born. Soon after, the wife of their friend Archer Taylor died, and the Thompsons took in two of his three children for a year.

March, 1931. Took a leave of absence and went to Cambridge, Massachusetts to work on his Motif-Index. "For my own development, it was high time that I was to have a period for catching up with myself and for seeing new faces. I had now behind me four textbooks in English and three important works in folklore. Though later I was on three occasions to receive higher appointments, I had achieved what normally is considered the highest rank in the academic field. My health was good and was improving. Though I was still unable to get beyond 135 pounds, I would soon be taking on middle-age weight. I was far enough through the Motif-Index to realize that I would be able to finish it.

"Without realizing how much responsibility I was leaving with Louise and her large family, a few days before my forty-sixth birthday I left for Harvard."[1]

From Cambridge, he went to Europe to continue his work.

1931. Indiana University continued to support him during the Depression. "I was beginning to receive financial help toward my research, even though the university had very little to give. I recall one day at the Faculty Club which was just opened that fall when President Bryan came to me and said, 'The depression seems to be descending upon us deeper and deeper, but I want you to know that insofar as the university can do it, we expect to support your research. It is very valuable in itself and it is bringing great honor to the university.' Of course this encouragement made me more eager than ever to go ahead."[1]

1935. Completed the Motif-Index. "As for my own work during that year, there is very little to report except that it was steady. I worked more at night than ever in my life. I was racing against time so as to finish the last stroke on the Motif-Index by my fiftieth birthday. Early in March, about three or four days before that eventful moment, I was able to say that the whole job was not complete."[1]

Thompson went to Sweden to attend the prestigious Congress for the Study of the Folktale. Only twenty-five specialists were invited from all over the world. During this Congress he was elected a member of the Gustav Adolphs Academi.

1936. On his return from Europe, Thompson spent the summer teaching at U.C.L.A., revisiting Oregon and taking his family camping.

He was elected President of the American Folklore Society and he completed *Our Heritage of World Literature*, a comparative literature anthology.

1939. Received a favorable offer to be a professor at New York University but finally decided to turn it down. "The choice was difficult, but in the end it was made easier since Indiana did what it could to meet all the conditions of the New York position. Not only could I stay on without financial sacrifice but also certain favorable understandings were reached about my work in the future. I was given a liberal fund for building up the library collection in folklore and was permitted to establish a Folklore Series of the Indiana University Publications with an adequate budget. I was also informed that a system of sabbatical leaves was to be put in within the next months and that as soon as I wished I might have my first sabbatical. Finally my title was added to so that I became the first Professor of English and Folklore in the United States. While this does not seem to be a very great change, it represented a certain autonomy in the folklore work at Indiana University, and had actually been important in promoting the success of the work there."[1]

1941. Took a sabbatical to California. His family went with him on a field trip to Northern Michigan to study Ojibwa Indian legends with a colleague.

While in California, Thompson completed *The Folktale*, a general introduction to the subject. Shortly after Christmas the family went to Mexico, returning to Indiana in time to start the spring semester.

1942. Founded the Folklore Institute at Indiana University. "Some time before we went on the California trip I had a talk with President Wells and told him that I had dreamed up a scheme which I thought would be important. He replied that it was only by following our dreams that we got anywhere. I then explained to him how, by means of a Folklore Institute extending through a whole summer, we might bring together a group of experts and therefore attract students to a session of real work and advance the whole cause of folklore. He gave his blessing to the plan, but I did nothing about it until I returned in January. The administration then furnished me with a small budget and told me in effect to go ahead. This, our first Folklore Institute, was small, but successful."[1]

1946. Awarded an Honorary Doctor of Letters from the University of North Carolina. The following year, Thompson went to South America at the invitation of the government of Venezuela who wished to foster folklore investigation. "One thing. . .which was important to me professionally was the fact that in Buenos Aires I was notified of my election to the American Philosophical Society. This was not only an honor, but. . .has brought about the most pleasant associations I could imagine."[1]

Thompson returned in November and was offered the Deanship of the graduate school at Indiana University. The graduate school instituted the first doctoral programs in the United States on folklore and comparative literature. They also began one of the early M.A.T. programs and initiated a University Press.

1955. A few months after his seventieth birthday, Thompson retired from Indiana University. Later that year he gave a talk at Michigan State College on Indian legends since Hiawatha. "In the course of my talk I mentioned the fact that this was for me the end of a long story; that these same Indians, or at least their very close cousins, the Potawatomis had held my great-grandmother in captivity for five years in the 1790's and that now I hoped we might finally bury the hatchet. Indians from the Isabella Reservation gave a number of dances under the general direction of Gertrude Kurath. In about the middle of their program the leader of these dances announced that they wanted to adopt Mrs. Kurath and Dr. Thompson into their tribe. Accordingly we went up and had the evil spirits driven out of us, and in other ways, were made members of the tribe. At the end the leader told me that now I was one of them and that when I came to their house I should walk right in, and, he added, 'We will do the same at your house.' I think Louise has had her eye out for wandering Indians ever since.''[1]

1956. Taught a semester at University of Texas, then returned to Europe on a Guggenheim Fellowship. Old age did not deter him. ''The let-down of vigor that comes with seventy has not yet arrived for me; as a matter of fact, I feel better physically and mentally than I did five or ten years ago, and I am just as eager to undertake new experiences and to make new friends as ever. Age has not yet taken on any of its melancholy aspects. To be sure, I have become somewhat reminiscent. I take pleasure in looking back over the thirty-four years of life at Indiana University and realizing how rich it has been in every way; I rejoice in the way the University has grown and prospered and become one of the lights in the country, and I think what a privilege it has been to be a part of the whole of that growth.

''I feel certain that no activities of mine could greatly influence any of the affairs of the world. To read about them in the daily papers is distressing enough; and yet I have a kind of natural optimism about the eventual issue. As I look back at the various bogeymen of the past, the Kaiser, Mussolini, Hitler, the Japanese overlords, Peron, and Huey Long, and Stalin, though I am troubled, I am not without hope; and I am glad that I have grandchildren who may see a world even better than that which my generation has enjoyed.

''It is hard to tell whether this optimism which I have always had would have succumbed under the onslaughts of ill health and misfortune. For in many ways I have been most fortunate—in my wife, in my daughters, in my grandchildren, in my friends and in my professional work. May I not also hope that this good fortune will continue into old age?''[1]

1962. Indiana University commissioned a bust of Dean Thompson by the sculptor Robert Laurent.

In later years, Thompson and his wife moved to a retirement home in Columbus, Indiana. Louise died in 1974. Thompson died of a sudden heart attack on **January 13, 1976,** shortly before his ninety-first birthday.

FOOTNOTE SOURCES

[1]Stith Thompson, ''Folklorist's Progress,'' Indiana University, 1956.
[2]S. Thompson, ''Narrative Motif-Analysis as a Folklore Method,'' *F. F. Communications*, Volume LXIV, number 161, 1955.

FOR MORE INFORMATION SEE:

W. Edson Richmond, editor, *Studies in Folklore*, Indiana University Press, 1957.
Wayland D. Hand and Gustave O. Arlt, editors, *Humaniora: Essays in Literature, Folklore, Bibliography*, J. J. Augustin, 1960.
Arv: Journal of Scandinavian Folklore, Volume XXI, 1965.

New York Times Book Review, January 5, 1969.
Western Folklore, October, 1976.
Journal of American Folklore, January, 1977.

OBITUARIES

New York Times, January 12, 1976.
Publishers Weekly, February 23, 1976.
Journal of American Folklore, January, 1977.

COLLECTIONS

Lilly Library at Indiana University.

VASS, George 1927-

PERSONAL: Born March 27, 1927, in Leipzig, Germany; son of Aloysius (a pathologist) and Minna (Blankfeld) Vass; married Theresa Shirley Miller, June 3, 1951; children: Sharon Elaine, Cynthia Diane. *Education:* Washington University, St. Louis, Mo., B.A., 1950; Northwestern University, M.S., 1952. *Religion:* Jewish.

CAREER: National Jewish Post, Indianapolis, Ind., managing editor, 1952-55; *Rockford Register-Republic*, Rockford, Ill., copy editor, 1955-58; *Chicago Daily News*, Chicago, Ill., sportswriter, beginning 1958; author. *Military service:* U.S. Army, 1945-47. *Member:* Authors Guild, Baseball Writers Association of America, National Hockey League Writers Association. *Awards, honors:* Illinois Associated Press Prize for stories on sports, 1968, 1970, and 1971.

WRITINGS:

JUVENILE

Champions of Sports, Reilly & Lee, 1970.
Reggie Jackson: From Superstar to Candy Bar, Childrens Press, 1979.
Steve Garvey: The Bat Boy Who Became a Star, Childrens Press, 1979.

ADULT

The Chicago Black Hawks Story, Follett, 1970.
(With Stan Mikita) *Inside Hockey*, Regnery, 1971.
George Halas and the Chicago Bears, Regnery, 1971.
(With Ferguson Jenkins) *Like Nobody Else: The Fergie Jenkins Story*, Regnery, 1973.

Contributor to *Baseball Digest* and *Hockey Digest*.

WORK IN PROGRESS: A historical novel.

VEVERS, (Henry) Gwynne 1916-1988

OBITUARY NOTICE—See sketch in *SATA* Volume 45: Born November 13, 1916, in Girvan, Scotland; died July 24, 1988. Scientist, curator, administrator, translator, editor, and author. Vevers was known for his vast canon of works in which the sciences were made accessible and discussed simply. He wrote or translated nearly one hundred books during his lifetime. He spent most of his career at the Zoological Society of London, where he was aquarium curator from 1955 to 1981, and assistant director of science from 1966 to 1981. His many writings include *The British Seashore, The Underwater World, The Pocket Guide to Aquarium Fishes*, and, as editor, *Practical Encyclopaedia of Freshwater Tropical Aquarium Fishes*.

Even though you may have a good shot, your linemate may have a better one. ■ (From *Inside Hockey* by Stan Mikita and George Vass. Photograph by Don Bierman.)

Vevers also wrote many science books for children, and he translated more than fifty zoological volumes.

FOR MORE INFORMATION SEE:

Contemporary Authors, Volume 113, Gale, 1985.

OBITUARIES

Times (London), July 27, 1988.

WALKER, Barbara M(uhs)   1928-

PERSONAL: Born in 1928, in Reading, Pa.; daughter of Elmer (a landscape architect) and Marie (a radio commentator; maiden name, Nading) Muhs; married Edward Walker (a physicist), October 15, 1960; children: Anna. *Education:* Vassar College, B.A., 1948. *Home and office:* Spring Valley Rd., Ossining, N.Y. 10562.

CAREER: Writer. Has worked in graphic design and writing for planners, architects and engineers. *Awards, honors:* Western Heritage Award from the National Cowboy Hall of Fame and Western Heritage Center, 1980, for *The Little House Cookbook.*

WRITINGS:

The Little House Cookbook: Frontier Foods from Laura Ingalls Wilder's Classic Stories (illustrated by Garth Williams), Harper, 1979.
(Editor) *The Little House Diary* (illustrated by G. Williams), Harper, 1985.

WORK IN PROGRESS: Building Rites: Ceremonies in the Rise of Structures.

SIDELIGHTS: "Our family's involvement with Laura and her food goes back to our first reading of *Little House in the Big Woods,* when I found myself making pancake men with my then four-year-old daughter Anna. Laura Ingalls Wilder's way of describing her pioneer childhood seemed to compel participation. Perhaps her native gift of observation and description was sharpened when she became the 'eyes' for her blind sister Mary.

"As time went by and Anna read and reread the series, we somehow acquired a coffee grinder in order to make 'Long Winter' bread, we experimented with sour-dough starter, and we tried our hands at drying blackberries. From other mothers I learned that our impulses were far from unique. One mother even advised me to 'skip *Farmer Boy* if you don't want to get into that ice cream making mess.' In fact, we skipped nothing.

"If the results were not always rewarding, the process was, and that is partly the reason for [*The Little House Cookbook*]. Cooking was for Laura Ingalls a social experience and an apprenticeship. By cooking with her elders she learned something about food, something about work, and something about human communion. Cooking remains one of the few essential household activities that adults and children or older and younger children can share in modern urban life. [*The Little House Cookbook*] is a gesture of sharing.

"Eventually I began looking for authentic recipes for dishes merely sketched or mentioned in the 'Little House' books. The search led to other writings of Laura Wilder, her daughter Rose, and their biographers, then on to sources of the period—pioneer diaries, local recipe collections, and cookbooks by professional authors. Always I have worked from the assumption that even in the fanciful *Farmer Boy* the details that illumine the fictional story line are true."[1]

BARBARA M. WALKER

FOOTNOTE SOURCES

[1]Barbara M. Walker, "Foreword," *The Little House Cookbook*, Harper, 1979.

WESTPHAL, Arnold Carl   1897-
(The Children's Shepherd)

PERSONAL: Born June 23, 1897, in Michigan City, Indiana; son of Henry H. (an iron worker) and Friedericka (a housewife; maiden name, Laborne) Westphal; married Esther Dysard, September 21, 1918 (died, 1954); married Addie Dysard Westphal, May 10, 1957 (died, 1980); children: Rex, Juanita, Arlo; five stepchildren. *Education:* Graduated from Valparaiso University, 1920, Moody Bible Institute, 1924, and Northern Baptist Theological Seminary, 1926; attended Chaplain's School at Harvard University, 1944, and Purdue University, 1948. *Politics:* Republican "with free choice by candidate." *Religion:* Baptist. *Home and office:* 1401 Ohio St., Michigan City, Ind., 46360.

CAREER: Licensed pastor and evangelist, 1918—, ordained, 1922. *Military service:* World War I, private; World War II, chaplain, captain; received three battle stars. *Member:* American Baptist Convention, Veterans of Foreign Wars. *Awards, honors:* Fifty-Year Ordination Award from the Evergreen Baptist Church, Michigan City, Ind., 1972; Sixty-Year Ordination Award from the Village Green Baptist Church, Michigan City, Ind., 1982.

WRITINGS:

Junior Surprise Visual Sermons with Handmade Objects (2 books), Fleming H. Revell, 1934, reissued, Visual Evangels, 1982.

Paper Tearing Trick Talks No. 1, Visual Evangels, 1967.

Fold 'n' Cut Surprise Sermonettes No. 2, Visual Evangels, 1968.

Paper Tearing Gospel Illustrations, No. 3, Visual Evangels, 1969.

Paper Tearing Bible Talks No. 4, Visual Evangels, 1970.

Paper and Scissors Truth Talks No. 5, Visual Evangels, 1971.

Gospel Magic with Home Made Stuff and Things No. 1, Visual Evangels, 1972.

Fold 'n' Cut Story Sermonettes No. 6, Visual Evangels, 1973.

Fold 'n' Snip Bible Bits No. 7, Visual Evangels, 1974.

Paper Tearing Evangels No. 8, Visual Evangels, 1975.

Surprise Paper Tearing Talks No. 9, Visual Evangels, 1976.

Trick Paper Tears with Gospel Truth No. 10, Visual Evangels, 1977.

Happy Surprise Junior Objectalks, Visual Evangels, 1978.

Visual Evangels No. 1, Visual Evangels, 1979.

Visual Evangels No. 2, Visual Evangels, 1979.

Visual Evangels No. 3, Visual Evangels, 1979.

Visual Evangels No. 4, Visual Evangels, 1979.

Visual Evangels No. 5, Visual Evangels, 1979.

Visual Evangels No. 6, Visual Evangels, 1979.

Eye-Gate Gospel Object Lessons No. 1, Visual Evangels, 1979.

Gospel Magic Made Easy, Visual Evangels, 1982.

Gospel Paper Tears with Surprise Climax No. 11, Visual Evangels, 1983.

The Voyage of Life on a Paper Boat, Visual Evangels, 1983.

Gospel Magic You Can Do No. 3, Visual Evangels, 1985.

ALIBI-ography: The Children's Shepherd: His Fears, Frenzies, Faith and Fun, Visual Evangels, 1985.

Gospel Surprise Paper Tears No. 13, Visual Evangels, 1986.

Bible Magic Trick Talks for Children's Church, Visual Evangels, 1987.

Magic Messages for Pulpit, Pew and Pint-Sized People, Visual Evangels, 1987.

WORK IN PROGRESS: Gospel Paper Tearing; Gospel Magic; Gospel Visual Aids with a Surprise Climax.

SIDELIGHTS: ''THAT'S AN ORDER.

''Soldiers know the meaning of 'That's an Order.' They obey or suffer the consequences—K.P. duty, company punishment or court martial.

''For years I had an order to write books, detailing what I had found effective in my nationwide Bible chautauquas in more than 5000 churches—but I was always too busy.

''Cortland, New York became my whipping post. I had just completed a three day Bible chautauqua and was loading my equipment in the rear of my station wagon. That's the last I remember.

''Along came a drunk driver without lights on his car and no control. He crushed me between his car and mine and threw me seventy feet. The bumpers crushed both legs and left one hanging by the skin. The unorthodox flight of seventy feet and the belly landing left me with a fractured skull, a demolished arm and a partly severed tongue, and an assortment of internal smash-ups.

''I spent five months in hospitals and for eight months was dressed in a mummy uniform of plaster. My almost weekly diet was surgery, totaling fourteen (now, twenty-three). I was bedfast and immobile. I was seventy-one with bones that did not knit readily. I finally emerged ambulatory.

''The Heavenly Commander-in-Chief queried, 'Now are you ready? Write those books. That's an order.' My new assignment was to be behind the scenes. No equipment was needed but a pencil and scrap paper.

''During the long nights of restlessness to the accompaniment of the clatter of bed pans and howls of fellow patient's pains, my mind suddenly became a developing tank for exposures that had pyramided through the years. Unable to write I sought the help of visitors who jotted down my thoughts, made crude drawings in a step by step procedure, under my direction to preserve the skeletons.

''Through the twenty-one years since, I spun flesh on the bones in book form. I had asked God to let me live long enough to write ten books. He has given me a bonus so now there are thirteen Gospel Paper Tearing books that largely originated in a hospital bed and that total 200 clever folds and cuts that produce Biblical Truth. Since the single snip symbols have no language barrier, they are in demand in all parts of the world by missionaries among those of whatever tongue.

''To the gold mine of paper tears I have added five books on Gospel Magic and nine books on Surprise Gospel Object Lessons, for those who teach children.

''My latest work is the 400 page *ALIBI-ography: The Childrens' Shepherd* which is the nickname awarded me because

of my work with children in mass meetings, sometimes numbering as many as 3600 in a meeting. It is the story of my checkered life, laced with humor over my seventy years of ministry as a Pastor, Evangelist and Army Wartime Chaplain. As a soldier I was obedient in two World Wars, but had to learn obedience as a soldier of the Cross by being re-assigned from the front line to a behind-the-scenes ministry.

''All of my books are published by Visual Evangels Publishing Company which I set up sixty years ago and have kept alive with the aid of my family. I am now the sole owner and also the sole employee.

''I write a book, send the manuscript to myself, approve it and set to work to publish it. I do the drawings, editing, proofreading, typesetting, photographing, printing, collating, covers, binding, advertising and mail order selling.

''For the past ten years I have been giving workshops on paper tearing at the International Convention of Christian Magicians at Winona Lake, Indiana Conference grounds made famous as the home of Billy Sunday and Homer Rodeheaver.

''Usually scouts in private enterprise frequent such places, looking for the freakiest freaks who might aid in their enterprise. One year I was selected for book material, and last year was chosen to make video tapes for world wide distribution to missionaries who in turn will train natives in this little known gospel approach. I went to Dallas, Texas and gave twenty-eight messages before lights and cameras, with how to do it demonstrations all in a single day. I had to make six changes of clothes, the most I have had since I was house broken. These tapes can now be rented by bookstores and churches who plan teacher training workshops in a six week series.

''For a hobby I construct musical instruments, musical bells and choral concert glasses guaranteed to self-destruct if dropped. They have thirty tones. About 500 have gone out as far as Germany, Japan, South America, Canada, Mexico, and Puerto Rico since 1961, the time I retired for two weeks. I have retired four times since.

''To occupy my spare time, I have just enrolled in a correspondence course in journalism to learn how to write for children. After my now twenty-seven books on the subject I want to learn how to do it.

''I praise God for giving me daily strength for the many tasks that pyramid day by day. He helps me put my priorities in order and supplies grace during this rapidly passing time while I am in his Waiting Room.

''Now ninety-one, I am still active serving as a 'girl friday' in local churches when pastors get sick, lazy or dead.''

WOODS, George (Allen) 1926-1988

OBITUARY NOTICE—See sketch in *SATA* Volume 30: Born January 26, 1926, in Lake Placid, N.Y.; died of lung cancer, August 11, 1988, in Englewood, N.J. Journalist, editor, and author. Woods was children's book editor for the *New York Times* from 1963 to 1984, when he became editor of the *New York Times Large Type Weekly.* Prior to working at the *Times,* Woods held a variety of positions with the *New York Times Book Review.* His own writings include *Vibrations,* and the mystery *Catch a Killer,* which won the 1974 Dorothy Canfield Fisher Award.

Woods also regularly contributed articles on children's literature to the *Encyclopedia Americana Yearbook* and taught classes on children's literature at Fordham University in 1976 and 1979, and at Marymount College in 1977 and 1978. His works are included in the Kerlan Collection at the University of Minnesota.

FOR MORE INFORMATION SEE:

Clare D. Kinsman and Mary Ann Tennenhouse, editors, *Contemporary Authors,* Volumes 29-32R, Gale, 1972.

OBITUARIES

New York Times, August 13, 1988.
Chicago Tribune, August 14, 1988.
Publishers Weekly, August 26, 1988.
School Library Journal, September, 1988.

WORK, Virginia 1946-

PERSONAL: Born September 26, 1946, in Moscow, Idaho; daughter of Vernon Melvin (a school employee) and Gloria (a housewife; maiden name, Salisbury) Stanton; married Daniel Work (a minister and teacher), December 21, 1969; children: Brian, Sherry, Vicki. *Education:* Multnomah School of the Bible, certificate, 1969. *Home address:* P.O. Box 1145, Lillooet, British Columbia, Canada VOK 1VO.

CAREER: Arctic Missions, Inc., Gresham, Ore., missionary teacher, 1969-75; independent missionary work, 1975-77; Canadian Sunday School Mission, Winnipeg, Manitoba, missionary, 1977—; author of books for young adults.

WRITINGS:

MYSTERY NOVELS FOR YOUNG ADULTS

Jodi: The Mystery of the Missing Message, Moody, 1980.
Jodi: The Secret of the Silver Box, Moody, 1980.
Jodi: The Curse of the Broken Feather, Moody, 1981.
Jodi: Mystery at Miser's Mansion, Moody, 1982.
Jodi: The Secret of the Alaskan Gift, Moody, 1983.
Apples of Gold: Proverbs for Today, Canadian Sunday School Mission, 1984.

Also author of *Ruth: A Beautiful Friend* (historical novel), published by Tyndale.

WORK IN PROGRESS: Dead Pigeons Don't Talk, a young adult mystery novel.

SIDELIGHTS: "For me, writing is a ministry whereby I can communicate God's timeless principles for living to young people. I wanted to write a mystery—a really good mystery—but a mystery with something more. I wanted to write a story that would not only entertain and captivate, but also teach some of the lessons I have learned that have been valuable in my own experience.

"I feel a burden for our young people of today. They face pressures and problems that are unique and often devastating. Many adults are afraid or too ignorant to show these young people a better way. We do not hear authoritative directives to young people about how they should live or make decisions. Somewhere there should be someone who can tell these children the principles of God's wisdom.

"I do not preach. I weave my message into the fabric of my story. I present my characters as real people with real problems

who find real answers based on the biblical principles that have influenced my own life.

"Writing, even rewriting, is pure joy for me. I recognize it is hard; it takes time and discipline and perseverance, but I love it. I read a great deal as well, and this fires my imagination and motivation. I find great personal satisfaction in learning how my books have helped others to grow and mature in their faith and walk with God. I do not look for the money that comes from writing, nor the prestige, nor recognition, but the joy of serving God."

ZARINS, Joyce Audy 1949-
(Joyce Audy dos Santos)

PERSONAL: Born January 14, 1949, in Methuen, Mass.; daughter of Armand Joseph (a glazier) and Marie Rose (an accountant; maiden name, Robidoux) Audy; married second husband, Egils Zarins (an electrical engineer), May 5, 1984; children: (first marriage) Carl Philip Emmanuel, Eric Ruben, Melody Aimee. *Education:* Attended Massachusetts College of Art, 1967-69, 1971-73, Harvard Graduate School of De-

Duffy put a kiss on his cheek. ■ (From *Piskies, Spriggans, and Other Magical Beings,* retold by Shirley Climo. Illustrated by Joyce Audy dos Santos.)

sign, 1980, and School of the Museum of Fine Arts, Boston, 1984-88. *Home:* Merrimac, Mass.

CAREER: Lawrence General Hospital, Lawrence, Mass., accounting clerk, 1966; while a student worked at a variety jobs including office work, waitress, and diet aide in the Boston area, 1966-74; author and illustrator, 1976—; ATSA Associates, Haverhill, Mass., designer, 1980-81; Merrimack Publishers Circle, Topsfield, Mass., designer, 1982-84; Ayer Publishing Co., Salem, N.H., free-lance designer, 1985-86; Andover Bookstore, Andover, Mass., part-time, 1988. Workshop leader, Continuing Education Division of Northern Essex Community College, 1987—. Town director of Merrimac Soccer Club (youth soccer program), 1983-84; member, Merrimac Arts Council, 1986-89. *Exhibitions:* Concord Art Association, Mass., 1975; Marblehead Art Association, Mass., 1975; Master Eagle Gallery, New York, N.Y., 1981. *Member:* Society of Children's Book Writers, Graphic Artist's Guild, Audubon Society, Museum of Fine Arts, Museum of Science. *Awards, honors: Mrs. Peloki's Snake* was named one of International Reading Assocation's Children's Choices, 1981; *Henri and the Loup-Garou* was named a Notable Children's Trade Book in the Field of Social Studies by the National Council for Social Studies and the Children's Book Council, 1982.

WRITINGS:

SELF-ILLUSTRATED

Toasted Bagels: A Break-of-the-Day Book, Coward, 1988.

ALL SELF-ILLUSTRATED; ALL UNDER NAME JOYCE AUDY DOS SANTOS

Sand Dollar, Sand Dollar, Lippincott, 1980.
The Diviner, Lippincott, 1980.
Henri and the Loup-Garou, Pantheon, 1982.
Giants of Smaller Worlds: Drawn in Their Natural Sizes, Dodd, 1983.

ILLUSTRATOR

Joanne Oppenheim, *Mrs. Peloki's Substitute,* Dodd, 1987.
L. Lawlor, *How to Survive Third Grade,* A. Whitman, 1988.
Joanne L. Henry, *Log Cabin in the Woods: A True Story about a Pioneer Boy,* Four Winds, 1988.

ILLUSTRATOR; ALL UNDER NAME JOYCE AUDY DOS SANTOS

Michelle Dionetti, *The Day Eli Went Looking for Bear,* Addison-Wesley, 1980.
J. Oppenheim, *Mrs. Peloki's Snake,* Dodd, 1980.
Shirley Climo, reteller, *Piskies, Spriggans, and Other Magical Beings,* Crowell, 1981.
Jane Thayer, *Gus Was a Real Dumb Ghost,* Morrow, 1982.
Barbara Heine Costikyan, *Be Kind to Your Dog at Christmas: And Other Ways to Have Happy Holidays and a Lucky New Year,* Pantheon, 1982.
Ron Roy, *Million Dollar Jeans,* Dutton, 1983.
Stephen Mooser, *Orphan Jeb at the Massacree,* Knopf, 1984.
J. Oppenheim, *Mrs. Peloki's Class Play,* Dodd, 1984.

Also illustrator of educational books and book jackets. Contributor of illustrations to periodicals, including *Cobblestone, Faces, Yankee, Cricket, Boston Globe,* and *New England Outdoors.*

WORK IN PROGRESS: Nymph, Naiad, Larva: Discovering Insect Young; The People of Little Round House; The Driftwood Dragon.

SIDELIGHTS: "Writing and illustrating, like all worthwhile disciplines, are demanding endeavors which offer exhilarating rewards. Patricia MacLachlan, speaking at a conference in Amherst, compared the publication of a book to having a baby. The conception of a story is a deeply personal experience; there is much emotion involved in nurturing the words into growth and sometimes considerable give and take with an editor. The end result, the book itself, is a jewel in your heart. For me it is a source of enormous pride and satisfaction.

"I've always been curious about the natural world. When I was in grammar school I read a series of natural history books for young readers. I would read about reptiles then find myself with a few friends in the field behind the cemetery where 'Butchie' showed me the best way to catch snakes. Butchie was a tough kid, the kind who would use the beam from his magnifying glass to fry ants just for the fun of it. His house was right behind ours, so my sister, brother and I couldn't avoid him. I watched him torment my sister with a garter snake (all she needed was the sight of anything crawly to set her off and crying). I determined not to let him frighten me that way. I thought that if I showed him that I wasn't afraid, he'd go away and leave us alone. Just saying so wasn't enough, though. That's when I learned to catch snakes, like it or not!

"I discovered wonderful things while out in the field. For instance, many blades of grass would have what we called 'snakespit.' Eventually I learned to look for the larvae of the spittlebug that was hiding in the protective 'spit.' Little finches and warblers would be harvesting seeds, and I would look them up later to find out what they were.

"The librarian in the children's room was very helpful. Although she had cerebral palsy, which affected her posture and made her struggle just to hold a pencil, she didn't let it distract her from her books. She introduced me to the 'Nancy Drew' series of adventure stories, and when I finished those, *Charlotte's Web, The Wind in the Willows, The Secret Garden, Alice in Wonderland, 20,000 Leagues under the Sea* and so many more.

"One reason there was so much time for reading was that I was sick often. Breathing was sometimes difficult for me and there would be more than one visit to the hospital and an oxygen tent before I became an adult. The books I read then were alter ego machines teleporting me into wonderful, exciting experiences.

"My early drawings gave me an avenue of escape from the mill city where I grew up. I wish I had saved some of them. I remember one that depicted an owl perched on a tree limb. Far below, a man and a boy were standing, looking up at the owl. I must have struggled with the foreshortening from this perspective, showing the upturned faces, the tops of their shoulders, and their shoes, because I've never been tall enough to really look down on anyone! I had never seen a real owl, but the drawing showed how fascinating I thought they were.

"Motherhood has been an inspiration to me, too. I have three lovely children, Carl, Eric, and Melody, who have brought a richness to my life I couldn't have found any other way. Of all the many things we do together the best was our bedtime stories. When Carl was very young I had an excuse to go back to reading picture books. Dozens would be carried home from the library and we'd all snuggle together on the bed to experience the wonderful stories and beautiful pictures. For years I channeled my creative instincts toward home and family. I made winter coats, curtains, and little dresses. I learned silk screen printing and jewelry making, macrame and other things. I had an opportunity to teach at a family-youth center nearby. One of the projects the children in my class worked on was a giant mural of a dinosaur. It was magnificent, with all kinds of designs on its body and lots of flowers and butterflies around it. Those inner city kids know all about such beautiful things, too. But of all the stimulants around me, sharing the picture books with my children fascinated me most.

"There is a peaceful wildlife reserve on Plum Island that offers salt marshes, beach plums, deer, egrets, ibises and much more. As you follow the meandering boardwalk from one of the parking lots down toward the ocean, the bayberry and false heather eventually give way to beachpeas with their charming flowers, sea grass drawing circles on the sand, then the rolling dunes. The sand carpets seven miles of beach fringing the surging ocean. A perfect place to bring a child!

"Carl, my oldest, loved it there. Eventually Eric and Melody joined him. They made sand castles and collected shells. They invented sock throwing contests where each filled a sock with sand, then clutched the open end, and swung it a full 360 degrees from the shoulder. The sock got long and skinny and spun faster and faster. Then they let it fly to see whose went the farthest.

"When I realized that the children and I would be starting a new life, I decided to make picture books. I could work at home where Carl, Eric and Melody needed me to be, and we all believed in what I was doing. My first book happened because Eric was afraid of the waves when we first took him to Plum Island. His fear came from his perception of how enormous and powerful the ocean was. *Sand Dollar, Sand Dollar* was my perception of the feelings Eric had to deal with.

"Melody helped in her own way with those pictures. While I sat drawing Peter, the boy in the story, she climbed onto my lap to watch. I asked Melody what kind of design I should put on Peter's beach hat. She suggested airplanes, a fine idea. It was only after *Sand Dollar, Sand Dollar* was published that I found out why. Melody explained to one of her friends that she had thought of airplanes because as we drive to the refuge on Plum Island we pass a small airport bustling with private planes. There is something else about that book that was a wonderful surprise. When the first copy of it came, I looked it over and read it and reread it—I was so proud of my first book—and I took off the paper dust jacket so I could look at the attractive three piece binding. There, embossed on the cover, was one of my sand dollar pictures.

"Sometimes the impetus for my commitment to work on an idea comes from outside sources as well. A visit to a museum

It was nothing but a fat gray string from a dirty old mop. ■ (From *Mrs. Peloki's Snake* by Joanne Oppenheim. Illustrated by Joyce Audy dos Santos.)

inspired my first book on insects, *Giants of Smaller Worlds.* When I started talking to the children who stream through this house every day, to show my enthusiasm for those giant insects, they gave the concept good reviews. While showing an editor my portfolio, I was asked what my plans were for future projects. I told her I wanted to write about the enormous specimens I had seen at the museum and she suggested that I send the manuscript to her when it was ready.

"I began my research in earnest, and discovered a good variety of giant insects with diversified lifestyles. The people who work with the specimens freely showed enthusiasm similar to my own. I enjoyed listening to Dr. Carpenter (who is a youthful eighty) discuss fossil insects over a cup of tea in his office. He showed me some of his meganeura specimens and publications. He gave me visual material specific enough to work from. When I thanked him for his generous hospitality he responded that he was merely 'spreading the word!' The thought crossed my mind that he and the other entomologists could feel that a simple forty-eight page book for children would not warrant their offering of time and information. Of course, this is not the case. These men, who have spent their entire lives learning and teaching, know quite well that the seeds of an inquiring mind are planted young. I hope to spend a good deal of energy sharing my curiosity, not only with my husband and children, but also with children everywhere.

"I've found other people who love children's books, and spend lots of time sharing beautiful things with them. Each of those people have helped me understand my work a little more. But children have taught me the most. Albert Einstein once said, 'Everything should be as simple as possible, but no simpler.' That is the way children see the world, with the pure uncluttered vision I admire.

"We live in a fine old Victorian house across the street from a brook and the town forest. The river is a half mile down the road and hummingbirds and hummingbird moths visit the tall pink phlox outside our kitchen windows. My husband Egils loves books, too. He reads with us, helps Carl build magic tricks, fixes the bikes, and we all go hiking and to concerts. We find feathers and oak galls and when we canoed down the Saco River we found strange cone shaped nets in the water. Were they made by some insect perhaps? I wonder. . . ."

FOR MORE INFORMATION SEE:

COLLECTIONS

De Grummond Collection at the University of Southern Mississippi.

ZELAZNY, Roger 1937-
(Harrison Denmark)

PERSONAL: Born May 13, 1937, in Cleveland, Ohio; son of Joseph Frank (a pattern maker) and Josephine (Sweet) Zelazny; married Judith Callahan (a social insurance specialist), August 20, 1966; children: Devin, Trent, Shannon. *Education:* Western Reserve University (now Case Western Reserve University), B.A., 1959; Columbia University, M.A., 1962. *Politics:* Democrat. *Home:* Santa Fe, New Mexico. *Agent:* Kirby McCauley Ltd., 432 Park Ave. S., Suite 1509, New York, N.Y. 10016.

CAREER: U.S. Social Security Administration, claims representative in Cleveland, Ohio, 1962-65, social insurance specialist in Baltimore, Md., 1965-69; writer, 1962—. Speaker;

ROGER ZELAZNY

teacher at writer's workshops and conventions. *Military service:* U.S. Army Reserve, 1960-66. *Member:* Science Fiction Writers of America (secretary-treasurer, 1967-68), Authors Guild, Authors League of America, National Space Society, Ohioana Library Association, Santa Fe Chamber of Commerce, Science Fiction Oral History Association, Science Fiction Research Association.

AWARDS, HONORS: Nebula Award for Best Novella from the Science Fiction Writers of America, 1965, for "He Who Shapes," and 1975, for "Home Is the Hangman"; Nebula Award for Best Novelette, 1965, for "The Doors of His Face, the Lamps of His Mouth"; Hugo Award from the World Science Fiction Convention, 1966, for Best Science Fiction Novel, ". . .And Call Me Conrad" (title as serialized), 1968, for Best Novel, for *Lord of Light,* 1976, for Best Novella, for "Home Is the Hangman," 1982, for Best Novelette, for "Unicorn Variation," 1986, for Best Novella, for "Twenty-four Views of Mt. Fuji, by Hohusai," and 1987, for Best Novelette, for "Permafrost."

Prix Apollo, 1972, for the French edition of *Isle of the Dead;* Guest of Honor, 1974, at the World Science Fiction Convention, Washington, D.C., and 1978, at the Australian National Science Fiction Convention, Melbourne; *Doorways in the Sand* was selected one of American Library Association's Best Books for Young Adults, 1976; Balrog Award for Short Fiction, 1980, for "The Last Defender of Camelot," and for Best Collection, 1984, for *Unicorn Variations;* Daicon Award, 1984, for the Japanese translation of "Unicorn Variation"; U.S. Guest of Honor, 1984, European Science Fiction Convention, Brighton, England; Locus Award for Best Fantasy Novel, 1986, for *Trumps of Doom; A Dark Traveling* was selected one of New York Public Library's Books for the Teen Age, 1988.

WRITINGS:

OF INTEREST TO YOUNG ADULTS

This Immortal (expanded version of ". . .And Call Me Conrad,'' first published as magazine serial, 1965), Ace Books, 1966.

The Dream Master (expanded version of ''He Who Shapes,'' first published as magazine serial, 1965), Ace Books, 1966.

Four for Tomorrow, Ace Books, 1967, published in England as *A Rose for Ecclesiastes,* Hart-Davis, 1969.

Lord of Light, Doubleday, 1967.

(Editor) *Nebula Award Stories 3,* Doubleday, 1968.

Isle of the Dead, Ace Books, 1969.

Damnation Alley, Putnam, 1969.

Creatures of Light and Darkness, Doubleday, 1969.

The Doors of His Face, the Lamps of His Mouth and Other Stories, Doubleday, 1971.

Jack of Shadows, Walker, 1971.

Today We Choose Faces, New American Library, 1973.

To Die in Italbar, Doubleday, 1973.

This Immortal, Ace, 1973.

Bridge of Ashes, New American Library, 1976.

My Name Is Legion, Ballantine, 1976.

(With Samuel R. Delany) *Dialogue for Dreams,* Algol, 1976.

Doorways in the Sand, Harper, 1976.

(With Philip K. Dick) *Deus Irae,* Doubleday, 1976.

The Illustrated Roger Zelazny, Baronet, 1978.

Four Roger Zelazny Novels (contains *Bridge of Ashes, Damnation Alley, Lord of Light,* and *Nine Princes in Amber*), G. K. Hall, 1979.

Roadmarks, Del Rey/Ballantine, 1979.

The Last Defender of Camelot, Underwood-Miller (paperback), 1980, (hardcover), 1981.

For a Breath I Tarry, Underwood-Miller, 1980.

When Pussywillows Last in the Catyard Bloomed (poetry), Norstrilia Press, 1980.

The Changing Land, Underwood-Miller, 1981.

(Jacket illustration by Margo Herr from *To Die in Italbar* by Roger Zelazny.)

Changeling, Ace, 1981.

Madwand, Phantasia Press, 1981.

(With Fred Saberhagen) *Coils,* Simon & Schuster, 1982.

To Spin Is Miracle Cat (poetry), Underwood-Miller, 1982.

Eye of the Cat, Simon & Schuster, 1982.

Dilvish, the Damned, Ballantine (paperback), 1982, Underwood-Miller (hardcover), 1983.

Unicorn Variations (collection), Simon & Schuster, 1983.

A Dark Traveling, Walker, 1987.

''AMBER'' SERIES

Nine Princes in Amber, Doubleday, 1969.

The Guns of Avalon, Doubleday, 1972.

Sign of the Unicorn, Doubleday, 1975.

The Hand of Oberon, Doubleday, 1976.

The Courts of Chaos, Doubleday, 1978.

The Chronicles of Amber, 2 Volumes, Doubleday, 1979.

A Rhapsody in Amber (chapbook), Cheap Street, 1981.

Trumps of Doom, Arbor House, 1985.

Blood of Amber, Arbor House, 1986.

Sign of Chaos, Arbor House, 1987.

ORIGINATOR; ''ALIEN SPEEDWAY'' SERIES

Clypsis, Bantam, 1987.

Pitfall, Bantam, 1988.

The Web, Bantam, 1988.

CONTRIBUTOR TO ANTHOLOGIES

Judith Merril, editor, *The Year's Best Science Fiction,* 10th annual edition, Delacorte, 1965.

J. C. Reid, editor, *40 Short, Short Stories,* Edward Arnold, 1965.

The Best from Fantasy and Science Fiction, Doubleday, annually, 1965-67.

Great Science Fiction from Amazing, Ultimate, 1966.

New Worlds, Compact Books, 1966.

Damon Knight, editor, *Nebula Awards Stories 1965,* Doubleday, 1966.

Fred Pohl, editor, *Ninth Galaxy Reader,* Doubleday, 1966.

Tom Boardman, Jr., editor, *An ABC of Science Fiction,* New English Library, 1966.

Harlan Ellison, editor, *Dangerous Visions,* Doubleday, 1967.

Michael Moorcock, editor, *The Best SF from New Worlds,* Berkely, 1967.

Terry Carr, editor, *New Worlds of Fantasy,* Ace Books, 1967.

The Last Defender of Camelot, Pocket Books, 1980.

Zelazny's works have been translated into French, Spanish, Portuguese, Italian, German, Dutch, Swedish, Greek, Hebrew, Japanese, Chinese, Russian, Polish, Finnish, Hungarian and Serbo-Croatian. Many have also been adapted into Braille and as Talking Books. Contributor of more than 150 short stories, some under pseudonym Harrison Denmark, to periodicals, including *Amazing Stories, Fantastic, Galaxy, Literary Cavalcade, Magazine of Fantasy and Science Fiction, Magazine of Horror, Worlds of Tomorrow, Worlds of If, Analog, Antaeus, Ariel, Destinies, Future Life, Heavy Metal, Isaac Asimov's Science-Fiction Adventure Magazine, Isaac Asimov's Science-Fiction Magazine, Knight, Omni, Satellite Orbit, Saturday Evening Post, Science-Fiction Digest, Sorcerer's Apprentice, Twilight Zone, Unearth, Whispers, Writer, Writers Digest Yearbook,* and *New Worlds.*

ADAPTATIONS:

''Damnation Alley'' (motion picture; starring Jan-Michael Vincent, George Peppard, and Dominique Sanda), Twentieth Century-Fox, 1977.

Poster advertising the Japanese run of "Damnation Alley."

"The Last Defender of Camelot" (television episode on "Twilight Zone"; starring Richard Kiley, Jenny Agutter, Norman Lloyd, and Cameron Mitchell), CBS-TV, April 11, 1986.

"Nine Princes in Amber" (computer game based on the first two novels in the "Amber" series), Telarium, 1985.

WORK IN PROGRESS: Ghostwheel; Frost and Fire; The Black Throne with Fred Saberhagen.

SIDELIGHTS: "I was born on May 13, 1937 and received my B.A. from Western Reserve University in 1959. I attended Columbia for graduate work and received my M.A. there in 1962, in English and Comparative Literature."[1] Zelazny did his graduate studies in the area of Elizabethan and Jacobean drama, which, he says, "probably influenced my writing considerably, both thematically and stylistically. I read French and German and am interested in general science, Oriental culture, poetry, martial arts, religion, dramatic literature, arms and armaments."

Zelazny began free lancing in 1962 while working for the Social Security Administration in Cleveland, Ohio. From that time until he became a full-time writer in 1969, he produced a multitude of stories that appeared in magazines like *Amazing Stories* and *Fantastic,* sometimes under the pseudonym Harrison Denmark. During those years he received sixteen nominations for the Hugo and Nebula Awards, winning each one twice. "For a little over seven years, from early 1962 to early 1969, I worked for the Social Security Administration as a claims representative in Ohio and, in the final four, as a claims policy specialist in the SSA Central Office. . .in Baltimore.

"I began that job and my first adult attempts at fiction in the same month, back in 1962. I kept the two sections of my life compartmentalized from the beginning. My first published story was 'Passion Play,' which appeared in the August, 1962 *Amazing Stories.* Before that, long before, somewhere between the ages of eleven and sixteen, I must have accumulated over a hundred rejection slips, but I stopped submitting stories after I graduated high school and did not begin again until February of '62.

"My first couple dozen sales were mainly short things—the two longest were 'A Rose for Ecclesiastes' and 'The Doors of His Face, the Lamps of His Mouth.' After about a year, I wrote 'The Ides of Octember,' which Cele Goldsmith, the editor of *Amazing,* rechristened 'He Who Shapes'—a much better title in my opinion—I had just slapped on the first thing that came into my mind. After that came '. . .And Call Me Conrad,' which was really my first novel. Subsequently, I expanded 'He Who Shapes' into its *The Dream Master* length. I had not attempted any novels prior to these efforts.

"No, there is no truth to the rumor that in order to escape my job with the government I undertook an excessive quantity of contracts that depressed the quality of my work; as well as presented me with a personal crisis of confidence in my ability to fulfill all those contracts."[1]

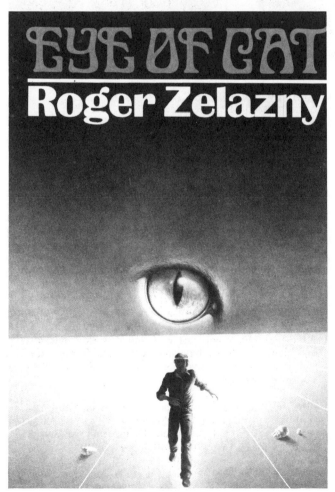

(Jacket illustration by Sonja Lamut and Nenad Jakesvic from *Eye of Cat* by Roger Zelazny.)

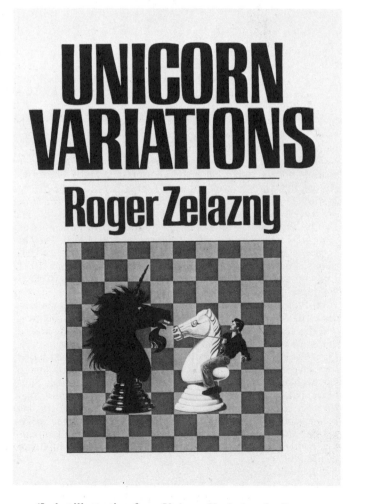

(Jacket illustration from *Unicorn Variations* by Roger Zelazny.)

(From the movie "Damnation Alley," starring Jan-Michael Vincent, Dominique Sanda and Paul Winfield. Copyright © 1977 by Twentieth Century-Fox Film Corp.)

In 1972 Zelazny was the recipient of the Prix Apollo for the French edition of *Isle of the Dead;* "Home Is the Hangman" garnered him both the Hugo and Nebula for best novella of 1975. In the 1970s he began devoting more of his time to writing novels rather than the shorter novelettes or stories. Among these are the well-known "Amber" series (*Nine Princes in Amber, The Guns of Avalon, Sign of the Unicorn, The Hand of Oberon,* and *The Courts of Chaos*), *Jack of Shadows,* and *To Die in Italbar.* His works have appeared in numerous anthologies, including *Four for Tomorrow* (Ace, 1967), *The Last Defender of Camelot* (Pocket Books, 1980), and *Unicorn Variations* (Pocket Books, 1983). "What have I done since 1972? I moved from Baltimore to Santa Fe, which is the most pleasant place I have ever lived. We are at an elevation of over 7000 feet, with the Sangre de Cristos Mountains to the east, the Ortiz Mountains to the south, the Sandias to the southwest and the Jemez to the west. It is generally sunny and clement, there are lots of pinon and juniper trees and no lawns to mow. I can easily see for sixty miles and the sunsets are spectacular. I had wanted a small town with all the amenities and none of the problems of a large urban center. As state capital, Santa Fe is that, with a population of 48,000 and no industry. New Mexico is the only state in the Union with two official languages spoken in the legislature, though you hear three spoken on the streets (Tewa's the other), and the cultural mixture makes life a bit richer. And Santa Fe is also filled with people in the arts."[1]

About his writing, Zelazny commented: "I like to keep my writing apart from the rest of my life. I make my living displaying pieces of my soul in some distorted form or other. The rest of it is my own.

"I am, by and large, against biographical criticism. Schiller used to keep rotting apples in his writing table. As he was working, he would open it every now and then and take a whiff. What does this tell you about Schiller?

"Communication is generally a form of self-expression, but the opposite does not necessarily apply. I considered myself in the communication business, not the self-expression business. They are necessarily bound up together in any piece of fiction, but I put in only as much of myself as I deem appropriate, no more, no less. If the story is a failure, it is not worth much consideration; if it is successful, then everything is in place, and it should not be necessary to ask for more.

"I never had the intention of writing the same sort of material *ad nauseum,* and. . .I have been doing a variety of things during the past few years, just as I intend to do other sorts of things in the future. I have no overall master plan for this which I can recite, however, because I would consider such a framework restrictive in itself.

"How did I get the idea for the Amber novels? I groped my way quickly through the first Amber novel, and saw my way about halfway through the second by the time I'd reached the end. By the time that I had written my way halfway through the second, the general outline of the entire series had fallen into place. Where did the initial idea come from? *Quien sabe?*"[1]

When asked to name some of the influences on his writing style, Zelazny answered: "I feel that I did my formative reading, style-wise, many years ago. I feel incapable as well as disinclined to pulling apart my way of telling things now and looking for influences. Somewhere along the line, my own style grew a protective pelt and set out scratching along its own line of development, as most writers do. You are pretty much immune to direct influence once this point is passed."[1]

FOOTNOTE SOURCES

[1] "Roger Zelazny," *Speaking of Science Fiction: The Paul Walker Interviews,* Luna Publications, 1978.

FOR MORE INFORMATION SEE:

BOOKS

Thomas D. Clareson, editor, *Many Futures, Many Worlds: Theme and Form in Science Fiction,* Kent State University Press, 1977.

Carl B. Yoke, *A Reader's Guide to Roger Zelazny,* Starmont House, 1979.

Joseph L. Sanders, *Roger Zelazny: A Primary and Secondary Bibliography,* G. K. Hall, 1980.

Dictionary of Literary Biography, Volume 8, part 2, Gale, 1981.

Contemporary Literary Criticism, Volume 21, Gale, 1982.

Tom Staicar, editor, *Critical Encounters II: Writers and Themes in Science Fiction,* Ungar, 1982.

Thomas P. Dunn and Richard D. Erlich, editors, *The Mechanical God,* Greenwood, 1982.

Daniel J. H. Levack, *Amber Dreams: A Roger Zelazny Bibliography,* Underwood-Miller, 1983.

Robert Reilly, editor, *The Transcendent Adventure: Studies of Religion in Science Fiction/Fantasy,* Greenwood, 1985.

C. B. Yoke and Donald M. Hassler, editors, *Death and the Serpent: Immortality in Science Fiction and Fantasy,* Greenwood, 1985.

Theodore Krulik, *Roger Zelazny,* Ungar/Continuum, 1986.

PERIODICALS

Baltimore Sun, January 29, 1967.

Algol, June, 1968 (p. 39ff), summer, 1976 (p. 8ff).

Extrapolation, December, 1973 (p. 6ff), summer, 1980 (p. 106ff), spring, 1984 (p. 20ff).

Foundation: The Review of Science Fiction, March, 1977 (p.142ff).

Science Fiction Studies, number 4, 1977 (p. 3ff), July, 1986 (p. 182ff).

Science Fiction: A Journal of Speculative Literature, December, 1979 (p. 129ff).

New Mexico, February, 1981 (p. 30ff).

Fantasy Newsletter, September, 1983 (p. 31ff).

Writer, October, 1984, March, 1988 (p. 9ff).

Michael R. Collings, "Words and Worlds: The Creation of a Fantasy Universe in Zelazny, Lee, and Anthony," *Scope of the Fantastic: Theory, Technique, Major Authors,* Greenwood, 1985.

COLLECTIONS

Roger Zelazny Manuscript Collection at George Arendts Research Library, Syracuse University.

Special Collections at the University of Maryland—Baltimore.

Foreign Language Collection at Kent State University.

Cumulative Indexes

Illustrations Index

(In the following index, the number of the volume in which an illustrator's work appears is given *before* the colon, and the page number on which it appears is given *after* the colon. For example, a drawing by Adams, Adrienne appears in Volume 2 on page 6, another drawing by her appears in Volume 3 on page 80, another drawing in Volume 8 on page 1, and another drawing in Volume 15 on page 107.)

YABC

Index citations including this abbreviation refer to listings appearing in *Yesterday's Authors of Books for Children,* also published by Gale Research Inc., which covers authors who died prior to 1960.

A

Aas, Ulf *5:*174
Abbé, S. van
   See van Abbé, S.
Abel, Raymond *6:*122; *7:*195; *12:*3; *21:*86;
   *25:*119
Abrahams, Hilary *26:*205; *29:*24-25; *53:*61
Abrams, Kathie *36:*170
Abrams, Lester *49:*26
Accorsi, William *11:*198
Acs, Laszlo *14:*156; *42:*22
Adams, Adrienne *2:*6; *3:*80; *8:*1; *15:*107 *16:*180;
   *20:*65; *22:*134-135; *33:*75; *36:*103, 112; *39:*74
Adams, John Wolcott *17:*162
Adams, Norman *55:*82
Adamson, George *30:*23, 24
Addams, Charles *55:*5
Adkins, Alta *22:*250
Adkins, Jan *8:*3
Adler, Peggy *22:*6; *29:*31
Adler, Ruth *29:*29
Adragna, Robert *47:*145
Agard, Nadema *18:*1
Agre, Patricia *47:*195
Ahl, Anna Maria *32:*24
Aichinger, Helga *4:*5, 45
Aitken, Amy *31:*34
Akaba, Suekichi *46:*23; *53:*127
Akasaka, Miyoshi *YABC 2:*261
Akino, Fuku *6:*144
Alain *40:*41
Alajalov *2:*226
Albrecht, Jan *37:*176
Albright, Donn *1:*91
Alcorn, John *3:*159; *7:*165; *31:*22; *44:*127;
   *46:*23, 170
Alda, Arlene *44:*24
Alden, Albert *11:*103
Aldridge, Andy *27:*131
Alex, Ben *45:*25, 26
Alexander, Lloyd *49:*34
Alexander, Martha *3:*206; *11:*103; *13:*109;
   *25:*100; *36:*131
Alexeieff, Alexander *14:*6; *26:*199
Aliki.
   See Brandenberg, Aliki
Allamand, Pascale *12:*9
Allan, Judith *38:*166
Alland, Alexandra *16:*255
Allen, Gertrude *9:*6
Allen, Graham *31:*145
Allen, Pamela *50:*25, 26-27, 28
Allen, Rowena *47:*75
Allison, Linda *43:*27
Almquist, Don *11:*8; *12:*128; *17:*46; *22:*110
Aloise, Frank *5:*38; *10:*133; *30:*92
Althea
   See Braithwaite, Althea
Altschuler, Franz *11:*185; *23:*141; *40:*48; *45:*29;
   *57:*181

Ambrus, Victor G. *1:*6-7, 194; *3:*69; *5:*15; *6:*44;
   *7:*36; *8:*210; *12:*227; *14:*213; *15:*213; *22:*209;
   *24:*36; *28:*179; *30:*178; *32:*44, 46; *38:*143;
   *41:*25, 26, 27, 28, 29, 30, 31, 32; *42:*87;
   *44:*190; *55:*172
Ames, Lee J. *3:*12; *9:*130; *10:*69; *17:*214;
   *22:*124
Amon, Aline *9:*9
Amoss, Berthe *5:*5
Amundsen, Dick *7:*77
Amundsen, Richard E. *5:*10; *24:*122
Ancona, George *12:*11; *55:*144
Anderson, Alasdair *18:*122
Anderson, Brad *33:*28
Anderson, Carl *7:*4
Anderson, C. W. *11:*10
Anderson, Doug *40:*111
Anderson, Erica *23:*65
Anderson, Laurie *12:*153, 155
Anderson, Wayne *23:*119; *41:*239; *56:*7
Andrew, John *22:*4
Andrews, Benny *14:*251; *31:*24; *57:*6, 7
Anelay, Henry *57:*173
Angel, Marie *47:*22
Angelo, Valenti *14:*8; *18:*100; *20:*232; *32:*70
Anglund, Joan Walsh *2:*7, 250-251; *37:*198,
   199, 200
Anno, Mitsumasa *5:*7; *38:*25, 26-27, 28, 29, 30,
   31, 32
Antal, Andrew *1:*124; *30:*145
Apple, Margot *33:*25; *35:*206; *46:*81; *53:*8
Appleyard, Dev *2:*192
Aragonés, Sergio *48:*23, 24, 25, 26, 27
Araneus *40:*29
Archer, Janet *16:*69
Ardizzone, Edward *1:*11, 12; *2:*105; *3:*258; *4:*78;
   *7:*79; *10:*100; *15:*232; *20:*69, 178; *23:*223;
   *24:*125; *28:*25, 26, 27, 28, 29, 30, 31, 33,
   34, 35, 36, 37; *31:*192, 193; *34:*215, 217;
   *YABC 2:*25
Arenella, Roy *14:*9
Armer, Austin *13:*3
Armer, Laura Adams *13:*3
Armer, Sidney *13:*3
Armitage, David *47:*23
Armitage, Eileen *4:*16
Armstrong, George *10:*6; *21:*72
Arno, Enrico *1:*217; *2:*22, 210; *4:*9; *5:*43; *6:*52;
   *29:*217, 219; *33:*152; *35:*99; *43:*31, 32, 33;
   *45:*212, 213, 214
Arnosky, Jim *22:*20
Arrowood, Clinton *12:*193; *19:*11
Arting, Fred J. *41:*63
Artzybasheff, Boris *13:*143; *14:*15; *40:*152, 155
Aruego, Ariane *6:*4
   See also Dewey, Ariane
Aruego, Jose *4:*140; *6:*4; *7:*64; *33:*195; *35:*208
Asch, Frank *5:*9
Ashby, Gail *11:*135
Ashby, Gwynneth *44:*26
Ashley, C. W. *19:*197
Ashmead, Hal *8:*70
Aska, Warabe *56:* 10
Assel, Steven *44:*153
Astrop, John *32:*56
Atene, Ann *12:*18

Atherton, Lisa *38:*198
Atkinson, J. Priestman *17:*275
Atkinson, Wayne *40:*46
Attebery, Charles *38:*170
Atwood, Ann *7:*9
Augarde, Steve *25:*22
Austerman, Miriam *23:*107
Austin, Margot *11:*16
Austin, Robert *3:*44
Auth, Tony *51:*5
Avedon, Richard *57:*140
Averill, Esther *1:*17; *28:*39, 40, 41
Axeman, Lois *2:*32; *11:*84; *13:*165; *22:*8; *23:*49
Ayer, Jacqueline *13:*7
Ayer, Margaret *15:*12; *50:*120

B

Babbitt, Bradford *33:*158
Babbitt, Natalie *6:*6; *8:*220
Bachem, Paul *48:*180
Back, George *31:*161
Bacon, Bruce *4:*74
Bacon, Paul *7:*155; *8:*121; *31:*55; *50:*42; *56:*175
Bacon, Peggy *2:*11, 228; *46:*44
Baker, Alan *22:*22
Baker, Charlotte *2:*12
Baker, Jeannie *23:*4
Baker, Jim *22:*24
Baldridge, Cyrus LeRoy *19:*69; *44:*50
Balet, Jan *11:*22
Balian, Lorna *9:*16
Ballantyne, R. M. *24:*34
Ballis, George *14:*199
Baltzer, Hans *40:*30
Bang, Molly Garrett *24:*37, 38
Banik, Yvette Santiago *21:*136
Banner, Angela
   See Maddison, Angela Mary
Bannerman, Helen *19:*13, 14
Bannon, Laura *6:*10; *23:*8
Baptist, Michael *37:*208
Bare, Arnold Edwin *16:*31
Bare, Colleen Stanley *32:*33
Bargery, Geoffrey *14:*258
Barker, Carol *31:*27
Barker, Cicely Mary *49:*50, 51
Barkley, James *4:*13; *6:*11; *13:*112
Barks, Carl *37:*27, 28, 29, 30-31, 32, 33, 34
Barling, Tom *9:*23
Barlow, Perry *35:*28
Barlowe, Dot *30:*223
Barlowe, Wayne *37:*72
Barner, Bob *29:*37
Barnes, Hiram P. *20:*28
Barnett, Moneta *16:*89; *19:*142; *31:*102; *33:*30,
   31, 32; *41:*153
Barney, Maginel Wright *39:*32, 33, 34; *YABC
   2:*306
Barnum, Jay Hyde *11:*224; *20:*5; *37:*189, 190
Barrauds *33:*114
Barrer-Russell, Gertrude *9:*65; *27:*31
Barrett, Angela *40:*136, 137
Barrett, John E. *43:*119
Barrett, Peter *55:*169

Einzig, Susan 3:77; 43:78
Eitzen, Allan 9:56; 12:212; 14:226; 21:194; 38:162
Eldridge, H. 54:109
Eldridge, Harold 43:83
Elgaard, Greta 19:241
Elgin, Kathleen 9:188; 39:69
Ellacott, S. E. 19:118
Elliott, Sarah M. 14.58
Ellison, Pauline 55:21
Emberley, Ed 8:53
Emberley, Michael 34:83
Emery, Leslie 49:187
Emmett, Bruce 49:147
Engle, Mort 38:64
Englebert, Victor 8:54
Enos, Randall 20:183
Enright, Maginel Wright 19:240, 243; 39:31, 35, 36
Enrique, Romeo 34:135
Epstein, Stephen 50:142, 148
Erhard, Walter 1:152
Erickson, Phoebe 11:83
Erikson, Mel 31:69
Ernst, Lisa Campbell 47:147
Escourido, Joseph 4:81
Esté, Kirk 33:111
Estoril, Jean 32:27
Estrada, Ric 5:52, 146; 13:174
Etchemendy, Teje 38:68
Ets, Marie Hall 2:102
Eulalie YABC 2:315
Evans, Katherine 5:64
E.V.B
    See Boyle, Eleanor Vere (Gordon)
Ewing, Juliana Horatia 16:92

F

Falconer, Pearl 34:23
Falls, C. B. 1:19; 38:71, 72, 73, 74
Falter, John 40:169, 170
Farmer, Andrew 49:102
Farmer, Peter 24:108; 38:75
Farquharson, Alexander 46:75
Farrell, David 40:135
Fatigati, Evelyn 24:112
Faul-Jansen, Regina 22:117
Faulkner, Jack 6:169
Fava, Rita 2:29
Fax, Elton C. 1:101; 4:2; 12:77; 25:107
Fay 43:93
Federspiel, Marian 33:51
Feelings, Tom 5:22; 8:56; 12:153 16:105; 30:196; 49:37
Fehr, Terrence 21:87
Feiffer, Jules 3:91; 8:58
Feigeles, Neil 41:242
Feller, Gene 33:130
Fellows, Muriel H. 10:42
Felts, Shirley 33:71; 48:59
Fennelli, Maureen 38:181
Fenton, Carroll Lane 5:66; 21:39
Fenton, Mildred Adams 5:66; 21:39
Ferguson, Walter M. 34:86
Fetz, Ingrid 11:67; 12:52 16:205; 17:59; 29:105; 30:108, 109; 32:149; 43:142; 56:29
Fiammenghi, Gioia 9:66; 11:44; 12:206; 13:57, 59; 52:126, 129
Field, Rachel 15:113
Fine, Peter K. 43:210
Finger, Helen 42:81
Fink, Sam 18:119
Finlay, Winifred 23:72
Fiorentino, Al 3:240
Firmin, Charlotte 29:75; 48:70
Fischel, Lillian 40:204
Fischer, Hans 25:202
Fischer-Nagel, Andreas 56: 50
Fischer-Nagel, Heiderose 56: 50
Fisher, Leonard Everett 3:6; 4:72, 86; 6:197; 9:59 16:151, 153; 23:44; 27:134; 29:26; 34:87, 89, 90, 91, 93, 94, 95, 96; 40:206; 50:150; YABC 2:169
Fisher, Lois 20:62; 21:7

Fisk, Nicholas 25:112
Fitschen, Marilyn 2:20-21; 20:48
Fitzgerald, F. A. 15:116; 25:86-87
Fitzhugh, Louise 1:94; 9:163; 45:75, 78
Fitzhugh, Susie 11:117
Fitzsimmons, Arthur 14:128
Fix, Philippe 26:102
Flack, Marjorie 21:67; YABC 2:122
Flagg, James Montgomery 17:227
Flax, Zeona 2:245
Fleishman, Seymour 14:232; 24:87
Fleming, Guy 18:41
Floethe, Richard 3:131; 4:90
Floherty, John J., Jr. 5:68
Flora, James 1:96; 30:111, 112
Florian, Douglas 19:122
Flory, Jane 22:111
Floyd, Gareth 1:74; 17:245; 48:63
Fluchère, Henri A. 40:79
Flynn, Barbara 7:31; 9:70
Fogarty, Thomas 15:89
Folger, Joseph 9:100
Folkard, Charles 22:132; 29:128, 257-258
Foott, Jeff 42:202
Forberg, Ati 12:71, 205; 14:1; 22:113; 26:22; 48:64, 65
Ford, George 24:120; 31:70, 177
Ford, H. J. 16:185-186
Ford, Pamela Baldwin 27:104
Foreman, Michael 2:110-111
Forrester, Victoria 40:83
Fortnum, Peggy 6:29; 20:179; 24:211; 26:76, 77, 78; 39:78; YABC 1:148
Foster, Brad W. 34:99
Foster, Genevieve 2:112
Foster, Gerald 7:78
Foster, Laura Louise 6:79
Foster, Marian Curtis 23:74; 40:42
Foucher, Adèle 47:118
Fowler, Mel 36:127
Fox, Charles Phillip 12:84
Fox, Jim 6:187
Fracé, Charles 15:118
Frame, Paul 2:45, 145; 9:153; 10:124; 21:71; 23:62; 24:123; 27:106; 31:48; 32:159; 34:195; 38:136; 42:55; 44:139
Francois, André 25:117
Francoise
    See Seignobosc, Francoise
Frank, Lola Edick 2:199
Frank, Mary 4:54; 34:100
Franké, Phil 45:91
Frankel, Julie 40:84, 85, 202
Frankenberg, Robert 22:116; 30:50; 38:92, 94, 95
Franklin, John 24:22
Frascino, Edward 9:133; 29:229; 33:190; 48:80, 81, 82, 83, 84- 85, 86
Frasconi, Antonio 6:80; 27:208; 53:41, 43, 45, 47, 48
Fraser, Betty 2:212; 6:185; 8:103; 31:72, 73; 43:136
Fraser, Eric 38:78; 41:149, 151
Fraser, F. A. 22:234
Frazetta, Frank 41:72
Freas, John 25:207
Freeman, Don 2:15; 13:249; 17:62-63, 65, 67-68; 18:243; 20:195; 23:213, 217; 32:155; 55:129
Fregosi, Claudia 24:117
French, Fiona 6:82-83
Friedman, Judith 43:197
Friedman, Marvin 19:59; 42:86
Frinta, Dagmar 36:42
Frith, Michael K. 15:138; 18:120
Fritz, Ronald 46:73
Fromm, Lilo 29:85; 40:197
Frost, A. B. 17:6-7; 19:123, 124, 125, 126, 127, 128, 129, 130; YABC 1:156-157, 160; 2:107
Fry, Guy 2:224
Fry, Rosalie 3:72; YABC 2:180-181
Fry, Rosalind 21:153, 168
Fryer, Elmer 34:115
Fuchs, Erich 6:84
Fuchshuber, Annegert 43:96
Fufuka, Mahiri 32:146

Fujikawa, Gyo 39:75, 76
Fulford, Deborah 23:159
Fuller, Margaret 25:189
Funai, Mamoru 38:105
Funk, Tom 7:17, 99
Furchgott, Terry 29:86
Furukawa, Mel 25:42

G

Gaberell, J. 19:236
Gackenbach, Dick 19:168; 41:81; 48:89, 90, 91, 92, 93, 94; 54:105
Gaetano, Nicholas 23:209
Gag, Flavia 17:49, 52
Gág, Wanda YABC 1:135, 137-138, 141, 143
Gagnon, Cécile 11:77
Gál, László 14:127; 52:54, 55, 56
Galazinski, Tom 55:13
Galdone, Paul 1:156, 181, 206; 2:40, 241; 3:42, 144; 4:141; 10:109, 158; 11:21; 12:118, 210; 14:12 16:36-37; 17:70-74; 18:111, 230; 19:183; 21:154; 22:150, 245; 33:126; 39:136, 137; 42:57; 51:169; 55:110
Gallagher, Sears 20:112
Galloway, Ewing 51:154
Galster, Robert 1:66
Galsworthy, Gay John 35:232
Gammell, Stephen 7:48; 13:149; 29:82; 33:209; 41:88; 50:185, 186-187; 53:51, 52-53, 54, 55, 56, 57, 58; 54:24, 25; 56:147, 148, 150; 57:27, 66
Ganly, Helen 56: 56
Gannett, Ruth Chrisman 3:74; 18:254; 33:77, 78
Gantschev, Ivan 45:32
Garbutt, Bernard 23:68
Garcia 37:71
Gardner, Earle 45:167
Gardner, Joan 40:87
Gardner, Joel 40:87, 92
Gardner, John 40:87
Gardner, Lucy 40:87
Gardner, Richard
    See Cummings, Richard, 24:119
Garland, Michael 36:29; 38:83; 44:168; 48:78, 221, 222; 49:161
Garnett, Eve 3:75
Garnett, Gary 39:184
Garraty, Gail 4:142; 52:106
Garrett, Agnes 46:110; 47:157
Garrett, Edmund H. 20:29
Garrison, Barbara 19:133
Gates, Frieda 26:80
Gaughan, Jack 26:79; 43:185
Gaver, Becky 20:61
Gay, Zhenya 19:135, 136
Geary, Clifford N. 1:122; 9:104; 51:74
Gee, Frank 33:26
Geer, Charles 1:91; 3:179; 4:201; 6:168; 7:96; 9:58; 10:72; 12:127; 39:156, 157, 158, 159, 160; 42:88, 89, 90, 91; 55:111, 116
Gehm, Charlie 36:65; 57:117
Geisel, Theodor Seuss 1:104-105, 106; 28:108, 109, 110, 111, 112, 113
Geldart, William 15:121; 21:202
Genia 4:84
Gentry, Cyrille R. 12:66
George, Jean 2:113
Gérard, Jean Ignace 45:80
Gérard, Rolf 27:147, 150
Gergely, Tibor 54:15, 16
Geritz, Franz 17:135
Gerlach, Geff 42:58
Gerrard, Roy 47:78
Gershinowitz, George 36:27
Gerstein, Mordicai 31:117; 47:80, 81, 82, 83, 84, 85, 86; 51:173
Gervase 12:27
Getz, Arthur 32:148
Gibbons, Gail 23:78
Gibbs, Tony 40:95
Gibran, Kahlil 32:116
Giesen, Rosemary 34:192-193
Giguère, George 20:111
Gilbert, John 19:184; 54:115; YABC 2:287

Pincus, Harriet _4_:186; _8_:179; _22_:148; _27_:164, 165
Pinkney, Jerry _8_:218; _10_:40; _15_:276; _20_:66; _24_:121; _33_:109; _36_:222; _38_:200; _41_:165, 166, 167, 168, 169, 170, 171, 173, 174; _44_:198; _48_:51; _53_:20; _56_:61, 68
Pinkwater, Daniel Manus _46_:180, 181, 182, 185, 188, 189, 190
Pinkwater, Manus _8_:156; _46_:180
Pinto, Ralph _10_:131; _45_:93
Pitz, Henry C. _4_:168; _19_:165; _35_:128; _42_:80; _YABC 2_:95, 176
Pitzenberger, Lawrence J. _26_:94
Plowden, David _52_:135, 136
Plummer, William _32_:31
Podwal, Mark _56_: 170, 173
Pogány, Willy _15_:46, 49; _19_:222, 256; _25_:214; _44_:142, 143, 144, 145, 146, 147, 148
Poirson, V. A. _26_:89
Polgreen, John _21_:44
Politi, Leo _1_:178; _4_:53; _21_:48; _47_:173, 174, 176, 178, 179, 180, 181
Polonsky, Arthur _34_:168
Polseno, Jo _1_:53; _3_:117; _5_:114; _17_:154; _20_:87; _32_:49; _41_:245
Ponter, James _5_:204
Poortvliet, Rien _6_:212
Portal, Colette _6_:186; _11_:203
Porter, George _7_:181
Potter, Beatrix _YABC 1_:208-210, 212, 213
Potter, Miriam Clark _3_:162
Powers, Richard M. _1_:230; _3_:218; _7_:194; _26_:186
Powledge, Fred _37_:154
Pratt, Charles _23_:29
Price, Christine _2_:247; _3_:163, 253; _8_:166
Price, Edward _33_:34
Price, Garrett _1_:76; _2_:42
Price, Hattie Longstreet _17_:13
Price, Norman _YABC 1_:129
Price, Willard _48_:184
Primavera, Elise _26_:95
Primrose, Jean _36_:109
Prince, Leonora E. _7_:170
Prittie, Edwin J. _YABC 1_:120
Provensen, Alice _37_:204, 215, 222
Provensen, Martin _37_:204, 215, 222
Pucci, Albert John _44_:154
Pudlo _8_:59
Purdy, Susan _8_:162
Pursell, Weimer _55_:18
Puskas, James _5_:141
Pyk, Jan _7_:26; _38_:123
Pyle, Howard _16_:225-228, 230-232, 235; _24_:27; _34_:124, 125, 127, 128

Q

Quackenbush, Robert _4_:190; _6_:166; _7_:175, 178; _9_:86; _11_:65, 221; _41_:154; _43_:157
Quennell, Marjorie (Courtney) _29_:163, 164
Quidor, John _19_:82
Quirk, Thomas _12_:81

R

Rackham, Arthur _15_:32, 78, 214-227; _17_:105, 115; _18_:233; _19_:254; _20_:151; _22_:129, 131, 132, 133; _23_:175; _24_:161, 181; _26_:91; _32_:118; _YABC 1_:25, 45, 55, 147; _2_:103, 142, 173, 210
Racz, Michael _56_: 134
Rafilson, Sidney _11_:172
Raible, Alton _1_:202-203; _28_:193; _35_:181
Ramsey, James _16_:41
Ramus, Michael _51_:171
Rand, Paul _6_:188
Randell, William _55_:54
Ransome, Arthur _22_:201
Rao, Anthony _28_:126
Raphael, Elaine _23_:192
Rappaport, Eva _6_:190
Raskin, Ellen _2_:208-209; _4_:142; _13_:183; _22_:68; _29_:139; _36_:134; _38_:173, 174, 175, 176, 177, 178, 179, 180, 181

Ratzkin, Lawrence _40_:143
Rau, Margaret _9_:157
Raverat, Gwen _YABC 1_:152
Ravielli, Anthony _1_:198; _3_:168; _11_:143
Ray, Deborah
See Kogan, Deborah Ray.
Ray, Ralph _2_:239; _5_:73
Raymond, Larry _31_:108
Rayner, Mary _22_:207; _47_:140
Raynor, Dorka _28_:168
Raynor, Paul _24_:73
Razzi, James _10_:127
Read, Alexander D. "Sandy," _20_:45
Reasoner Charles,_53_:33, 36, 37
Reed, Tom _34_:171
Reid, Stephen _19_:213; _22_:89
Reinertson, Barbara _44_:150
Reiniger, Lotte _40_:185
Reiss, John J. _23_:193
Relf, Douglas _3_:63
Relyea, C. M. _16_:29; _31_:153
Rémi, Georges _13_:184
Remington, Frederic _19_:188; _41_:178, 179, 180, 181, 183, 184, 185, 186, 187, 188
Renlie, Frank _11_:200
Reschofsky, Jean _7_:118
Réthi, Lili _2_:153; _36_:156
Reusswig, William _3_:267
Rey, H. A. _1_:182; _26_:163, 164, 166, 167, 169; _YABC 2_:17
Reynolds, Doris _5_:71; _31_:77
Rhead, Louis _31_:91
Rhodes, Andrew _38_:204; _50_:163; _54_:76
Ribbons, Ian _3_:10; _37_:161; _40_:76
Rice, Elizabeth _2_:53, 214
Rice, Eve _34_:174, 175
Rice, James _22_:210
Richards, George _40_:116, 119, 121; _44_:179
Richards, Henry _YABC 1_:228, 231
Richardson, Ernest _2_:144
Richardson, Frederick _18_:27, 31
Richman, Hilda _26_:132
Richmond, George _24_:179
Rieniets, Judy King _14_:28
Riger, Bob _2_:166
Riley, Kenneth _22_:230
Ringi, Kjell _12_:171
Rios, Tere.
See Versace, Marie
Ripper, Charles L. _3_:175
Ritz, Karen _41_:117
Rivkin, Jay _15_:230
Rivoche, Paul _45_:125
Roach, Marilynne _9_:158
Robbin, Jodi _44_:156, 159
Robbins, Frank _42_:167
Robbins, Ruth _52_:102
Roberts, Cliff _4_:126
Roberts, Doreen _4_:230; _28_:105
Roberts, Jim _22_:166; _23_:69; _31_:110
Roberts, W. _22_:2, 3
Robinson, Charles _3_:53; _5_:14; _6_:193; _7_:150; _7_:183; _8_:38; _9_:81; _13_:188; _14_:248-249; _23_:149; _26_:115; _27_:48; _28_:191; _32_:28; _35_:210; _36_:37; _48_:96; _52_:33; _53_:157
Robinson, Charles 1870-1937 _17_:157, 171-173, 175-176; _24_:207; _25_:204; _YABC 2_:308-310, 331
Robinson, Charles _56_: 15
Robinson, Jerry _3_:262
Robinson, Joan G. _7_:184
Robinson, T. H. _17_:179, 181-183; _29_:254
Robinson, W. Heath _17_:185, 187, 189, 191, 193, 195, 197, 199, 202; _23_:167; _25_:194; _29_:150; _YABC 1_:44; _2_:183
Roche, Christine _41_:98
Roche, P. K. _57_:151, 152
Rocker, Fermin _7_:34; _13_:21; _31_:40; _40_:190, 191
Rockwell, Anne _5_:147; _33_:171, 173
Rockwell, Gail _7_:186
Rockwell, Harlow _33_:171, 173, 175
Rockwell, Norman _23_:39, 196, 197, 199, 200, 203, 204, 207; _41_:140, 143; _YABC 2_:60
Rodegast, Roland _43_:100
Rodriguez, Joel _16_:65
Roever, J. M. _4_:119; _26_:170
Roffey, Maureen _33_:142, 176, 177

Rogasky, Barbara _46_:90
Rogers, Carol _2_:262; _6_:164; _26_:129
Rogers, Frances _10_:130
Rogers, Walter S. _31_:135, 138
Rogers, William A. _15_:151, 153-154; _33_:35
Rojankovsky, Feodor _6_:134, 136; _10_:183; _21_:128, 129, 130; _25_:110; _28_:42
Rorer, Abigail _43_:222
Rosamilia, Patricia _36_:120
Rose, Carl _5_:62
Rose, David S. _29_:109
Rosenbaum, Jonathan _50_:46
Rosenblum, Richard _11_:202; _18_:18
Rosier, Lydia _16_:236; _20_:104; _21_:109; _22_:125; _30_:151, 158; _42_:128; _45_:214
Ross
See Thomson, Ross
Ross, Clare Romano _3_:123; _21_:45; _48_:199
Ross, Dave _32_:152; _57_:108
Ross, Herbert _37_:78
Ross, John _3_:123; _21_:45
Ross, Johnny _32_:190
Ross, Larry _47_:168
Ross, Tony _17_:204; _56_:132
Rossetti, Dante Gabriel _20_:151, 153
Roth, Arnold _4_:238; _21_:133
Rotondo, Pat _32_:158
Roughsey, Dick _35_:186
Rouille, M. _11_:96
Rounds, Glen _8_:173; _9_:171; _12_:56; _32_:194; _40_:230; _51_:161, 162, 166; _56_:149; _YABC 1_:1-3
Rowan, Evadne _52_:51
Rowe, Gavin _27_:144
Rowell, Kenneth _40_:72
Rowen, Amy _52_:143
Roy, Jeroo _27_:229; _36_:110
Rubel, Nicole _18_:255; _20_:59
Rubel, Reina _33_:217
Rud, Borghild _6_:15
Rudolph, Norman Guthrie _17_:13
Rue, Leonard Lee III _37_:164
Ruff, Donna _50_:173
Ruffins, Reynold _10_:134-135; _41_:191, 192-193, 194-195, 196
Ruhlin, Roger _34_:44
Ruse, Margaret _24_:155
Rush, Peter _42_:75
Russell Jim,_53_:134
Russell, E. B. _18_:177, 182
Russo, Susan _30_:182; _36_:144
Ruth, Rod _9_:161
Rutherford, Meg _25_:174; _34_:178, 179
Rutland, Jonathan _31_:126
Ryden, Hope _8_:176
Rymer, Alta M. _34_:181
Rystedt, Rex _49_:80

S

Saaf, Chuck _49_:179
Sabaka, Donna R. _21_:172
Sabin, Robert _45_:35
Sacker, Amy _16_:100
Saffioti, Lino _36_:176; _48_:60
Sagsoorian, Paul _12_:183; _22_:154; _33_:106
Sahlberg, Myron _57_:165
Saint Exupéry, Antoine de _20_:157
Saldutti, Denise _39_:186; _57_:178
Sale, Morton _2_:31
Sambourne, Linley _YABC 2_:181
Sampson, Katherine _9_:197
Samson, Anne S. _2_:216
Sancha, Sheila _38_:185
Sand, George X. _45_:182
Sandberg, Lasse _15_:239, 241
Sanders, Beryl _39_:173
Sanderson, Ruth _21_:126; _24_:53; _28_:63; _33_:67; _41_:48, 198, 199, 200, 201, 202, 203; _43_:79; _46_:36, 44; _47_:102; _49_:58
Sandin, Joan _4_:36; _6_:194; _7_:177; _12_:145, 185; _20_:43; _21_:74; _26_:144; _27_:142; _28_:224, 225; _38_:86; _41_:46; _42_:35
Sandland, Reg _39_:215
Sandoz, Edouard _26_:45, 47

Author Index

The following index gives the number of the volume in which an author's biographical sketch, Brief Entry, or Obituary appears.

This index includes references to all entries in the following series, which are also published by Gale Research Inc.

YABC—*Yesterday's Authors of Books for Children: Facts and Pictures about Authors and Illustrators of Books for Young People from Early Times to 1960,* Volumes 1-2

CLR—*Children's Literature Review: Excerpts from Reviews, Criticism, and Commentary on Books for Children,* Volumes 1-16

SAAS—*Something about the Author Autobiography Series,* Volumes 1-8

Brand, Christianna
   See Lewis, Mary (Christianna)
Brandenberg, Aliki (Liacouras) 1929- 35
   Earlier sketch in SATA 2
Brandenberg, Franz 1932- 35
   Earlier sketch in SATA 8
Brandhorst, Carl T(heodore) 1898- 23
Brandon, Brumsic, Jr. 1927- 9
Brandon, Curt
   See Bishop, Curtis
Brandreth, Gyles 1948- 28
Brandt, Catharine 1905- 40
Brandt, Keith
   See Sabin, Louis
Branfield, John (Charles) 1931- 11
Branley, Franklyn M(ansfield) 1915- 4
   See also CLR 13
Branscum, Robbie 1937- 23
Bransom, (John) Paul 1885-1979 43
Bratton, Helen 1899- 4
Braude, Michael 1936- 23
Brautigan, Richard (Gary) 1935-1984 56
Braymer, Marjorie 1911- 6
Brecht, Edith 1895-1975 6
   Obituary 25
Breck, Vivian
   See Breckenfeld, Vivian Gurney
Breckenfeld, Vivian Gurney 1895- 1
Breda, Tjalmar
   See DeJong, David C(ornel)
Breinburg, Petronella 1927- 11
Breisky, William J(ohn) 1928- 22
Brennan, Gale Patrick 1927-
   Brief Entry 53
Brennan, Joseph L. 1903- 6
Brennan, Tim
   See Conroy, Jack (Wesley)
Brenner, Anita 1905-1974 56
Brenner, Barbara (Johnes) 1925- 42
   Earlier sketch in SATA 4
Brenner, Fred 1920- 36
   Brief Entry 34
Brent, Hope 1935(?)-1984
   Obituary 39
Brent, Stuart 14
Brett, Bernard 1925- 22
Brett, Grace N(eff) 1900-1975 23
Brett, Hawksley
   See Bell, Robert S(tanley) W(arren)
Brett, Jan 1949- 42
Brewer, Sally King 1947- 33
Brewster, Benjamin
   See Folsom, Franklin
Brewster, Patience 1952- 51
Brewton, John E(dmund) 1898- 5
Brick, John 1922-1973 10
Bridgers, Sue Ellen 1942- 22
   See also SAAS 1
Bridges, Laurie
   See Bruck, Lorraine
Bridges, William (Andrew) 1901- 5
Bridwell, Norman 1928- 4
Brier, Howard M(axwell) 1903-1969 8
Briggs, Carole S(uzanne) 1950-
   Brief Entry 47
Briggs, Katharine Mary 1898-1980
   Obituary 25
Briggs, Peter 1921-1975 39
   Obituary 31
Briggs, Raymond (Redvers) 1934- 23
   See also CLR 10
Bright, Robert 1902- 24
Brightfield, Richard 1927-
   Brief Entry 53
Brightfield, Rick
   See Brightfield, Richard
Brightwell, L(eonard) R(obert) 1889-
   Brief Entry 29
Brimberg, Stanlee 1947- 9
Brin, Ruth F(irestone) 1921- 22
Brinckloe, Julie (Lorraine) 1950- 13
Brindel, June (Rachuy) 1919- 7
Brindze, Ruth 1903- 23
Brink, Carol Ryrie 1895-1981 31
   Earlier sketch in SATA 1
   Obituary 27

Brinsmead, H(esba) F(ay) 1922- 18
   See also SAAS 5
Briquebec, John
   See Rowland-Entwistle, (Arthur) Theodore
   (Henry)
Brisco, Pat A.
   See Matthews, Patricia
Brisco, Patty
   See Matthews, Patricia
Briscoe, Jill (Pauline) 1935- 56
   Brief Entry 47
Brisley, Joyce Lankester 1896- 22
Britt, Albert 1874-1969
   Obituary 28
Britt, Dell 1934- 1
Brittain, Bill
   See Brittain, William
   See also SAAS 7
Brittain, William 1930- 36
Britton, Kate
   See Stegeman, Janet Allais
Britton, Louisa
   See McGuire, Leslie (Sarah)
Bro, Marguerite (Harmon)
   1894-1977 19
   Obituary 27
Broadhead, Helen Cross 1913- 25
Brochmann, Elizabeth (Anne) 1938- 41
Brock, Betty 1923- 7
Brock, C(harles) E(dmund)
   1870-1938 42
   Brief Entry 32
Brock, Delia
   See Ephron, Delia
Brock, Emma L(illian) 1886-1974 8
Brock, H(enry) M(atthew) 1875-1960 42
Brockett, Eleanor Hall 1913-1967 10
Brockman, C(hristian) Frank 1902- 26
Broderick, Dorothy M. 1929- 5
Brodie, Sally
   See Cavin, Ruth (Brodie)
Broekel, Rainer Lothar 1923- 38
Broekel, Ray
   See Broekel, Rainer Lothar
Bröger, Achim 1944- 31
Brokamp, Marilyn 1920- 10
Bromhall, Winifred 26
Bromley, Dudley 1948-
   Brief Entry 51
Brommer, Gerald F(rederick) 1927- 28
Brondfield, Jerome 1913- 22
Brondfield, Jerry
   See Brondfield, Jerome
Bronowski, Jacob 1908-1974 55
Bronson, Lynn
   See Lampman, Evelyn Sibley
Bronson, Wilfrid Swancourt
   1894-1985
   Obituary 43
Brook, Judith Penelope 1926-
   Brief Entry 51
Brook, Judy
   See Brook, Judith Penelope
Brooke, L(eonard) Leslie 1862-1940 17
Brooke-Haven, P.
   See Wodehouse, P(elham) G(renville)
Brookins, Dana 1931- 28
Brooks, Anita 1914- 5
Brooks, Barbara
   See Simons, Barbara B(rooks)
Brooks, Bruce
   Brief Entry 53
Brooks, Charlotte K. 24
Brooks, Gwendolyn 1917- 6
Brooks, Jerome 1931- 23
Brooks, Lester 1924- 7
Brooks, Maurice (Graham) 1900- 45
Brooks, Polly Schoyer 1912- 12
Brooks, Ron(ald George) 1948-
   Brief Entry 33
Brooks, Walter R(ollin) 1886-1958 17
Brosnan, James Patrick 1929- 14
Brosnan, Jim
   See Brosnan, James Patrick
Brothers Hildebrandt, The
   See Hildebrandt, Tim(othy)

Broun, Emily
   See Sterne, Emma Gelders
Brower, Millicent 8
Brower, Pauline (York) 1929- 22
Browin, Frances Williams 1898- 5
Brown, Alexis
   See Baumann, Amy (Brown)
Brown, Bill
   See Brown, William L.
Brown, Billye Walker
   See Cutchen, Billye Walker
Brown, Bob
   See Brown, Robert Joseph
Brown, Buck 1936- 45
Brown, Cassie 1919-1986 55
Brown, Conrad 1922- 31
Brown, David
   See Myller, Rolf
Brown, Dee (Alexander) 1908- 5
Brown, Drollene P. 1939- 53
Brown, Eleanor Frances 1908- 3
Brown, Elizabeth M(yers) 1915- 43
Brown, Fern G. 1918- 34
Brown, (Robert) Fletch 1923- 42
Brown, George Earl 1883-1964 11
Brown, George Mackay 1921- 35
Brown, Irene Bennett 1932- 3
Brown, Irving
   See Adams, William Taylor
Brown, Ivor (John Carnegie)
   1891-1974 5
   Obituary 26
Brown, Joe David 1915-1976 44
Brown, Joseph E(dward) 1929-
   Brief Entry 51
Brown, Judith Gwyn 1933- 20
Brown, Laurene Krasny 1945- 54
Brown, Lloyd Arnold 1907-1966 36
Brown, Marcia 1918- 47
   Earlier sketch in SATA 7
   See also CLR 12
Brown, Marc Tolon 1946- 53
   Earlier sketch in SATA 10
Brown, Margaret Wise 1910-1952 .....*YABC* 2
   See CLR 10
Brown, Margery 5
Brown, Marion Marsh 1908- 6
Brown, Myra Berry 1918- 6
Brown, Palmer 1919- 36
Brown, Pamela 1924- 5
Brown, Robert Joseph 1907- 14
Brown, Rosalie (Gertrude) Moore
   1910- 9
Brown, Roswell
   See Webb, Jean Francis (III)
Brown, Roy (Frederick) 1921-1982 51
   Obituary 39
Brown, Vinson 1912- 19
Brown, Walter R(eed) 1929- 19
Brown, Will
   See Ainsworth, William Harrison
Brown, William L(ouis) 1910-1964 5
Browne, Anthony (Edward Tudor)
   1946- 45
   Brief Entry 44
Browne, Dik
   See Browne, Richard
Browne, Hablot Knight 1815-1882 21
Browne, Matthew
   See Rands, William Brighty
Browne, Richard 1917-
   Brief Entry 38
Browning, Robert 1812-1889 ....*YABC* 1
Brownjohn, Alan 1931- 6
Bruce, Dorita Fairlie 1885-1970
   Obituary 27
Bruce, Mary 1927- 1
Bruchac, Joseph III 1942- 42
Bruck, Lorraine 1921- 55
   Brief Entry 46
Bruemmer, Fred 1929- 47
Bruna, Dick 1927- 43
   Brief Entry 30
   See also CLR 7
Brunhoff, Jean de 1899-1937 24
   See also CLR 4